BRITISH ELECTIONS
AND
PARTIES YEARBOOK 1996

BRITISH ELECTIONS AND PARTIES YEARBOOK 1996

EDITED BY

David M. Farrell
David Broughton
David Denver
Justin Fisher

FRANK CASS
LONDON • PORTLAND, OR

First published in 1996 in Great Britain by
FRANK CASS & CO. LTD
Newbury House, 900 Eastern Avenue
London IG2 7HH

and in the United States by
FRANK CASS
c/o ISBS, 5804 N.E. Hassalo Street, Portland, Oregon 97213-3644

Printed in Great Britain by
Bookcraft (Bath) Ltd, Midsomer Norton, Avon

CONTENTS

PREFACE

This is the sixth volume of the British Elections and Parties Yearbook, the annual publication of the Elections, Public Opinion and Parties (EPOP) specialist group of the Political Studies Association. Like its predecessors, the volume contains a selection of the best papers delivered at the annual EPOP conference, in this case hosted by London Guildhall University in September 1995. We are especially grateful to the following organizations for supporting the EPOP conference: the Economic and Social Research Council (Award No. A47126006), the British Academy, the Arthur McDougall Fund, and London Guildhall University.

Again like its predecessors, this volume also contains a comprehensive selection of reference material of interest to EPOP members and others involved in the analysis of elections and political parties.

The editors are grateful to the authors for keeping to such a tight schedule in turning around papers. We wish to express our gratitude to Cathy Jennings of Frank Cass Ltd. for her advice, encouragement, and support throughout the preparation of this volume. Further details about membership of EPOP and its activities may be obtained from any of the editors.

David M. Farrell   David Broughton   David Denver   Justin Fisher

May 1996

NOTES ON CONTRIBUTORS

Tim Bale took his first degree, in history, at Cambridge University and his Masters at Northwestern University. He is a final-year doctoral candidate in the Department of Politics at Sheffield University, working under Professor Patrick Seyd. His thesis aims to apply the 'Cultural Theory' pioneered by Mary Douglas and developed by Aaron Wildavsky to a study of the 1964–70 Labour Government. He has also published work on qualitative data, on Labour and the Social Chapter and on the think-tank, Demos.

Shaun Bowler is Associate Professor of Political Science at the University of California, Riverside. His principal research interests are electoral systems (with a particular emphasis on preferential systems), voting behaviour, and legislatures. He is editor (with David Farrell) of *Electoral Strategies and Political Marketing* (Macmillan, 1992), and (with David Farrell and Richard Katz) of *Party Cohesion, Party Discipline and the Organization of Parliaments* (Ohio State University Press, forthcoming, 1997).

David Broughton is a Lecturer in Politics in the School of European Studies at the University of Wales in Cardiff. He has recently published a book on *Public Opinion Polling and Politics in Britain*. His other research interests focus on parties and party systems in comparative perspective, and religion and politics in Europe.

Philip Cowley is a temporary Lecturer at the University of Hull. He is currently researching the behaviour of the Conservative Party in parliament under John Major.

David Denver is a Reader in Politics at Lancaster University and co-convenor of EPOP. He is the author of *Elections and Voting Behaviour in Britain*, and has been a co-editor of the first six volumes of the *British Elections and Parties Yearbook*.

Daniel Dorling is a Lecturer in Geography at University of Bristol. His research interests are in the visualization of spatial social structure and the changing economic, medical and political geographies of Britain.

Niall Farrall is a graduate in Communication Studies from Bournemouth University, and holds a postgraduate degree in Mass Communication from Leicester University.

David M. Farrell is the Jean Monnet Lecturer in European Politics at the University of Manchester. He co-edits *Party Politics, Representation*, and the *British Elections and Parties Yearbook* (1994–96). Author of *Comparing Electoral Systems* (Prentice Hall, 1996), his research interests include parties, elections, and campaigning. In 1997 he will be a visiting Fellow at the Joan Shorenstein Center on the Press, Politics and Public Policy at the Kennedy School, Harvard.

Justin Fisher is Lecturer in Political Science at London Guildhall University. He is the author of *British Political Parties* (Prentice Hall, 1996) and numerous articles on political and party finance. He was co-organizer (with David Farrell) of the 1995 Elections, Public Opinion and Parties conference hosted by London Guildhall University.

Neil T. Gavin is Lecturer in the School of Politics and Communication Studies at the University of Liverpool. His current interests include voting behaviour, media effects analysis and methodology.

Gordon Hands is a Senior Lecturer in Politics at Lancaster University. He has collaborated with David Denver on a number of projects and has co-authored numerous articles on elections and electoral behaviour.

Bernadette C. Hayes is a Reader in Sociology at Queen's University of Belfast, Northern Ireland. Previous appointments include Lecturer in Sociology at the University of Surrey and a Research Fellowship at the Australian National University. She has published widely in the area of gender and social stratification.

Anthony Heath is Official Fellow at Nuffield College, Oxford. He is co-director of the Centre for Research into Elections and Social Trends (CREST). He has been the co-director of the British Election Study since 1983 and co-author of the three books resulting from those studies: *How Britain Votes, Understanding Political Change* and *Labour's Last Chance*. He will also be the co-director of the next British Election Study in 1996–97 (with Roger Jowell, John Curtice and Pippa Norris).

Ron Johnston is Professor of Geography at the University of Bristol. His main research interests are in electoral and political geography, and he is currently involved in studies of the Boundary Commissions, of local campaign spending, and of the influence of perceptions of the health of regional economies on voting.

Graham Kinshott is a Ph.D. student in the Department of Government at the University of Essex. He is currently working on an Economic & Social Research Council funded study into the possible causes of differences between voting behaviour in local and general elections in England and Wales from 1976 to 1992.

Michael Levy is an Instructor of Political Science at Southeast Missouri State University. His research interests focus on the regional effects of Thatcherism and its impact on Labour and the smaller parties. He is completing a dissertation on regional polarization in British elections (1979–92) at the University of Kentucky.

Peter Lynch is a Lecturer in Politics at the University of Stirling. He has written on European regionalism, political parties and constitutional politics in the UK and is currently working on a study of political parties in Scotland.

Ian McAllister is Professor of Government at the University of Manchester. He has held positions at the University of Strathclyde, the University of New South Wales and the Australian National University. He is author of *The Loyalties of Voters* (Sage, 1990, with Richard Rose), *Political Behaviour: Citizens, Parties and Elites in Australia* (Longman Cheshire, 1992) and *Russia Votes* (Chatham House, 1996, with Stephen White and Richard Rose).

Iain McLean is Official Fellow in Politics at Nuffield College, Oxford. He was co-author of an article on the impact of the poll tax on the 1992 general election in *British Elections and Parties Yearbook 1994*. Most recently, he has edited a *Dictionary of Politics* (Oxford University Press, 1996). He is a co-editor of *Electoral Studies*.

Anthony Mughan is a Professor in the Department of Political Science at Ohio State University. He has previously held positions at University College, Cardiff and the Australian National University. He has published widely on electoral politics and is currently working in the fields of public opinion, the mass media and democratic politics.

Charles Pattie is a Senior Lecturer in Geography at University of Sheffield. His primary research interests are in electoral geography. Recent publications have included work on local economic conditions and voting, and political campaigning. He is currently working with Johnston and Rossiter on a Leverhulme-funded project investigating parliamentary redistricting and the work of the Boundary Commissions.

Colin Rallings is Reader in Electoral Politics and a Director of the Local Government Chronicle Elections Centre at the University of Plymouth. With Michael Thrasher, he compiled and edited *The Media Guide to the New Parliamentary Constituencies*. He was a co-editor of *British Elections and Parties Yearbook 1993–95*.

David Rossiter is a Research Associate at the University of Bristol. He is currently employed on a research project into the operations of the Parliamentary Boundary Commissions, funded by the Leverhulme Trust.

David Sanders is a Professor in the Department of Government at the University of Essex. His interests include political forecasting, the political economy of post-war Britain, and European elite attitudes.

Bridget Taylor is a Research Officer at Nuffield College, Oxford. She has been involved in a number of research projects for CREST, including recent British Social Attitudes Surveys (BSAS).

Michael Thrasher is Reader in Public Policy and a Director of the Local Government Chronicle Elections Centre at the University of Plymouth. Together with Colin Rallings, he is the author of *Local Elections in Britain*.

ABSTRACTS OF ARTICLES

Were the 1994 Euro- and Local Elections in Britain Really Second-Order? Evidence from the British Election Panel Study

Iain McLean, Anthony Heath and Bridget Taylor

This article introduces the concept of 'second-order elections'. We then use evidence from the panel survey of the British electorate that has been running since the 1992 general election to discuss whether British voters in the 1994 elections to local authorities and to the European Parliament behaved in the way that theorists of second-order elections would expect.

Forecasting Vote and Seat Share in Local Elections

Colin Rallings and Michael Thrasher

This article describes a model developed to monitor national movements in electoral opinion based on the results of local government by-elections held regularly throughout the country. Since 1992, this model has proved very successful in projecting the share of vote likely to be gained by the political parties at the annual round of local elections in May; the model has been less good at forecasting the number of seats likely to be won and lost by each party. Some of the reasons for this discrepancy are discussed with particular reference to the under-estimation of the seat gains made by the Liberal Democrats in both 1993 and 1994.

Missing Voters in Britain, 1992–96: Where and with What Impact?

Daniel Dorling, Charles Pattie, David Rossiter and Ron Johnston

Several hundred thousand adults are eligible, but are not registered, to vote in Great Britain. This article looks in detail at where these potential voters probably live and asks what difference their exclusion makes to the process of electing the next government. In doing so, we consider the implications of the constituency boundary changes on this process and the recent increase in electoral registration. We confirm the results of Jeremy Smith and Iain McLean (1994) – that as many as ten seats may have been won by Conservative candidates at the last election due to missing voters. We show that, although the recent boundary changes have had the effect of concentrating these missing voters in fewer constituencies, they are still electorally important as a result.

A *Comparative Analysis of Ward and Constituency Level Effects on Voting Behaviour in England and Wales 1986–92*

Graham Kinshott

Differences between voting behaviour in local government and general elections are often attributed to protest voting or turnout bias, as supporters of the governing party express their discontent with mid-term government performance. However, the evidence suggests that these factors cannot explain these disparities in their entirety. This article seeks to test an alternative hypothesis: the possibility that individuals have different voting criteria in each type of election and consciously make contradictory electoral choices between local and national government levels. Using a database of election results and ward/constituency level census data, the article constructs a comparative local/national model of electoral behaviour. A series of regression analyses are conducted to examine any differential effects of socio-economic variables between local and national level elections.

The Impact of Television News on Public Perceptions of the Economy and Government, 1993–94

Neil T. Gavin and David Sanders with Niall Farrall

The article looks at economic coverage on prime time BBC and ITN news in 1993–94. It assesses the relationship between this coverage and measures of government popularity, and the economic attitudes of the public. Content analysis was deployed to assess the weight of good and bad news, and Gallup 9000 weekly polls were used to measure changes in the climate of public opinion. What the analysis shows is that at the aggregate level there is indeed a relationship – albeit an indirect one – between the overall pattern of economic news coverage that the BBC and ITN collectively provide, and the extent to which the UK electorate is prepared to express its support for the governing Conservative Party.

Constituency Campaigning in the 1992 General Election: The Peculiar Case of the Conservatives

David Denver and Gordon Hands

Recent research, using various measures of party performance and surrogate indicators of campaign strength, has challenged the orthodox view that constituency campaigning makes no difference to election results. Analysis of the 1992 general election, using a survey-derived index of campaign intensity, confirms the 'revisionist' view – that the level of campaigning does make a difference – with regard to Labour and Liberal Democrat campaigns, but suggests that Conservative campaigning had no effect. A possible explanation for the absence of impact in the case of the Conservatives may be that Conservative supporters are likely to turn out and vote for the party irrespective of the strength of the local campaign although the evidence is not conclusive.

Reasoning Voters, Voter Behaviour and Institutions: The Decision Dependence of Voting Behaviour
Shaun Bowler

The article argues two broad points concerning the impact of institutions upon voter decision making and mass behaviour. First, electoral institutions help shape voter decisions and decision making in predictable ways. Second, provided we sharpen our theoretical expectations about institutions and their likely impact on voting behaviour, we can begin to study the impact of institutions even within single countries by exploiting institutional variations in electoral practice. Empirical examples are given from Australia, Britain and Germany.

Television Can Matter: Bias in the 1992 General Election
Anthony Mughan

For politicians, television is a potent medium of political communication and persuasion, whereas students of politics generally see it as having few implications for the party that voters choose. This analysis of the 1992 general election shows that a good number of voters do in fact think that the news programmes of both the BBC and ITN show a partisan prejudice. Interestingly, though, this bias influences voting patterns only in the case of the BBC. The demonstrated electoral bonus for the Conservative Party is argued to be the result of its aggressive campaign alleging left-wing bias in the BBC's coverage of politics.

Political Outcomes, Women's Legislative Rights and Devolution in Scotland
Bernadette C. Hayes and Ian McAllister

The political representation of women and constitutional change were two major party political issues in Scotland during the 1992 general election campaign. This article uses the 1992 Scottish Election Study to examine popular attitudes towards these issues and their influence on the vote. The results show that Scottish voters blame political parties for the lack of women representatives, although there is support for the view that insufficient women come forward for nomination. The constitutional issue, however, overshadows the question of female representation and is a major influence on voting behaviour, net of a wide range of other factors. Although the political parties have placed female representation high on their agendas, voters consider it less important. The reasons for this are discussed, as well as the conditions under which it might become a salient election issue.

The Death of the Past': Symbolic Politics and the Changing of Clause IV

Tim Bale

Analysts of parties, like most political scientists, do not delve too deeply into symbols and symbolism and as a result tend towards an exclusively instrumental view of their role in party life. There are approaches to organizational culture which go beyond the idea that symbols are merely a means of manipulation, but arguably even these do not go far enough. Unfortunately, the interpretative approaches that do are difficult to integrate with traditional modes of political explanation. This is a problem, though, which may yet be resolved – primarily by turning to 'the new institutionalism'. All this is illustrated by applying each approach to attempts – past and present, successful and unsuccessful – to change Clause IV of the Labour Party's constitution. Blair's victory owed much to his skill in appealing to changing popular conceptions about the nature of organizations. Though vitally important, his victory is unlikely to prove total.

Modernization and Clause IV Reform: The Attitudes of Labour Backbench MPs

Michael Levy

After the 1983 electoral debacle, Labour began to moderate its manifesto and to mould its image, abandoning many socialist pledges so as to appeal to the centre of the political spectrum, and particularly to southern England and the Midlands. These reforms started under Kinnock, were followed by Smith and by Blair, and culminated in the reform of Clause IV. This article examines the relative warmth of Labour backbench MPs towards some of these reforms (Europe, Clause IV, unilateralism). Based on interviews with 36 MPs and a survey of a further nine MPs, the article finds that, while most MPs express attitudes favourable towards modernization, a significant proportion oppose it, and there are a large number of MPs who are not exactly enthusiastic about 'New Labour'.

How Did He Do That? The Second Round of the 1990 Conservative Leadership Election

Philip Cowley

This article is a systematic analysis of the individual voting behaviour of the 372 Conservative MPs who chose John Major to lead the Conservative Party in November 1990. It analyses the support for all three candidates by examining a variety of socio-economic and political factors suggested by the extant literature: ideology, career status, education, previous occupation, age, parliamentary experience, and marginality. By and large the extant explanations are found to be correct: the dominant factors were ideology, socio-economic background, and the career position of those voting. But there are subtle distinctions (for example, between the different factions on the right of the party) which previous studies had overlooked.

Professionalization, New Technology and Change in a Small Party: The Case of the Scottish National Party
Peter Lynch

Electoral professionalization has affected small parties as well as large. However, small parties face significant obstacles in embracing new campaigns and communications techniques, as well as the technology related to financial and personnel resources. This article examines the efforts of the SNP to catch up with the professionalization of its competitors through improving its fundraising, communications and campaigning abilities. The key question is whether small parties are subject to a similar electoral-professional transformation as that apparently experienced by large parties.

Were the 1994 Euro- and Local Elections in Britain Really Second-Order? Evidence from the British Election Panel Study

Iain McLean, Anthony Heath and Bridget Taylor

Introduction: Second-Order Elections

Reif and Schmitt (1980) introduced the term 'second-order elections' as 'a conceptual framework for the analysis of European Election results':

> [T]he 'first-order' elections in parliamentary systems are the national parliamentary elections, and in presidential systems, the national presidential elections.... There is a plethora of 'second-order elections': by-elections, municipal elections, various sets of regional elections, those to a second chamber and the like.... Side-effects of these outcomes are ...felt in the main arena of each nation. Many voters cast their votes in these elections not only as a result of conditions obtaining [in] ... the second-order arena, but also on the basis of factors in the main political arena of the nation.

They predict that second-order elections will have a lower level of participation than first-order ones; that they offer brighter prospects for small and new political parties; that there will be a higher percentage of invalid ballots; and the governing parties will do badly. A similar list of predictions is to be found in Reif (1984).

The literature on second-order elections does not always distinguish clearly between defining features and consequential or accompanying ones. For this article, we will accept the simplest stipulative definition offered by Reif and Schmitt. By definition, first-order elections are those to the national parliament or presidency, whichever is the more important; second-order elections are all others. This stipulative definition enables us to take all the other claimed features of second-order elections as predictions or hypotheses that may be tested by data. We will test them on evidence from the British Election Panel Survey (BEPS) about the behaviour of British voters (and non-voters) in elections to the European Parliament and to local authorities.

Elections to the European Parliament

The first direct elections to the European Parliament were held simultaneously in all EU member states in 1979. Since then, they have taken place at five-yearly intervals. As predicted by Reif and Schmitt, all four elections have generally been marked by low turnout, by voters' concentration on issues in their national political arenas, and by generally poor performances by the national governing party or parties (see, for example, *Electoral Studies* 3:3, 1984: *passim*; 8:3, 1989: *passim*; 13:4, 1994: 331–67). Analysts have detected only faint transnational movements, such as a pale Green tide in 1989 (Curtice, 1989), and the uncertain emergence of a federalist *versus* nationalist dimension in 1994 (Irwin, 1995; van der Eijk, Franklin, and Marsh, forthcoming). For whatever reason – perhaps in part because electors are aware that the European Parliament has strictly limited powers – these elections have done little to address the notorious 'democratic deficit' of the European Union.

Local Elections in the UK: Turnout, Knowledge and Accountability

Reformist concern at generally low levels of turnout and information at UK local elections is even more venerable. The Maud Committee on Management of Local Government (Ministry of Housing and Local Government, 1967: paras 34–40) identified low turnout and interest in local affairs as two of the threats to the legitimacy it perceived in the local government system. It quoted overall turnout in contested seats for England as 40 per cent. The overlapping Royal Commission, with the same chairman, expressed similar anxieties ('Local government is, at present, apt to be irrelevant to people's problems': Cmnd 4040/1969, para. 96), although it did not specifically consider turnout. The Layfield Committee on Local Government Finance (Cmnd 6453/1976, para. 1:30) complained of widespread ignorance of how rates were calculated and of which services were delivered by local authorities. The Widdicombe Committee on the Conduct of Local Authority Business (Cmnd 9797/1986, paras 2.71–2.85) noted that 'the reorganisation of local government into larger more coherent councils in 1974' had not 'remed[ied]' low turnout, quoting mean turnouts in the same range as Maud's 40 per cent of twenty years earlier. The report continued:

> It is clear that turnout in British local elections is lower than in most European local elections ... but compares less badly with English speaking countries.... What is perhaps more a cause for concern is that, within Great Britain, local election turnout remains so much lower than that in recent general elections.... [Our] analysis ... suggests that those who vote in local elections are in most respects a fair cross-section of the

community and of those who vote in general election; and that low turnout therefore produces no serious distortion in the results (Cmnd 9797, paras 2.73–2.74).

The most explicit policy conclusions in this reformist literature were those drawn by the UK government Green Paper which introduced the Community Charge (poll tax): *Paying for Local Government* (Cmnd 9714/1986, esp. 1.36–1.37; 3.11–3.12). It drew attention to the 'poor linkage between those who vote and those who pay' for local government services and stated that only about half of local government electors in Great Britain were also ratepayers. The principal justification of the poll tax was that for the first time those who voted on local services would be individually billed. The government argued that this would increase local accountability. Many critics of the poll tax pointed out that a two-tier local government structure makes local accountability hard to pin down. In those areas in the UK with a two-tier structure, one council presents the bills and collects payment on behalf of both – a feature which has survived the transitions from rates to poll tax and from poll tax to council tax. Even in the unlikely event of the majority of citizens knowing which council delivered which service, the two councils always have the option of blaming the bills on each other. The citizen is unlikely to have sufficient information to adjudicate.

The scholarly evidence on turnout and participation, much of it conducted on behalf of the authors of the official reports summarized in the previous paragraph, presents a more nuanced picture. There is, first, a divergence between policymakers who are puzzled and upset because some people do not vote and political scientists who are puzzled because anybody at all does vote. As is well known, in the model of rational political participation proposed by Downs (1957) and since elaborated by a host of other writers, a voter votes if their 'party differential' multiplied by the probability that they are decisive exceeds the cost of voting. But the probability of being decisive in a national election is infinitesimal. Therefore the turnouts of 70 per cent and above observed in national elections should be ascribed to notions such as feelings of civic duty, Kantian morality (that is, disapproval of free-riding on ethical grounds), and the triviality of the cost of voting. The impact of these factors varies in different ways in different varieties of second-order election. The probability of being decisive in a local election, while still low, is orders of magnitude higher than in a national election, while at a European election it is orders of magnitude lower. But both of these varieties of second-order election feature roughly the same level of turnout as each other, typically some 30 per cent below that at a national election. This is prima facie evidence against the subjective probability of decisiveness playing a large role, but the hypothesis can be tested against the contrasting backgrounds of the European and local elections.

Less demanding versions of rational choice lead to various models of voting as a form of rewarding or punishing politicians. There are two dimensions giving four possible combinations. Voters may be modelled as *egocentric* or *sociotropic,* and they may reward or punish politicians *retrospectively* or *prospectively.* Here again the two sorts of second-order elections may be regarded differently. Very few voters could have the degree of information required to evaluate the European Parliament, but some would be able to evaluate the performance of their local council(s).

There is a considerable body of academic evidence as to British voters' factual knowledge of local government and its services. Typical results are those in Lynn (1990). Without prompting, 95 per cent of respondents could name at least one council service, with services conspicuous to the public named most often (refuse collection by 70 per cent of respondents, road maintenance by 44 per cent, schools by 37 per cent). Degree of knowledge was positively related with degree of formal education. Lynn's results show a similar profile to those found by the Layfield Committee's researchers in 1975. When prompted to say whether each of a list of services was provided by local councils or not, most respondents correctly placed most services as being either council services or not. In areas with two-tier councils, there was much less knowledge of which council was responsible for which service – not at all surprisingly, particularly in the case of highways and planning matters, where even councillors are not always sure. The main 'false-positive' was hospitals, which 48 per cent of people in two-tier areas and 32 per cent of people in single-tier areas assigned to councils; the main 'false-negatives' were police and fire, which substantial proportions failed to identify as local government services (police: 52 per cent in two-tier areas, 67 per cent in single-tier; fire: 28 per cent and 49 per cent). Especially in the case of police, this may have been a sophisticated rather than an ignorant answer from some respondents. In London, there is no local control of the police service at all; in the rest of the country, it is very weak. In many parts of the country, the police (and sometimes the fire) service covers more than one county and is run by a board on which each county council is represented. This, combined with the roles of magistrates and the Home Office, means that it is very dubious whether the police and fire services can correctly be described as being under local control.

In this article we aim to show that some second-order elections are more second order than others. In particular, respondents' decisions on whether and how to vote in the European elections owed little or nothing to European issues, whereas their decisions on the local elections did owe something to their perceptions and experience of local matters.

The Context of the 1994 Wave of British Election Panel Study Interviews

In the summer of 1994 the incumbent Conservative government wallowed in the deepest mid-term trough of unpopularity recorded up to that time. Interviews took place shortly after two sets of elections. There were local elections on 5 May in most parts of Britain.[1] The results were the worst for the governing Conservatives since the current pattern of three-party competition began (though the Conservatives were to do still worse in 1995). The Liberal Democrats did better than their current poll ratings, as they normally do in British local elections. The fourth direct election to the European Parliament took place on 9 June. The Conservatives did not do so badly as projections from the local election results and national opinion polls implied, but their share of the vote in Great Britain slumped from the 42.6 per cent achieved in the 1992 general election to 28.1 per cent; the Labour Party's vote share rose from 35.0 per cent to 44.6 per cent. (For fuller detail, including detail of the composition of the BES panel, see Heath, Jowell, Curtice, and Taylor, 1995, and the appendix to this article.) As with past Euro-elections in the UK, the Liberal Democrats did not outperform their current poll rating.

Voting in the 1994 Local Elections

In both 1994 and 1995, Conservative spokesmen excused their poor local election performance by saying that Conservative voters had stayed at home, denying that people who formerly voted Conservative had switched to another party. Table 1 shows the relative contribution of these two factors in the 1994 BES panel's voting in 1994. The fact that it was a panel enables us to compare respondents' local vote in 1994 with their 1992 statement of how they voted in the general election. This provides a more accurate measure than that reported by cross-sectional polls, which asked people interviewed in 1994 how they had voted in 1992. This type of recall question is vulnerable to under-reporting of vote for the currently unpopular party.

Table 1 is restricted to those members of the panel who faced local elections in 1994. It confirms that the loyalty rate of 1992 Conservatives was lower than that of other party supporters. Thirty-four per cent of those who stated in 1992 that they voted Conservative in the general election did so again in the 1994 local election. The analogous loyalty rate for 1992 Labour voters was 63 per cent, for Liberal Democrats 52 per cent, and for other voters (largely Nationalists) 43 per cent.

TABLE 1a
VOTE IN 1992 AND VOTE IN THE 1994 LOCAL ELECTIONS: ROW PERCENTAGES

Vote in 1994

		Con	Lab	LD	Other	DNV	% of all voters	N
	Con	34	7	13	2	43	38	413
	Lab	0	63	8	2	27	33	362
Vote	LD	3	13	52	5	28	15	169
in	Other	0	14	6	43	37	4	38
1992	Did not vote	4	15	4	1	75	10	112
	% of all voters	14	28	16	4	38	100	1093

TABLE 1b
VOTE IN 1992 AND VOTE IN THE 1994 LOCAL ELECTIONS: TOTAL PERCENTAGES

Vote in 1994

		Con	Lab	LD	Other	DNV	% of all voters	N
	Con	13	3	5	1	16	38	413
	Lab	0	21	3	1	9	33	362
Vote	LD	0	2	8	1	4	15	169
in	Other	0	1	0	2	1	4	38
1992	Did not vote	0	2	0	0	8	10	112
	% of all voters	14	28	16	4	38	100	1093

Note: Data were weighted to correct for the oversampling of Scots in the 1992 survey.
Sample: Respondents who reported that there were local elections in their area.

By studying the 'total percentage' figures in Table 1b, we can treat it as a transition matrix, although not a perfect one (it necessarily omits both those who departed from the electorate, or at least from our panel, between 1992–94, and new electors in 1994). It shows that the Conservative lead over Labour (among those voters on our panel who believed that they faced local elections in 1994) declined by 18 percentage points between 1992–94. Of this, 6 points were attributable to direct switching from Conservative to Labour voting, 5 points to movements to and from the other parties (broadly, both big parties lost support to the Liberal Democrats, but the Conservatives lost more), and 9 points to changes in turnout. Thus changes in turnout accounted for around half of the Conservative decline. These calculations follow the standard method described by Butler and Stokes (1974: 267). Unlike Butler and Stokes, however, we have not attempted to adjust the transition matrix so that the marginal distributions correspond to the official vote distributions.

TABLE 2a

VOTE IN 1992 AND VOTE IN THE 1994 EUROPEAN ELECTIONS: ROW PERCENTAGES

Vote in 1994

		Con	Lab	LD	Other	DNV	% of all voters	N
	Con	34	4	8	4	50	41	746
	Lab	0	57	3	2	37	30	536
Vote	LD	3	15	39	5	38	17	314
in	Other	0	15	3	41	41	3	47
1992	Did not vote	5	10	3	2	80	9	163
	% of all voters	15	22	11	4	47	100	1806

TABLE 2b

VOTE IN 1992 AND VOTE IN THE 1994 EUROPEAN ELECTIONS: TOTAL PERCENTAGES

Vote in 1994

		Con	Lab	LD	Other	DNV	% of all voters	N
	Con	14	2	3	2	21	41	746
	Lab	0	17	1	1	11	30	536
Vote	LD	1	3	7	1	7	17	314
in	Other	0	0	0	1	1	3	47
1992	Did not vote	0	1	0	0	7	9	163
	% of all voters	15	22	11	4	47	100	1806

Note: Data were weighted to correct for the oversampling of Scots in the 1992 survey.

Table 2 presents the same sort of information as Table 1, this time comparing respondents' reported vote in the 1992 general election with their vote in the 1994 *European* election. The loyalty rates (Table 2a) were lower than for the 1994 local elections: 34 per cent for Conservatives, 57 per cent for Labour, 39 per cent for the Liberal Democrats and 41 per cent for other parties. The main political difference between Table 1a and Table 2a is that in the local elections, disgruntled Conservatives turned in considerable numbers to other parties, whereas for the European elections they stayed at home. The Liberal Democrats did badly both at retaining their 1992 supporters and at attracting refugees. Table 2b shows, using the Butler–Stokes transition matrix procedure again, that of the 18 percentage point diminution of Conservative lead over Labour from the 1992 general election to the 1994 European election, 8 points arose from net switching to other parties, and 10 points from differential abstention. We have shown elsewhere that 1992 Conservatives who abstained in the European election were more likely to have dropped their previous party identification than were 1992 supporters of the other parties who abstained in 1994 (Heath *et al.,* 1995: Table 4).

Did the panel treat the European and local elections as second-order in a substantive sense? In other words, did they tend to use them as 'cheap talk' gestures to send signals about something other than their ostensible purpose? One measure of this is the simple question: 'would you say you cared a good deal which party did best in the European election in Britain (45 per cent of respondents) or didn't you care very much which party did best?' (55 per cent). By contrast, 60 per cent of respondents claimed to have 'cared a great deal which party did best in the recent council elections'. Another is the proportion who say it makes a difference which party wins. The proportions saying 'not very much' or 'none at all' slope sharply up from general elections (combined proportion 14 per cent) to local elections (28 per cent) to European elections (37 per cent). A third measure is the proportion of those who voted in the European elections who claimed they did so for national reasons. The BES 1994 panel questionnaire did not ask respondents whether national or European issues played a more important role in their European election vote, but the EU-wide Eurobarometer survey, in the field in April 1994, did. In the UK, twice as many respondents (63 per cent to 31 per cent) opted for 'national' as compared to 'European' issues. This compared with an EU-wide ratio of 55 per cent to 37 per cent (*Eurobarometer* 41, 1994: Fig.1.5).

We did find some association between voters' attitude to Europe and their behaviour in the European election. The most distinctive group were those who, on a five-point scale between 'leaving the European Union' and 'a single European government', preferred the second-most Eurosceptic position, namely staying in but reducing the powers of the European Union. In the 1994 European election this was roughly the position of the

Conservatives, whereas all other parties including the Nationalists were more Europhile. If we concentrate on Conservative supporters, we find that this Eurosceptic group were the most likely subgroup of 1992 Conservative voters to turn out and vote Conservative in 1994. Furthermore, Eurosceptic voters, who comprised 40 per cent of the total, provided no less than 62 per cent of the Conservative vote in 1994. In this sense, Conservative Euroscepticism was well aligned with their supporters' views. But no such consistent pattern was found among voters who wanted to leave the EU altogether. Elsewhere we have tested whether policy differences on Europe accounted for Conservative defections by running a series of logistic regressions comparing Conservative loyalists (who identified with and voted for the Conservatives in both the general election and the European election) with 1992 Conservatives who showed varying degrees of disloyalty in 1994. Their attitudes to European policy were only mildly significant as predictors: the more anti-European they were in 1992, the more likely they were to be loyal to the Conservatives in 1994. However, these effects were overshadowed by their 1992 attitudes to the other parties and their 1992 positions on a left–right scale (Heath *et al.*, 1995: Table 8). On the whole, then, our conclusions support those of other academic observers who have stressed that the Europolicy impact on European election voting was modest.

We do have BES data on our respondents' reasons for voting in the 1994 local elections. Of those who voted, almost equal proportions said that they voted 'mostly according to what was going on in your local area' (45 per cent) and 'mostly according to what was going on in the country as a whole' (42 per cent). However, there was a sharp difference by party (Table 3).

TABLE 3
LOCAL OR NATIONAL CONSIDERATIONS?

		local	national	both	other	N
	Con	51	37	8	5	158
Vote	Lab	31	54	11	3	307
in	LD	61	28	8	3	182
1994	Other	58	30	7	5	43

Sample: respondents who reported voting in the 1994 local elections. Weighted figures.

Conservative and Liberal Democrat voters chose the local option by substantial margins. Apart from the few respondents who voted for an 'other' party at the local elections, Liberal Democratic voters were clearly the most localist, by 61 per cent to 28 per cent. Conservative voters were some way behind, preferring the local option by 51 per cent to 37 per cent. In contrast

Labour voters chose the national option (by 54 per cent to 31 per cent).

We do not know what is cause and what is effect here. One possible explanation is that causation runs from party to 'localism', so that, for example, Conservative supporters take refuge in localism as a rationalization of a Conservative vote in hard times, Liberal Democrat voters absorb their party's 'localist' ideology, and Labour voters take the only means open to them of punishing the incumbent government. But this is a rather weak explanation for the sharp difference between Liberal and Labour voters. Perhaps, rather, the arrow runs the other way for many people. Those whose ideology is localist tend to support parties that make local appeals (the Liberal Democrats because they always do, and the Conservatives because, in 1994, it was sensible to do so). Those who view local elections as a way of giving their opinion of the national government tend to cast a protest vote for Labour. If we calculate column percentages instead of the row percentages given in Table 3, those who gave the 'local' answer split their votes among the three main parties in the proportion (Cons: Lab: LD) 26 per cent: 31 per cent: 35 per cent. Those who gave the 'national' answer split them in the proportion 20 per cent: 58 per cent: 18 per cent.

One interpretation of these results is that there was a substantial element of gesture politics in both sets of voting, but more in the European than in the local elections. In the local elections, local considerations were claimed to be primary by nearly half the voters, and this fits uneasily with the notion that local elections are simply second-order ones in which voters record their views of the national government.

'Conservative Councils Cost You Less'?

As we noted earlier, one aim of the Conservatives' reforms of local taxation has been to make local councils more accountable. 'Conservative Councils Cost You Less' was a major Conservative slogan during the 1994 election campaign. If voters were indeed voting on the basis of local issues, rather than engaging in national protest politics, then a good place to start our search for evidence might be with perceptions of Labour profligacy and Conservative prudence in managing local affairs.

To be sure, the Conservatives' slogan was, on the face of it, a singularly unsuccessful slogan: as detailed above, the Conservatives suffered their second-worst performance ever in the 1994 local elections. Yet analysis of our panel shows that the slogan may have been shrewd. Respondents who believed that their local council was controlled by the Conservatives consistently thought that they got better value for money from their council tax bills than those who thought their council was controlled by Labour. Therefore the slogan may have implanted, or reinforced, an image of

Conservative financial prudence which saved them from an even worse disaster. Unfortunately for the Conservatives, after their further disaster in 1995 there are hardly any Conservative councils left, which will make it difficult to reuse the slogan.

We asked respondents whether they thought their council tax represented good value for money, offering them a five-point response from 'very good value for money' to 'very poor value for money'. The first thing to note is that the council tax evokes widespread contentment, unlike its predecessor, the poll tax. If responses are scaled from 1 ('very poor value') to 5 ('very good value'), the average score was 3.1, slightly on the good side of 'neither good nor bad'. By contrast, of respondents to our poll tax question in 1992, 7 per cent accepted the statement that 'the poll tax was a good idea and should have been kept', 28 per cent that 'it was a good idea but too unpopular to keep' and 65 per cent that it was 'a bad idea and should never have been introduced'. The 1992 and 1994 questions and circumstances are not directly comparable, but there is no doubt about the comparative popularity of the two taxes (see Lynn, 1990: Tables 9.1 and 9.2; Smith and McLean, 1994, 1995).

Table 4 breaks down these responses by the party each respondent thought controlled their council and by their party identification.[2]

TABLE 4
EVALUATION OF THE COUNCIL TAX: AVERAGE SCORES FOR EACH GROUP

		All respondents	Con ID	Lab ID	LD ID	no ID
	Con	3.18 (225)	3.35 (104)	2.85 (58)	3.29 (38)	2.96 (20)
Perceived party control	Lab (543)	2.99 (137)	3.11 (260)	3.06 (65)	2.62 (59)	2.79
	LD	3.17 (81)	3.37 (20)	2.86 (21)	3.07 (31)	3.83 (6)
	NOC	3.20 (54)	3.38 (17)	2.98 (19)	3.19 (12)	3.37 (5)
	DK	2.86 (148)	3.03 (34)	2.69 (53)	3.17 (24)	2.76 (30)

Note: The main figure in each cell gives the average score reported by members of that group (1 = 'very poor value for money'; 5 = 'very good value for money'). The figures in brackets give the base Ns. Weighted data. Respondents who reported that they had local elections in their area.

Looking at the first column of Table 4, we see that Conservative, Liberal Democrat (LD) and NOC (no overall control) councils obtained rather higher average scores than did Labour councils. As there were many more Labour than Conservative or Liberal Democrat identifiers in the sample, this cannot simply be a result of partisans praising councils run by their own party. The following columns of Table 4 amplify this. What we see is that in general partisans tend to give their 'own' councils a more favourable rating than do our respondents as a whole. Thus Conservative partisans gave an average rating of 3.35 to Conservative councils, compared with the overall average of 3.18; Labour partisans gave an average rating of 3.06 to their own councils compared with the average 2.99. Only Liberal Democrat partisans did not demonstrate this favouritism, but as we can see there were very few LD partisans whose councils were controlled by the LDs, so this anomaly could be the result of sampling error.

However, when we allow for this partisan favouritism, there is still a clear tendency for Labour councils to get lower ratings. We can test this formally with a regression model in which the individual's rating of the 'value for money' they get from the council is the dependent variable and the explanatory variables are the perceived party control and a measure of congruence between the respondent's partisanship and the party in control of their local council. (Formally, we construct a variable which takes the value 1 if the perceived party control is the same as the respondent's partisanship; 0 otherwise.)

We find a significant effect of partisan congruence ($b = 0.15$, se $= 0.07$). Taking as our reference category councils where the respondent did not know who was in control, we find a small positive but nonsignificant parameter estimate for Labour councils ($b = 0.06$, se $= 0.10$), but estimates for Conservative councils ($b = 0.25$, se $= .11$), Liberal Democrat councils ($b = 0.25$, se $= 0.14$), and for councils where there was believed to be no overall control ($b = 0.34$, se $= 0.16$). While the Liberal Democrat parameter is not quite twice its standard error, and therefore does not reach the standard criterion of statistical significance, we would nonetheless be unwise to conclude that it was only Conservative councils which were perceived to give good value for money. The parameter estimate for councils where there was perceived to be no overall control is also of considerable interest. On this evidence, our respondents have rather favourable views of 'hung councils'.

Did these responses derive from perceived differences in the quality of the services run by local councils? We asked respondents whether each of the following services had improved, stayed the same, or got worse in the last two years:

- street and pavement repairs
- 'standards in hospitals around here'

- 'control of crime in this area'
- rubbish collection
- control of traffic locally

As we noted earlier, hospitals are not a local authority responsibility, and it is arguable how far local authorities can be held responsible for control of crime. We therefore asked our respondents, if they said that services had improved or got worse, whether they gave the credit/blame to their local council, the government, or some other body.

Table 5 shows that our respondents did have a reasonable understanding of the extent of local responsibility, confirming the evidence from previous research (such as Lynn, 1990). Our respondents were particularly unlikely to credit or blame their local councils for standards in hospitals or for control of crime. They did however correctly perceive the council's responsibility for street repairs, rubbish collection and traffic control. It is also noticeable that our respondents felt that local councils had done a better job of their responsibilities than the government had done with hospitals or crime. Thus, local councils had a favourable balance of credit and blame for street repairs (25 per cent giving them credit versus 21 per cent giving them blame) and rubbish collection (24 per cent versus 5 per cent), although a less favourable one on traffic control (11 per cent versus 21 per cent). Government however had very unfavourable balances of credit and blame on hospitals (8 per cent versus 41 per cent) and crime (1 per cent versus 32 per cent).

TABLE 5
PERCEPTIONS OF LOCAL SERVICES

	Street repairs	Hospitals	Crime	Rubbish	Traffic
Improved and credited (%)					
Council	25	4	4	24	11
Government	1	8	1	1	1
Other	3	8	6	1	2
Stayed the same (%)	38	33	33	66	48
Got worse and blamed (%)					
Council	21	1	4	5	21
Government	10	41	32	1	6
Other	3	4	21	1	10
N	1101	937	1067	1096	1082

Note: Weighted data. Respondents who reported that they had local elections in their area.

These perceptions, particularly those of street repairs and rubbish collection, were quite strongly related to our respondents' judgements of whether they received value for money from their local council tax. When we included these variables in our regression analysis of the council tax, we found that traffic control, street repairs and rubbish collection all had significant effects on perceptions of 'value for money'. Rather comfortingly, perceptions of standards in hospitals and of control of crime were not related to perceived 'value for money' once the other variables had been entered in the equation.

However, these variables did not appear to account for the lower general evaluation of the council tax when Labour was in control of the local council. There was no significant association between the political complexion of the council and perceptions of the various local services. The one exception was repair of streets and pavements. In line with the conventional wisdom, our respondents did tend to give more favourable evaluations of this service in areas where the Liberal Democrats were perceived to be in office.[3] However, the generally lower evaluation of value for money where Labour was believed to control the local council persisted even when we controlled for these evaluations of specific services.

It is possible, therefore, that Conservative campaigning succeeded in planting, or maintaining, the impression that Conservative councils were prudent and that Labour councils were spendthrift. As the question we asked about council tax was a 'value for money' one, it is perhaps not surprising that this impression was not associated with a feeling that Labour councils were bad at delivering any service in particular. Central Office may have succeeded in persuading the electorate that Conservatives were good in general and Labour bad in general, without persuading them (or needing to persuade them) that this goodness and badness was manifested in any particular council service. On the other hand, we must not ignore the finding that both Liberal Democrat councils and councils where there was no overall control also got relatively good ratings from our respondents. There may be more behind our results than Central Office campaigning.

Of course, another possibility is that, even though the services were not perceived to be any worse under Labour councils, council tax charges were perceived to be higher. We are currently assembling data on the actual levels of the council tax in respondents' areas, and will add these to the analysis.

Local Effects on Local Voting?

A crucial question now arises. Is there any evidence that this belief that Conservative and Liberal Democrat councils gave better value for money helped win them votes (or at least helped them avoid losing votes)? As a first step, let us compare the electoral fortunes of the Conservatives and Liberal

Democrats in seats where they were the incumbent and those where Labour was the incumbent. Is there any sign that incumbency gave the Conservatives and the LDs an electoral advantage?

In Table 6 we look at the vote transition matrices, dividing respondents up according to their perceptions of which party was in control of the local council prior to the local elections on 5 May. The table suggests that incumbency may have brought some advantages to the Conservatives and Liberal Democrats. The Conservative loyalty rate was somewhat higher (44 per cent compared with 36 per cent and 32 per cent) where they were perceived to be in control than when the Labour or Liberal Democrats were perceived to be in control. However, when we test for significance, we find that the Conservative loyalty rate was not significantly higher when the Conservative Party was incumbent. The results are suggestive, then, but far from conclusive.

However, significant differences are found among the Liberal Democrats. Their loyalty rate was significantly higher (81 per cent compared with 42 per cent and 36 per cent) when the LDs were perceived to be in control. Moreover, the LDs also fared better among former Labour and Conservative voters when the LDs were in control. There does, then, appear to be a decided LD advantage from incumbency.

TABLE 6
VOTE TRANSITION MATRICES BY PERCEIVED PARTY CONTROL

Perceived Conservative control

		Con	Lab	*Vote in 1994* LD	Other	DNV	N
Vote	Con	44	5	13	2	36	127
in	Lab	0	69	6	0	25	52
1992	LD	10	13	42	0	36	31

Perceived Labour control

		Con	Lab	*Vote in 1994* LD	Other	DNV	N
Vote	Con	36	10	11	3	40	242
in	Lab	0	68	5	4	24	314
1992	LD	1	22	36	6	35	81

Perceived Liberal Democrat control

		Con	Lab	*Vote in 1994* LD	Other	DNV	N
Vote	Con	32	3	32	0	32	31
in	Lab	5	57	19	0	19	21
1992	LD	0	0	81	3	17	36

This also fits with our respondents' reports of whether they were voting on the basis of local or national issues. Thus Labour voters were the least likely to say that they were voting on local issues, and it is for Labour that local incumbency seems to be least important. Conversely, Liberal Democrat voters were the most likely to say that they were voting on local issues, and for them local incumbency does appear to matter. This pattern also inclines us to the view that the causal direction is indeed from local issues to voting, rather than from partisanship to justifications in terms of local issues.

However, Table 6 on its own does not prove that it was 'value for money' that explains the LD advantage from incumbency. It suggests that incumbency had an effect, but it does not tell us why it did so. It could simply be that Conservatives (and LDs) were less likely to stay at home if they felt that their failure to vote would have real consequences for their party. Most voters were presumably aware that the electoral tide was running in the Labour direction, and hence more was at stake when the LDs were in control.

To explore this further we construct a combined variable which incorporates both the identity of the party in control and its perceived value for money. We then enter this into a logistic regression, controlling for previous vote.

In Table 7 we report the results of three logistic regressions. In the first one (reported in the first column) our dependent variable is whether respondents voted Conservative or not in the 1994 local elections. In order to take account of the effects of partisanship, we include as an explanatory variable the party which our respondents voted for in the 1992 general election. Our main interest, however, is in our new variable which incorporates respondents' perceptions of the value for money given by the party they believed to be in control of their local council prior to the local elections. As usual in a logistic regression, the parameter estimates can be interpreted as fitted log odds ratios.

In the case of our incumbency/value for money variable, we take as our reference category people who believed that the Conservatives had been in control of their local council and that their local council tax offered poor value for money. We can see from column 1 that, controlling for 1992 vote, only one group of respondents were significantly more likely to vote Conservative than this reference group – namely respondents who believed that the Conservatives offered good value for money (the parameter of 0.97 is just twice its standard error). With this one exception, however, Conservative voting was not affected by the political complexion of the local council or by the value for money which it offered.

There are no significant 'value for money' parameters in the Labour analysis, although it is noticeable how many of the parameters are negative. These negative signs suggest that the groups in question (for example, people who believed their local council to be controlled by the Liberal Democrats) were rather less likely to vote Labour than were members of the reference category (people who believed their Conservative councils offered poor value for money).

TABLE 7
LOGISTIC REGRESSION OF VOTING IN THE 1994 LOCAL ELECTIONS

Parameter Estimates

	Con vs.	non-Con	Lab vs.	non-Lab	LD vs.	non-LD
Conservative control						
Poor value	0		0		0	
Neither	0.42	(.54)	0.00	(.54)	0.57	(.58)
Good value	**0.97**	(.45)	-0.47	(.46)	0.62	(.49)
Labour control						
Poor value	0.17	(.44)	0.08	(.38)	0.25	(.47)
Neither	0.21	(.50)	-0.11	(.41)	0.36	(.52)
Good value	0.43	(.43)	0.24	(.37)	0.20	(.47)
Liberal Democrat control						
Poor value	0.14	(.87)	-1.05	(.84)	**1.54**	(.65)
Neither	-0.77	(1.13)	-1.10	(.76)	**1.84**	(.63)
Good value	0.50	(.63)	-0.94	(.64)	**1.80**	(.55)
Vote in 1992						
Conservative	2.26	(.50)	-0.94	(.36)	1.26	(.56)
Labour	-2.49	(.99)	2.14	(.32)	0.58	(.58)
Liberal Dem	-1.45	(.93)	-0.11	(.40)	2.93	(.57)
Other	*		0.04	(.58)	0.67	(.92)
Did not vote	0		0		0	
Constant	-4.35	(2.40)	-1.66	(.19)	-1.63	(.21)
Model improvement						
	228.0	(12 df)	281.9	(12 df)	137.7	(12 df)
N	838		838		838	

Note: Significant parameters are in bold. Standard errors are given in brackets. Sample: respondents with local council elections in their area. *Too few cases for reliable estimation

In the third column, reporting the analysis of Liberal Democrat voting, we find three statistically significant parameters, corresponding to the three groups of people whose council was controlled (they believed) by the Liberal Democrats. This demonstrates the beneficial effects of incumbency for Liberal Democrat support in the local elections. However, if it was value for money that explained this incumbency effect, we would expect to find that Liberal Democrat voting was higher only when respondents believed that the incumbent Liberal Democrat council gave good value for money, while there would be no Liberal Democrat advantage if the council was believed to give poor value for money. However, the results show that there is a Liberal Democrat advantage from incumbency whether or not the council is perceived to give good value for money.

Conclusion

Local elections, given our stipulative definition, must be regarded as second-order ones. They clearly have some of the characteristics that Reif and Schmitt predicted for second-order elections – their turnout is substantially lower than in general elections, the governing party tends to do badly, and many voters cast their votes in local elections on the basis of factors in the main political arena of the nation.

But in other respects, in Britain the local elections seem to be less second-order than the European elections: more of our respondents cared about the outcome; more felt that the result would make a difference, and fewer reported that they voted on the basis of national issues. Like other analysts, we have found only very faint evidence that European issues affected turnout or vote in the European election. We also find that instrumental tactical voting was lower in the European elections – 2.8 per cent compared with 4.8 per cent in the local elections – although both were lower than in the 1992 general election.

Gesture politics were clearly present in our respondents' local election behaviour in 1994, especially among those who voted for the Labour party, but Liberal Democrat voters were especially likely to claim that they had voted on local issues. Given that the Liberal Democrats typically fare better in local elections than their national opinion poll standings, there seems no reason to disbelieve our respondents' reports. Moreover, we found clear evidence that control of the local council helped gain the Liberal Democrats votes. In this respect, local factors did translate into local votes.

We have been less successful so far in discovering what it was that gave the Liberal Democrats their advantage from incumbency. It does not appear to have been the 'value for money' that voters attributed to the council. Possibly it was due to tactical voting, or more strictly to an absence of tactical voting for other parties by supporters of the Liberal Democrats, although the numbers in our sample are too small to permit thorough investigation of this. More probably it was due to a general awareness of LD concern for local voters' wishes rather than to any specific service. We asked our respondents whether they felt that 'local councils ought to be controlled by central government more, less, or about the same as now'. Forty-two per cent of our respondents felt that local councils should be controlled less (while only 12 per cent felt they should be controlled more). Moreover, former Conservatives who felt that local councils should be controlled less by central government were significantly more likely to switch to the Liberal Democrats.

The fact that we were unable to pin down value for money, or evaluation of specific local services, as a direct influence on voting should not, however, be taken as lack of local accountability. The conditions for local accountability do seem to be in place: voters were aware which services were the responsibility of local government, and they were happy to give an evaluation of these services. Interestingly they were not so willing to give evaluations of standards in local hospitals, on which of course fewer people will have direct experience. They were also happy to evaluate the value for money they received from their local council tax, and after allowing for the effects of partisanship, there were consistent differences in the evaluations which councils of different political complexion received.

So voters could have decided on the basis of value for money if they had wished to do so. But perhaps voters felt that value for money was not the only relevant local consideration.

APPENDIX
THE BRITISH ELECTION PANEL STUDY

Our data come from the 1992–97 British Election Panel Study (BEPS). The panel is a follow-up of respondents to the 1992 British Election Survey, and the plan is to re-interview them annually until the time of the next general election in 1996 or 1997. Of the original 3534 respondents to the 1992 BES, 13.5 per cent said that they were unwilling to be re-interviewed. As many as possible of the remaining 3057 were contacted by post in 1993 and by face-to-face interview in 1994. Altogether 2622 usable questionnaires were returned in 1993 and 2277 interviews were achieved in 1994.

The original 1992 BES oversampled in Scotland in order to enable a detailed study to be undertaken of Scottish voting behaviour (Brand *et al.*, 1994). In order to adjust for this oversampling, the 1992 voters in the sample have been weighted. See Brook and Taylor (1996) and Taylor, Heath, and Lynn (1996) for details on: panel attrition, its effect on the representativeness of those left in the panel, and the measures taken to minimize it; and investigations of whether membership of our panels conditioned voters into behaving differently than they would otherwise have done.

ACKNOWLEDGEMENTS

The BEPS is funded through the ESRC Research Centre for Research into Elections and Social Trends. We are very grateful to the ESRC and to our colleagues in the Centre – Roger Jowell, John Curtice, Daphne Arendt, Lindsay Brook, Alison Park and Katarina Thomson – for their help with the design and fieldwork of the BEPS.

NOTES

1. All the metropolitan areas in England, including London, and the whole of Scotland had an election. Most of Wales did not (4 councils out of 37 had an election). In England outside the

metropolitan conurbations, a minority of authorities (114 out of 296) held elections. In all, 1129 out of 1859 respondents in the 1994 panel (60.7 per cent) believed that there was a local election in their area.

2. If our respondents had frequently been mistaken as to who controlled their council there would be further complications; but they were not. Seventy-two per cent of those who faced local elections correctly identified the party or parties that controlled the council in question, and only 4 per cent believed that a council was Labour controlled when it was actually Conservative controlled or vice versa.

3. We first selected respondents who blamed (or credited) the local council as opposed to government or some other body. We then found that, of respondents who believed that the Conservatives were in control, 49 per cent felt repairs had improved. Of those who believed that Labour was in control, 54 per cent believed repairs had improved, while of those who believed that the Liberal Democrats were in control, 72 per cent felt repairs had improved.

BIBLIOGRAPHY

Brand, J., J. Mitchell and P. Surridge (1994) 'Will Scotland Come to the Aid of the Party?' in A. Heath *et al.*, (eds) *Labour's Last Chance?* pp.213–28. Aldershot: Dartmouth.

Brook, L. and B. Taylor (1996) 'The British Election Panel Study 1992–5: Technical Report', London and Oxford: Centre for Research into Elections and Social Trends, CREST Working Article No.41.

Butler, D. and D. Stokes (1974), *Political Change in Britain.* (2nd edn) London: Macmillan.

Curtice, J. (1989), 'The 1989 European Election: Protest or Green Tide?', *Electoral Studies* 8: 217–30.

Downs, A. (1957), *An Economic Theory of Democracy* New York: Harper and Row.

Heath, A., R. Jowell, J. Curtice and B. Taylor (1995), 'The 1994 European and Local Elections: Abstention, Protest, and Conversion', paper presented at the PSA annual conference, York, April.

Irwin, G. (1995) 'Second-order or Third-Rate? Issues in the Campaign for the Elections to the European Parliament 1994', *Electoral Studies* 14: 183–99.

Lynn, P. (1990), *Public Perceptions of Local Government: its Finance and Services.* London: HMSO for Department of the Environment.

Reif, K. and H. Schmitt (1980), 'Nine Second-Order National Elections', *European Journal of Political Research* 8: 3–45 and 145–62.

Reif, K. (1984), 'National Electoral Cycles and European Elections 1979 and 1984', *Electoral Studies* 3: 244–55.

Smith, J. and I. McLean (1994), 'The Poll Tax and the Electoral Register', in A. Heath, R. Jowell, J. Curtice, and B. Taylor (eds), *Labour's Last Chance? The 1992 Election and Beyond.* pp.229–53. Aldershot: Dartmouth.

Smith, J. and I. McLean (1995), 'The Poll Tax, the Electoral Register and the 1991 Census: an Update', in D. Broughton, D. Farrell, D. Denver, and C. Rallings (eds.), *British Elections and Parties Yearbook 1994.* pp.128–47. London: Frank Cass.

Taylor, B., A. Heath and P. Lynn (1996) 'The British Election Panel Study 1992–5: Response Characteristics and Attrition', London and Oxford: Centre for Research into Elections and Social Trends , CREST Working Article No. 40.

Van der Eijk, C., M. Franklin and M. Marsh (1996) 'What Can Voters Teach us about Europe-Wide Elections; What Can Europe-Wide Elections Teach us about Voters?', *Electoral Studies* 15: 149–66.

Forecasting Vote and Seat Share in Local Elections

Colin Rallings and Michael Thrasher

For political scientists, developing an accurate model for election forecasting is the equivalent of inventing the perfect mouse-trap. Such models that currently exist fall into one of two main types. On the one hand, there are those attempts, often very sophisticated, to model the pattern of future electoral preferences according to the impact of policy and economic conditions on voters' perceptions and partisanship. The current doyen of work in this field is David Sanders (1991, 1993, 1993a) of the University of Essex. On the other hand, prediction over the very short term is provided by election exit polls which ask respondents how they have voted in order to forecast both the share of the vote and the number of seats gained by parties as soon as the polling booths close (Curtice and Payne, 1995; Mathias and Cowling, 1995). A similar role is played by opinion polls at the end of an election campaign, although pollsters consistently and correctly point out that their findings are a snapshot of how voters intended to behave at the time they were asked and are not a prediction of how they will actually behave even in just a few hours time (Worcester, 1991). What both these approaches have in common, however, is that they have been used almost exclusively to predict the result of general elections. Limited exit polling has been conducted during elections to the European Parliament, but not at local elections (Braunholtz and Atkinson, 1996). There has been no work relating prior economic conditions and perceptions to the result of either type of 'second-order' contest.

The purpose of this article is to outline and test a third approach specifically designed to forecast the outcome of local elections. It derives from a model we have developed for monitoring movements in electoral opinion based on the results of local government by-elections regularly held throughout the country. Since 1992 this model has proved very successful in projecting the share of vote likely to be gained by the political parties at the annual round of local elections in May; it has been less good at forecasting the number of seats likely to be won and lost by them. We explore some of the reasons for this discrepancy with particular reference to the underestimation of the seat gains made by the Liberal Democrats in both 1993 and 1994.

Calculating Party Vote Shares

Each week in Britain there are, on average, eight local council by-elections. Like their parliamentary counterparts, they occur as the result of death or resignation and they give the electorate in wards where they fall an additional and unexpected opportunity to exercise their franchise. Unlike parliamentary by-elections, however, these contests generally take place far from the glare of national media and party attention and may be said to be a more accurate reflection of voters' underlying and unprompted partisanship. Of course, some of these local by-elections will be dominated by local issues and local personalities, but in most cases those electors who turn out are likely to be expressing their current party preference at least as far as the running of their local council is concerned.

The results of individual contests help to flesh out a pattern of ebbs and flows in party support. Changes in share of the vote and 'swing' can easily be calculated by comparison with the last time the ward was contested in a 'general' local election. However, just as added interest in parliamentary by-elections stems from comparing the result in terms of what would have happened across the nation rather than just in one constituency at the previous general election, so it is the case that drawing wider conclusions from local by-elections requires the establishment of a benchmark against which all results can be measured. Without such a benchmark we have no way of knowing how far the electoral behaviour in any ward accorded with, or deviated from, the national average and thus the significance of the vote movements it displays.

It is relatively straightforward to calculate a share of the vote figure for each party at each set of local elections that may be seen as a surrogate for its national level of support if those elections had been contested in every part of the country as in a general election. For the past decade two independent calculations of this 'national equivalent vote share' have been published in the days immediately following the May local elections. The reliability and robustness of the measure may partly be gleaned from the degree to which these estimates have been in accord over that period (Curtice and Payne, 1991; Rallings and Thrasher, 1993). Its role in enabling forecasts of the results of future local elections to be made is crucial.

Quite simply, the model relies on estimating what impact each individual local by-election result has had on the national standing of the parties. The first step in this process is to record the shares of the vote obtained by the three major parties in the ward both at that by-election and on the last occasion it was fought in the May contests. Only local elections which feature Conservative, Labour and Liberal Democrat candidates are used. Next, the year in which those May elections occurred and the national equivalent vote share published at the time are noted. Then, the change in each party's share of the vote between the by-election and the relevant May elections is calculated and those change figures applied to the appropriate national equivalent vote. Naturally, as when a party's local election share increases or decreases by a factor greater than its national equivalent level of support, some of the results produced by this model will be nonsensical. However, it has become clear that by taking the mean change in all those by-elections which occur over the period of either a fixed or rolling quarter, extreme results are smoothed out and an accurate gauge of each party's national level of support in local elections can be produced.

The only empirical test of this model is its ability to forecast the results of each May's local elections ahead of the event. In 1993, 1994 and 1995 applying the model to local by-elections occurring in the three months prior to May has produced a national equivalent vote share very similar to that calculated after the elections had taken place. As Table 1 makes clear, the largest error in projection produced by this method for any party at any of the elections was the 2 per cent overestimate of the Labour vote in 1993. This contrasts sharply with some of the opinion poll projections published close to the election which have over- or underestimated party shares of the vote by a much greater factor.[1]

TABLE 1
PROJECTED AND ACTUAL NATIONAL EQUIVALENT SHARES OF THE VOTE AT
LOCAL ELECTIONS

	1993		1994		1995	
	Proj.	Actual	Proj.	Actual	Proj.	Actual
Conservative	32	31	29	28	26	25
Labour	43	41	41	40	47	47
LibDem	23	24	27	27	23	24

Note: All figures as published in *The Sunday Times* before and after elections.

Predicting Seat Gains and Losses

The model was designed, of course, not simply to produce a forecast national equivalent share of the vote, but also to project how many seats each party was likely to win or lose. Assuming uniform change between the national equivalent vote at the previous set of May local elections at the same point in the cycle and our current vote share projection, we presented that calculation in terms of the net gains or losses to be expected for each party. Unfortunately, as Table 2 shows, this aspect of our prediction proved much less reliable. In 1993 and 1994 Conservative losses and Liberal Democrat gains, and in 1995 Conservative losses and Labour gains, were seriously underestimated. The fact that such errors occurred despite the proven accuracy of our vote share projection has led us to examine the patterns of changing party support in different types of ward. The analysis reported here focuses on the 1993 and 1994 elections and our failure to predict the extent of Liberal Democrat gains.

TABLE 2
PROJECTED AND ACTUAL SEAT GAINS AND LOSSES

| | 1993 | | 1994 | | 1995 | |
	Proj.	Actual	Proj.	Actual	Proj.	Actual
Conservative	-100	-470	-300	-450	-1750	-2100
Labour	–	+90	+50	+110	+1150	+1800
LibDem	+150	+380	+250	+380	+600	+500

Note: All projection figures as published in *The Sunday Times*. Actual figures from C. Rallings and M. Thrasher, *Local Elections Handbook* (Plymouth: Local Government Chronicle Elections Centre, various years).

The Link Between Vote Share and Seat Share in 1993

One possible cause of our error in estimating seat gains and losses can be addressed immediately. If a party puts up a candidate for the first election but not for the subsequent one, or vice versa, any calculation of the numbers of seats to be won by each party based on changing shares of the vote is bound to be wrong. As it happens this has not influenced the accuracy of the model unduly, but to eliminate the influence of such cases we consider only those 1605 out of a total 3500 county council divisions where the boundaries were unchanged and where all three parties contested the elections in both 1989 and 1993.

In Table 3 we report the impact a uniform swing model would have had in these 1605 seats using two sets of national equivalent vote share figures calculated after the 1993 local elections. The first set are our own calculations for the *Sunday Times*, while the second are those figures prepared for the BBC and the *Guardian* by John Curtice and colleagues. The respective changes in party vote shares between 1989 and 1993 implied by these estimates were then applied to the 1989 voting figures and, assuming uniform swing, the number of seats projected to be won by the different parties recalculated.

TABLE 3
NATIONAL EQUIVALENT VOTE SHARES, SEAT PROJECTIONS WITH UNIFORM
SWING AND ACTUAL SEAT OUTCOMES

	Sunday Times		BBC		
	% Change 1989–93	Proj. seats	% Change 1989–93	Proj. seats	Actual seats
Conservative	-6.5	659	-7.0	663	512
Labour	-0.5	522	–	547	549
LibDem	+6.0	424	+4.0	395	531

The BBC's national equivalent vote figures for 1989 and 1993 imply a 7 per cent fall in the Conservative vote, no change for Labour and a 4 per cent rise in the Liberal Democrat share. Applied to those seats in this analysis the BBC figures are very accurate for Labour, but they overestimate Conservative seats by 151 and underestimate Liberal Democrat seats by 136. The *Sunday Times* figures are slightly different, suggesting the Liberal Democrat vote rose by 6 per cent, while Labour's fell by half a percentage point and the Conservatives' by 6.5 per cent. These figures underestimate Labour strength by 27 seats and the Liberal Democrats by 107 seats, while overestimating the number of Conservative seats by 147 seats. Both sets of national estimated vote shares, therefore, produce inaccurate figures for seats on the uniform swing model. In order to make the seat predictions from the uniform swing model coincide with the actual allocation of seats it is necessary to leave the Labour vote exactly as it was in 1989 (as both models effectively do), and to decrease the Conservative vote and increase the Liberal Democrat vote by 11 per cent. In other words, instead of a Conservative–Liberal Democrat swing of either 5.5 per cent (BBC) or 6.3 per cent (*Sunday Times*), the uniform swing model would have to assume an 11 per cent swing in order to predict the correct number of seats. Neither estimation of the national equivalent vote was likely to have been that far from the mark!

To explore this problem further we examined how far tactical voting might provide an explanation for the failure of uniform swing accurately to project seat gains and losses. Local electors, perhaps, had been keen to deliver the Conservatives a bloody nose and had voted for the party most likely to unseat the incumbent Tory. We sub-divided Conservative-held seats in 1989 into Conservative/Labour (N=369) and Conservative/Liberal Democrat (N=426) according to which party had finished as runner-up. These categories were then further sub-divided into those seats with a Conservative majority of 20 per cent or less and those with a similar majority, but where the gap between the second and third parties was greater than 10 per cent. The intention was to discover whether the marginals had behaved differently from other seats and whether the size of the gap between the second and third placed parties had any impact on the outcome. Tactical voting might be more likely where the voters were not confused about which of the opposition parties to support.

If there had been tactical voting we would expect that in Conservative/Labour marginals the Liberal Democrat vote would be squeezed, while in Conservative/Liberal Democrat marginals it would be Labour's support which felt the pinch. In fact, as Table 4 shows, in the Conservative/Labour marginals the Liberal Democrat vote did rise by less than average while Labour's vote was 1 per cent higher. But this is only part of the story. In the Conservative/Liberal Democrat marginals the Labour vote is virtually unaffected by the circumstances of the contest, whereas for the Liberal Democrats the movement is, if anything, contrary to the direction expected. Certainly, on this evidence it does not appear that tactical voting contributed significantly to the inaccuracy of our seats forecast.

TABLE 4
VOTING IN THE CONSERVATIVE MARGINALS: 1993 COUNTY ELECTIONS

	Cons % Δ 89–93	Labour % Δ 89–93	LibDem % Δ 89–93	Seats N=
All	-7.4	+0.6	+9.0	1605
All Con/Lab	-9.6	+2.2	+9.7	369
Con/Lab marginal	-7.0	+3.2	+5.9	149
Con/Lab marginal and >10% lead over LibDem	-7.4	+3.1	+6.6	125
All Con/LibDem	-9.7	+0.3	+10.7	426
Con/LibDem marginal	-7.9	+0.6	+9.0	189
Con/LibDem marginal and >10% lead over Lab	-7.7	+0.6	+8.6	164

Two further possible explanations for the non-uniform vote swing suggest themselves. First, it could be that there was a marked, non-proportional decline in the Conservative vote so that the party's support fell most in its safest seats. A second, and related, possibility is that traditional Conservative voters in these same seats failed to perceive that there was any threat to their party and allowed their ward to be lost through higher than average rates of abstention. Table 5 divides those seats won by the Conservatives in 1989 into four categories based on the party's share of the vote at that time, ranging from seats where it gained more than 60 per cent of the vote to those where it scored 30–40 per cent. Although the vote changes are higher in the party's safest seats the vote decline is, in fact, roughly proportional in each of the four categories. Similarly, the pattern of turnout does not suggest that Conservative voters were more complacent in their safest seats. In these, turnout declined by one per cent compared with 1989. In those invariably more marginal seats with a 1989 Conservative vote share between 30 per cent and 40 per cent, however, the turnout fell by 2.6 per cent. Neither finding is consistent with the proposition that the variability in the county council elections was a function of irregular fluctuations in Conservative support.

TABLE 5
CHANGE IN CONSERVATIVE PERCENTAGE VOTE AND TURNOUT: 1989–93
COUNTY COUNCIL ELECTIONS

	Cons % Δ 89–93	Turnout % Δ 89–93	Wards N=
Con share in 1989 >60%	-12.7	-1.1	204
Con share in 1989 >50% and <60%	-10.1	-0.7	311
Con share in 1989 >40% and <50%	-7.4	-1.6	375
Con share in 1989 >30% and <40%	-6.3	-2.6	336

Tactical voting requires a proactive electorate willing and able to assess the relative chances of the different parties in individual wards and to cast a ballot in the most effective manner. In the case of these elections such a description would seem unjustified. However, if the electorate was not proactive, can we uncover any evidence that it was reactive? One way to proceed is by examining those seats lost by the Conservatives in 1993. It was expected that the Conservatives would lose about 100 seats. Instead they lost almost five times as many. If tactical voting does not appear to be the explanation, what was so different about these seats that a uniform swing model could not detect their vulnerability beforehand?

First, we looked solely at the 233 seats in our sample which the Liberal Democrats captured from the Conservatives in 1993. In these seats the change in share of the vote compared with 1989 was: Conservative -13.5 per cent; Labour -3.4 per cent; Liberal Democrat +20.0 per cent. In effect the Conservative decline was 6.1 per cent more than the average for all cases, Labour's decline compared with its 0.6 per cent increase overall, while the increase in the Liberal Democrat vote was fully 11 per cent higher than its overall average (Table 4). Clearly, there was something unusual going on in these particular seats. The 1989 average Conservative majority in those seats lost to the Liberal Democrats in 1993 was no less than 17.4 per cent, ranging from less than 1 per cent to a maximum of 52.9 per cent. Of the 233 Liberal Democrat gains, 130 (55.8 per cent) were in seats that would have been classified as 'marginal' because the Conservative majority had been 20 per cent or less in 1989. In these particular cases the Conservative vote fell by 11 per cent, Labour's by 2.3 per cent and the Liberal Democrat vote rose by 15.7 per cent, compared with a Conservative fall of -7.9 per cent, a Labour increase of +0.6 per cent and a Liberal Democrat advance of +9.0 per cent in all 189 Conservative/Liberal Democrat marginals. Such figures imply that the Conservative share in those Conservative/Liberal Democrat marginal seats retained by the party in 1993 fell by less than 2 per cent while the Liberal Democrat vote in the same divisions rose by only 2.5 per cent.

Such figures, together with the size and range of the majorities in seats lost by the Conservatives, highlights the irregular pattern in the Liberal Democrat performance. When the party's gains are examined in more detail it appears that in no less than 135 cases out of 233, the Conservative-to-Liberal Democrat swing was higher than that used as the basis for our seat prediction. In each of three districts (Wokingham, Poole and New Forest) the Liberal Democrats gained four divisions where the Conservative lead had been higher than the 12 per cent majority deemed vulnerable by the assumed change in vote between 1989 and 1993. Further support for the idea of a reactive electorate responding to campaign messages can be found in the 49 out of 233 divisions where the Liberal Democrats not only gained the seat from the Conservatives but also overtook Labour which had finished second in 1989. Leapfrogging is not entirely unknown, especially in three-way marginals, but in these examples the Conservative vote fell by an average 17 per cent, Labour's by 7 per cent and the Liberal Democrat vote rose by a massive 31 per cent. Few of these seats would have been described as three-way competitive before the elections took place. These particular seats, comprising 21 per cent of all Liberal Democrat gains from the Conservatives in our party competition controlled data set, do not sit easily within any tactical voting model but do support a view which puts more emphasis on the capacity of local party campaigns to determine the electoral outcome.

In order to test whether this behaviour was specific to the Liberal Democrats we then looked at Labour gains from the Conservatives to see if there were similarities. Within the truncated data set there were 77 cases where Labour had gained a Conservative seat. In these divisions the changes in share of the vote were Conservative -10.0 per cent (compared with an average of -7.4), Labour +9.2 per cent (+0.6 per cent) and Liberal Democrat +2.8 per cent (+9.0 per cent). For each party these changes in support also demonstrate greater variation from the average than in the case of all Conservative/Labour marginals. However, it is worth recording that 68 (88.3 per cent) out of the 77 Labour gains came in divisions where the Conservative lead was less than 20 per cent, that is, the marginals. There were only five divisions where Labour had leapfrogged the Liberal Democrats to gain a seat from third place so it was not really possible to replicate that particular analysis. However, as with the case in seats where they were challenged by the Liberal Democrats, the Conservative share held up much better in those Conservative/Labour marginals the party held (-4 per cent), whereas Labour's share was unchanged compared with 1989 in the same seats.

The Link between Vote Share and Seat Share in 1994

In order to determine whether these findings were the product of an exceptional set of elections in 1993, we decided to replicate the analysis for the 1994 local elections. Once again our seat forecasting had underestimated Liberal Democrat gains despite our computer model of local election shares proving an accurate predictor of the eventual national equivalent outcome (see Tables 1 and 2 again). There were elections in more than 3400 wards in 1994 covering some shire districts and all the metropolitan and London boroughs. Controls introduced to allow for changes in boundaries and party competition between the previous elections in this cycle in 1990 and 1994 reduced the number of cases in the 1994 dataset to 884 wards in the shires, 446 in the metropolitan authorities and 496 in the London boroughs. Table 6 shows the mean change in vote share in those wards held by the Conservatives going in to the election according to the type of authority, the party which was in second place, and the seat's marginality in 1990. Because of the problems created by the existence of many multi-member wards we have not reproduced the category identifying the size of the gap between the second and third placed parties used in the 1993 county elections analysis above.

Once again the figures in Table 6 do not provide much prima facie evidence of tactical voting in either Conservative/Labour or Conservative/Liberal Democrat marginals. Taking Conservative/Labour marginals first, we found that far from Labour squeezing the Liberal Democrat vote in the marginals, Labour's own vote fell by more than it did in safer Conservative seats in both the districts and metropolitan boroughs. The exception to this pattern was in London where Labour's vote rose by 2 per cent more in the marginals compared with all Conservative/Labour seats and the Liberal Democrat vote increased by 1 per cent less. Even in these cases, however, the Conservative vote fell by less in the marginal seats compared both with all Conservative/Labour seats and across London as a whole.

In Conservative/Liberal Democrat marginal seats evidence of tactical voting would be expected to show a steeper decline in the Labour vote as that party's support was squeezed. The only case where this happens to any extent is in the districts where Labour's vote fell by 0.6 per cent more in the 71 marginals than in all Conservative/Liberal Democrat seats. However, the Liberal Democrat vote also rose by less than average in these wards. The consistent pattern in all types of authority is that the Conservatives are better able to preserve their own vote in their marginal wards than in the contests as a whole, whereas there is little evidence to suggest that the opposition parties do best in their target seats. Such figures do not present an image of a proactive electorate efficiently seeking the most effective way to register a protest vote against the Conservatives.

TABLE 6
VOTING IN CONSERVATIVE WARDS: 1994 ELECTIONS

	Cons % Δ 90–94	Labour % Δ 90–94	LibDem % Δ 90–94	Wards N=
Shire districts	-4.7	-3.9	+10.8	884
All Con/Lab	-8.4	-6.0	+16.5	124
Con/Lab marginal	-7.5	-7.1	+16.2	74
All Con/LibDem	-7.2	-4.7	+12.7	119
Con/LibDem marginal	-5.5	-5.3	+10.9	71
Metropolitan boroughs	-4.7	-3.3	+9.6	446
All Con/Lab	-7.0	-0.9	+12.4	57
Con/Lab marginal	-6.4	-1.4	+12.0	31
All Con/LibDem	-6.5	-0.9	+8.8	15
Con/LibDem marginal	-4.8	0.0	+5.8	9
London boroughs	-6.0	+2.2	+7.1	496
All Con/Lab	-6.6	+2.6	+7.8	188
Con/Lab marginal	-5.1	+4.6	+6.7	79
All Con/LibDem	-9.3	-0.2	+12.9	43
Con/LibDem marginal	-6.7	-0.5	+9.9	13

Note: Marginal is defined as 20% majority or less in 1990.

Once again we extended our analysis by looking at those Conservative wards in our data set which changed hands between 1990 and 1994. The figures in Table 7 show quite significant differences in the change of share of the vote in those wards won by Labour and, most particularly, the Liberal Democrats compared with the overall averages in Table 6. The 'uniform swing with hindsight' model indicated a likely fall in the Conservative vote of 4 per cent and a Liberal Democrat rise of 11 per cent – a 7 per cent swing. However, in the 154 cases in our dataset where the Liberal Democrats gained a Conservative seat the *average* swing was at least twice what we expected. A much smaller swing of 0.5 per cent had been anticipated between Conservative and Labour because of Labour's strong local election performance in 1990, but in the 60 seats which Labour won from the Conservatives the average swing ranged from 6.4 per cent in the metropolitan boroughs to 8.1 per cent in London. Given that the swing across all cases (with the partial exception of London where Labour increased its vote compared with 1990 and thus achieved a swing of 4 per cent) corresponded with the national swing, we appear to have a set of wards that behaved quite out of the ordinary. And yet, as Table 6 indicated, there was little about these seats in terms of marginality and the ordering in which the parties finished in 1990 to suggest the seats changed hands through tactical voting.

TABLE 7
AVERAGE PERCENTAGE CHANGE AND SWING IN WARDS LOST BY CONSERVATIVES:
1994 ELECTIONS

	Cons % Δ 90–94	Labour % Δ 90–94	LibDem % Δ 90–94	Wards N=
Labour gains				
Districts	-8.7	+6.4	+5.0	16
Mets	-7.3	+5.5	+7.3	10
London	-7.8	+8.4	+5.0	34
Liberal Democrat gains				
Districts	-10.0	-9.4	+21.6	112
Mets	-11.1	-7.7	+21.4	14
London	-15.3	-5.1	+23.3	28

Such an assertion receives further support when we discover that in no fewer than 60 of the 154 cases where the Liberal Democrats gained a seat from the Conservatives it had been Labour which was in second place in 1990. In these seats the Conservative vote fell by an average 12 per cent and Labour's vote fell by an even greater 12.5 per cent while the Liberal Democrat share rose by some 27.5 per cent. These gains were divided between 42 local authorities with only Bath (4), Hastings (3) and Sheffield (3) recording more than two gains of this type. Indeed the broad spread of wards where the Liberals overtook both Labour and Conservative to win seats in 1994 suggests that such extraordinary victims would have been extremely difficult to predict beforehand.

Election Forecasts and the Erratic Liberal Democrat Vote

Further evidence of how erratic the Liberal Democrat vote has proved to be can be found in Table 8. In their analysis of the 1982 local elections, Curtice and his colleagues noted that the Alliance's performance had suffered from a 'plateau effect' (Curtice *et al.,* 1983). Thus, the higher the Liberal performance in 1980, the lower the improvement on that performance by the Alliance in 1982. At the other end of the scale, where the Liberal vote had been low in 1980, the Alliance improved the most – to little avail of course in terms of seats won. Across the two elections, therefore, there was a clear linear pattern to the change in the Liberal and Alliance vote. Although using slightly different vote share categories, Table 8 replicates that earlier analysis for the Liberal Democrats in 1993 and 1994 compared with elections four years earlier.

Two features of this table are worthy of note. First, the plateau is barely noticeable compared with that found in 1982 and a sizeable increase in Liberal Democrat support is recorded in all categories. True, there is a tapering off above the 40 per cent level but there is no clear left to right decline in the vote change between the two sets of elections. Second, the standard deviations for these mean scores are considerably higher than were those either for the Alliance in 1982 or for the other main parties in 1994. This suggests that even within these categories the Liberal Democrat vote is not behaving uniformly.

TABLE 8
LIBERAL DEMOCRATS AND THE MISSING PLATEAU

Previous election	%vote 0–20	%vote 20–30	%vote 30–40	%vote >40	All wards
1993 elections					
% Δ since 1989	8.6	9.6	8.8	6.3	8.4
Std. deviation	9.6	12.9	10.6	9.2	10.3
N	(836)	(259)	(207)	(303)	(1605)
1994 elections					
% Δ since 1990	9.7	12.5	9.2	7.8	9.5
Std. deviation	9.5	12.4	10.9	9.0	10.0
N	(1087)	(186)	(219)	(339)	(1831)

This leaves us with the possibility that the Liberal Democrat vote is influenced by the *local* context. Within each of the four vote share categories there will be instances of Liberal Democrat candidates fighting seats in areas where the party is weak in the ward but strong in the district or, conversely, where the party is strong in the ward but weak in the district as a whole. Thus, a Liberal Democrat candidate fighting to gain an additional ward in Bath or Eastbourne will benefit from the fact that the party is already strong in the area, whereas fellow candidates in Barnsley or Barrow would not experience the same sort of contextual support for their campaign.

To examine this proposition we divided districts according to the Liberal Democrat share in the authority as a whole at the previous election. For the 1993 and 1994 results we devised three categories of local authority based on the party's performance in 1989 and 1990. Those where the Liberal Democrat vote was 25 per cent or less, those where it was between 25 per cent and 40 per cent and those where it was in excess of 40 per cent. Changes in the Liberal Democrat vote share were looked at from three perspectives: those seats which the party won at neither election; those which the party gained; and those which the party held in both sets of election. If there was a local authority level impact on the fate of Liberal Democrat candidates in individual wards we would expect that in areas where the party was strong their candidates might do better than in areas where no Liberal Democrat presence had yet been established. The results of this analysis are presented in Table 9.

TABLE 9
LOCAL AUTHORITY CONTEXT AND MEAN CHANGE IN THE LIBERAL DEMOCRAT VOTE

	Liberal Democrat vote share in local authority at previous election			
	less than 25%	26%–40%	40%+	Overall
1993 Counties (change on 1989)				
Seats not won by LibDem	4.8	8.2	9.9	5.5
Seats gained by LibDem	22.9	18.8	16.2	20.5
Seats held by LibDem	7.3	8.2	7.2	7.8
1994 Elections (change on 1990)				
Seats not won by LibDem	6.7	7.0	-2.5	6.6
Seats gained by LibDem	23.2	21.6	17.6	22.3
Seats held by LibDem	10.4	10.4	4.6	9.5

We have already referred to the large swings enjoyed by Liberal Democrat candidates when they succeed in gaining a seat, and these figures give immediate clarification of that. What they do not show, however, is any clear link between the context of a seat in terms of the local authority area and the relative increase in vote share for Liberal Democrats. In both 1993 and 1994 the largest increases in Liberal Democrat share were in the seats they gained in areas which had been the party's weakest four years previously. There is some evidence of 'plateauing' in strong Liberal Democrat districts where the party held its seats, but even in these districts the average increase in vote share in those wards captured by the party is impressive. On the whole, however, the figures appear to be telling us that the Liberal Democrat vote in individual wards does not depend on strong district-wide support for the party in order for it to increase sufficiently for the party to win the seat. In short, if there are the activists, organizers and candidates in a ward the Liberal Democrats have as good a chance of winning new wards, and winning them spectacularly, in Barnsley and Barrow as they have in Bath and Eastbourne.

Conclusion

Our analysis began by setting out a method for calculating the national share of the vote and number of seats likely to be obtained by the political parties at each set of May local elections. The method has succeeded in projecting accurate vote shares in each of the last three local elections, but has proved less useful in forecasting the number of seats gained and lost. It is clear that much of this error is the result of the lack of uniform swing in local election results across the country.

Our curiosity was especially prompted by the Liberal Democrats' success in 1993 and 1994 in winning many more seats than a strict application of their share of the vote would have implied. Liberal Democrat seat gains were often associated with huge swings. The existence of prior favourable conditions such as the marginality of the ward and the party's occupation of second place did not appear to be necessary prerequisites for success. In particular, there was little indication that the Liberal Democrats – or indeed any other party – benefited substantially at the local level from tactical voting. Rather, whereas the Conservatives did manage to retain a greater share of its vote than average in those marginal seats it was defending and whereas most of Labour's successes occurred in wards which were already marginal (both likely rewards for campaigning effort), Liberal Democrat gains took place in widely different circumstances and often involved a straight move from third to first place.

Such victories may well represent less a case of tactical voting than of tactical campaigning, an electorate reacting to cues from the parties rather than itself assessing each party's chances of victory and voting accordingly. In the often numerically and geographically small wards of local government it is relatively easy to mount intense election campaigns. Moreover, as the 'centre' party, the Liberal Democrats are well placed to exploit a volatile electorate disenchanted with either of its traditionally preferred choices. Given the right local candidates, issues and campaigns the Liberal Democrats can potentially win anywhere. It is this ability to defy electoral gravity which dooms any attempt to relate share of the vote and seats won on the basis of uniform swing. The lesson may next need to be learned by those who attempt to forecast the result of general elections by the application of similar assumptions.

Unfortunately, therefore, our model for forecasting the outcome of local election results has proved only a partial success. Compared with opinion polls, the use of local by-election data does appear to provide a more reliable base from which to predict the main parties' likely national equivalent vote share. For a variety of reasons, ranging from changing patterns of party competition to local campaigning effects, the model is less secure in its forecast of seat gains and losses. The immediate goal must be to seek some modification of the uniform swing hypothesis to provide a more accurate seat prediction. It seems likely, for example, that there is a spatial dimension particularly to the performance of the Liberal Democrats in local elections (Dorling et al., 1995). Applying different changes in vote share in different geographical regions based on historical precedent may have a positive impact on our forecasts. Similarly, closer attention to the impact of candidates (especially where incumbent councillors do not put themselves forward for re-election) and campaigns (as measured by changes in levels of turnout) may reap dividends.

ACKNOWLEDGEMENTS

The research reported on here forms part of a larger ESRC funded project on local elections (research grant R000234540).

NOTE

1 For example, a MORI poll published in *The Times* on 28th April 1995 recorded that 55 per cent of respondents intended to vote Labour in the following week's local election, 22 per cent Conservative and 18 per cent Liberal Democrat.

BIBLIOGRAPHY

Braunholtz, Simon and Simon Atkinson (1996) 'What Can We Learn from June 9? Voters in the 1994 European Parliament Elections', in Colin Rallings, David Farrell, David Denver and David Broughton (eds) *British Elections and Parties Yearbook 1995*, pp.1–13. London: Frank Cass.

Curtice, John, Clive Payne and Robert Waller (1983) 'The Alliance's First Nationwide Test: Lessons of the 1982 English Local Elections', *Electoral Studies* 2: 3–22.

Curtice, John and Clive Payne (1991), 'Local Elections as National Referenda', *Electoral Studies* 10: 3–17.

Curtice, John and Clive Payne (1995) 'Forecasting the 1992 Election: the BBC Experience', pp.213–41 in Ivor Crewe and Brian Gosschalk (eds), *Political Communications: the General Election Campaign of 1992*. Cambridge: Cambridge University Press.

Dorling, Daniel, Colin Rallings and Michael Thrasher (1995) 'The Epidemiology of the Liberal Democrat Vote', paper presented to the EPOP annual conference, London Guildhall University, September.

Mathias, Glyn and David Cowling (1995) 'The ITN Exit Poll', pp.242–6 in Ivor Crewe and Brian Gosschalk (eds), *Political Communications: the General Election Campaign of 1992*. Cambridge: Cambridge University Press.

Rallings, Colin and Michael Thrasher (1993) 'Explaining Uniformity and Variability in Local Election Outcomes', *Electoral Studies* 12: 366–84.

Sanders, David (1991) 'Government Popularity and the Next General Election', *Political Quarterly* 62: 235–61.

Sanders, David (1993) 'Forecasting the 1992 General Election Result: the Performance of an Economic Model', in David Denver, Pippa Norris, David Broughton and Colin Rallings (eds), *British Elections and Parties Yearbook 1993*, pp.100–115. Hemel Hempstead: Harvester Wheatsheaf.

Sanders, David (1993a) 'Economic Influences and the Vote: Modelling Electoral Decisions', in Ian Budge and David McKay (eds), *Developing Democracy: Research in Honour of J.F.P. Blondel.* London: Sage.

Worcester, Robert (1991) *British Public Opinion: A Guide to the History and Methodology of Political Opinion Polling.* Oxford: Basil Blackwell.

Missing Voters in Britain, 1992–96: Where and with What Impact?

Daniel Dorling, Charles Pattie, David Rossiter and Ron Johnston

Introduction

The number of people able to vote at elections in the United Kingdom has increased virtually continuously over the last two centuries. This has been partly due to population growth, but mainly to the various extensions of the democratic franchise to men without property, women, and then to adults aged 18–20. This relatively steady rise came to an end roughly ten years ago, and the electorate fell sharply in the latter half of the 1980s, despite an increase in the numbers of people of voting age. Although there has been some recovery in the number of people registered on the electoral roll in the 1990s, this has not offset the majority of the losses which had occurred before then. The electoral implications of this situation are difficult to quantify as, by definition, we can know very little of the views of people who are 'missing' and choose not to vote or who are unable, to register on the electoral roll. However, it is possible to determine which constituencies these potential voters were most likely to be living in at the time of the 1992 general election. We also look at the nature of electoral competition both in those constituencies and in the new constituencies created by the recent boundary review in order to speculate on what might be the possible effect of the voluntary abstention of adults not eligible to vote at both the last general election and the next.

Finding the Missing Millions

'Left-wing council will give homeless the vote' (*The Times*, 19 August 1995)

The story which the above headline was taken from addresses an issue we know so little about, but have heard so much of: the missing millions. The story started when it emerged that 1.2 million people living in Britain had not been counted in the 1991 census. The story grew as it became apparent that the narrow Conservative victory at the 1992 general election may have been aided by people not registering to vote, so as to avoid the poll tax (Smith and

McLean, 1994; McLean and Smith, 1995). One result of this attention was that the Economic and Social Research Council (ESRC) funded a project to estimate where people were missing from: Estimating with Confidence (EWC). This work was recently completed at the Universities of Manchester and Southampton and the results have been released to the academic community for research purposes. The results estimate, for every ward in the country, the actual number of people who lived there in 1991 by age and sex (for further details see Simpson *et al.*, 1995).

Even given good estimates of the number of people living in small areas, estimating how many electors there should be in each constituency is far from easy. First you need to know which wards constitute which constituency. Prior to the recent boundary changes, constituencies were defined in terms of the ward boundaries which were in place when they were created (in 1983, approximated here by 1981 census wards). The new constituencies are defined in terms of 1991 census wards. This means that estimates of missing people for both sets of basic spatial units are needed if a comparison over the period is to be made. The problem is particularly tricky in Scotland (as digital 1981 Scottish ward boundaries are not available to the academic community for research and as the Scottish Boundary Commission used Regional Electoral Divisions in the fourth review). Worrying about shifting ward boundaries may sound pedantic, but misplacing half a large ward's population can make it appear as if ten thousand voters were missing from a constituency.

The second problem is that 'people' don't equate to 'eligible electors'. Firstly, of course, only adults have the vote, so those aged under 18 have to be excluded. The data on the number of missing people is organized into five-year age groups, so we have assumed that half the number of missing people aged 15–19 in July 1991 in each ward would have been adults by the time of the 1992 general election. More problematic is the fact that not all adults resident in each area are eligible. For example, members of the House of Lords and some people in psychiatric institutions cannot vote at general elections. People in the armed services do not have to be registered where they live. People with multiple homes can be registered at two or more addresses – students as a group are the most concentrated example of this phenomenon: many universities register their students automatically and many students are also registered at their parental address. People who live overseas can register to vote. Most importantly, people who are neither Commonwealth citizens nor citizens of the Irish Republic may not vote at general elections. It is very difficult to take any of these factors into account using the available data. We have only addressed the last problem here by calculating from the 1991 Census how many people living in each ward were born outside the Commonwealth or Ireland and we use this as a proxy for the number of adults ineligible to vote in each ward. This will be an overestimate of the numbers unable to vote because many of these people are British citizens. It also includes children, but they can be taken as a very loose estimate of the numbers of missing adults who would not be eligible to vote in each constituency.

TABLE 1
OLD CONSTITUENCIES WITH MOST VOTERS MISSING IN 1992

Seat		1992 Winner	Adults	NCborn	Electors	Missing	Missing (%)
1	Buckingham*	Con	74378	2300	56063	16015	22
2	Stretford	Lab	68989	2650	54467	11872	18
3	Birmingham Erdington	Lab	64527	816	52398	11313	18
4	Bassetlaw**	Lab	69681	756	58583	10342	15
5	Bristol South	Lab	75913	1169	64309	10435	14
6	Cardiff Central	Lab	69815	2759	57716	9340	14
7	Hammersmith	Lab	62327	8206	47229	6892	13
8	Islington North	Lab	72023	7698	56270	8055	13
9	Portsmouth South	Con	90292	1874	77645	10773	12
10	Westminster North	Con	88284	21667	58847	7770	12
11	Birmingham Hall Green	Con	68356	1038	60091	7227	11
12	Bristol North West	Con	83338	1959	72726	8653	11
13	Poole	Con	90721	2377	79221	9123	10
14	Wolverhampton N.E.	Lab	71038	1164	62695	7179	10
15	Salford East	Lab	60304	1800	52616	5888	10
16	Hackney S. & Shoreditch	Lab	71109	6723	57935	6451	10
17	Kingston-upon-Hull N.	Lab	80460	1183	71363	7914	10
18	Surbiton	Con	49520	2581	42421	4518	10
19	Plymouth Drake	Con	58214	1131	51667	5416	9
20	Fulham	Con	67516	9337	52740	5439	9

Notes: The respective figures for Britain as a whole were: Adults, 43,729,094; NCborn, 1,283,514; Electors, 42,113,792; Missing, 655,382; Missing (%), 2. The total number of eligible electors estimated to be missing at the last election is the total of all the (positive) numbers of missing people estimated to be resident and eligible to vote in each seat.

Adults is the EWC estimate of the number of adults in 1991. NCborn is the census estimate of the number of non-Commonwealth/Irish born. Electors is the number of electors registered to vote at the 1992 election. Missing = Adults – NCborn – Electors. If Missing <0 then Missing = 0. Missing (%) = 100* Missing / (Adults – NCborn).

*Buckingham appears to have had the highest number of missing voters in Britain due to a processing error. At the time of planning the geography of the 1991 census three wards – Stony Stratford, Wolverton and Wolverton Stacey Bushes – were in Buckingham. Prior to the 1992 general election these wards were allocated to the new seat of North East Milton Keynes (Dorling 1995). Hence, it appears that Buckingham was missing 22% of its electors when most of them had actually been transferred to another seat. This error is included here to show how sensitive the statistics are to even minor misallocations.

**Bassetlaw is another constituency which should not be in this list. This is because its actual electorate was 68,583 (Rallings and Thrasher, 1995). The electorate given above was that reported in publications such as *The Times* and *Dod's Guide to the House of Commons*. We have left it here as it is indicative of the level of uncertainty which exists over the true size of electorates, even at elections. We have also recalculated all the statistics in this article using an alternative set of electorates published by OPCS in *Electoral Statistics* which include attainers and the effects of boundary changes around the time of the election. This has allowed us to estimate how robust our results are.

The reason we are not too unhappy with this compromise is that it produces plausible results. Table 1 lists the twenty seats which had the highest proportion of eligible adults not registered at the last general election according to our estimates. The total is less than official estimates of the number of missing electors, but the geographical distribution is plausible. These twenty seats contained 26 per cent of all voters thought to be missing in Britain under the model (24 per cent excluding Buckingham and including Hemsworth, and even lower if Bassetlaw is excluded: see table footnotes). They also contained a fairly even mix of Conservative and Labour areas.

The Missing Millions and the 1992 Election

The number of voters actually missing from the Buckingham constituency is irrelevant to the political process because the Conservative candidate there had a majority of almost 20,000 at the last election. What may matter is how many voters were missing in the most marginal Conservative seats or, to be precise, in how many seats was the number of missing voters greater than the Conservative majority – how many seats were 'vulnerable'. The answer is 20 and the seats are shown in Table 2. In four of them, if less than 2 per cent of the missing voters had registered and voted for the main opponent, the Conservatives would have lost. We have labelled the percentage of the margin of victory which could be accounted for by missing voters as 'vulnerability'. In 10 seats, less than 50 per cent of these missing voters could have altered the outcome had they voted for the main opposition candidate.

It may be worth recapping how the estimates in Table 2 were derived, using the example of Westminster North constituency. The census (corrected by the EWC project) estimates that 88,284 adults lived there, but 21,667 of them were not born in the Commonwealth or Ireland, leaving a potential electorate of 66,617. At the election there were only 58,847 electors registered, leaving 7,770 unaccounted for. Sir John Wheeler's majority over the closest (Labour) candidate was 3,733 votes. Thus if 48 per cent of those missing electors had registered and voted for Labour, Sir John would have lost. Note that the Conservatives only won the general election as a whole by 10 seats, and Westminster North is seat number 10 in the table.

Did the missing voters keep the Conservative Party in office for another five years by not registering and voting? That would depend on how many of them might have voted against the government if they had voted at all. By definition (as the people are missing from many official statistics!) these questions are almost impossible to answer (Smith, 1993).

One thing which is reassuring, however, is the similarity between our findings and those of an earlier study (Smith and McLean, 1994), which also identified ten constituencies where the Conservative candidate only won

TABLE 2
OLD CONSTITUENCIES WHERE MISSING VOTERS MATTERED IN 1992

Seat		1992 Winner	Adults	NCborn	Electors	Missing	Vulner -ability
1	Bristol North West	Con*	83338	1959	72726	8653	1
2	Vale of Glamorgan	Con*	69992	1381	66672	1939	1
3	Hayes & Harlington	Con*	60236	1890	54449	3897	1
4	Portsmouth South	Con*	90292	1874	77645	10773	2
5	Norwich North	Con*	65955	1135	63308	1512	18
6	Edmonton	Con	69431	3604	63052	2775	21
7	Ayr	Con*	66541	814	65481	246	35
8	Plymouth Drake	Con	58214	1131	51667	5416	37
9	Bolton North East	Con*	59952	811	58659	482	38
10	Westminster North	Con	88284	21667	58847	7770	48
11	Birmingham Hall Green	Con	68356	1038	60091	7227	51
12	City of Chester	Con	66881	1593	63370	1918	57
13	Blackpool South	Con	59938	778	56801	2359	71
14	Exeter	Con	83915	2104	76723	5088	80
15	Amber Valley	Con	71763	714	70155	894	80
16	Birmingham Edgbaston	Con	59714	1985	53041	4688	92
17	Southampton Test	Con	75937	2376	72932	629	93
18	Brighton Pavilion	Con	64788	3267	57616	3905	94
19	Northampton North	Con	75315	2075	69139	4101	95
20	Conwy	Con	55600	997	53576	1027	97

Notes: The respective figures for Britain as a whole were: Adults, 43,729,094; NCborn, 1,283,514; Electors, 42,113,792; Missing, 655,382.

All variables are the same as in Table 1 except that: Vulnerability = 100 * (The Conservative majority / Missing). Thus it shows the proportion of non-registered adults who would have had to register and vote for the main opposition party in each of the twenty seats if the Conservatives were to lose.

* Seats which an alternative study suggests would have been lost (see below).

** For those readers interested in the robustness of these results, if the alternative set of electorates is used (see Table 1) then only eight Conservative seats were won by a margin of less than 50% of the missing voters. In essence, Bolton North East and Ayr appear to be slightly less vulnerable if attainers or slight boundary changes are taken into account.

because of missing electors (specifically due to the effect of the poll tax). Seven of those ten seats are included in the top half of Table 2 (marked by an asterisk). The three seats which they also included but which we did not were Tynemouth, Brecon and Radnor, and Edinburgh West. One reason these are excluded here is that the earlier study had to rely on district level estimates of missing people and assumed no intra-constituency variation. Tynemouth constituency is the most affluent part of North Tyneside district. It is unlikely that many of the missing of North Tyneside are to be found in Tynemouth; they are more likely to live in the other less advantaged wards in that district. The same may be true of the other two constituencies. Similar reasons might also explain the exclusion of the three constituencies in the top ten of our list which were not in Smith and McLean's 1994 article. Another reason for their inclusion here is that Smith and McLean only considered the most marginal seats but, where there were a large number of people missing, seats did not have to be that marginal to be 'vulnerable'. Nevertheless the 70 per cent overlap between the two studies is reassuring, given that they were based on such very different methodologies and data, and that they had such different purposes.

The broad conclusion concerning the 'missing millions' and the 1992 election, then, is that the missing voters may have helped the Conservatives win between four and ten seats. The missing mattered, but it is difficult to say that they were crucial to the Conservative victory. That would depend on who they would have voted for, had they been registered and decided to vote.

Musical Chairs – The Missing Voters in 1995

What is most interesting now is not whether the missing voters allowed the Conservatives to win the last general election, but how important they will be at the next. Three factors will be different at the next election: different numbers of people will register to vote; due to boundary changes many will vote in different constituencies; and many may vote for a different party than they did before. If we knew what all these changes would be then we could predict the result of the next election, but we don't know how people are likely to change their vote. What we do know now is how the areas they vote in have changed and how the numbers registering to vote have changed. Table 3 shows how many people have been registered each year in Great Britain since 1991. The total has increased by over a quarter of a million, despite falling numbers of service voters, attainers, voluntary patients and overseas registrations. As there has not been a dramatic fall in mortality or a halt in emigration, it would appear that more people are choosing to be counted and to count electorally again. This effect needs to be included in understanding the implications of fewer missing voters at the next general election.

TABLE 3
THE REGISTERED ELECTORATE IN BRITAIN ('000s)

Year	Total	Service	Attainers	Patients	Overseas
1991	42424	268	540	2	34
1992	42583	271	532	2	32
1993	42565	262	498	2	22
1994	42624	248	483	1	18
1995	42727	227	463	1	17
Change 91–95	303	-41	-77	-0	-17

Sources: OPCS, Electoral Statistics, series EL No.21, Monitor EL91/1, London: HMSO, and OPCS Newsletter issue No.4, December 1995.

The total electorate given in Tables 1 and 2 is slightly lower than in Table 3 because many of the attainers (people becoming 18 over the period) would not have been eligible to vote at the last general election. One simple way in which this rise can be modelled is to include attainers in the electorate (and ignore losses such as deaths). This is done in the remaining tables, which give a projected total electorate for Britain of 42,528,000 by the time of the next election. Such a figure would not be out of line with the statistics in Table 3. Thus to calculate electorates for the new constituencies, we sum the 1991 electorates of wards including attainers to simulate the increase in people registering to vote (still excluding people not born in the Commonwealth or Ireland).

The number of adults living in each of the new constituencies was calculated as before, although this time the 1991 wards were used as basic spatial units. The number of people born outside the Commonwealth and Ireland but living in each constituency was again subtracted from the estimated number of adults to give an estimate of the number of people who are eligible to vote in each of the new constituencies. We have not made any estimate for the effects of population change and migration between 1991 and 1996 as this is likely to be minor compared to the effect of changing the boundaries and it is also extremely difficult to do. The first results of this exercise are shown in Table 4, which produces identical statistics to those in Table 1, but for the new constituencies using the slightly larger electorates. The estimate of which party would win each seat was made by transferring the results from the old seats to the new assuming no local variation (they are thus approximate, but fine for our purposes).

If Table 4 is compared to Table 1, the most obvious difference is that fewer people will be missing in 1996. Less obvious however is that the missing will have become more concentrated. The 20 seats in Table 4 contain 31 per cent of all the missing voters. The 20 old seats containing the most missing voters in 1992 accounted for less than a quarter of that year's total. This may well be one effect of the boundary changes which, of course, ignored the missing people and so could easily have had the effect of concentrating them into particular areas. The average Conservative constituency now has 2754 fewer electors than before, whereas the average Labour constituency has 2787 more (these figures can be calculated from Table 5). This is to be expected as the primary purpose of the boundary review was to equalize the size of constituencies. Although the average Conservative-held constituency now contains 4220 more electors than the average Labour-held one, only 3739 of these are adults eligible to vote. By ignoring the missing voters the Boundary Commissioners have made the House of Commons more equal than they know!

TABLE 4
NEW CONSTITUENCIES WITH THE MOST VOTERS MISSING IN 1996

Seat		1992 Winner*	Adults	NCborn	Electors	Missing	Missing (%)
1	Islington North	Lab	72032	7698	55650	8684	13
2	Plymouth Sutton	Con	77134	1427	66756	8969	12
3	Folkestone & Hythe	Con	74309	2395	64443	7500	10
4	Hammersmith & Fulham	Con	94476	13522	72731	8223	10
5	Glasgow Maryhill	Lab	59249	1092	56969	5866	10
6	Islington South & Finsbury	Lab	66307	5831	54443	6033	10
7	Aldershot	Con	86987	3465	7536	8201	10
8	Spelthorne	Con	73456	2318	64291	6890	10
9	Vauxhall	Lab	84387	9479	67962	6947	9
10	Regents Park & Kensington N.	Con	98576	21487	69959	7130	9
11	Kingston & Surbiton	Con	81869	4744	70238	6887	9
12	Hamilton North & Bellshill	Lab	58228	458	58879	4977	9
13	Bethnal Green & Bow	Lab	75181	3710	65485	5986	8
14	Streatham	Lab	84361	6964	71008	6389	8
15	Birmingham Ladywood	Lab	79332	1556	71943	5833	7
16	Bristol West	Con	88017	3867	77906	6244	7
17	Acton & Shepherds Bush	Con	86511	12911	68324	5276	7
18	Newport West	Lab	60420	1134	55294	3992	7
19	Blackpool South	Con	81523	1103	75039	5411	7
20	Poplar & Canning Town	Lab	70421	3756	62190	4475	7

Notes: The respective figures for Britain as a whole were: Adults, 43,730,035; NCborn, 1,283,514; Electors, 42,528,137; Missing, 412,731; Missing (%), 1.
*The party which is marked as having won each seat in 1992 is an estimate made by examining the socio-economic characteristics of the wards which changed constituencies due to boundary changes (using the 1991 census).

TABLE 5
ARITHMETIC AVERAGE CONSTITUENCY POPULATIONS BY PARTY

Party	Adults	NCborn	Eligible	Electorate	Missing
Old Constituencies					
Conservative	73957	2504	71453	71276	785
Labour	64053	1513	62540	61515	1412
Liberal Dem	60135	1415	58720	58804	461
Nationalists	56071	919	55152	55682	54
New Constituencies					
Conservative	70644	2413	68231	68522	509
Labour	66021	1529	64492	64302	862
Liberal Dem	59761	1458	58303	59333	301
Nationalists	51807	745	51062	52718	25

The Missing in the Next General Election

What will be the political importance of the missing voters at the next election? Table 6 was created by the same procedure used to create Table 2, but using the new seats and new electorates. The results are quite surprising. Despite a fall in the average number of missing voters by a third in Conservative constituencies, there are nine constituencies where the number of eligible adults missing is more than twice the Conservative majority. Three of these are seats which were identified in Table 2 but five of them are essentially new seats (some information on their old parts is given in the table in parentheses). These are new seats which are both vulnerable and contain many unregistered adults who would be eligible to vote if they chose to register.

TABLE 6
NEW CONSTITUENCIES: WHERE MISSING VOTERS WILL MATTER IN 1996

Seat	1992 Winner	Adults	NCborn	Electors	Missing	Vulner-ability
1 Acton & Shepherds Bush	Con new	86511	12911	68324	5276	1
2 Vale of Glamorgan	Con*	69847	1381	67244	1314	5
3 Portsmouth South	Con*	83831	1874	77282	4699	5
4 Blackpool South	Con*	81523	1103	75039	5411	5
5 Regents Park & Kensington N	Con new	98576	21487	69959	7130	10
6 Plymouth Sutton (was Drake)	Con new	77134	1427	66756	8969	28
7 Lincoln (mostly old Lincoln)	Con new	68327	1589	65119	1651	37
8 Croydon North	Con new	87055	4318	80076	2661	39
9 Mitcham & Morden	Con	68269	2837	61603	3829	44
10 Exeter	Con*	83917	2104	76605	5226	58
11 Hammersmith & Fulham	Con new	94476	13522	72731	8223	71
12 Edinburgh West	Con new	66372	1359	66074	3018	103
13 Folkestone & Hythe	Con	74309	2395	64443	7500	116
14 Bristol West (with part NW)	Con new	88017	3867	77906	6244	138
15 Brighton Pavilion	Con*	71753	3459	66008	2286	151
16 City of Chester	Con*	71733	1730	68570	1446	154
17 Torbay	Con	75997	1653	70764	3598	160
18 Dover	Con	71884	1798	69646	440	190
19 Eastbourne (mostly old area)	Con new	75890	2936	70623	2352	205
20 Aldershot (mostly old area)	Con new	86987	3465	75369	8201	209

Notes: The respective figures for Britain as a whole were: Adults, 43,730,035; NC born, 1,283,514; Electors, 42,528,137; Missing, 412,731.

Modelling the Missing

Finally, where are the missing voters? Are particular types of constituencies, or special combinations of local conditions, associated with the incidence of missing voters? A preliminary answer can be obtained through regression analyses in which the dependent variable is our missing voter estimate. In the following analyses, we use two dependent variables: the number of estimated missing voters, and the missing voters as a percentage of the constituency electorate. The analyses are carried out for the old (the 1983) constituencies (Table 7).

TABLE 7
MISSING VOTERS: REGRESSION MODELS (SIGNIFICANCE LEVELS IN PARENTHESES)

	Missing voters		Missing voters (%)	
Tory vote % t-1	-11.25	(0.520)	-0.02	(0.574)
Tory margin t-1	-19.71	(0.018)	-0.03	(0.050)
House price (£ '000s) 1991	-6.83	(0.526)	-0.02	(0.400)
% with negative equity 1993	9.26	(0.303)	0.01	(0.633)
% change in house prices 1989–91	2.60	(0.583)	0.00	(0.585)
% migrants 1991	204.60	(0.000)	0.36	(0.000)
Winning party 1987				
Labour	714.82	(0.016)	1.24	(0.012)
Alliance	-383.21	(0.425)	-0.63	(0.431)
Nationalist	-62.38	(0.940)	-0.10	(0.940)
Region				
Strathclyde	-474.40	(0.457)	-0.47	(0.656)
East Scotland	-1138.51	(0.100)	-1.88	(0.103)
Rural Scotland	-1268.10	(0.088)	-2.17	(0.080)
Rural North	-234.06	(0.677)	-0.55	(0.555)
Industrial N East	-653.05	(0.320)	-1.21	(0.268)
Merseyside	418.78	(0.534)	0.64	(0.567)
Greater Manchester	354.05	(0.551)	0.73	(0.459)
Rest North West	-280.82	(0.606)	-0.45	(0.617)
West Yorkshire	-268.38	(0.672)	-0.57	(0.589)
South Yorkshire	-932.38	(0.192)	-1.71	(0.149)
Rural Wales	-844.43	(0.228)	-1.35	(0.247)
Industrial S Wales	281.54	(0.666)	0.48	(0.657)
West Midlands	599.39	(0.287)	1.08	(0.248)
Rest West Midlands	-479.97	(0.340)	-0.74	(0.378)
East Midlands	-126.50	(0.777)	-0.17	(0.818)
East Anglia	-775.57	(0.128)	-1.23	(0.145)
Devon/Cornwall	304.14	(0.569)	0.49	(0.582)
Wessex	54.37	(0.895)	0.02	(0.979)
Inner London	222.54	(0.659)	1.00	(0.232)
Outer London	173.83	(0.684)	0.70	(0.321)
Outer Metropolitan	433.39	(0.258)	0.80	(0.212)
Constant	-186.03		-0.39	
R^2	0.12		0.13	

Possible explanations for the size of the 'missing' electorate in a constituency include: the political situation in the constituency; the economic situation there; levels of migration; the region in which the constituency is situated; and local differences in the working practices of electoral registration officers.

Much of the discussion of missing voters to date has suggested that the largest groups of missing voters are poll tax evaders, the homeless, and those alienated from contemporary politics. None of these groups is likely to be Conservative supporters. The implication is that missing voters should be most numerous in seats where the Conservatives are weak. Conservative electoral strength at the 1987 election is included in the regression models, therefore, as are dummy variables for which party won the seat then (Conservative seats are excluded and serve as the comparison group). Going missing from the electoral register may also be an extreme form of abstention. We already know that abstention rates are lower in marginal seats (where each vote is more likely to count) than in safe seats. It seems plausible, therefore, to expect that the size of the missing electorate is related to the marginality of the seat. We therefore also include a measure of marginality for the Conservatives in 1987. Where the party won the seat, the marginality measure is the Conservatives' percentage share of the vote minus the share of the party in second place; where the Conservatives did not win, the measure is the winning party's percentage share minus that of the Conservatives. The marginality measure is always positive, therefore, but tends towards zero as seats become more marginal for the Conservatives.

A corollary of the argument that missing voters are largely non-Conservatives is that they are likely to be drawn from among less affluent groups of the population. To assess this, we include a series of measures of local affluence, based on local housing market conditions in the early 1990s. The three measures are: the average house price in each seat in 1991 (in £'000s); the change in house prices between 1989 and 1991 (the period was marked by a property recession); and an estimate of the proportion of the electorate with negative equity (where the resale value of a house is less than the mortgage) in 1993. If missing voters are from less affluent areas, we would expect that there would be more missing voters in areas with low and falling house prices and with many affected by negative equity.

Disappearing from the electoral register might be a simple consequence of moving house and not being included in the enumeration. To the extent that this is the case, missing voters are a relatively short-term phenomenon. It also implies that there should be more missing voters in areas where there are many migrants than in areas where few people move house. To assess this, we include a measure from the 1991 Census indicating the proportion of the population in each seat who had been resident at a different address in the previous year. This gives us a surrogate for population mobility.

Finally, there may be some regional factor at play. Missing voters may be more numerous in some parts of the country than in others. We therefore include a series of dummy variables for geographic regions (the Outer South East region is omitted and serves as the comparison group). For instance, well known cultural factors such as the tradition of high turnouts in Wales often have clear geographical characteristics.

As the final regression models show, few of these factors had any bearing on the distribution of missing voters. Only the marginality of the seat, whether Labour controlled it, and the proportion of migrants there had impacts. As we expected, there were more missing voters in seats where the population was relatively mobile than in seats where the population was static. This makes clear intuitive sense. Furthermore, missing voters were more common in Labour-held seats than they were in Conservative ones. However, against our expectations, the more marginal the seat was for the Conservatives the greater the number of missing voters. On the assumption that missing voters are mainly non-Conservatives (the preponderance of missing voters in Labour seats supports this), the implication is that the Conservatives may well have been helped by the missing voter phenomenon in 1992, since it meant the absence from the register of potential voters opposed to the Conservative party in key marginals during an unusually close-fought election (compared to the 1980s).

Overall, however, the equations provided a poor fit to the data: only around 12 per cent of the original variance was accounted for. There remains a large unexplained element underlying the geography of the missing voters. This may reflect differences between local Electoral Registration Officers in how they pursue non-registration.

Conclusion

In short – as *The Times* article with which we began this article implied – it may well be in the Labour Party's interest to get more adults to register to vote and in the interests of the Conservative Party to hinder this process. The creation of new constituencies was more important in areas where the missing voters could make a difference. We may assume that many of the voters who have already come back are likely to vote Labour, if they vote, and that Labour will do better among voters as a whole. The next election could then be very close (Cornford *et al.*, 1995). Given that scenario, the 'missing of Shepherds Bush' may well count more than the 'disgusted of Tunbridge Wells'.

ACKNOWLEDGEMENT

Part of this work was funded by a grant from the Leverhulme Trust, which is gratefully acknowledged.

BIBLIOGRAPHY

Cornford J., D. Dorling and B. Tether (1995) 'Historical precedent and British electoral prospects', *Electoral Studies* 14: 123–142.

Dorling, D., (1995) *A New Social Atlas of Britain.* Wiley: Chichester, pp.i–xxxviii and 1–247.

McLean, Iain and Jeremy Smith (1995) 'The Poll Tax, the Electoral Register and the 1991 Census: An Update', in David Broughton, David Farrell, David Denver and Colin Rallings (eds) *British Elections and Parties Yearbook 1994.* pp.128–47. London: Frank Cass.

Rallings C. and M. Thrasher (1995) Personal communications with the authors.

Simpson, S., R. Tye and I. Diamond (1995) 'What was the real population of local areas in mid-1991?', Working Article 10 of the Estimating with Confidence Project (EWC), Social Statistics Department, University of Southampton.

Smith, J. and I. McLean (1994) 'The poll tax and the electoral register' in A. Heath, R. Jowell and J. Curtice (eds) *Labour's Last Chance? The 1992 Election and Beyond,* pp.229–53. Aldershot: Dartmouth.

Smith, S., 1993, *Electoral registration in 1991.* HMSO: London.

A Comparative Analysis of Ward and Constituency Level Effects on Voting Behaviour in England and Wales 1986–92

Graham Kinshott

Introduction

Disparities between patterns of voting in local and general elections now appear to be a semi-permanent feature of British politics (Rallings and Thrasher, 1993). Yet comparatively little seems to be known about why people sometimes vote for different parties at local and national level. The key question is whether these disparities result primarily from the *contexts* in which local and national voting take place or whether voters actually make *different calculations* in deciding how to cast their local and national votes. Existing explanations of the observed disparities between local and general elections have focused mainly on the importance of context. Newton's (1976) 'annual general election' hypothesis suggests that local elections are merely an opportunity to express dis/approval of mid-term government performance in a kind of costless referendum. Local issues are largely irrelevant and voting is determined by national level influences such as partisan identification. Similarly, *turnout* is suggested to be a contributory factor to local/national disparities. Turnout in local elections is so low as to be unrepresentative of the electorate; thus local/national disparities may be caused by turnout bias. This supposed 'turnout bias' may be a consequence of the popular view of local elections as the 'annual general election': in the mid-term of parliament, disillusioned government supporters might fail to vote while opposition supporters are more likely to turn out for their parties to register their disapproval of the government's performance. Finally, Burnham (1990) suggests that some of the differences between local and national level electoral outcomes derive from a *proportionality* effect. For example, a party's ward-level distribution of support is critical in local elections, but irrelevant within a constituency – a fact that may account for variations in the vote share/seat share ratios between local and national elections.

Each of these hypotheses, however, suffers from an important defect. The 'annual general election' hypothesis cannot explain why the parties achieve different percentage shares of the vote in local elections and simultaneous national level opinion polls. The turnout bias hypothesis, while plausible, is unproven, as the results of several panel surveys demonstrate (Miller, 1988). And, the proportionality hypothesis cannot account for the differing percentage shares of the *vote* achieved by the parties in local and general elections. This suggests that one other possible explanation should be considered; the possibility of inconsistent individual-level voting behaviour. Individuals are consciously voting for different parties in local and national elections, possibly because they recognize the differing roles of local and central government and thus have differing priorities at each level, a fact reflected in their seemingly contradictory voting choices. It is this hypothesis that I seek to test here.

This article presents the results of a model of comparative local/national electoral behaviour between 1986 and 1992. It includes both of the general elections that took place during this time, but excludes the county council elections of 1989. The analysis is presented in four sections. The first explains the data reduction technique that was used to construct a series of socio-economic and demographic variables that were used in the analysis. The second reports the results of a series of regression analyses which use the socio-economic variables to explain the variance in party support. The third and fourth stages feature political intercept and slope shift terms respectively in order to test the differential effects that may result from incumbency; that is, do variables become more or less important when one party has an established presence? It must be stressed that the results presented in this article are preliminary findings. Accordingly, the inferences that can be drawn from the data must be limited.

The Core Model

The aim of the model presented here is to test whether people behave differently in local and national elections. Its premise is that the probability that a given voter will support a particular party in a given area is significantly affected by the prevailing socio-economic and political conditions. For instance, it might be assumed that the higher the level of deprivation in a given area, individuals living in that area would have a higher propensity to vote Labour. Using the major parties' percentage shares of the vote as the dependent variables and socio-economic/demographic variables as the independent variables, identical regression analyses are undertaken at local and national level. The general functions for the local and national level equations are expressed below.

Local Level Probability that the ith voter in a given ward at time t will vote Con (or Lab or Lib)

= f(ward level socio-economic conditions + council

National Level

characteristics t-1)

Probability that the ith voter in a given constituency at time t will vote Con (or Lab or Lib)

= f (constituency level socio-economic conditions + parliamentary characteristics t-1)

In order to analyse the aggregate level behaviour of voters in local and general elections the model utilizes local and national level databases, each consisting of socio-economic and demographic variables that have been extracted from the Local Base Statistics of the 1991 Census of Population and aggregated to ward and constituency level respectively; also contained within their respective databases are ward and constituency level election results. Thus by employing a local level database comprising ward level election results and census data, and a national level database containing constituency-level general election results and constituency-level census data, a comparative analysis of voting behaviour can be undertaken.

Using regression coefficients that are calculated for the independent variables at local and national level, it is possible to compare the relative strength of voter sensitivities to a number of socio-economic variables at local and general elections. The relative magnitude of the regression coefficients allows inferences to be made about aggregate level voter sensitivity to socio-economic conditions in each form of election. For instance, if the Conservative percentage share of the vote (CONPC) is the dependent variable, and per cent unemployment (%un) is the independent variable, it might be found that %un has a coefficient of -5.25, indicating a significant negative effect on CONPC at national level. If the equivalent local model revealed a lower coefficient, or a statistically insignificant relationship, it could be concluded that unemployment was not such an important factor in individual voter's calculations in local elections. In essence, the model uses the regression coefficients to answer the question of whether, and if so to what extent, people are voting differently in different forms of election.

However, before any analysis of the results can take place, it is necessary to note potential pitfalls and also to explain the structure of the socio-economic factors that are used in the model. There is little doubt that a comparative analysis of local and national election results will encounter problems of 'applicability'. Indeed, the very character of local government elections compounds the problem. In a general election voting takes place in all areas by definition. However, in any one round of local elections, large areas of England will be excluded from the voting. For instance, all seats in the London boroughs are contested once every four years (1986, 1990, 1994), whereas most of the non-metropolitan authorities hold elections on a similar basis but on a different cycle (1987, 1991). In the remaining years (excluding county council election years 1989 and 1993), only the metropolitan authorities outside London and a minority of non-metropolitan authorities go to the polls to elect councillors on a rolling or one-third basis. Whether this factor is sufficient to distort a local/national comparison is uncertain, but it needs to be considered as a possibility.

A second potential problem is 'aggregation bias'. This is the phenomenon whereby correlations between observed variables can be inflated purely as a consequence of the use of larger aggregation units.[1] The well known – and related – ecological fallacy involves the danger of spuriously deriving inferences about *individual* level behaviour from observed correlations involving data which describe the relationships between social aggregates. Although both of these problems are potentially relevant to the analysis conducted here, the evidence that is reported suggests that neither problem is so serious as to render the results invalid. With regard to aggregation bias, the findings show that there is no systematic difference between the magnitudes of the various coefficients observed at different levels of aggregation. With regard to the ecological fallacy, there is no reason to suppose that the results reported here are any more distorted than those observed in other studies based on aggregate level data. However, it is possible that the extent of the problems associated with aggregate level analyses explain the paucity of cross-sectional analyses of local/national level electoral behaviour.[2]

The Structure of the Socio-economic Variables

A number of socio-economic and demographic variables were extracted from the Local Base Statistics section of the 1991 Census of Population. At this stage of the analysis it would have been possible to conduct an estimated series of regression models, using the percentage shares of the vote for the major parties as the dependent variables and the raw census data as the independent variables. However, such an approach would have encountered two difficulties. First, given the nature of the census variables, multicollinearity would almost certainly have been a significant problem with its likely distorting effects on coefficient estimates and second, the census variables in their 'raw' state would not have provided a clear representation of the way in which cases (wards and constituencies) differed from each other in basic socio-economic terms. In order to eliminate these problems, data reduction techniques were applied. A factor analysis of all the relevant census variables was undertaken at both ward and constituency level to identify the main dimensions along which the variables lie. The factor scores for each case were saved as new variables in the dataset. The variables involved in the factor analysis are as follows: percentage born outside EC/Old Commonwealth (bosecoc), percentage households with > 1.5 persons per room (Housing/density), percentage economically active residents, males/females, youths unemployed (earesun/eamun/eafemun/youthun respectively), percentage male and female residents (maleres and femres respectively), percentage managers/administrators (manad), percentage residents and males employed in manufacturing (manuf and mmanuf respectively), percentage households with no/more than one car (nocar/multicar respectively), percentage single-parent households (onepar), percentage residents over 65 years old (over65), percentage owner-occupier households (ownocc), percentage households renting from local authorities/new towns (rentlant), percentage head of households in socio-economic classes 1 + 2, 3 (manual and non-manual), 4 and 5 (sc1plus2, sc3, sc4, and sc5 respectively), percentage residents under 15 years old (under15) and percentage residents with vocational/professional qualifications (vocqual).

TABLE 1

WARD LEVEL FACTOR LOADINGS

VARIMAX rotation   1 for extraction   1 in analysis
1 – Kaiser Normalisation.

VARIMAX converged in 7 iterations.
Rotated Factor Matrix:

Bosecoc	.24066	.15523	-.07016	-.09279	.83270
Density	.33628	.04567	-.03715	-.013645	.77849
Eafemun	.84412	.15747	-.05553	.00476	.31429
Eamun	.89464	-.25276	.03405	.05949	.18547
Earesun	.89781	-.23042	.00238	.04499	.22219
Femres	.19798	-.00195	.90606	.05099	.06282
Maleres	-.19798	.00195	-.90606	-.05099	-.06282
Manad	-.41976	.66581	-.01889	-.25671	-.09747
Manuf	.03188	.17450	-.10271	.94044	-.10699
Mmanuf	.02929	-.16674	-.06708	.95124	-.10132
Multicar	-.82393	.31863	-.23259	-.07256	-.26027
Nocar	.82393	-.31863	.23259	.07256	.26027
Onepar	.80252	-.13179	-.03658	.05181	.22289
Over65	-.07209	-.00441	.83472	-.16860	-.21363
Ownocc	-.84075	.07567	.07092	.12803	-.04442
Profess	-.22747	.81221	.13182	.02821	.15035
Rentlant	.80850	-.24157	-.05199	.09382	-.14096
Sc1plus2	-.46175	.84877	.05499	-.10308	.02480
Sc3	.02024	-.86195	.09585	.23185	.12130
Sc4	.47852	-.49870	-.08044	.06062	-.22494
Sc5	.60751	-.33920	.01063	-.08163	-.19425
Under15	.33052	-.21360	-.60793	.20142	.03505
Vocqual	-.32350	.84949	.07798	-.07628	.17847
Youthun	.82535	-.14371	.09572	.07061	.16279

The ward and constituency level factor loadings for the variables are shown in Tables 1 and 2 respectively. The ward level factor analysis reveals five underlying dimensions, or hypothetical composite variables, that can be extracted from the original raw variables. The first and most important factor is that of economic deprivation. A varimax rotation of the factor matrix shows that the following variables load heavily on this factor: economically active females unemployed (0.84), economically active males unemployed (0.89), economically active residents unemployed (0.89), households with one or more cars (-0.82), households with no car (0.82), one parent households (0.8), owner-occupiership (-0.84), renting from councils/new towns (0.8) and youth unemployment (0.82). Thus the importance of unemployment among economically active groups, patterns of tenure, and car non-/ownership can be seen within this dimension. Factor 2 is more specifically occupational class-related. The varimax factor matrix shows heavy factor loadings for managers/administrators (0.665), professionals (0.81), social classes 1+2 (0.84), social class 3 (-0.86), and vocational qualifications (0.849), denoting the divide between the salariat of classes 1 and 2 and the routine non-manual and skilled manual workers of the merged social class 3. Demographic variables dominate factor 3, with the varimax rotation showing heavy loadings for percentage female residents (0.90), percentage male residents (-0.90), percentage over 65 (0.83) and percentage under 15 (-0.60). The fourth factor is a straightforward manufacturing dimension with only percentage employed in manufacturing (0.94) and percentage males employed in manufacturing (0.95) showing significant loadings. A pseudo-race/living conditions dimension appears within factor 5, with percentage born outside EC/Old Commonwealth and housing density yielding factor loadings of 0.83 and 0.778 respectively.[3] Replication of the local level factor analysis at national level produces a similar, although not identical, set of results.

The economic dimension contains the same variables as the local level analysis, albeit with significantly higher factor scores (apart from percentage renting from local authorities/new towns). Factor 2 also yields a similar class-related variable, although the signs denoting the direction of the variables' loadings seem to have been reversed. Significantly, social class 4 (0.75) loads far more heavily on this factor than in the ward level model. The demographic dimension in factor 3 is also reproduced although the +/- signs for the variables are once again reversed. Thus, for presentational purposes, the national level coefficients presented in Tables 3–6 for the social class and demographic variables (sclass and age/gender) are multiplied by -1. Factor 4 produces an almost identical manufacturing based dimension. Possibly the only notable difference between the ward and constituency level based models is the fact that the constituency level solution is four dimensional rather than five dimensional; it has no race/living conditions factor. Instead, percentage born outside EC/Old Commonwealth and housing density load more heavily on the economic deprivation dimension, recording 0.59 and 0.66 respectively. This may reflect greater disparities between wards than are present between constituencies, where disparities may be dissipated due to the larger area size. In essence, the factor analysis yielded broadly similar underlying variables at both ward and constituency level which could be used in a simplified model of comparative local/national level electoral behaviour; economic deprivation, social class/salariat, gender/age, manufacturing activity, and race/living conditions.

TABLE 2
CONSTITUENCY LEVEL FACTOR LOADINGS

VARIMAX rotation   1 for extraction   1 in analysis
1 – Kaiser Normalisation

VARIMAX converged in 6 iterations
Rotated Factor Matrix:

Bosecoc	.59557	-.47818	.21406	-.18973
Density	.66743	-.35636	-.17237	-.26231
Eafemun	.94882	.14405	.05087	-.00576
Eamun	.92053	.29285	-.04616	.04528
Earesun	.93564	.26073	-.01079	.03293
Femres	.26490	-.12233	-.89885	-.13796
Maleres	-.26490	.12233	.89885	.13796
Manad	-.53327	-.72040	-.06782	-.24616
Manuf	-.06024	.24596	.21070	.92515
Mmanuf	-.04469	.24867	.16558	.94369
Multicar	-.93233	-.22532	.14234	-.02158
Nocar	.93233	.22532	-.14234	.02158
Onepar	.94406	.05351	-.00251	-.06264
Over65	-.25907	.12064	-.84824	-.04122
Ownocc	-.88725	-.04501	-.06079	.10572
Profess	-.07304	-.90359	-.10566	-.03135
Rentlant	-.53327	.34804	.12880	.07623
Sc1plus2	-.42030	-.87685	-.07648	-.15136
Sc3	-.03357	.84422	.03937	.16559
Sc4	.39406	.75928	.09224	.24423
Sc5	.60507	.62991	-.03440	-.09037
Under15	.35919	.38213	.61043	.16382
Vocqual	-.14604	-.94097	-.07720	-.15294
Youthun	.90927	.24804	-.10887	.05210

Knowledge of the composition of the five factors extracted from the data reduction exercise enables us to make simple predictions regarding the effects of these variables upon the support for the respective parties. The traditional sociological model of electoral behaviour suggests that the salariat index would have a positive effect on Conservative support, due simply to the middle classes' higher propensity to vote Conservative. The sociological model also implies that the economic deprivation, manufacturing activity and race/living conditions indices should have a positive effect on Labour support (Butler and Stokes, 1974). The accuracy (or otherwise) of these predictions can be gauged from the analysis of the local/national level results in the next section.

Empirical Findings 1:
The Effects of Socio-economic Conditions on Party Support

Using the reduced census data obtained by the factor analysis of the original variables it is possible to specify the regression models of party support for the major parties at each level. For example, the Conservative model (to be run at both local and national level) is as follows:

CONPC = a + b1 (economic deprivation) + b2 (salariat) + b3 (age/gender) + b4 (manufacturing activity) +b5 (race/density) + error

The first stage of the regression analysis uses the above-mentioned independent variables to explain the percentage shares of the vote attained by the parties in each constituency in 1987 and 1992, and in each ward in 1986, 1987, 1988, 1990, 1991 and 1992. No examination of the political characteristics of a ward or constituency is undertaken at this stage. Table 3 summarizes the regression coefficients extracted from the models of local/national level party support for each of the parties. With this information it is possible to compare local and national level coefficients and observe any differential effects.

Looking at the models of *Conservative* support in Table 3, the similarity between the economic deprivation coefficients at local and national level suggests that this factor is equally important to the determination of Conservative support in local and national level elections. Thus the expected negative impact of economic deprivation upon the Conservative support at ward and constituency level is confirmed by the large negative coefficients.

There appears to be a significant difference in the importance of social class to Conservative support between local and national level. This is shown by the local level coefficients of the salariat variable, which are significantly higher than their national equivalents; the ratio of economic deprivation/salariat coefficients reaches almost 1:1 in 1990–91 while the national figures remain constant at 1.4:1. This suggests that the salariat index is more important at local level, although it still remains secondary to economic deprivation in its impact upon Conservative support. Demographic factors also appear to be more significant at local level, as indicated by the age/gender coefficients. At local level, Conservative support appears to be positively influenced by the percentages of women and elderly people in an area with an average coefficient of 1.65, compared with a tiny and statistically insignificant figure at national level.

TABLE 3
PARTY SUPPORT COEFFICIENTS

Year	Econ/ Dep	Salariat	Age/ Gender	Manuf.	Race/ Density
Conservative Party					
1987	-8.29	5.87	-0.17	-1.34	na
1992	-8.40	5.95	-0.09	-1.15	na
1986	-8.40	6.35	2.08	-1.45	0.66
1987	-8.22	6.83	1.78	1.91	4.39
1988	-9.22	7.39	1.39	-0.46	0.49
1990	-7.92	7.19	1.88	-0.74	1.81
1991	-7.65	7.16	1.59	1.69	3.16
1992	-8.55	5.87	1.22	0.99	0.51
Labour Party					
1987	11.39	-7.77	1.61	3.20	na
1992	11.70	-8.14	-2.11	2.88	na
1986	12.99	-9.83	-1.50	4.21	2.00
1987	14.07	-9.51	-1.71	5.74	2.09
1988	14.26	-11.23	-1.25	3.76	0.52
1990	11.59	-10.28	-1.37	4.30	1.03
1991	13.84	-10.34	-1.65	5.99	2.76
1992	11.86	-9.82	-0.83	2.70	0.76
Liberal Democrats					
1987	-3.11	1.95	-1.17	-1.38	na
1992	-3.47	2.27	1.90	-1.40	na
1986	-3.70	2.38	0.72	-1.12	-0.60
1987	-1.55	1.37	1.33	0.95	3.63
1988	-3.22	1.92	1.58	-1.10	1.29
1990	-3.37	2.04	1.12	-1.48	-0.97
1991	-2.48	1.95	2.05	0.34	3.41
1992	-2.79	2.22	1.20	1.34	1.13

Note: Dependent variable is party percentage share of the vote. The first two rows in each part of the Table give the national level support coefficients for the 1987 and 1992 general elections. The remaining six rows give the support coefficients for the local elections 1986–1992.
Conservatives: National level age/gender coefficients non-significant in 1987 and 1992. Local level coefficient for manuf(acturing) non-significant in 1988, as were the race/density coefficients for 1988 and 1992.
Labour: Local level race/density coefficient non-significant in 1988–92.
Liberal Democrats: Local level manuf. coefficient non-significant in 1991.

The level of manufacturing employment shows a curious difference in its effect between local and national level. At constituency level, an increase in manufacturing employment produces a negative effect on Conservative support, as one might expect. However, at local level, the coefficients are positive in 1987, 1991 and 1992, and insignificant in 1988. It is interesting to note that the highest coefficients were achieved in 1987 and 1991, when a greater number of rural, and thus presumably Conservative-orientated, wards were contested.

The positive local level coefficients for the race/density factor may seem surprising, suggesting that local level Conservative support is positively influenced by greater population density and a higher percentage of residents who were born outside Europe and the Old Commonwealth, despite conventional wisdom which suggests the contrary. However, it may be a simple case of the ecological fallacy. In deprived inner-city areas, people from the ethnic minorities are less likely to be on the electoral register, and even if they are registered, they are less likely to vote than other groups. So, in such areas it could merely be a case of a swing to the right by white voters rather than large numbers from the ethnic minorities voting for the Conservatives.

The increasing importance of social class at local level is repeated when influences on the *Labour* vote are observed. While the Labour vote at local level is also more sensitive to economic deprivation, as shown by the high positive coefficients, the increase in magnitude of the salariat factor is proportionately greater. The ratio between the mean coefficients of economic deprivation/salariat at national level is >1.4:1, while at local level it is less than 1.3:1. It is noticeable that the magnitude of the econ/dep and social class coefficients is greater in the model of Labour support at local and national levels, suggesting that more of the Labour vote can be explained in terms of class and economic deprivation. In addition, Labour support at local level appears to be significantly more sensitive to the scale of manufacturing industry with coefficients that in some cases are almost double the size of their national level equivalents. Again, a comparison of the ratios of the mean coefficients yielded by economic deprivation/manufacturing activity produces a figure of approximately 3.8:1 at national level, but less than 3:1 at local level. Finally, the impact of demographic factors on Labour support at national level is variable, yielding small positive and negative coefficients at different times. However, greater numbers of women and the elderly seem to have a more consistent negative effect on Labour support at ward level.

The local/national comparisons of support for the *Liberal Democrats* is more problematic, partly due to the absence of a class/economic interest basis to their support, which makes the prediction of Liberal Democrat support with socio-economic and demographic variables very difficult as well as less reliable. In addition, the relatively low barriers to entry at local government level (both economic and psephological) means that local level political activity is relatively easy for candidates of the Liberal Democrats, as it is for other parties.

Economic deprivation has a negative effect on Liberal Democrat support at both local and national level, a fact that is supported by its failure to challenge Labour in the most deprived inner-city areas. However, the small coefficients denote a fairly minor effect, being slightly more important at national level. Social class seems to have a similar effect on Liberal Democrat support across the two levels, but again the small coefficients confirm the generally non-class basis of the party's support. Demographic effects on Liberal Democrat support are more consistent at local level, but even at local level there is significant variation over time. Manufacturing employment has a consistent negative effect on the party's national level support, but its local level effect appears to be so variable as to preclude any meaningful conclusions. Again, no local-national comparison of race and population density is possible, but it is noteworthy that this variable's effect is greater when all the non-metropolitan authorities are contested, and reversed in the years when elections are held in the London boroughs, suggesting a differential effect across different types of local authority.

Empirical Findings 2:
The Effects of Socio-economic and Political Conditions on Party Support

This stage of the analysis features the inclusion of a series of intercept shift political control dummy variables which are used to test for incumbency effects. The local level dummies are based on the control of the council (in which the ward is situated) after the previous round of elections. So, if the party in question controlled a council at time t-1, all the wards contained in that area score 1 on ptyM1 (the dummy variable). If the council was controlled by another party, or there was no overall control at time t-1, ptyM1 is equal to 0. The constituency, or national level, dummies are simply representations of whether the party in question won the constituency in the previous general election. For example, if the Conservatives won constituency A in the 1987 general election, it scores 1 on ptyM1 for the analysis of the 1992 general election. Otherwise ptyM1 equals 0. It could be argued that this comparison of council and constituency level dummies is inappropriate and that a proper comparison should be based either on a comparison of ward and constituency level dummies or on the basis of the composition of councils and Parliament. Unfortunately, the latter would be useless at national level as it would mean that all constituencies would have the same scores on their dummy variables, while the use of ward level dummies could yield distorted results given the relative homogeneity and small size of wards.

Table 4 shows the coefficients for the original variables once the political control dummies are included. The results of these models are as follows:

First, when the intercept shift dummy is included in the model of *Conservative* support, it becomes apparent that incumbency effects are much greater at constituency level, apart from in 1987 and 1991 when the local level dummy's values increase dramatically, possibly due to the greater number of non-metropolitan seats that were contested in these years.

TABLE 4
PARTY SUPPORT COEFFICIENTS (WITH INTERCEPT SHIFT DUMMY)

Year	Econ/ Dep	Salariat	Age/ Gender	Manuf	Race/ Density	PtyM1
Conservative Party						
1987	-4.31	2.77	0.16	-0.83	na	15.31
1992	-4.31	2.90	0.32	-0.72	na	15.07
1986	-7.56	6.08	2.15	-0.93	0.59	6.42
1987	-5.79	5.74	1.76	2.24	4.09	17.95
1988	-8.52	7.06	1.81	-0.38	0.82	7.01
1990	-7.23	6.80	1.97	-0.52	1.78	6.43
1991	-5.96	6.18	1.79	1.60	2.95	13.62
1992	-8.05	5.61	1.50	1.22	0.63	8.08
Labour Party						
1987	7.19	-4.68	1.19	2.41	na	16.23
1992	7.80	-5.28	-1.79	2.13	na	14.60
1986	11.48	-9.39	-1.54	3.52	2.02	8.64
1987	11.35	-8.61	-1.51	4.24	1.30	14.29
1988	12.23	-10.16	-1.50	3.00	0.35	12.78
1990	9.81	-9.68	-1.63	3.48	0.61	9.82
1991	11.61	-9.39	-1.48	4.63	2.21	12.37
1992	9.95	-8.72	-1.06	2.09	0.16	11.20
Liberal Democrats						
1987	-3.17	2.15	-1.13	-1.18	na	20.96
1992	-3.61	2.37	1.78	-1.03	na	23.45
1986	-3.65	2.49	0.60	-1.05	-0.58	22.77
1987	-1.54	1.41	1.22	0.99	3.58	20.37
1988	-3.08	2.09	1.22	0.91	1.17	17.74
1990	-3.30	1.97	1.11	-1.39	-1.17	24.05
1991	-2.43	1.98	2.05	0.27	3.52	22.98
1992	-2.62	2.29	0.72	-1.36	1.15	20.54

Note: Dependent variable is party percentage share of the vote. The first two rows show the national level coefficients.
Conservatives: National level coefficients for age/gender non-significant in 1987, 1992. Local level coefficient for manufacturing non-significant in 1988, as was the race/density coefficient for 1992.
Labour: Local level coefficients for race/density non-significant in 1988, 1992.
Liberal Democrats: Local level coefficients for age/gender non-significant in 1986 and 1992, as was the coefficient for manufacturing in 1991.

The introduction of a dummy variable has a considerable effect upon the national level coefficients of economic deprivation and salariat, the values of which are almost halved. Yet at local level it has comparatively little effect, except in 1987 and 1991. Little can be said about the effect of the dummy upon age/gender, manufacturing, and race/density due to the small initial coefficients or, in the latter case, the absence of national level figures to provide a comparison. However, the primary inferences that can be drawn from this model are that Conservative support is significantly more sensitive to levels of economic deprivation and the middle class population at local level than at national level where incumbency effects appear to be of greater importance.

A similar pattern emerges when the political dummy variable is added to the model of *Labour* support in Table 4. National level coefficients for economic deprivation and salariat drop by approximately one third while their local equivalents are consistently more resilient. Interestingly, the difference in magnitude between the local and national level dummies is noticeably less than in the model of Conservative support, with the local level coefficients being comparatively high, suggesting that local level incumbency is more important to Labour support. The two outliers are 1986 and 1990, both years when London borough elections were held. The dummy's introduction also results in small changes in the coefficients of age/gender, manufacturing and race/density, but again the initial coefficients are so small that these effects can be regarded as secondary. The importance of incumbency to *Liberal Democrat* support at local and national level is evidenced by the magnitude of the dummy variable, typically around 20 (per cent) at both levels. The dummy has little impact on the existing variables' coefficients at either level.

Empirical Findings 3:
The Effects of Slope Shift Political Dummy Variables on Party Support

The final stage of the analysis re-runs the model with a series of slope shift political control dummy variables in order to test for differential effects of variables in wards and constituencies controlled by Labour and the Conservatives at time t-1. Econ/dep, salariat, age/gender, manuf and race/density are multiplied by the intercept shift dummy ptyM1 to create slope shift dummy variables economic deprivation * (ptyM1), salariat * (ptyM1), age/gender * (ptyM1), manufacturing * (ptyM1), and race/density * (ptyM1) respectively.

The results of these analyses are shown in Tables 5 and 6. In Conservative-held constituencies, economic deprivation exerts a substantial additional influence upon that party's support, as evidenced by the consistent national level coefficients of between -3.1 and -3.2. At local level, the extra effects of economic deprivation in Conservative-held wards is rather more complex. The coefficients are much smaller and in some cases non-significant except in 1987 and 1991. This is partly counterbalanced by the fact that the original coefficients are substantially larger than their national level equivalents, but it does appear that incumbency effects have a greater influence on voter sensitivity to economic deprivation at national level.

TABLE 5
CONSERVATIVE SUPPORT COEFFICIENTS
(WITH INTERCEPT AND SLOPE SHIFT DUMMY VARIABLES)

Year	Econ/ Dep	Salariat	Age/ Gender	Manuf	Race/ Density	PtyM1
1987	-3.11	3.11	2.37	0.46	na	15.50
1992	-3.14	2.73	-1.94	0.44	na	15.30
1986	-7.20	5.74	2.79	-0.10	0.86	7.28
1987	-5.14	5.39	2.11	3.15	4.97	16.05
1988	-8.40	7.10	2.46	0.03	0.99	7.61
1990	-7.16	6.59	1.73	0.08	1.57	6.29
1991	-5.39	5.86	2.04	2.23	3.90	12.03
1992	-7.97	5.63	1.71	1.61	0.68	8.61

Year	Econ/ PtyM1	Salar/ PtyM1	Agender/ PtyM1	Manuf/ PtyM1	Race/ PtyM1
1987	-3.19	-0.34	-2.88	-1.81	na
1992	-3.13	0.44	1.95	-1.76	na
1986	-1.20	0.98	-1.77	-3.93	-0.95
1987	-4.88	0.88	-0.49	-3.62	-3.74
1988	-0.64	-0.31	-2.42	-2.24	1.11
1990	-0.12	0.98	0.22	-2.73	0.64
1991	-4.04	0.88	-0.43	-2.46	-3.97
1992	-1.66	0.03	-1.14	-4.80	-1.19

Note: Dependent variable is Conservative percentage share of the vote, as per Tables 3 and 4. The first series of figures in this Table show the coefficients for the basic factors and the intercept shift dummy variable. As before, the first two rows display the national level coefficients while the remaining rows show the local level coefficients. The second series of figures show the coefficients for the slope shift dummy variables. The following coefficients were statistically non-significant:
(National level) manufacturing (1987) salar(iat)/ptyM1 (1987 and 1992)
(Local level) manufacturing (1986, 1988, and 1990), race/density (1992), econ/ptyM1 (1988, 1990, and 1992), salar(iat)/ptyM1 (1987–92), agender/ptyM1 (1990–91) and race/ptyM1 (1988 and 1990).

Surprisingly, incumbency effects on class voting for the Conservatives are non-significant at national level and in all but one case at local level, as the coefficients for salariat demonstrate. The introduction of the slope shift dummies produces a change in the size and status of the coefficients for age/gender at national level. Previously non-significant, it now yields a substantially greater effect. The slope shift variable itself (age/gender*ptyM1) appears to have a greater influence at national level, although both this and the age/gender variables exert inconsistent effects at national level between their 1987 and 1992 general election scores.

The effect of manufacturing on Conservative support diminishes to the point of non-significance in half the cases at local/national level following the introduction of the manuf/ptyM1 variable. When all cases are considered at national level, manufacturing activity has little or no influence upon Conservative support, a pattern repeated at local level in 1986, 1988 and 1990. However, when only Conservative-held wards and constituencies are analysed by the manufacturing (ptyM1) dummy, significant negative effects on Tory support are identified by the coefficients. In 1987, 1988 and 1992, positive local level manuf coefficients are more than counterbalanced by the negative effects of the manufacturing (ptyM1) variable, denoting a strong and consistently negative effect upon Conservative support.

The only notable point that can be extracted from the local level coefficients for race/density (ptyM1) is that they are much larger in 1987 and 1991. Even so, in 1987 the race/density (ptyM1) coefficient is insufficient to counteract the surprisingly positive relationship between race/pop. density which is shown by the coefficient for the original race/density variable.

Looking at the model of Labour support, econ/ptyM1 yields strong negative coefficients at both local and national level, presumably due to the operation of the dummy variable ptyM1(Lab). The negative effects are significantly greater at national level. Salariat (ptyM1) is statistically non-significant at both levels in most cases. The only year of interest is that of 1990 where a coefficient denotes a positive relationship between the percentage of middle class voters in a Labour -held ward and Labour support, possibly due to the effect of the Poll Tax. However, the negative salariat coefficient is so large that it may not have any substantial impact. It is impossible to draw any inferences about the effect of age/gender(ptyM1) on Labour support at either local or national level as the results do not appear to have any discernible pattern over time.

The negative coefficients for manuf/ptyM1 are greater at local level, mirroring the higher positive coefficients for manufacturing at local level. The strength of the negative manufacturing (ptyM1) coefficients could be due to the operation of the intercept shift dummy. No local/national comparison is possible for race/ptyM1, but the local level coefficients are consistently negative which is somewhat puzzling.

TABLE 6
LABOUR SUPPORT COEFFICIENTS (WITH INTERCEPT AND SLOPE SHIFT DUMMY VARIABLES)

Year	Econ/ Dep	Salariat	Age/ Gender	Manuf	Race/ Density	PtyM1
1987	11.49	-4.41	2.22	2.44	na	18.56
1992	12.61	-5.49	-2.87	2.69	na	14.17
1986	14.98	-8.78	-1.57	4.96	3.38	14.58
1987	13.71	-7.84	-1.88	5.24	3.16	15.60
1988	16.14	-8.82	-1.28	4.67	1.94	16.07
1990	14.12	-9.99	-1.45	5.74	1.42	14.26
1991	14.94	-9.07	-1.86	5.98	3.77	14.53
1992	14.48	-8.14	-1.19	4.31	2.31	14.14

	Econ/ PtyM1	Salar/ PtyM1	Agender/ PtyM1	Manuf/ PtyM1	Race/ PtyM1
1987	-8.28	-0.19	-3.48	-1.38	na
1992	-9.03	0.91	3.81	-2.68	na
1986	-6.91	0.02	-1.67	-3.81	-3.81
1987	-4.40	-2.21	0.99	-4.08	-3.89
1988	-6.49	-1.89	-1.33	-3.90	-2.83
1990	-7.32	1.77	-1.84	-4.70	-2.23
1991	-6.45	-0.52	0.58	-4.97	-3.75
1992	-6.48	-0.17	-0.62	-4.93	-3.12

Note: Dependent variable is Labour percentage share of the vote, as per Tables 3 and 4. The first series of figures in this Table show the coefficients for the basic factors and the intercept shift dummy variable. As before, the first two rows display the national level coefficients while the remaining rows show the local level coefficients. The second series of figures show the coefficients for the slope shift dummy variables.
The salar(iat)/ptyM1 coefficients were statistically non-significant at local /national level in 1987 and 1992, and at local level in 1986, 1991, and 1992. The agend/ptyM1 coefficients were non-significant at local level in 1988, 1991 and 1992.

Conclusion

The model may have its limitations, but it does at least facilitate a plausible comparative analysis of local/national level electoral behaviour. The similar local/national level results of the factor analysis and the general pattern of the regression coefficients in the results section suggests that aggregation bias is not a serious problem. Yet the results show that there appear to be significant differences in the composition of the parties' support at each level. The most striking difference is the increasing importance of the salariat/social class in the patterns of local level support of Labour and the Conservatives relative to the other variables. One might have expected the opposite, given the electoral volatility associated with recent local elections. Perhaps the possibility of neighbourhood effects in local elections requires examination.

The results also provide some insight into the effect of incumbency on parties' support, as indicated by the coefficients for both the intercept and slope shift variables. The coefficients for the dummy variables in Table 4 show that incumbency is generally more important for the Conservatives and Labour at national level, while Liberal Democrat support is equally dependent on incumbency at both local and national level. The proportionally greater Liberal Democrat dependence on incumbency factors would be consistent with the party's tactics of concentrating effort on particular seats, especially at local level. The effects of incumbency upon voters' reactions to the levels of different socio-economic variables are shown in Tables 5 and 6; the prime examples being the effects of economic deprivation on Conservative and Labour support in areas where they held the parliamentary seat or controlled the council at time t-1. In such cases, the effects of the economic deprivation factor are significantly diminished due to the presence of the econ/ptyM1 variables. However, even controlling for incumbency, the significant difference between the effects of economic deprivation at local and national level on Labour support still remains. The stronger *local* level relationship could indicate that Labour supporters *do* believe that local authorities have an important role in service provision and economic development despite the erosion of local government powers. A similar analysis of the relationship between economic deprivation and Conservative support (after incumbency considerations) is more problematic. The inflation of the local level coefficients for 1987 and 1991 is presumably due to the different character of the authorities in which elections were contested in those years and possibly indicates a divide in Conservative support between prosperous rural districts and areas on the economic periphery which suffer from economic problems more commonly associated with the inner-cities. Disparities within the local level results themselves suggest that tests for differential effects across different types of local authority may be necessary, which in turn suggests that patterns of local election results may be more complex than the proponents of the 'annual general election' theory would have us believe.

ACKNOWLEDGEMENTS

The author would like to thank David Sanders and John Bartle for their comments and suggestions on various drafts of this article.

NOTES

1. Openshaw (1984) refers to this phenomenon as the 'Modifiable Areal Unit Problem'.
2. Gibson and Stewart (1991, 1992) analysed the electoral impact of the Poll Tax on the 1990/1991 local elections. However, their data allowed analysis only at local authority rather than ward level, this being due to the simple fact that the Poll Tax was set at the same level for people in all wards within an authority.

3. The local level analysis was based on the data for all 9527 wards (less the cases where the LBS data are suppressed for reasons of confidentiality). If one conducted a factor analysis in a given year for just those wards where elections took place, the data from those wards could yield significantly different results. However, an analysis for 1990 (including London), using the same variables and rotation, yields a similar dimensional solution but with the race/living conditions factor being absorbed into the economic deprivation factor.

BIBLIOGRAPHY

Burnham, J. (1990), 'District Councils In The South Of England: Is Labour Doing Well?', *Local Government Studies* 16: 9–16.

Butler, D. and D. Stokes (1974), *Political Change In Britain. The Evolution Of Electoral Choice*, (2nd Edn). London: Macmillan.

Gibson, J. G. and J.D. Stewart (1991), 'Electoral Accountability And The Poll Tax: An Analysis Based On 1990 Ward Results', *Local Government Studies* 17: 63–71.

Gibson, J. G. and J.D. Stewart (1992), 'Poll Tax, Rates And Local Elections', *Political Studies* XL: 516–531.

Miller, W. L. (1988), *Irrelevant Elections: The Quality Of Local Democracy In Britain*. Oxford: Clarendon.

Newton, K. (1976), *Second City Politics*. Oxford: Clarendon.

Openshaw, S. (1984) *The Modifiable Areal Unit Problem*. Norwich: Geo-Abstracts.

Rallings, C. and M. Thrasher (1993), 'Exploring Uniformity And Variability In Local Electoral Outcomes: Some Evidence From English Local Elections 1985–1991', *Electoral Studies* 12: 366–84.

The Impact of Television Economic News on Public Perceptions of the Economy and Government, 1993–94

Neil T. Gavin and David Sanders with Niall Farrall

Background

The fields of economic voting and mass media impact represent two widely developed sub-disciplines of the social sciences. The economy has figured in a wide variety of electoral and inter-electoral studies of political support (Dunleavy and Husbands, 1985; Heath *et al.*, 1985; Whiteley, 1986; Sanders *et al.*, 1987; Heath *et al.*, 1990; Miller *et al.*, 1990; Price and Sanders, 1993; Clarke *et al.*, 1994). In the aggregate-level analyses the focus has been on the impact of the 'real economy' (represented by aggregate government statistics) on government popularity, though attention has now turned to perceptions of the national economy, and attitudes toward the family's economic circumstances and future prospects. The precise way in which the economy affects public perceptions, however, is still a live issue (Gavin, 1992b; Nannestad and Paldam, 1994). Although the explanation offered by Downs for the manner in which economic fluctuations translate into public concern is often deployed, work on individual-level processes has been limited, and specifying the individual-level decision calculus of the public has proved particularly problematic for aggregate analyses (Downs, 1957; Husbands, 1985).

The literature on media effects on public opinion is equally well developed, though here the results are rather more perplexing. A great deal of the early work suggested that the media have fairly modest effects on mass perceptions (Lazarsfeld *et al.*, 1944; Klapper, 1960). On the other hand, more recent studies on 'agenda setting' and 'priming' suggest that the media do have important, if elliptical, effects on public opinion (McCombs and Shaw, 1972; Iyengar and Kinder, 1987; Iyengar, 1991). Indeed, in both the USA and UK there is a growing body of research that is testimony to the significant, but subtle, impact of the media on political attitudes (Mutz, 1992; Newton, 1992; Miller *et al.*, 1990). This research tends to suggest that the impact of the press is more significant than that of television. The available aggregate-level evidence suggests that television does have an impact, though this is contingent on media structure, and on audience composition: Page *et al.* (1987) emphasize the types of news sources that are significant; Weatherford (1983) suggests that media-attentive audience members are more prone to influence.

But in Britain, as elsewhere, the issue of the inter-relationship between the economy, the media and public opinion has been greatly under-researched in quantitative terms. In the USA, a few studies have shown that press coverage can influence perceptions of economic problems, and thereby affect political evaluations (Benton and Frazier, 1976; Mutz, 1992; Blood and Phillips, 1995). Another study, again focusing on the press, suggested that newspaper coverage had a significant impact on the accuracy of people's expectations about the economy (Pruitt et al., 1988). This study was laboratory-based but at least went beyond some of the more speculative and provisional work on the role of media in fashioning economic attitudes (Van Raaij, 1989). In Britain there is comparatively little work in this area, though Mosley (1984) and Sanders et al. (1993) are the exceptions. The former was billed as a pilot study, and the latter has shown a modest impact of the press on personal prospective perceptions (and thereby voting behaviour). The results from the latter study are interesting but perhaps not surprising, given that newspapers are not the first choice of the public for reliable information (Dunleavy and Husbands, 1985) and are not wholly trusted by their audience (Barnett, 1989). The British results differ from the more substantial effects highlighted by American researchers, though the difference in media structures prevents direct comparison.

The British work has focused almost exclusively on the press. This is partly because it is easier to apply content analysis techniques to written text and partly because data from a national archive are readily accessible. In addition, there is the tacit assumption that the ideological positioning and express ideological project of many papers are more likely to influence the public than the notionally impartial and balanced output of the BBC and ITN. The only sustained empirical work on television and the economy in Britain (Glasgow University Media Group, 1976, 1980) is now rather long in the tooth, and it had a qualitative rather than a quantitative thrust. Comparable work has been undertaken in the USA (Jensen, 1987). The Glasgow team only looked at content (in its latent and manifest forms), and were roundly criticized for lack of attention to the audience (that is, to public opinion). The following discussion seeks to address this gap in the literature, and presents the preliminary findings of a larger project.

The Basic Analytic Model

In this section, we consider the possible connections between television coverage of economic news and the UK public's political and economic perceptions. The basic hypothesis that we advance is that, since (a) economic performance matters to most voters and (b) television news is an obvious source of information for the average voter, support for the incumbent government will tend to increase (*ceteris paribus*) when news about the economy is good and decrease when it is bad. This is not to suggest that either the economy or television news coverage are the only sources of voter preferences: merely that preferences are influenced to some degree by these phenomena. The broad analytic strategy that we pursue follows that adopted by Sanders *et al.* (1993) in their analysis of the electoral consequences of press coverage of economic news.

Our basic concern here is to assess how far BBC and ITN coverage of economic news might have been associated with the changing pattern of Conservative fortunes as measured by standard opinion poll questions about electoral preferences. We do this in two broad ways. Our initial approach is to test a series of simple models which take the general form:

$$Con_t = f(Coverage_t...Coverage_{t-n})$$

where Con_t is Conservative support at time t and $Coverage_t$ measures the weekly balance of positive versus negative television news items about various aspects of the UK's economic performance. The limitation of this basic model, however, is that it ignores a critical variable which previous research has suggested is an important influence upon variations in support for the Conservatives: the electorate's views of the Conservatives' (as opposed to Labour's) economic management capabilities (Gavin, 1992a; Sanders, 1995). There is comparable research in the USA that explores this notion (Monardi, 1994). Accordingly, our amended approach develops a two-stage model of the connections between Coverage and Conservative support as follows:

$$Con_t=f(Conhandle_t...Conhandle_{t-n})$$
$$Conhandle_t = f(Coverage_t...Coverage_{t-n})$$

where $Conhandle_t$ measures the electorate's sense that, 'with Britain in economic difficulties...', the Conservatives (as opposed to Labour) 'could handle the problem best'. The logic underlying this two-stage approach is extremely simple. It assumes that television coverage of economic news exerts an indirect rather than a direct effect on voters' electoral preferences: coverage affects voters' perceptions of the government's economic management competence which in turn affects their propensity to support it politically.

Measurement of Variables

The primary data that we employ on television coverage of the economy come from the midweek, flagship nine and ten o'clock broadcasts on BBC and ITV. The coding regime draws on and develops the work of Gavin (1993), Sanders *et al.* (1993) and Page *et al.* (1987), in the sense that the emphasis is placed on what is said by anchors, as well as experts and commentators. The pronouncements of politicians, while obviously significant in relation to the agenda, were excluded on the grounds that these, as partial and interested voices, were least likely to have a strong impact on political attitudes. This is consistent with a great deal of evidence on the dynamics of persuasive communication, from psychology (for a brief introduction, see Gergen and Gergen, 1981; and Severin, 1988).

The coding strategy, however, did have to be tailored to the distinctive expositional forms that are characteristic of televisual presentation of the economy[1] (an approach differing from that taken to analyse campaign agendas, where the presence or absence of an issue is the primary concern: Semetko *et al.*, 1991, 1994). Unlike the editorializing of the press, the BBC and ITN, with their remit to present impartial and balanced news, tend to present the economy in a very distinctive style. With the exception of politicians' special pleading, there is little judgmental commentary on the pros and cons of particular economic policies. Instead, there is much more on the dynamics and health of the economy generally – focusing particularly on which indicators are trending down, which up, and the likely implications of this for the overall vitality of the economy. The coding strategy had to reflect this focus and, as a result, the emphasis was on the form that these economic trends took (was inflation going up, was unemployment going down, were increases in interest rates likely?).

A further refinement led to the focus on eleven broad economic themes. These were: inflation and prices; taxation; jobs and unemployment; sales and spending; wages, pay and disposable income; balance of payments and foreign trade; short-time working; interest rates; state borrowing and PSBR; and the housing market. A final broad category encompassed 'the economy generally': this included news about recovery and recession, production, investment and growth, as well as references to the general health of the economy.[2] (The coding guidelines for each of these themes are described in more detail in the Appendix.) The general aim was to produce a set of measurements that could be aggregated to give an overall picture of the economy, while retaining sufficient flexibility to allow analysis of the impact of particular economic themes and temporal aspects of the news on public opinion. The main all-encompassing aggregate measure that we employ is 'Allnews'. This composite variable takes all the thematic codes for the whole of a particular story and calculates whether there is a positive or negative balance (was it, on balance, a 'good' news story or a 'bad' news story, taking into consideration all the themes included?). Each weekly period might have three or four such stories. If three of these were 'good news' stories, and one

a 'bad news' story, the overall media coverage indicator would register +2 for
that week's observation. The justification for this tactic is that, while coding
errors might throw up the occasional mis-specified code for a specific item of
news, it is extremely unlikely that they would unbalance the overall coding
for an entire news story.

A second aggregative indicator used the same technique of subtracting
good news codes from bad news, then adding these positive and negative
scores over the particular week. The difference was that this indicator
('Headline') focused only on the headline and introduction to any particular
economic news story. There is some theoretical justification for this. Not only
is the opening to a story rarely at odds with the bulk of the following copy,
but it usually distills the essence in a readily accessible form (focused, pithy,
and without the elaboration given by specialists and commentators). Framing
analysis, too, places emphasis on the leading elements of news stories,
suggesting quite strongly that this sort of introduction dominates and gives
direction to the subsequent text (Pan and Kosicki, 1993). Lastly, this
procedure of aggregation was carried out for each of the themes already
outlined (such as inflation and unemployment). The object was to develop an
indicator of how the respective aspects of news were covered (was it a good
or bad news week on jobs; was it a good or bad news week on inflation; and
so on). So, the thematic elements (such as inflation, jobs, tax) were isolated
within each story. Then, for each story the 'bad' news was subtracted from the
'good'. When each of these story indicators are aggregated across a week, this
gives a fairly robust measure of the overall 'good' or 'bad' news for each
particular theme.

The content analysis procedure described above generates 'Coverage'
data that can be integrated into conventional time series analysis. Our
television news coverage variables were collected on a weekly basis for the
period 17 November 1993–29 November 1994. (Resource constraints
prevented us from sampling a longer period.) This periodization was chosen
because it corresponds exactly to that employed by Gallup for the collection
of their monthly 'Gallup 9000' data. The measurement of the attitudinal
components of the models that we examine here, therefore, is entirely
conventional in the sense that the Gallup questions used are identical to those
deployed in numerous other studies which use monthly data ('If there were a
general election tomorrow, which party would you support?'; 'With Britain in
economic difficulties, which party do you think could handle the problem best
– the Conservatives under Mr Major, or Labour under Mr. Smith/Blair?'). The
difference is that the public opinion data that we employ are drawn from
weekly breakdowns (typical sample size: 1500–2000 respondents) of the
'omnibus' Gallup 9000 polls. Grouping the data in this way gives us total of
54 observations to analyse over the November 1993–November 1994 period.

Figure 1 describes what happened to Conservative support, on a weekly basis, during the November 1993–November 1994 period. The next section reviews our efforts to specify and estimate statistical models that might enable us to assess the impact of television news on this varying pattern of political support.

FIGURE 1
WEEKLY VARIATIONS IN SUPPORT FOR THE CONSERVATIVE PARTY,
17 NOVEMBER 1993 TO 29 NOVEMBER 1994

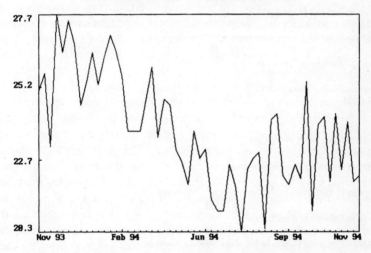

Source: Gallup 9000 data. Percentage Intending to Vote Conservative 'if there were a General Election tomorrow'. Don't Knows excluded from percentage base.

Empirical Results 1:
Simple One-stage Models of the Coverage–Conservative Support Relationship

The pattern of Conservative support in 1993–94 which is displayed in Figure 1 suggests an obvious difficulty for any time-series analysis. Although the data cover only a one-year period, the series is clearly non-stationary in the sense that (in this case) its mean is not constant over time: Conservative support appears to exhibit a distinct downward trend for the first six months or so, followed by a slight recovery thereafter. The difficulties encountered in deciding whether or not to detrend data of this sort prior to analysis have been discussed extensively elsewhere (Sanders and Ward, 1994). Throughout the ensuing analysis, we work with first-differenced, de-trended data. This ensures that we do not over-estimate any possible effects of television coverage on party support: since our primary concern here is to show, for the

TABLE 1
THE EFFECTS OF TELEVISION COVERAGE OF ECONOMIC NEWS AND AGGREGATE
PERCEPTIONS OF CONSERVATIVE ECONOMIC MANAGEMENT COMPETENCE ON
CONSERVATIVE SUPPORT, DECEMBER 1993–NOVEMBER 1994

	Model 1	Model 2	Model 3	Model 4	Model 5	Model 6
Change in Unemployment Coverage, t-1	+0.12 (.12)	+0.12 (.11)	-0.21 (.15)		-0.09 (.14)	
Change in Inflation Coverage, t-1	+0.23 (.17)	+0.17 (.16)	-0.12 (.18)		-0.18 (.16)	
Change in Housing Coverage, t-1	+0.45 (.40)	+0.59 (.35)	+0.59 (.33)		+0.18 (.31)	
Change in Other Economic Coverage, t-1		+0.09 (.11)	+0.04 (.10)		+0.02 (.09)	
Change in Borrowing Coverage, t-1	-0.25 (.40)					
Change in Trade Coverage, t-1	+0.29 (.22)					
Change in Interest Rate Coverage, t-1	-0.06 (.23)					
Change in Taxation Coverage, t-1	+0.01 (.21)					
Change in General Economic Coverage, t-1	-0.08 (.22)					
Change in Overall Balance of Coverage, t-1 (δAllnews)			+0.30* (.12)	+0.13* (.05)	+0.23* (.11)	+0.07 (.05)
Change in Balance of Headlines, t-1				-0.05 (.12)	-0.09 (.11)	
Change in Perceived Conservative Management Competence$_t$					+0.43* (.12)	+0.48* (.10)
Constant	-0.13 (.22)	-0.13 (.22)	-0.09 (.20)	-0.09 (.10)	-0.04 (.18)	-0.03 (.08)
LM(3) Serial Correlation Test [significance in parentheses]	15.08 [.002]	14.67 [.002]	11.18 [.011]		12.63 [.006]	
AR(1)				-0.58* (.14)		-0.52* (.17)
AR(2)				-0.28* (.14)		-0.39* (.17)
Corrected R^2	0.03	0.07	0.19	0.37	0.38	0.56
N	51	51	51	49	50	50
Sample	1/12/93–29/11/94	1/12/93–29/11/94	1/12/93–29/11/94	15/12/93–29/11/94	8/12/93–29/11/94	8/12/93–29/11/94

Note: Dependent variable is change in percentage intending to vote Conservative t-1 to t.
Estimation by OLS in Models 1, 2, 3, and 5. Estimation by Maximum Likelihood in
Models 4 and 6; AR(n) specification determined by the lag-structure of the error term in
the corresponding OLS equation. Standard errors in round parentheses. Starred
coefficients (*) significant at the .05 level.

first time, that such effects do exist, this conservative approach to hypothesis testing is entirely appropriate. We make no effort here, however, to 'recover' any possible trend effects through error correction models (Clarke *et al.*, 1994; Harris, 1995). Such models attempt to incorporate information about the long-term equilibrium relationships between variables analysed. We eschew them because of the difficulty of assessing the character of such long-term equilibria with data that cover a period of only one year.

The initial differenced model that we estimated was:

$$dCon_t = a + b_1 \, djob_{t-1} + b_2 \, dpri_{t-1} + b_3 \, dira_{t-1} + b_4 \, dhou_{t-1}$$
$$+ \, b_5 \, dtax_{t-1} + b_6 \, dstb_{t-1} + b_7 \, dftr_{t-1} + b_8 \, deco_{t-1} + u_t \qquad [1]$$

where Con is Conservative support; job measures the weekly balance ('good' minus 'bad' news items) of unemployment coverage; pri denotes the balance of prices coverage; ira is interest rates; hou is housing; tax is taxation; stb is state borrowing; ftr is foreign trade; eco is general economic news; d represents the first difference operator; and u_t is a random error term.[3] Since the Conservative popularity and the coverage data were collected over the course of each week, in order to avoid the possibility that coverage late in the week could be falsely deemed to influence popularity measured early in the week, all coverage variables were lagged by one time-point.

The results of estimating this initial model are shown in Table 1, Model 1. (Although we do not report the results here, lagged effects of greater than one week were also examined – but they invariably produced non-significant results.) What is clear from the table is that none of the individual coverage variables yields a significant coefficient. This suggests that television coverage of particular economic issues fails to exert any measurable effect on Conservative support.

The sort of specification outlined in Model 1, however, takes no account of the salience of the various issues involved. Table 2 shows which issues were rated as 'the most urgent problem(s) facing the country at the present time' by UK voters during the 1993–94 period. The three most frequently cited economic issues were unemployment (on average cited as most important by 50 per cent of the electorate), prices (8 per cent) and housing (3 per cent). 'Other economic issues' were cited, on average, by 6 per cent of voters. In order to reflect this pattern of differential salience, the interest rates, taxation, borrowing, trade, short-time working and general economic coverage variables were additively combined to create a single 'other economic issues' variable ('other'). The simpler model specification thus implied was

$$dCon_t = \quad a + b_1 \, djob_{t-1} + b_2 \, dpri_{t-1} + b_3 \, dhou_{t-1}$$
$$+ \, b_4 \, dother_{t-1} + u_t \qquad\qquad\qquad [2]$$

However, the results of this simpler specification, which are shown in Table 1, Model 2, again yield no significant coefficients: even grouping the coverage categories together in this way fails to produce a significant effect on Conservative popularity.

TABLE 2
SALIENCE OF ECONOMIC ISSUES AMONG THE UK ELECTORATE,
NOVEMBER 1993–NOVEMBER 1994

	Unemployment	Housing	Other Economic Issues	Prices
Nov 1993	47	2	8	9
Dec 1993	54	2	7	9
Jan 1994	50	3	8	7
Feb 1994	45	2	9	10
Mar 1994	na	na	na	na
Apr 1994	47	3	7	7
May 1994	51	3	7	6
Jun 1994	53	3	4	5
Jul 1994	57	3	5	6
Aug 1994	48	3	4	6
Sep 1994	52	2	4	8
Oct 1994	52	2	4	6
Nov 1994	47	3	5	8

But if specific categories of coverage are apparently unrelated to variations in support for the incumbent government, it is possible that public opinion is influenced by the overall thrust of reported economic news. As outlined earlier, an 'overarching' measure ('allnews') was constructed which attempted to specify whether, on balance, each week's news items were 'good' or 'bad' as far as the government's broad policy aims were concerned. An analogous measure was also constructed purely on the basis of the content of the news headlines ('headline'). These two measures were then added to the specification described in equation [2] above to produce:

$$dCon_t = a + b_1 \, djob_{t-1} + b_2 \, dpri_{t-1} + b_3 \, dhou_{t-1} + b_4 \, dother_{t-1} + b_5 \, dallnews_{t-1} + b_6 \, dheadline_{t-1} + u_t \qquad [3]$$

The OLS findings derived from this specification are reported in Table 1, Model 3. As the table indicates, only the 'Overall Balance of Coverage' variable yields a significant coefficient (though the housing coefficient is close to significance), suggesting that the overall tenor of television coverage of economic news may indeed affect the public's views of the governing party. However, the diagnostics from the table indicate that the model as a whole suffers from a variety of problems associated with non-random residuals. The model outlined in Model 3 was accordingly revised along the following lines. First, following the strategy advocated by Hendry (1983), all non-significant variables were dropped from the specification. Second, the resultant 'reduced form' specification was estimated by OLS as follows:

$$dCon_t = a + b_1 \; dallnews_{t-1} + u_t \tag{4}$$

Third, the residuals from [4] were inspected for serially correlated error. This inspection revealed an AR(2) process in the error term. Equation [4] was accordingly re-estimated as a maximum likelihood AR(2) model, producing the results shown in Model 4.[4] The critical feature of Model 4 is the significant coefficient which attaches to the Overall Balance variable (b=.13). This finding lends powerful support to the idea that television news coverage does influence the political views of voters. It suggests that, at least during the period analysed, a unit increase in the balance between favourable and unfavourable economic news in any given week, as portrayed by the BBC and ITN, increased support for the Conservatives by .13 of a percentage point the following week; a unit decrease exerted a proportionately reductive effect. These might appear to be very small effects and, in absolute terms, they are. It needs to be recognized, however, that public opinion generally changes very slowly and that there are very many weeks in a 'long election campaign'. In these circumstances, the slow drip of good (or bad) economic news can exert a powerful long-term effect. Indeed, it would be surprising if the statistical effects that we observe here were anything other than very tiny. What matters is that they are consistent and that they have been estimated on the basis of a specification that seeks to take account of all of the major distortions that typically afflict time-series models of this sort.

Empirical Results 2:
Two-stage models of the Coverage-Conservative Support Relationship

The foregoing results demonstrate that there is undoubtedly a measurable statistical relationship between the overall (favourable/unfavourable) balance of television news coverage and support for the incumbent government. What the results cannot 'prove' however is that this relationship is in any sense 'causal'. We can certainly hypothesize that changes in coverage 'cause' variations in support and argue that our data are 'consistent with' this hypothesis. However, purely on the basis of the models reported above, we cannot demonstrate that government popularity changes because of changes in coverage. One alternative explanation for our findings runs as follows: 'Television coverage of economic news reflects "real" changes in voters' economic experiences: if it failed to do so over the long-term, people would cease to watch. Insofar as the economy is important to voters' preferences, it is their own economic experiences, rather than television coverage of the economy, that lead voters to adjust their political allegiances. Both coverage and shifts in political preferences, therefore, derive from economic experience; the statistical association between coverage and party support is a classic example of a theoretically spurious correlation.'

There are a number of ways, in principle, in which this sort of counter hypothesis could be tested. The most obvious would be to apply statistical controls for 'voters' economic experiences', as measured by 'objective' economic statistics such as inflation, unemployment and interest rates, to the coverage-support relationship. If the coverage-support relationship either disappeared or weakened substantially when these controls were applied, it could reasonably be concluded that the relationship was indeed theoretically spurious. Unfortunately, 'objective' data such as these are not available on a week-by-week basis and so no such controls can be applied to the specific models developed here.

A second approach to countering the spurious correlation accusation is to attempt to strengthen the theoretical and empirical case for believing that coverage and support are indeed causally connected. On the face of it, simply to assert that voters increase (reduce) their support for the government because the overall balance of television economic news coverage has been more (less) favourable says nothing of the calculation that is assumed to operate inside the heads of individual voters. We hypothesize that the critical intervening variable in this context is the extent to which the average voter believes that the governing party is capable of managing the economy effectively – particularly in comparison with the capabilities of the main opposition party. On this account, the crucial effect of 'good' or 'bad' economic news is to change voters' assessments of the governing party's relative economic management competence. These changes in assessments of management competence then lead voters to adjust their political preferences in favour of the party that they consider to be best able to handle the economy. Clearly, if empirical corroboration for these propositions could be obtained, this would go some way towards reinforcing the conclusion that the coverage-support relationship is non-spurious. It would simply imply, rather, that the relationship is an indirect one which operates through voters' assessments of party management competence.

Fortuitously, since early 1991, Gallup have been collecting information on a weekly basis about the relative economic management capabilities of the Conservative and Labour parties by asking the following question: 'With Britain in economic difficulties, which party do you think could handle the problem best – the Conservatives under Mr Major or Labour under Mr (Blair)?'. The responses to this question enable us to do two things. First, by subtracting the percentage of respondents who cite Labour as best able to handle economic problems from the percentage who cite the Conservatives, we can devise a simple aggregate measure of relative competence. Second, we can develop a very precise test of the claim that voter perceptions of economic management competence act as an intervening variable between coverage and support. Using simple causal modelling logic, if relative competence assessments mediate the coverage support relationship, we should expect to find: (1) that, controlling for relative competence, coverage exerts no effect on Conservative popularity; and (2) that coverage has a significant effect on relative competence. It should be stressed in this context that, although aggregate-level measures of relative competence and Conservative popularity are closely correlated with one another, the available evidence suggests that they do not 'measure the same thing' (Sanders, 1995). In the 9-month period before the 1992 general election, the Conservatives enjoyed a large and consistent lead over Labour on the question of competence. In terms of measured popularity, however, Conservative and Labour support were consistently at very similar levels. This strongly suggests that the Gallup competence measure is not a simple surrogate for (comparative) party popularity.

The logic of the intervening-variable argument outlined above is followed through in the equations reported in Models 5 and 6 of Table 1 and in Table 3. Model 5 shows the consequences of adding a relative economic management competence term to the OLS specification shown in equation [3] above. With this OLS specification, it appears that overall coverage continues to exert a significant direct effect on Conservative popularity. However, it is clear from the model's diagnostic statistics that the model is afflicted by serially correlated error. (In fact the residuals exhibit a second order autoregressive process, or AR(2).) When the correct error specification is incorporated into the equation, as shown in Model 6, the coefficient on the coverage term is non-significant – suggesting that, over and above the effects of competence assessments, coverage exerts no effect on government popularity. Finally, Table 3 shows the results of regressing competence assessments on overall coverage. When the appropriate error correction is specified, coverage does indeed exert a significant impact on competence. All of these findings support the notion that coverage indirectly affects government popularity through its effects on voters' assessments of the relative economic management competence of the two major parties. This does not – indeed it could not – 'prove' that the coverage-support relationship is non-spurious. However, it certainly lends theoretical and empirical credence to the claim that television news coverage does exert a small, but consistent, effect on the political preferences of British voters.

TABLE 3
THE EFFECTS OF TELEVISION COVERAGE OF ECONOMIC NEWS ON AGGREGATE
PERCEPTIONS OF CONSERVATIVE ECONOMIC MANAGEMENT COMPETENCE, DECEMBER
1993–NOVEMBER 1994

Independent Variable	Coefficient
Change in Overall Balance of Coverage t-1	+0.16* (.06)
Constant	-0.12 (.08)
AR(1)	-0.73* (.20)
AR(2)	-0.55* (.20)
AR(3)	-0.41* (.20)
Corrected R^2	0.46
N	50

Note: Dependent variable is the change in the Conservatives' Perceived Economic Management Competence rating t-1 to t. The model is estimated as a Maximum Likelihood AR(3) because the OLS specification exhibited a third order autoregressive process in the originals. Standard errors are in parenthesis.

Conclusion

It is easy to assert that television news coverage 'obviously' affects popular economic and political perceptions because television is a major source of information for most voters. It is equally easy to assert that coverage 'obviously' fails to affect popular opinions because voters' interpretations of news are strongly coloured by their prior political preferences. Assertion, however, is a luxury of post-modernism that serious empirical researchers can ill afford. It is much more difficult to specify a testable model that might enable an impartial assessment to be made of the possible effects of media coverage on voter perceptions and preferences. Ideally, of course, a research design based on a long-term panel would provide the sort of data that are required. Such data, however, would be inordinately expensive to collect and are not at present available. In their absence, we have sought here to develop an aggregate-level model of the relationship between television coverage and patterns of party support.

We recognize, obviously, that we have not established any sort of relationship between media messages and individual-level changes in partisan support. What we have shown, however, is that at the aggregate level, there is indeed a relationship – albeit an indirect one – between the overall pattern of economic news coverage that the BBC and ITN collectively provide and the extent to which the UK electorate is prepared to express its support for the governing Conservative Party. We cannot specify which individuals (or which sort of individuals) are likely to change their political preferences in accordance with either improving or deteriorating economic news. But we can assert with some confidence that changes in party preference are strongly related to changes in perceived management competence and that competence perceptions are, in turn, clearly influenced by the overall balance of television news coverage. In short, economic news which is on balance 'bad' reduces voters' confidence in the managerial capabilities of government, while news which is on balance 'good' serves to increase it. In terms of practical politics, this result offers some crumbs of comfort to Conservative strategists who are desperate to see their opinion poll ratings improve in the run-up to the next general election. A continuing series of 'good news' weeks would help, cumulatively, to restore the Conservatives' lost – and vital – reputation for competent economic management.

APPENDIX

The coverage was divided by theme for the purpose of coding. There were eleven themes, including:

1. *Prices*: Under this heading were stories concerning the price or cost of goods; inflation; reference to cheaper or more costly goods; bills, charges or fares; and discounts.
2. *Tax*: This grouped references to tax, VAT and National Insurance; and duties, tariffs, excise, levies and customs.
3. *Jobs*: Under this heading came items on closures and companies going 'out of business', 'bust', 'to the wall' or 'shutting'; jobs, jobless, redundancies and (un)employment; staffing and posts; and axing and lay-offs. Not coded were increases in part-time, seasonal or women's as opposed to men's jobs.
4. *Consumption*: News on buying, shopping for, or purchasing goods; the sale of, or spending on goods; consumption, and benefit for the consumer; and demand, fell under this rubric.
5. *Disposables*: This category was reserved for news on living standards; pay, wages, income and earnings; wealth; and consumer confidence.
6. *Foreign Trade*: References to the deficit, imports and exports; the trade balance or surplus; trade figures; and the balance of payments.
7. *Short-time Work*: References to night shifts, short-time working, holiday truncation, and shortening of the working week.
8. *Interest Rates*: All references to interest rate, base rates, mortgage rates, loan and lending rates were coded under this rubric.
9. *State Borrowing*: Under this category were classified references to PSBR, public borrowing, government borrowing, and public debt; and to government or public debt.
10. *Housing*: A separate category was set up to include house prices; house buying, purchasing, selling and turnover; and the housing market.
11. *General Economic*: This large and catch-all category included general references to the economy, trade, business, and industry; to recovery, upswing, upturn, 'boom' and prosperity; to recession, downturn, slow-down, slump and 'bust'; also included were references to production, output, growth and GDP; finally this category included references to invest(ment) and business confidence.

The tagging of these pieces of news coverage proceeded as one might expect: more jobless coded negative; sales down negative; interest rates down positive; and so on. The exception to this was the prices/inflation and pay coding. In the former case it was noted that prices rarely if ever decrease. So, there was a danger of any mention of inflation being negative, when, in fact, much news on inflation was positive. It was decided to code as negative if inflation was 'rising', 'going up', 'coming back' or 'starting up'. On the other hand if inflation was 'steady', 'stable', 'slight', 'low', 'unchanged' or 'zero', this was coded positive. Likewise with references to inflation 'decreasing', 'falling', 'threatening to turn negative', 'down' or 'slashed'. On pay a similar sort of coding strategy was applied. If pay was 'declining', 'diminishing', 'being squeezed' or 'reduced' it was coded as negative. If pay was rising, but at less than inflation, this too was coded negative (likewise, if pay was 'static', at the 'same level', or 'not rising'). A positive code was registered for references to pay 'increasing' or 'getting better'.

ACKNOWLEDGEMENTS

The authors are indebted to Harold Clarke, David Farrell, David Broughton and Shaun Bowler for their helpful comments on an earlier draft of this article. They are also grateful to Bob Wybrow and Peter Duffyn of Gallup for supplying the weekly Gallup 9000 data used here. The research was sponsored by the ESRC (Ref. R000221336).

NOTES

1. For full details, contact Neil Gavin, Department of Politics, University of Liverpool.
2. State spending was, finally, excluded from the coding scheme: it was seen as highly politicized. Stories in this sphere were not handled like other economic stories (that is, there was no consensus on whether increases or decreases in state spending were intrinsically 'good' or 'bad'). Increases in inflation and unemployment were on the whole placed in a negative frame; likewise increases in growth or investment were viewed positively. This, of course, embodies political values at one step removed, but in terms of commentary comes close to the notion of 'valency'. State spending was, in contrast, a political football, and was at some points viewed in a positive (particularly with respect to Government departments 'winning' and 'losing' in the Budget disposition of funds), and at other points in a negative light.
3. Coverage variables relating to short-time working, consumption and state borrowing were excluded from the analysis because they were mentioned so infrequently in the news broadcasts sampled.
4. We do not reflect on the precise character of the AR(n) residual processes reported here. Our primary aim is not to assess the determinants of either Conservative popularity or perceived Conservative economic management competence. Rather, it is to assess the possible connections between popularity, competence and television news. We use the AR(n) error specifications simply to obtain the best possible 'fix' on the possible effects of television news coverage.

BIBLIOGRAPHY

Barnett, Steve (1989) 'Broadcast News', British Journalism Review 1: 49–56.
Benton, Mark and Jean P. Frazier (1976) 'The Agenda-Setting Function of the Mass Media at Three Levels of 'Information Holding', Communication Research 3: 261–74.
Blood, Deborah and Peter Phillips (1995) 'Recession Headline News, Consumer Sentiment, the State of the Economy and Presidential Popularity: A Time Series Analysis 1989–1993', International Journal of Public Opinion Research 7: 2–22.
Clarke, Harold D., William Mishler and Paul Whiteley (1990) 'Recapturing the Falklands: Models of Conservative Popularity 1979–83', British Journal of Political Science 20: 63–81.

Clarke, Harold D., Marianne Stewart and Paul Whiteley (1994) 'Tory Trends: The Dynamics of Conservative Party Support, 1992–94', paper presented at EPOP annual conference, University of Wales, Cardiff, 27–29 September.

Downs, Anthony (1957), *An Economic Theory of Democracy*. New York: Harper & Row.

Dunleavy, Patrick and Christopher T. Husbands (1985) *Democracy at the Crossroads: Voting and Party Competition in the 1980s*. London: Allen & Unwin.

Gavin, Neil T. (1992a) *The Impact of the Mass Media on the Structure of Economic Perceptions: Britain in the 1980s*. (PhD, London University).

Gavin, Neil T. (1992b) 'Television News and the Economy: The Pre-Campaign Coverage' *Parliamentary Affairs* 45: 596–611.

Gavin, Neil T. (1993) 'Recovery and Recession: Economic Explanation and Expectations in the Near-Term Election Campaign 1992', paper presented to the PSA annual conference, Leicester University, April.

Gergen, Kenneth J. and Mary M.Gergen (1981) *Social Psychology*. New York: Harcourt Brace Jovanovich.

Glasgow University Media Group (1976) *Bad News*. London: Routledge and Kegan Paul.

Glasgow University Media Group (1980) *More Bad News*. London: Routledge and Kegan Paul.

Harris, Richard (1995) *Using Cointegration Analysis in Econometric Modelling*. Hemel Hempstead: Prentice Hall/Harvester Wheatsheaf.

Hendry, David F. (1983) 'Econometric Modelling: The "Consumption Function" in Retrospect', *Scottish Journal of Political Economy* 30: 193–220.

Heath, Anthony, Roger Jowell and John Curtice (1985) *How Britain Votes*. Pergamon Press: Oxford.

Heath, Anthony, Roger Jowell, John Curtice, Geoffrey Evans, Julia Field and Sharon Witherspoon (1990) *Understanding Political Change*. Oxford: Pergamon Press.

Husbands, Christopher T. (1985) 'Government Popularity and the Unemployment Issue, 1986–93', *Sociology* 18: 1–18 .

Iyengar, Shanto (1991) *Is Anyone Responsible?: How Television Frames Political Issues*. Chicago: University of Chicago Press.

Iyengar, Shanto and Donald R. Kinder (1987) *News That Matters*. Chicago: Chicago University Press.

Jensen, Klaus B. (1987) 'News as Ideology: Economic Statistics and Political Ritual in Television Network News', *Journal of Communication* 37: 8–27.

Klapper, James (1960) *The Effects of Mass Communication*. New York: The Free Press.

Lazarsfeld, Paul F., Bernard Berelson, and Hazel Gaudet (1944) *The People's Choice*. New York: Columbia University Press.

McCombs, Max E. and Shaw, Donald L. (1972) 'The Agenda-Setting Function of the Mass Media', *Public Opinion Quarterly* 36: 176–87.

Miller, William, Harold Clarke, Martin Harrop, Lawrence LeDuc and Paul Whiteley (1990) *How Voters Change: The 1987 British Election Campaign in Perspective*. Oxford: Clarendon Press.

Monardi, Fred M. (1994) 'Primary Voters as Retrospective Voters', *American Politics Quarterly* 22: 88–103.

Mosley, Paul (1984) 'Popularity Function and the Role of the Media: A Pilot Study of the Popular Press', *British Journal of Political Science* 14: 117–33.

Mutz, Diane C. (1992) 'Mass Media and the Depoliticization of Personal Experience', *American Journal of Political Science* 36: 483–508.

Nannestad, Peter and Martin Paldam (1994) 'The V-P Function: A Survey of the Literature on Vote and Popularity Functions after 25 Years', *Public Choice* 79: 213–45.

Newton, Ken (1992) 'Do People Read Everything They Read in the Papers? Newspapers and Voters in the 1983 and 1987 Election', in Ivor Crewe, Pippa Norris, David Denver, David Broughton (eds) *British Parties and Elections Yearbook, 1991*, pp.51–74. Hemel Hempstead: Harvester Wheatsheaf.

Page, Benjamin I., Robert Shapiro, and Glenn Dempsey (1987) 'What Moves Public Opinion?', *American Political Science Review* 88: 23–43.

Pan, Zhondang and Gerald Kosicki (1993) 'Framing Analysis: An Approach to News Discourse',

Political Communication 10: 55–75.

Price, Simon and David Sanders (1995) 'Economic Expectations and Voting Intentions in the UK, 1979–1987: A Pooled Cross-Section Approach', *Political Studies* 43: 451–71.

Pruitt, Stephen W., Robert J. Reilly, and George E. Hoffer (1988) 'The Effects of Media Presentation on the Formation of Economic Expectations: Some Initial Evidence', *Journal of Economic Psychology* 9: 315–25.

Sanders, David (1991) 'Government Popularity and the Next General Election', *Political Quarterly* 62 : 235–61.

Sanders, David (1995) 'Forecasting Political Preferences and Electoral Outcomes in the UK: Experiences, Problems and Prospects', *Electoral Studies* 14: 251–72.

Sanders, David and Hugh Ward (1994) 'Time Series Techniques for Repeated Cross-Sectional Data' in Richard Davies and Angela Dale (eds) *Analyzing Social and Political Change*, pp.198–223. London: Sage.

Sanders, David, Hugh Ward, David Marsh, and Tony Fletcher (1987) 'Government Popularity and the Falklands War: A Reassessment', *British Journal of Political Science* 17: 281–314.

Sanders, David, Hugh Ward and David Marsh (1991) 'Manipulating the Manipulation?: The Political Impact of Press Coverage of the UK Economy, 1979–87', paper presented at EPOP annual conference, Worcester College, Oxford, 28–29 Sept.

Sanders, David, David Marsh and Hugh Ward (1993) 'The Electoral Impact of Press Coverage of the Economy, 1979–87', *British Journal of Political Science* 23: 175–210.

Semetko, Holli, Jay G. Blumler, Michael Gurevich and David Weaver (1991) *The Formation of Campaign Agendas: A Comparative Analysis of Party and Media Roles in the Recent American and British Elections*. New Jersey: Lawrence Erlbaum.

Semetko, Holli, Margaret Scammell and Tom Nossiter (1994) 'The Media's Coverage of the Campaign', in Anthony Heath, Roger Jowell and John Curtice (eds) *Labour's Last Chance?: The 1992 Election and Beyond*, pp.24–42. Aldershot: Dartmouth.

Severin, Werner J. (1988) *Communication Theories*. London: Longman.

Van Raaij, W. Fred (1989) 'Economic News, Expectations and Macro-Economic Behaviour', *Journal of Economic Psychology* 10: 473–93.

Weatherford, M. Stephen (1983) 'Economic Voting and the "Symbolic Politics" Argument: A Reinterpretation and Synthesis', *American Political Science Review* 77: 158–74.

Whiteley, Paul (1986) 'Predicting the Labour Vote: Social Backgrounds versus Subjective Evaluations', *Political Studies* 34: 82–98.

Constituency Campaigning in the 1992 General Election: The Peculiar Case of the Conservatives

David Denver and Gordon Hands

Introduction

In terms of media attention, academic analysis and the commitment of the national party organizations, the main focus of campaigning in British general elections remains the national campaign. In recent years, however, the parties have devoted more attention than before to the campaigns fought by individual party branches or associations in the constituencies. Thus, the Labour Party had a very rigorous and thorough 'key seats' strategy in the 1992 election and was very successful in focusing the party's efforts and resources on winnable marginal seats (see Denver and Hands, 1993: 235). The Conservatives are less able to direct local campaigning strategy from the centre – because local associations have greater autonomy – and they have less need to do so, since their local organization is generally stronger. Nonetheless, reports since 1992 suggest that Conservative Party headquarters has begun to take more seriously the task of managing local campaign efforts (for example, *The Guardian*, 8 February 1995).

There has also been a considerable increase in interest in local campaigning among students of elections. In particular, a number of recent studies have challenged what has been the orthodoxy up until now – the view, largely associated with the Nuffield studies, that local campaigning is merely a ritual. Rituals in many spheres of life are extremely important, of course, but the word is used in this context to imply that local campaigning is simply a matter of going through a series of set patterns of activity which are really of very little significance, and in particular have no impact on the outcomes of elections. What might be called the 'revisionist' literature has argued, to the contrary, that constituency campaigning can have a significant impact. It is not suggested that the impact is very large – a very well organized constituency campaign may produce a change in the share of the vote which is three to four percentage points better than a poor or average campaign. But this can make a considerable difference and clearly could crucially affect the election result in a number of constituencies.

The work in question has been largely carried out by three pairs of researchers – Ron Johnston and Charles Pattie, Patrick Seyd and Paul Whiteley, and ourselves – and as we shall see, there are some important differences in the methods used. But although all of these authors agree in contradicting the traditional view of the effects of local campaigning, this work has also thrown up a puzzle. Johnston and Pattie and Seyd and Whiteley have argued that in recent elections the campaigns of *all* parties have had an impact. In contrast, our work on the 1992 election campaign suggests that in that election, while Labour and Liberal Democrat constituency campaigns did significantly affect their performance, variations in the strength of Conservative campaigning were not associated with variations in their performance. We have tested this result using a variety of measures and procedures and it seems to be robust. The puzzle is, therefore, why there is this discrepancy – why do the results reported by Johnston and Pattie and Seyd and Whiteley differ from ours in this respect? And, if our results are correct, why is it that Conservative constituency campaigns, at least in 1992, had no effect? In this article, we set out the differences between our own and earlier work, and explore reasons why Conservative campaigns seem to be less effective than those of the other parties.

The Basic Approach

All of the 'revisionist' literature uses the same basic approach to testing the impact of local campaigns. The technique is to start with two measures, one of the party's performance in the constituency and the other of the strength or intensity of the campaign mounted by the local party. Multiple regression analysis is then used to assess the effects of variations in campaign strength on party performance across constituencies, while incorporating a number of control variables into the analysis. The various studies have used different measures of both party performance and campaign strength, however, and we begin, therefore, by considering the various measures used.

The Independent Variable: Campaign Strength

Until our own recent work on the 1992 election, based on a postal survey of election agents, no direct measure of the strength of local campaigns has been available and various alternatives have been employed. Johnston and Pattie use election expenditure – the proportion of the legally allowed maximum expenditure actually spent by a party in a constituency – as a surrogate measure of campaign strength (Johnston, 1987; Johnston *et al.*, 1989; Johnston and Pattie, 1995). The assumption is that better organized and more intense campaigns are likely to spend a higher proportion of the allowed expenditure. This measure has a major advantage in that the relevant data are easily available from the official returns of expenditure published after each election.

The disadvantage is that it is not clear that expenditure is actually a good guide to the level of campaign activity. Partly because of the stringent legal restrictions on spending at constituency level, many of the campaign activities undertaken by British parties are not expensive in terms of money – they are more likely to be labour intensive. It seems likely, therefore, that expenditure will be at best only an approximate guide to the strength of local campaigns.

Seyd and Whiteley have also used election expenditure as an indicator of campaign strength but, in addition, they have also used two rather different measures (Seyd and Whiteley, 1992; Whiteley and Seyd, 1992). The first is the size of local party membership. Initially, this seems to make good sense. As we have just noted, much local campaign activity is labour intensive – local campaign organizers in our survey were more likely to complain about shortages of workers than about shortages of money. But there are a number of problems. What really matters for campaigning is not the number of members in a local party, but the number of *active* workers available. But this seems likely to depend, among other things, on the age profile of the membership, and Seyd and Whiteley's work on the Conservative Party, for example, has shown that many of its members are well into middle age. The age structure of party memberships seems likely to vary not only between parties, but also between the constituency branches of any one party. This may mean that membership is not a particularly good guide to the number of active workers available and, therefore, not a good guide to the overall level of campaign activity. A further problem is that of obtaining accurate membership figures for local parties. Seyd and Whiteley were not able to get such figures for the Conservative Party. In their study of the Labour Party, they base their figures on a postal survey of Labour Party members sent to 1 in 30 of party members in 480 selected constituencies, multiplying the returns from each constituency by 30 to get an estimate of the party's membership. Clearly, there must be a considerable margin of error in figures arrived at in this way.

The second measure used by Seyd and Whiteley in their study of the Labour Party is a constituency activism scale. This is based on a series of questions asked in their survey of party members concerning the number of occasions on which, during the previous five years, respondents had displayed election posters, delivered leaflets during an election or canvassed voters. The index is calculated by assigning a score for the frequency with which each activity was carried out, and then summing these scores for all respondents in each constituency. Thus, this measure takes account both of the level of activity and the size of the membership in a constituency. But there are two problems with this approach. First, since it makes use of the membership estimates described above, it is subject to the same problems as those figures. Second, it is not clear that questions assessing levels of activity over the past five years are a particularly good guide to what happens in a particular general election campaign.[1]

Our own analysis is based on an index of intensity of campaigning derived from a postal survey of agents in the 1992 election. This is the first time that a study of the effects of local campaigning has developed and made use of a direct measure of local campaign strength. Responses to questions on seven dimensions of campaign activity (preparation, organization, election workers, canvassing, literature, use of computers, polling day operation) were used to carry out a principal components analysis. This produced a single factor solution to which all seven dimensions were strongly and positively related and the index was then constructed on the basis of the factor weightings produced by the analysis.[2] This index directly measures what we are interested in – the range and intensity of local campaign activity – but it is not without problems. First, we have scores only for those campaigns for which the agent responded to the survey. The number of responses for each of the three main parties is healthy, however, and analysis of the constituencies from which we received responses shows that, again for all three parties, they are highly representative in terms of a number of political and socio-economic variables. A second disadvantage of our index is that it is derived from responses to a fairly complex questionnaire. This means that scores will not be readily available for comparison in future elections unless comparable surveys are carried out. Seyd and Whiteley have also questioned the reliability of a postal survey of agents as a basis for the index, arguing that agents may have exaggerated or otherwise distorted information in their responses (Whiteley *et al.*, 1994: 195–7). This cannot be ruled out, of course, but we see no reason to suppose that the responses in this case would be any less reliable than those to any other confidential questionnaire. Indeed, it is election agents who make the returns of election expenditure on which Seyd and Whiteley and others are happy to rely. Overall, although our measure is one that it will not be easy to reproduce for future elections, we feel confident that it gives the most accurate guide available so far to the level of campaigning in constituencies.

TABLE 1

CORRELATIONS BETWEEN PARTY MEMBERSHIP, ACTIVISM, ELECTION EXPENDITURE AND INDEX OF CAMPAIGN INTENSITY

	Conservative campaign intensity	Labour campaign intensity	Lib. Dem campaign intensity
Membership	0.55	0.57	0.74
(N)	(242)	(338)	(379)
Activism	–	0.45	–
(N)		(272)	
Campaign expenditure	0.70	0.72	0.80
(N)	(265)	(356)	(383)

Note: Membership is measured as a percentage of constituency electorate. All coefficients are significant at the .01 level.

If our confidence in our index of campaign strength is justified, then we can use the index to test the reliability of the surrogate measures which have been used by other authors. Table 1 presents simple correlations between our index and the three alternative measures.[3] It can be seen that the correlation with the Labour Party activism index, while positive and significant, is the least satisfactory of the three surrogates. The measure of party membership which we test here is not based on Seyd and Whiteley's figures – which in any case were only available for Labour – but on our own questionnaire responses. We asked agents to report their local party membership figures, and we are confident that these responses are at least as reliable as those used by Seyd and Whiteley – overall estimates for national party membership based on them are close to the parties' official membership figures. The correlation coefficients in this case are moderately good – especially those for the Liberal Democrats. But even in the case of the Liberal Democrats variations in campaign expenditure accounts for less than 50 per cent of the variance in the campaign intensity index, and in the case of Labour and the Conservatives the figure is less than 33 per cent. Election expenditure appears to be the best of the three surrogates. The correlation coefficients are all over 0.70, although even here the fit is far from perfect – expenditure accounts for only about 50 per cent of the variance in the campaign intensity index for Labour and the Conservatives. Nonetheless, this simple analysis suggests that, in the absence of a direct measure of local campaigning, expenditure is the best surrogate to use.

The Dependent Variable: Party Performance

In studies of the effect of local campaigning there is also considerable variation in the operationalization of the dependent variable – party performance. We consider each of the alternatives in turn.

Share of the vote. The most obvious measure of party performance in a constituency would appear to be the share of the vote won by the party concerned, and this has been used by Seyd and Whiteley in some of their work (Seyd and Whiteley, 1992; Whiteley *et al.*, 1994). Though simple and initially attractive, however, there are problems with this measure. There is, without doubt, a significant positive correlation between campaign strength and share of the vote for all three parties in 1992 (the figures from our study are 0.65 for the Conservatives, 0.46 for Labour and 0.80 for the Liberal Democrats). This certainly indicates that where a constituency party mounted a stronger campaign, its share of the vote was larger. But to draw any causal inference from this about the effectiveness of campaigning is surely unwise. It would seem more plausible to suggest that parties campaign better where they are already strong, rather than that they win a larger share of the vote because they have campaigned well. In the 1992 election, for example, the

Conservatives campaigned most intensively in their safe seats, and all three parties made much less effort where their position was already weak. We would suggest, then, that strong correlations between campaign intensity and share of the vote are not unexpected and cannot be taken as evidence of a campaign effect.

Party vote-share ratios. In a number of publications, Johnston and Pattie have used a rather more complex indicator of party performance (for example, Johnston and Pattie, 1995). Rather than taking the share of the vote gained by any one party, they have used ratios of shares of the vote gained by pairs of parties. Thus they test to see whether campaign strength (as measured by expenditure) affects, for example, the ratio of the Conservative share to the Labour share. When strong campaigning by the Conservatives is associated with higher scores for that ratio, or strong campaigning by Labour is associated with lower scores, they argue that this shows a campaigning effect. In their 1995 article, Johnston and Pattie offer no justification for using this dependent variable, and an earlier (and fuller) discussion by Johnston (1987: 48–50) is not very clear on this point.

Using two-party vote ratios to measure party performance seems problematical. What matters, both to the parties themselves and for any assessment of the effects of campaigning, is the *overall* effect that campaigning has on the parties' votes. To look separately at two-party ratios tells us nothing about this. Thus, for example, a Labour campaign might have no effect on the Conservative:Labour vote ratio, but at the same time increases the Labour:Liberal Democrat ratio. But what matters is the combined effect – whether Labour does better overall. Looking at the effects separately, while it may illuminate interesting details, may well be misleading as to the overall effect.

There is another oddity about Johnston and Pattie's approach. When they carry out their multiple regression analyses, they usually divide constituencies into those which were held by the Conservatives and those held by Labour and analyse the two groups separately (the number of seats held by the Alliance being too small to make separate analysis worthwhile). In *Money and Votes* Johnston justifies this by arguing firstly that 'party incumbency is much more important than candidate incumbency as an influence in British election results' (Johnston, 1987: 46) and secondly, that introducing a dummy variable for party incumbency would cause problems of collinearity between this variable and, for example, party share of the vote. In their later analysis of the elections of 1983, 1987 and 1992 Johnston and Pattie simply state that 'earlier studies have shown that there is much less variation in spending by incumbent than by challenger parties, especially in marginal seats' (1995: 265), although it is not clear why this justifies dealing with the two sets of seats separately. Whether party incumbency has the significance that Johnston claims is not clear. If it has, however, this seems likely to arise largely because incumbent parties are in a position to fight stronger campaigns, so that taking account of party incumbency will simply serve to mask any campaign effect. Certainly, treating Conservative-held and Labour-held seats separately seems likely to have the effect of reducing the variation in both the dependent (vote ratio) and the independent (expenditure) variables and thus will give misleading results as far as the overall relationship between the two is concerned.[4]

Flow of the vote. A third measure of party performance, which has been widely used by Johnston and Pattie in other contexts, is employed by Pattie, Whiteley, Johnston and Seyd in an analysis of constituency campaigning in the 1987 election (Pattie *et al.*, 1994). This is based on 'flow of the vote' tables. Electoral change between two elections, over the country as a whole as well as in individual constituencies, can be measured and described using flow of the vote tables, sometimes called election transition matrices. These are simple two-way tables which cross-tabulate the voting behaviour of individual electors at one election with their behaviour at the previous election. These data enable us to measure the proportion of its previous voters that a party has retained or has lost, and the proportion of its current voters that has been newly recruited from other parties, from previous non-voters or from those who were too young to vote at the previous election.

Clearly, the construction of such tables requires survey data, and they are routinely produced using national surveys (see Denver, 1994: 21–3). Suitable surveys in individual constituencies are rare, but Pattie and his colleagues have used 'entropy maximizing' techniques to estimate flow of the vote tables for individual constituencies in recent elections. In this instance, they use vote flows between 1983 and 1987 as dependent variables – more specifically, the proportion of its 1983 vote that a party retained or lost to each of the other parties or to non-voting in 1987 – to test the effects of Labour campaigning in 1987, using a composite measure of campaigning based on election expenditure, Seyd and Whiteley's activism scale, and responses to a question on canvassing in the 1987 British Election Study (BES) survey. They also examine the impact of campaigning by each of the three parties in 1987, using expenditure figures alone as a surrogate indicator of campaign intensity, and on the basis of these analyses conclude that in 1987 strong campaigning paid off in terms of improved performance for all three parties.

This approach is certainly interesting and ingenious, but we again have considerable doubts about it. The problem is fundamentally the same as that with Johnston and Pattie's two-party vote ratio measure. In this case, rather than looking at the overall impact of campaigns, it is the impact on particular flows that is examined. Thus, Pattie *et al.* run separate regressions for the Conservative to Labour flow, the Labour to Conservative flow, the

Conservative to Liberal Democrat flow, and so on. This provides much fascinating detail, and may be useful in exploring questions such as the extent to which Liberal Democrat campaigns were effective in encouraging tactical voting by detaching former Labour supporters. But it is the overall effect of campaigning that is at issue – whether good campaigning will result in a net improvement in a party's performance – and the presence or absence of an effect on one particular flow tells us little about the *overall* effect.

Change in share of the electorate. The aim of local party campaigning is to achieve a better level of support than would have resulted from the party's national campaign alone. If local campaigns are effective, then, we would expect to find a correlation across constituencies between variations in campaign strength and variations in levels of party support. As compared with the previous election parties would be expected to get a bigger increase (or a smaller decrease) in their share of the vote, in constituencies where they put in a big effort than in constituencies where they put in a small effort. In this case, there is clearly no reason to expect that larger increases in party support would be related to existing party strength. Change in share of the vote, therefore, appears to be a better measure of party performance for our purposes than simple share of the vote.

There is a further qualification to be made, however. From the point of view of a specific party campaign, increasing the share of vote received is an indirect consequence of the primary aim – maximizing the number of votes received. What a constituency party seeks to do in its campaign is to increase the proportion of the constituency electorate which votes for its candidate. Parties are not just seeking to attract the votes of those who had previously voted for other parties, but also those of new voters and of those who abstained last time. Thus, although the difference is not likely to be large, change in share of the *electorate* obtained seems a more appropriate basis for testing the efficacy of campaigning than change in share of the *vote* and this is the measure of party performance which we have adopted in our study.

Results of Previous Studies

We have no disagreement with the conclusions of previous 'revisionist' studies about the effects of constituency campaigning by Labour and the Liberal Democrats, and we are not in a position to challenge their conclusions about Conservative campaigns in previous elections. It is the case of Conservative campaigning in the 1992 election that we focus on here.

In a recently published article, Johnston and Pattie analyse the results for three general elections – 1983, 1987 and 1992 – using expenditure as the measure of campaign activity and vote share ratios as the measure of party performance (Johnston and Pattie, 1995). They find that in all three elections, constituency campaigning by the Alliance/Liberal Democrats had a significant impact on their performance, and Conservative campaigns, if anything, had a stronger impact than those of Labour. They argue that, in all three elections, 'although Labour spending assisted its challenges in Conservative-held seats, its campaign activity had no measurable impact on the constituencies it was defending' (1995: 269). Their results show that in 1992 Conservative spending had a positive effect on Conservative:Labour vote ratios in both Conservative and Labour seats, and on Conservative:Liberal Democrat ratios in Conservative-held seats. Whiteley *et al.* offer two analyses of Conservative campaigning in 1992 with election expenditure as the indicator of campaign strength (Whiteley *et al.,* 1994). The first has share of the vote in 1992 as the dependent variable and finds (unsurprisingly, as we have suggested) that Conservative campaigns had a positive impact. The second again uses vote share in 1992 as the dependent variable but also has vote share in 1987 as one of the control variables. In addition, in this case all of the variables are transformed logarithmically, on the grounds that cross-tabulation analysis suggested a non-linear relationship between spending and 1992 vote share. Whiteley *et al.* conclude that this analysis confirms that Conservative constituency campaigning had a significant impact upon Conservative performance. Finally, although the analysis by Pattie *et al.* (1994) using flow of the vote data does not deal with the 1992 election, we replicated for that election the method they used to examine the Conservatives in 1987 and found the same result – Conservative campaigning had a significant impact on the relevant vote flows.[5]

Results using Campaign Intensity Index and Change in Share of Electorate

The puzzle generated by our findings is already apparent if we consider simple bivariate correlations between campaign intensity scores and change in share of the electorate between 1987 and 1992. For Labour and Liberal Democrat campaigns the correlation coefficients are 0.43 (N=349) and 0.32 (N=379) respectively, and both coefficients are significant at the 0.1 per cent level. The figure for Conservative campaigns, however, is 0.08 (N=259) which is not significant, suggesting that Conservative constituency campaigns had no significant impact on their performance. This broad pattern is confirmed by a variety of multiple regression analyses.

Table 2a shows the results of multiple regression analyses using data derived from our survey respondents from each of the three main parties, with dummy variables for candidate incumbency and region as controls (for clarity of presentation the coefficients for the control variables are not shown). The coefficients for campaign intensity for Labour and Liberal Democrat campaigns are significant, even when the control variables are included in the equations. Campaign intensity for Conservative campaigns, on the other hand, is not significant.

Table 2b repeats this analysis, but is restricted to the 95 constituencies for which we have survey responses from all three parties and now incorporates the campaign intensity scores for all three parties in each equation. The pattern is the same, although in this case the figures suggest that stronger Conservative campaigns actually increased the Liberal Democrat share of the electorate. The number of cases analysed in Table 2b is not large, and it is possible that the group of constituencies is skewed in some way and therefore not representative. We have shown, however, that there is a significant correlation between campaign intensity and election expenditure and we can use this relationship as a basis for estimating approximate levels of campaign intensity for those party campaigns for which we do not have responses.

TABLE 2

THE INFLUENCE OF CAMPAIGNING UPON CHANGE IN SHARE OF THE ELECTORATE 1987–92

	Conservative	Labour	Lib Dem
a. All respondents			
Own campaign intensity	–	0.379	0.229
Adjusted r^2	0.192	0.465	0.165
(N)	(259)	(349)	(379)
b. Cases with intensity measures for all three parties (N=95)			
Con campaign intensity	–	–	0.240
Lab campaign intensity	-0.346	0.374	-0.259
Lib Dem campaign intensity	–	-0.394	0.369
Adjusted r^2	0.262	0.376	0.369
c. All constituencies (N=618)			
Con campaign intensity	–	0.114	0.105
Lab campaign intensity	-0.153	0.290	-0.274
Lib Dem campaign intensity	–	-0.190	0.166
Adjusted r^2	0.226	0.500	0.234

Note: In Tables 2–5 the figures shown are beta-weights and only significant coefficients are reported. To simplify presentation, coefficients for regional and incumbency variables are not reported. In section c estimated campaign intensity scores are used where survey responses were not available.

For each of the three parties, for the constituencies for which we have survey data, we calculated regression equations with campaign intensity as the dependent variable, and expenditure and a range of political, regional and socio-demographic variables as predictors.[6] We used these equations to estimate approximate values of campaign intensity in the remaining cases. Using actual scores for campaign intensity where they were available, and estimated scores in the remaining cases, we are now in a position to replicate the analysis of Table 2b using a much larger number of cases. The results are shown in Table 2c. (The N in this analysis is 618 because here, as in the other multivariate analyses reported, we have excluded constituencies in which there were significant by-elections between 1987 and 1992 or in which there were 'other' candidates who significantly affected the election result.) The broad pattern of the results shown in 2b is clearly confirmed.

It might be argued that if we take 'change in share of electorate' as our dependent variable, then the appropriate independent variable to use is not campaign intensity in 1992, but change in campaign intensity between 1987 and 1992. An improvement in a party's performance in 1992, as measured by change in share of the electorate, could be just as much a result of poor campaigning in 1987 as of strong campaigning in 1992. We have, of course, no direct measure of campaign strength in the 1987 election to enable us to analyse the effect of changes in campaign intensity. There are, however, two possible solutions to this problem. One is to take a party's share of the electorate in 1992 as the dependent variable with its share of the electorate in 1987 as one of the controls. By controlling for 1987 performance we are effectively analysing change in support in 1992 while holding constant all the factors – including the level of local campaigning – which affected the result in 1987.

Table 3 reports the results of three sets of regression models of this form. The analysis follows the course that we have already established – the first part of the table concerns all cases for which we have responses; the second relates to constituencies for which we have returns from all three main parties; the third involves all constituencies, using estimated figures for campaign strength where we do not have survey returns. In all of the regressions we controlled for region and incumbency, as well as for 1987 performance, but for clarity of presentation we have not reported the beta weights for the regional and incumbency dummy variables. It can be seen that in every case the r^2 statistic is very large – share of the electorate in 1987 is a very good predictor of share of the electorate in 1992. But it is the campaign intensity variables that we are concerned with, and once again our original conclusions stand up well. In the analyses involving only each party's own campaign intensity score, Conservative campaigning is again not significant, while the strength of Labour and Liberal Democrat campaigning is positively associated with their 1992 performance. When campaign strength scores for all three parties are incorporated into the analysis (section b), Labour and Liberal Democrat campaigning is associated with their respective 1992 shares of the electorate in the expected ways and stronger Labour campaigning is associated with weaker Conservative performances, but Conservative campaigning has no significant effect on the performance of any of the three parties. These results are broadly confirmed when the analysis is repeated for all constituencies using estimated intensity scores where necessary (section c).

TABLE 3
THE INFLUENCE OF CAMPAIGN INTENSITY UPON ELECTORATE SHARE 1992

	Conservative	Lab	Lib Dem
a. All respondents			
Electorate share 1987	1.007	0.956	0.595
Own campaign intensity	–	0.112	0.243
Adjusted r^2	0.972	0.962	0.880
(N)	(259)	(349)	(379)
b. Cases with intensity measures for all three parties (N=95)			
Electorate share 1987	0.935	0.857	0.684
Con campaign intensity	–	–	–
Lab campaign intensity	-0.061	0.109	-0.112
Lib Dem campaign intensity	–	-0.103	0.241
Adjusted r^2	0.967	0.962	0.869
c. All constituencies (N=618)			
Electorate share 1987	0.952	0.897	0.532
Con campaign intensity	–	–	–
Lab campaign intensity	-0.028	0.112	-0.144
Lib Dem campaign intensity	–	-0.079	0.280
Adjusted r^2	0.973	0.965	0.898

Note: In section c estimated campaign intensity scores are used where survey responses were not available.

An alternative way of trying to measure change in intensity of campaigning is again to make use of the fact that the proportion of the allowable expenditure that a party spends is a rough guide to its level of campaigning. Changes in that proportion are approximate measures of changes in campaign intensity. In Table 4, therefore, we report the results of regression analyses using change in share of the electorate as the dependent variable and change in party expenditure, incumbency and region (coefficients not reported) as the control variables. The pattern is the familiar one that we have found when using our survey data as the basis for analysis – changes in Conservative spending had no significant effect, while change in Labour expenditure and change in Liberal Democrat expenditure are both significantly related to changes in their level of support in 1992.

These results demonstrate very clearly and, we would argue, with remarkable consistency, that Labour and Liberal Democrat campaigns had a significant impact upon their performance in the 1992 election, whereas Conservative campaigns did not. As we have seen, the results for the Conservatives clearly contradict the conclusions reached by other studies. How can this discrepancy be explained?

Clearly, one possible explanation would focus on the different approaches to measuring party performance used by Johnston and Pattie and Seyd and Whiteley. We have suggested a number of problems with their use of party vote ratios and flow of the vote figures, but we can modify their approaches to remove or mitigate what we see as being their least satisfactory aspects. When we do so, we find that analysis using our index of campaign strength confirms our conclusions.

Table 5a shows the results of a modified version of Johnston and Pattie's analysis, with vote ratios as the dependent variables. The analysis uses our survey-based index of campaign strength and is restricted to constituencies for which we have a campaigning measure for all three parties, with the corresponding two-party ratio at the 1987 election, incumbency and region as control variables. However we have not followed Johnston and Pattie in analysing Conservative-held and Labour-held seats separately. The results do not support the conclusions drawn by Johnston and Pattie. The figures suggest that Liberal Democrat campaigning improved their performance relative to both of the other parties and that, although Labour campaigning did not significantly affect the Conservative:Labour ratio, it was positively associated with increases in the Labour:Liberal Democrat ratio. But this analysis now confirms our view that Conservative campaigning had no significant effect on any of the three vote ratios.

TABLE 4
THE EFFECT OF CHANGE IN EXPENDITURE ON CHANGE IN SHARE OF ELECTORATE 1987–92
(ALL CONSTITUENCIES, N=618)

	Con	Lab	Lib Dem
Change in Con expenditure	–	–	–
Change in Lab expenditure	–	0.131	-0.089
Change in Lib Dem expenditure	–	-0.287	0.394
Adjusted r^2	0.204	0.497	0.287

TABLE 5
THE EFFECT OF CAMPAIGN INTENSITY ON 1992 PARTY VOTE RATIOS
AND NET INTER-PARTY FLOWS (N=95)

a. Party vote ratios

	Cons: Labour	Cons: Lib Dem	Labour: Lib Dem
1987 ratio	0.929	0.607	0.769
Con campaign intensity	–	–	–
Lab campaign intensity	–	0.209	0.104
Lib Dem campaign intensity	0.117	-0.290	-0.152
Adjusted r^2	0.959	0.775	0.861

b. Net inter-party flows

	Net Con– Lab flow	Net All– Con flow	Net Lab– LD flow
Con campaign intensity	–	-0.320	–
Lab campaign intensity	0.438	0.323	-0.257
Lib Dem campaign intensity	-0.488	-0.453	0.375
Adjusted r^2	0.517	0.506	0.340

We have also expressed doubts about the usefulness of using individual vote flows as indicators of party performance. As we saw above, Pattie *et al.* use as their dependent variables the proportions of a party's 1983 vote that it retained or lost to each of the other parties or to non-voting in 1987. However, if flow of the vote tables are to be used, a more accurate indicator of electoral change is the proportion of the total electorate falling within the relevant cells of the matrix. Since all the resulting percentages are then calculated on the same base, this has the advantage that we are able to add and subtract the various flows. We therefore recalculated Pattie's data on this basis, and produced a score measuring the *net* flows between the parties. Thus the net flow from Conservative to Labour is the percentage of the electorate moving from Conservative to Labour minus the percentage moving from Labour to the Conservatives. These net flow figures are still only partial measures of change between elections, but they give a better picture than concentrating on individual cells in the flow of the vote matrix. The combined impact of party campaigns on net flows between the parties, again in the constituencies for which we have campaign intensity scores for the three parties and using incumbency and region as controls, is shown in part b of Table 5. These multiple regression results suggest that Labour and Liberal Democrat campaigns had the expected effects on flows. In striking contrast, however, the only significant effect of Conservative campaigning was to decrease the net flow from the Alliance to the Conservatives! The stronger the

Conservative campaign in 1992, the more their 1987 voters deserted to the Liberal Democrats.

These results are consistent with our original conclusion that Conservative campaigning in 1992 did not affect Conservative performance.[7] We would argue, therefore, that the difference between ourselves and others in this respect does not simply result from the particular measure of party performance that we have used. In part, it stems from the fact that the latter were not able to use precise measures of campaign intensity but had to rely on the various surrogates we have discussed, and in part from the way in which the measures of party performance used have been operationalized. We are confident, therefore, that our results are the more accurate – that there was indeed a significant difference between the effect of Conservative constituency campaigns in 1992 and of those mounted by Labour and the Liberal Democrats.

Why Did Conservative Campaigns have no Effect?

How are we to explain the lack of impact of Conservative campaigns? There are a number of possible explanations that we can suggest. Firstly, this finding may result from what might be termed 'technical' problems with our survey. It is conceivable, for example, that our results are unreliable because we have a skewed sample of responses from Conservative campaigns. Our response rate for the Conservatives was somewhat lower than those for the other two parties, and it is possible that the sample is in some way misleading. We think that this is extremely unlikely, however, since analysis of the constituencies from which we had Conservative responses suggests that they are representative of British constituencies as a whole.[8] Furthermore, we checked our results using all constituencies and estimates of campaigning where we do not have responses, and the pattern is broadly similar to that found using survey responses only. We also checked our conclusions by simply using election expenditure in all constituencies as a surrogate measure of campaigning and again found that Conservative spending had no significant impact. We are inclined, therefore, to discount skewed Conservative responses as a possible explanation for the lack of effect we have reported.

A second possible 'technical' explanation is that in some way our measure of campaign intensity does not capture important elements of the Conservative style of constituency campaigning. It is possible, though again we think unlikely, that Conservative campaigns were doing things, or doing things in a way, that our questionnaire did not cover. The most obvious possibility, perhaps, would concern telephone canvassing. We did ask about this, but we suspect that our replies were not all that reliable. It is unclear under existing electoral law whether or not the costs associated with telephone canvassing – which could be very considerable if it were carried out on a large scale – should be counted as part of a candidate's allowed election expenditure. Agents may, therefore, have been reluctant to go into detail on the matter. Certainly, in the aftermath of the election there was a good deal of comment from people in the Labour Party and from political commentators about the extent of telephone canvassing by the Conservatives and the impact it might have made. There may also be other things our measure missed – perhaps the Conservatives with their preponderance of full-time agents were able to employ organizational techniques in their marginal seats which were simply superior to those of their rivals. The very nature of this argument makes it difficult to counter – we simply have no systematic evidence about other things they may have been doing. Some support for our argument that we have not missed anything substantial may be drawn from interviews we conducted with Conservative agents in a number of constituencies we studied in detail and with party officials at national and regional level. These did not suggest that there was any significant element of campaigning that had been overlooked in our questionnaire.

We are inclined, then, to reject these explanations for the peculiar result we find for Conservative campaigns. Rather, we suggest three substantive hypotheses to account for their lack of impact.

One explanation worth considering is that the failure of Conservative campaigns to reap significant electoral rewards may have been due to factors specific to the 1992 election. In particular, it may be that in specific elections, where the political 'tide' is running strongly in favour of one party and against another, the local campaigns of the party swimming with the tide will have more success than those of one swimming against. Even though the Conservatives won the 1992 election, there was certainly a belief throughout most of the campaign – largely based on opinion poll results – that things were going Labour's way. Perhaps, then, Labour and Liberal Democratic campaigns were successful in 1992 because (to change the metaphor) they were pushing at an open door, whereas the Conservatives were desperately trying to keep the door shut.

We can attempt to cast some light on this explanation by looking at evidence from previous general elections. Although we do not have campaign intensity measures, we can make some progress using expenditure figures. If the effect of campaigns is related to the direction of the political tide, then the impact of local party campaigns will differ from election to election, depending on the national political situation. In Table 6, we present the results of some simple analysis which shed some light on this suggestion. The first part of the table reports bivariate correlation coefficients showing the relationship between changes in shares of the electorate for three pairs of elections and the election expenditure in the relevant second election. The second part of the table has correlation coefficients for changes in shares of the electorate and changes in expenditure between the corresponding two elections. The figures give no support to the 'direction of the tide' argument. In the 1979 election there was clearly a strong movement in favour of the Conservatives and against Labour (the two-party swing was 6.4 per cent). On that basis we would expect to find weak or insignificant correlations for Labour expenditure and strong correlations for Conservative expenditure, but if anything the reverse is the case. The position in 1987 is less clear. On this occasion, there was a somewhat weaker movement from the Conservatives to Labour (a two-party swing of 3 per cent), so that we might anticipate a similar pattern to that found in 1992 – weak or insignificant correlations in the case of Conservative campaigns, and strong correlations for Labour campaigns. In fact, the correlation with expenditure in 1987 is significant and fairly strong for the Conservatives, and the correlation with change of expenditure from 1983, while not strong, is significant at the 5 per cent level. Both figures for Labour are significant at the 0.1 per cent level. There is little evidence, then, that the results for the Conservatives in 1992 can be explained in terms of the direction in which the national political tide was running.

TABLE 6

SIMPLE CORRELATIONS BETWEEN PARTY SUPPORT, ELECTION EXPENDITURE AND CHANGE IN ELECTION EXPENDITURE

	Conservative	Labour	Lib. Democrat
a. Election expenditure			
Change in share of electorate 1974(O)–79	0.10*	0.22**	0.21**
Change in share of electorate 1983–87	0.31**	0.31**	0.43**
Change in share of electorate 1987–92	0.11*	0.23**	0.31**
b. Change in expenditure from previous election			
Change in share of electorate 1974(O)–79	(0.05)	0.14**	0.33**
Change in share of electorate 1983–87	0.10*	0.15**	0.42**
Change in share of electorate 1987–92	(0.04)	0.21**	0.42**

Note: ** = significant, p < .001; * = significant, p < .05; coefficients in brackets not significant. Ns: 1974(O)–79 Con 622, Lab 622, Lib Dem 573 (section a) and 569 (section b); 1983–87 633 in all cases; 1987–92 in section a Con 617, Lab 618, Lib Dem 617; in section b Con 615, Lab 616, Lib Dem 616.

A second explanation for the apparent lack of impact of Conservative campaigns may be suggested. In this case it may be helpful to use the metaphor of squeezing the juice out of an orange: a relatively small amount of pressure will produce plenty of juice to begin with; but when the orange has already been thoroughly squeezed, even a fairly large amount of pressure will produce only a small amount of juice. In the past, it has been generally accepted that the Conservatives have had the strongest grass-roots organization of the major parties, and our research has demonstrated that in 1992 they mounted their strongest campaigns in their safest seats (Denver and Hands, 1993). It may be, then, that in these safe seats all the juice has been squeezed – even though their campaigns were very strong, there were few if any additional votes to be won for the party. By contrast, in other seats, though their campaigns were less strong, there was still some juice available, there were still some additional votes to be won. So relatively modest campaigning in these other seats may have produced greater rewards than the strong campaigns in safe seats. This pattern would give rise to results for the Conservatives consistent with the lack of impact of local campaigning which we have found. A similar effect would not operate for Labour because they do not have the history of strong campaigns in their safest seats, and in 1992 their strongest campaigns were in their marginal seats, where there would be, relatively speaking, plenty of votes to be won.

If this hypothesis were valid, then we might expect there to be a significant relationship between campaign intensity and Conservative performance in seats other than those which were very safe for them. A simple test of this yields negative results, however: the correlation between campaign intensity and change in share of electorate remained non-significant even when these seats were excluded. It may be, then, that 'the juice' has been squeezed in all categories of seat – the Conservatives have after all won the past four general elections, with little change in their national share of the vote.

A final and rather different explanation might be that Conservative constituency campaigns generally have little impact because Conservative supporters are likely to turn out and vote regardless of the strength of the local campaign. By contrast, it might be argued, Labour and Liberal Democrat supporters – for different reasons – are more affected by local campaigning. The argument would be that Conservative voters – typically middle class and well-educated – have a stake in the community, a greater understanding of the working of the electoral system and so on, and that this makes it more likely that they will vote. There is ample evidence from other political systems of an important link between socio-economic class and education and electoral turnout – the link is very marked, for example, in the United States (for example, Wolfinger and Rosenstone, 1980). Until fairly recently, the broadly accepted view has been that there was no significant relationship between class and turnout in Britain (see Crewe *et al.*, 1977), but Swaddle and Heath (1989), using official voting records for the 1987 election in conjunction with the BES survey of the electorate, showed that in 1987 – to a small but significant extent – middle-class electors were more likely to vote than those in the working class. In another recent analysis, Rallings and Thrasher (1990) suggest that, at the aggregate level, there is a clear link between socio-economic factors and turnout in local government wards in English local elections. It may be, then, that there is an emerging link between class and turnout, that the Conservatives benefit from this, and that, as a result, their local campaigns have less impact.

Once again, we may be able to shed some light on this hypothesis by looking at earlier elections. If there is a generally stronger tendency for Conservative supporters to vote irrespective of the local campaign then we would expect that the pattern found in 1992 would be repeated in earlier elections – Labour and Liberal Democrat campaigns would have a clearly stronger impact than Conservative campaigns. The figures in Table 6 again provide some relevant evidence and give slightly more support to this final explanation. If the hypothesis were valid, we would expect low correlations at all elections for Conservative campaigns. It is certainly the case that for the three pairs of elections analysed in the table the coefficients for Conservative campaigns are clearly smaller than those for Labour and the Liberal Democrats (with the exception of the correlation between election expenditure and change in share of electorate between 1983 and 1987). Indeed, none of the correlations between change in the Conservative share of the electorate and change in expenditure from the previous election is significant at the 1 per cent level.

Of the three substantive hypotheses we have tested, then, only the third – that Conservative voters are likely to turn out and vote regardless of the strength of the campaign – seems to be at all consistent with the data, and our test is certainly far from conclusive.

Although, as we have explained, we have some doubts about the particular measures and methods that they use, our analysis has partially confirmed the general view taken by Johnston and Pattie and Seyd and Whiteley – that constituency campaigning has an electoral effect. In the 1992 general election Labour and Liberal Democrat constituency campaigns clearly affected the performances of these parties. On the other hand, we have shown that the same cannot be said of Conservative campaigning. Even using modified versions of Johnston and Pattie's and Seyd and Whiteley's measures, we have been unable to find evidence of a campaign effect for the Conservatives. On the basis of our detailed analysis, we are confident that this conclusion is robust and that the contrast in this respect between Labour and the Liberal Democrats, on one hand, and the Conservatives on the other is something that requires explanation. Our brief analysis of earlier elections suggests that the absence of a Conservative campaign effect may not have been unique to the 1992 election but, lacking satisfactory campaign intensity measures for earlier elections, we cannot be certain of that. It may be that a study of local campaigning in the next election would throw more light on the problem but, for the moment, what is certain is that the lack of impact of the Conservatives' constituency campaigns in the 1992 election is a puzzling and peculiar case which needs further exploration.

ACKNOWLEDGEMENTS

The research on which this article is based was financed by a grant from the ESRC (ref: Y304 25 3004). A copy of the questionnaire can be obtained from the authors on request.

NOTES

1. In their work on the 1987 election Seyd and Whiteley also used a question asked in the 1987 BES survey about whether respondents had been canvassed or not. However this question was not asked in the 1992 BES survey (see Pattie *et al.*, 1994).
2. In constructing the index we used responses from 1051 election agents (265 Conservative, 356 Labour, 383 Liberal Democrat and 47 Nationalist).
3. The scores for Labour party activism were kindly made available by Patrick Seyd and Paul Whiteley.
4. In a more recent article, Pattie *et al.*, (1995) have adopted a rather different approach. Following work by Jacobson on elections to the US House of Representatives, they have used two-stage least squares analysis and claim to demonstrate that whereas spending by challenger parties (those not holding the seat concerned) has a significant impact on vote share, the impact of spending by incumbent parties is generally not significant, regardless of whether Labour, Conservatives or the Liberal Democrats are the incumbents or challengers. We have reservations about the statistical techniques employed in this work, however, especially since the analysis again involves treating Conservative-held and Labour-held seats separately.
5. Constituency flow of the vote estimates for 1987–1992 were kindly supplied by Charles Pattie.
6. In addition to election expenditure, 1987 vote share and 1987 constituency marginality were significant in predicting Conservative campaign intensity (adjusted $r^2 = 0.574$); 1987 vote share, percentage owner occupiers, incumbency and a Welsh regional dummy in predicting Liberal Democrat campaign intensity ($r^2 = 0.698$); and 1987 marginality, incumbency, 1987 vote share and seven regional dummy variables in predicting Labour campaign intensity ($r^2 = 0.662$).
7. We also attempted to replicate the logarithmic transformations employed by Whiteley *et al.* (1994) but were unable to produce regression equations in which Conservative spending or campaign intensity were statistically significant.

8. Some social and political comparisons between the constituencies in which we had
    Conservative respondents and all British constituencies are as follows.

	Conservative response constituencies	All British constituencies
% council tenants	21.3	22.2
% owner occupiers	66.1	65.7
% managerial & technical employees	28.7	27.9
% unemployed	6.3	6.4
Persons per hectare	18.8	19.0
% Conservative 1992	42.1	41.1
% Labour 1992	34.7	37.0
% Liberal Democrat 1992	18.6	17.6
% turnout 1992	77.7	77.6
Size of electorate	66940	66471

BIBLIOGRAPHY

Crewe, I., T. Fox and J. Alt (1977) 'Non-voting in British General Elections, 1966–October 1974' in C. Crouch (ed.) *British Political Sociology Yearbook 3*, pp.38–109. London: Croom Helm.

Denver, D. (1994) *Elections and Voting Behaviour in Britain*. Hemel Hempstead: Harvester Wheatsheaf, second edition.

Denver, D. and Hands, G. (1993) 'Measuring the Intensity and Effectiveness of Constituency Campaigning in the 1992 General Election' in D. Denver, P. Norris, D. Broughton and C. Rallings (eds) *British Elections and Parties Yearbook 1993*, pp.229–42. Hemel Hempstead: Harvester Wheatsheaf.

Johnston, R. (1987) *Money and Votes*. London: Croom Helm.

Johnston, R. J. and C. J. Pattie (1995) 'The Impact of Spending on Party Constituency Campaigns at Recent British General Elections', *Party Politics* 1: 261–73.

Johnston, R.J., C. J. Pattie and L. C. Johnston (1989) 'The Impact of Constituency Spending on the Result of the 1987 British General Election', *Electoral Studies* 8: 143–155.

Pattie, C., P. Whiteley, R. Johnston and P. Seyd (1994) 'Measuring Local Campaign Effects: Labour Party Constituency Campaigning at the 1987 General Election', *Political Studies* 42: 469–79.

Pattie, C., R. Johnston and E. Fieldhouse (1995) 'Winning the Local Vote: The Effectiveness of Constituency Campaign Spending in Great Britain, 1983–1992', *American Political Science Review* 89: 969–83.

Rallings, C. and M. Thrasher (1990) 'Turnout in English Local Elections – an Aggregate Analysis with Electoral and Contextual Data', *Electoral Studies* 9: 79–90.

Seyd, P. and P. Whiteley (1992) *Labour's Grass Roots: the Politics of Party Membership*. Oxford: Clarendon Press.

Swaddle, K. and A. Heath (1989) 'Official and Reported Turnout in the British General Election of 1987', *British Journal of Political Science* 19: 537–51.

Whiteley, P. and P. Seyd (1992) 'Labour's Vote and Local Activism', *Parliamentary Affairs* 45: 582–95.

Whiteley, P., P. Seyd and J. Richardson (1994) *True Blues: The Politics of Conservative Party Membership*. Oxford: Clarendon Press.

Wolfinger, R. and S. Rosenstone (1980) *Who Votes?* New Haven: Yale University Press.

Reasoning Voters, Voter Behaviour and Institutions: The Decision Dependence of Voting Behaviour

Shaun Bowler

Introduction

This article contains four broad sections. In the first section the literature on electoral institutions and voting behaviour is discussed: the argument is developed that institutional effects are likely to be persistent but more subtle and typically harder to uncover than that developed by Duverger's Law. In the second section a distinction is made between preferences over alternatives and preferences over outcomes, and the possible impact of institutions upon both is outlined. Since electoral institutions help shape both preferences and choices, in turn they also play a role in framing or setting up the decision that voters are asked to make; and as this decision varies so should voter behaviour. The third section presents some partial and suggestive evidence consistent with this argument, using German and Australian data. In the concluding section the argument is advanced that theoretically informed case studies are likely to be a profitable way of understanding the micro-level effects of electoral systems.

The literature on the political consequences of electoral laws comprises a large and growing body of work. Within this literature there exist two broad, and complementary, approaches. On the one hand there is the familiar set of aggregate-level studies (Rae, 1971; Lijphart, 1994; Taagepera and Shugart, 1989) which have developed our understanding of the issue of proportionality. On the other hand there are studies which tend to a fuller understanding of the workings of specific systems (for example, Lakeman, 1974; Silva, 1964), often within a formal framework (for example, Riker, 1982, Ordeshook, 1992). Occasionally, studies such as Rae's combine the two approaches.

While providing a rich mix of aggregate-level empirical results, as well as formal and historical examples, this body of work has tended not to develop models of individual-level voting behaviour and how it may be affected by institutions. The one notable exception is, of course, the considerable body of work concerning Duverger's Law and the related phenomenon of tactical voting in single member, simple plurality (SMSP) systems.[1] Beyond this, however, there has been relatively little attempt to examine the impact of electoral institutions at the micro-level.

To some extent it may not be that important to pay so much attention to individual models of vote choice. After all, one of the great successes of the election systems literature as a whole is the finding that electoral systems can shape outcomes in ways that are not necessarily dependent on how voters choose. It may also be the case that many of the effects of fractionalization or coalescence are brought about by elite rather than mass actions (for example, Gunther, 1989). Thus there may be little need to build well-developed micro-level models of electoral system effects. One example of this, in terms of electoral outcomes, is the link between proportionality and district magnitude, which may depend more upon simple arithmetic rather than a specific model of vote choice.[2] In fact the preoccupation of this literature with proportionality, especially in aggregate-level cross-national studies, seems unlikely to be shared by voters at an individual level. Given what we know about the 'minimally informed' electorate, it seems difficult to sustain, a priori, an argument that voters share a keen appreciation for the distinctions produced by the d'Hondt method of counting as opposed to any of its rivals, although it seems quite likely that elites would care.[3]

Despite the fact that some of the 'political consequences of electoral laws' may not require much analytical development at the micro-level, some other effects may well do so. In fact, it may not be possible to build general, comparative, models of vote choice unless and until we develop models which take account of institutional effects. For example, there are differences in the way that party identification works cross-nationally (Harrop and Miller, 1987), and one possible source of explanation for this lies in institutional effects. But if electoral institutions have an impact on voter behaviour, what kind of impact do we expect? At least part of the answer depends on how we conceive of institutional effects. And, in quite sharp contrast to the aggregate-level studies, which have repeatedly stressed the large distinction between SMSP and proportional (PR) systems, institutional effects at the level of individual voters may be quite hard to detect.

Identifying the impacts of institutions is made difficult by the fact that there may not be unique effects associated with a given institutional arrangement. Either broadly similar institutional arrangements can produce disparate results; or very different institutions can produce similar results. An example of the first of these can be found when comparing Australia and Ireland.

Both the Senate elections in Australia and the Dáil elections in Ireland use the single transferable vote system of proportional representation (STV). Even within a broadly similar set of electoral rules, however, voters may still be given different options. For example, Australian STV bears a great deal of similarity to Irish practice, except that voters do not have the option of expressing only one preference. Voters in Australia are required to express a preference across 90 per cent of the candidates running, in order for the ballot to be considered valid. Clearly, they could have a very hard time dealing with this amount of complexity. In the 1993 Senate election for New South Wales, for example, voters were supposed to rank order 66 candidates from 22 different ideological blocs. These burdens for the electorate are compounded by the fact that voting is compulsary in Australia. Voters who elsewhere might be expected to stay at home at election day are forced to turn out and vote. Australian practice thus differs markedly from that of Ireland in the level of informational demands that the ballot itself places upon voters.

There are, however, two devices which help Australian voters deal with difficulties of the ballot, devices which illustrate the way in which it is possible for parties to help shape the expression of preferences and sidestep some of the effects of the electoral system itself. The first of these is a campaign device, the second a feature of the ballot. The campaign device is the widespread use of 'How to Vote' cards in which all candidates on the ballot are rank-ordered by the party. Second, there is the 'ticket vote' which allows voters to treat STV as if it were a party list system. Since 1984 voters have been able to mark a box next to one party's name and the preferences are redistributed according to the party's ordering. This ordering is registered and public prior to the election.

One immediate effect of the 'ticket vote' has been to reduce the number of spoiled ('informal') ballots in Senate elections.[4] But what did not change in any substantial way was the manner in which preferences transfer. Voter preferences in Australia transfer largely *en bloc*. For example in the Senate elections in New South Wales in 1984 the preferences of an Australian Labor Party (ALP) candidate were to be divided on the second count between three other ALP candidates (40 candidates in total; over three million voters). Of these transfers 99.8 per cent went to Childs. Subsequently Morris received 99.8 per cent of transfers from Child's surplus.[5] This pattern is typical for the major parties and, it is important to note, in part it is a function of party campaign activity – not just ballot structure – since at least some patterns were not materially affected by the introduction of the party vote option.

Table 1 compares the number of first preferences going to the candidate listed first by the party. In 1984 voters could vote for this list by marking a single box; in 1983, by contrast, voters had to mark all the boxes (many of the same candidates ran in 1983 and 1984), perhaps by following 'How to Vote' cards. If we are to see a difference in voting behaviour brought about by changes in allowing ticket voting then this is likely to be in the form of an increase in the vote going the party's declared way, that is, more preferences to the candidate placed first by the party. One way of seeing this is to compare the votes of first-placed candidates in 1983 and 1984. In principle, voters in

1983 could simply reorder candidates on the list from within the same block and then follow the party line for the remainder of the ballot. This option is, of course, open to voters in 1984, but the big distinction is that the ticket vote was not available in 1983. As can be seen, the party's first candidates did generally do better when the electorate could choose by party label (1984) rather than having to vote for the candidates individually (1983). But this difference is very small and in many cases negligible.

TABLE 1

A COMPARISON OF FIRST PREFERENCES GOING TO THE PARTY'S NUMBER-1 LISTED CANDIDATE BEFORE AND AFTER THE 1984 INTRODUCTION OF 'TICKET VOTING' (%)

	Labor		Liberal		National		Democrats	
	1983	1984	1983	1984	1983	1984	1983	1984
Queensland	96.9	98.99	99.2	98.33	98.7	98.97	98.94	98.88
South Australia	98.5	99.43	98.3	99.2	91.2	98.22	98.6	98.79
New South Wales	99.22	99.25	99.01	98.8			98.7	98.92
Victoria	99.4	99.58	99.05	99.44		98.72	99.04	99.07

Thus, we see relatively little difference in voter behaviour under the two systems. The use of the party list does not subvert the STV system any more than the widespread reliance by voters on 'How to Vote' cards and other campaign material provided by the parties.

Irish transfer patterns are generally less tidy than this in two ways. First there is leakage from the party bloc to rival party blocs. It may be the case, for example, that some Fine Gael party transfers may leak out to non-Fine Gael candidates even at the earliest stages of the count. The Fianna Fáil party has the strongest record of party solidarity. From 1927 (its first election) to 1989 its average was around 82 per cent, dropping to 70 per cent in the 1992 election. Even at its most solid, then, party solidarity of transfers within Ireland approaches but nowhere matches Australian levels. A second way in which transfers are less neat and tidy in the Irish case is in cases where there are more than two alternatives from within the same party, so that the voters may split the transfers between them. For example in the Cork North Central constituency in the 1987 general election we see Wallace's (FF) surplus go, on the second count, to three remaining Fianna Fáil (FF) candidates in the following proportions: 20.3 per cent, 32.9 per cent and 21 per cent (17 total candidates).[6]

Thus, the expression of preferences and the pattern of transfers can be seen to differ even under the same electoral system.[7] But this is not the only difficulty facing attempts to sort out institutional effects, since not only may similar institutions produce different outcomes, but different institutions may produce similar outcomes. Within the broader literature on institutions an example of this effect may be found in the work of Tsebelis (1995). He argues that a multi-party parliamentary system (such as Italy) can produce remarkably similar outcomes to that of a two-party presidential system (such as the USA). The relevance of this finding to institutionally grounded theories of voting behaviour is that if very different institutional structures may produce similar, even identical, results the same may be true for electoral systems.

One possible example may be seen in the workings of the preferential Alternative Vote (AV) system and the single member simple plurality (SMSP) system, both of which seem to help produce larger and fewer parties. Duverger's Law is the well-known mechanism which helps support outcomes under SMSP. Something similar seems to occur under AV: candidates from smaller parties are eliminated first and their preferences re-distributed, while large parties can survive most of the early eliminations. The re-distribution process, then, typically involves a steady flow of preferences from smaller parties to larger ones. Consequently, voters' relative preference ranking of the bigger parties, even if low down on the preference schedule, may ultimately shape the final choice and may be a more meaningful decision than simply deciding on whom to place first; a form of tactical voting can thus affect AV elections in a manner similar to that found in SMSP. Perhaps strategic considerations of this kind were one reason for Rae's intriguing 'negative finding' that ordinal vote systems did not produce as much fractionalization as hypothesized (Rae, 1971).

Table 2 illustrates the continued dominance of the Australian Labor Party and Liberal/National blocs of the legislature even under a preferential system. This is so despite the rise in the average number of counts over the decade (row 6), and despite the fact that transfers from minor parties such as the Democrats have become more important in shaping the result. Even the arrival of the two independents elected in 1993 shows evidence of the importance of the big parties, as the results of the lower panel illustrates. As can be seen, the decisive event here is the numbers of transfers from the larger parties to the independent candidate. This is a pattern consistent with voters preferring an independent to one of the 'other' side. If true, this illustrates how preferences over the main candidates can structure the ballot.

TABLE 2
SMALL PARTIES AND THE ALTERNATIVE VOTE IN AUSTRALIAN LEGISLATIVE ELECTIONS

	1983	1984	1987	1990	1993
Labor seats	75	82	86	78	80
Liberal seats	33	45	43	55	49
National seats	17	21	19	14	16
Other seats	0	0	0	1	2
Total seats	125	148	148	148	147
Average count	1.56	1.72	1.80	2.85	3.02
% counts where Democrat vote important	23	27	28.5	45.95	33.33

TWO CONSTITUENCIES WHERE INDEPENDENTS WON IN 1993

Wills

	Labor	Independent	Liberal
6th count	31011	21564	17773
	44.08	30.65	25.26
7th count	33412	36816	excluded
	47.58	52.42	
		ELECTED	

North Sydney

	Labor	Independent	Liberal
3rd count	13211	34781	27082
	17.6	46.3	36.07
4th count	excluded	36154	38912
		48.1	51.8
			ELECTED

The broader point these examples serve to illustrate is that institutions may seem to have indeterminate effects: either broadly similar institutions producing different outcomes or seemingly different institutions producing similar outcomes, depending upon specific circumstances. Either way, these features of institutions can make understanding their impact extremely difficult. This problem is especially pronounced in cross-national studies where many institutions may vary simultaneously, creating huge problems of statistical control, especially given the larger set of democratic states resulting

from the end of the Cold War. Unless we have strong prior theory we are
unlikely to know ahead of time the cause of a given effect, whether it was
produced by federalism, by the party system, the electoral system, or some
combination.

TABLE 3a
BONNER'S EXAMPLE OF STV AT WORK

	Group A 12 votes	Group B 11 votes	Group C 10 votes	Group D 9 votes
1	x	z	y	w
2	y	x	w	z
3	w	y	z	x
4	z	w	x	y

2 seats to be filled, 4 candidates, 42 voters, Quota=15

1st Count x=12, y=10, z=11, w=9   w eliminated. All of w's
                                       2nd preferences go to z

2nd Count x=12, y=10, z=20   z elected; 5 surplus votes
                                       and all of w's 3rd prefs
                                     go to x

3rd Count x=17, y=10   x elected

Source: Bonner (1986: 88–91)

TABLE 3b
ORDESHOOK'S EXAMPLE OF STV AT WORK

	Group A 18 votes	Group B 17 votes		Group C 32 votes	Group D 32 votes
1	a	a	(c)	c	b
2	b	c	(a)	b	a
3	c	b	(b)	a	c

If everyone votes sincerely, a is elected first, then b.
If, however, one member of Group B changes their preferences to the schedule in parentheses, a
and c are elected and this is an equilibrium result.

Source: Ordeshook (1992: 154)

A second broad reason for suggesting that institutional effects are typically going to be smaller and less obvious than those produced by Duverger's Law comes from the formal literature on electoral systems. In this literature examples abound of the problems created by any electoral system. The broader argument of this literature is, of course, to establish the absence of 'true and fair amalgamations' (Riker, 1982: 111) under any given electoral system. And so, in this literature, the very existence of a given paradox (for example, Dummett's paradox for STV) sufficiently establishes the broader argument. But the examples given in such work, even the historical or 'real world' examples, are typically quite fragile; they may depend upon a fairly specific set of circumstances in order to produce a given paradox. Relatively small shifts in preference profiles may destroy the particular paradox, especially if rival voters are allowed to counter-strategize (that is, change what they are doing in response to other voters' tactical voting). Bonner (1986: 88–91) provides a clear example of such a case, examining STV.

Table 3a displays Bonner's example which shows x and z being elected. In a fairly typical account, Bonner notes that group C could upset this result by simply voting all 1's next to w and not voting for anyone else. Their triumph, however:

> depends upon detailed knowledge of everyone's voting intentions, of the procedures for elimination and strong group discipline. It may also be watched by group A who could try to stop the ploy by offering to plump all their first preferences on candidate y (Bonner, 1986: 91).

Of course, a one vote shift from group C to group D results in w and z winning the election and pretty much removes the point of C acting strategically.

Ordeshook shows a similar example whereby one person acting strategically may change the outcome (Table 3b). In his example the result is an equilibrium since no other player can change the (strategically produced) outcome. In providing examples of where STV can be manipulated both Bonner and Ordeshook make an important contribution to general issues of manipulability when considering the interplay between preferences and institutions. For our purposes, however, the point is not so much that these examples exist but that they may be quite fragile. In the examples of Bonner and Ordeshook, changing a single preference profile changes the results.

The general literature on institutions as well as the more specific work on electoral institutions thus suggests that while institutions have deep and important effects, they are also likely to be subtle, and possibly fragile, ones. Institutions clearly 'matter', and matter a lot, but it may be difficult to see continued, persistent and obvious effects. But having said this, and after having also argued that voters are unlikely to share the literature's concern for (dis)proportionality of outcomes in any direct manner, how can we begin to understand the impact of electoral institutions upon voters? The next two sections outline ways in which voters may be affected by electoral institutions. The first of these rests on a distinction between preferences over alternatives and choices.

The 'Menu-Dependence' of Choice: Voter Preferences over Alternatives

In elections voters are typically offered a choice between competing candidates and/or parties. The major exceptions are, of course, referendum and initiative elections which typically focus on single issues. Putting this last category aside we can turn to candidate and/or party elections and note that, in these elections, voter choices are – to use Sen's apt phrase – 'menu-dependent' (Sen, 1995). A voter may choose alternative x from a set of alternatives, but this may not remain the choice if the set of alternatives changes.

Consider, for example, a group of diners sitting in a restaurant thinking about dessert. The menu lists three sorts of pies – apple, blueberry and cherry – and the people are thinking about these choices as the waiter approaches. The waiter arrives and informs the diners that there is no more apple pie, leaving the diners to choose between cherry and blueberry. A second scenario might see the waiter arriving to tell the table that not only were all three pies available, but the chef had just made their specialty chocolate cake. It seems clear that in either instance the choices people make are conditioned by the alternatives open to them. In the first scenario it would seem silly for people to insist on apple pie when there is none; in the second, we might reasonably expect some of the diners to abandon their choice of pie for the chocolate cake. The analogy drawn between diners in a restaurant and voters is that it seems reasonable to suppose that electoral choice is similarly menu-dependent.

> For example, the presence of a 'green' candidate z may make a voter go for a somewhat 'greenish' x over environmentally naive but otherwise sensible candidate y, even though she might have voted for y over x had there been no fully 'green' candidate (Sen, 1995: 94).

If the hypothesis of menu dependence is correct then we should see much more fundamental shifts in attachments when voters may choose a given party under one set of alternatives that they would not consider from another set. This is most obviously true where the new set of alternatives contains more alternatives than the original, and it suggests that voter choices should vary as the set of alternatives vary.

It is feasible, although much harder, to see this menu dependence where the set of alternatives narrows. This does raise potential problems with independence from irrelevant alternatives. An example of independence from irrelevant alternatives applied to the restaurant scenario is where the diners choose apple only to have the waiter return and tell them that while there were lots of apple pies there were no cherry ones left. Clearly this is a more difficult case to argue, although it is implied within the example given above by Sen (the absence of ecologically sound z prompts the voter to prefer y).[8]

More generally, in terms of voter preferences over alternatives this argument suggests that either voter choice will differ – and/or strength of voter attachment to a given choice will vary – as the set of alternatives varies. So, in addition to the kinds of short term, campaign-led, shifts in party identifications and policy preferences noted in a growing body of literature (for example, Gerber and Jackson, 1993; Franklin, Marsh and McLaren, 1994), we should also be able to locate shifts in preferences as the set of alternatives shift, and some evidence suggests that this is the case. For example, the importance of extremist candidates and parties may not be so much in terms of vote shares or even their impact on the platforms of other parties, but in the way they help frame the choice facing voters. Perhaps, then, the true impact of racist parties, such as the UK National Front, lies in convincing centrist voters to vote for a right wing party such as the Conservatives, rather than for Labour.

Using party identification as an indicator of underlying voter preferences illustrates the importance of menu dependence even further. To take a simple – and perhaps crass – survey example, voters in England are unlikely to express a party identification in favour of the Scottish National Party even if they were asked. Likewise, Australian voters rarely give much thought to the Parti Quebecois or Ross Perot. Childhood socialization processes clearly have less to do with this than the fact that the SNP only exists in Scotland, the PQ and Perot only in North America. Simple though these examples may be, a number of consequences follow from them. Unless we are to believe that asking such questions makes sense, these examples illustrate that party identifications are identifications with respect to particular – nationally bound – objects on the political landscape. At least part of what drives the Michigan model is thus implicitly country- and institution-specific, and so some understanding of institutional factors cannot be posed within this model. Since attitudes and behaviour are conducted with regard to a specific system, we cannot understand anything about voting behaviour unless we take account of that system. Thus, one important consequence is that standard Michigan models of party identification are not likely to be the best vehicle from within which to explore institutional effects on voting behaviour, since identifications are logically endogenous to a given set of alternatives on offer.

One simple illustration of this comes from our standard measure of party identification which implicitly carries with it a particular systemic setting.

Typically this measure is one-dimensional. Within the USA – and especially the USA of the 1950s – this makes a great deal of sense. Moving from one end of the standard 5 point scale to the other we can place strong Republicans, then weak Republicans, Independents, weak Democrats and then strong Democrats. Debates over the status of Independents to one side, there are still problems in applying this one-dimensional scale outside the USA. By contrast, consider an example of a very simple non-US setting, such as the UK which has three parties: Labour, Conservative and Liberal. Do we place weakly identifying Conservatives to the right of, the left of, or at the same place as strongly identifying Liberals? There is no easy or obvious answer to this question; a question which becomes all the harder when the number of parties increases. Clearly, then, the presence of more than two parties demands the use of a measure that is of greater than one dimension. Is this an innocuous shift? Perhaps; but then again perhaps not. Results from formal theories, however, strongly suggest that dimensionality is not an innocuous issue (for example, Laver and Schofield, 1990).[9]

In short, since party identification is identification with respect to a given array of options, it implicitly assumes the institutional features which may be interesting to explore. It is the 'with respect to' that defines institutional effects. This is not to say, however, that party identification is a completely useless concept, only that it may not provide a theoretical basis from within which to understand institutional effects upon voters. Party identification may, however, provide a means of detecting institutional effects. An example of this is presented below. For the time being, however, it may be noted that institutions may not only shape preferences, they may also shape choices. And, while preference and choice are generally related, they are not necessarily identical.

The Strategic Dependence of Choice

The study of the aggregate-level properties of electoral systems has made considerable progress in establishing a number of factors fundamental to how we understand and judge electoral systems. Chief among these properties is that of proportionality. However, this feature need not be of paramount concern to voters and their direct choice. More fundamental strategic considerations arise from the number of alternatives on offer and the chance that any alternative will become an outcome.

While voters may well have preferences over the alternatives on offer, these alternatives could have little or no relevance to the likely outcome. Where the election imposes a binary choice – most straightforwardly in direct democracy elections or two candidate/party elections – the alternatives on offer map directly into outcomes, and voters should vote sincerely. But this is not the case where more than two alternatives are on offer. In such settings choice is linked not only to preferences over alternatives, but also preferences over outcomes. In multi-party contests voters may choose with respect to preferred outcomes rather than preferred alternatives. The simplest example here is, of course, that of tactical voting under single member district plurality elections. While voters may well greatly prefer the British National Party or the Peace and Freedom Party over all others, it is not a relevant preference in terms of outcome. Such a difference between preferences over alternatives and preferences over outcomes is the cleanest example of an institutional effect on voter behaviour. Of course, if institutions are so important in shaping voters, perhaps voters will not even exhibit such a distinction. The fact that tactical voting occurs in Britain seems quite strong evidence of an institutional effect.[10]

Thus while two-party or two-alternative contests essentially invoke only the voter's first preference, multi-candidate or multi-alternative elections invoke lower order preferences over both alternatives and outcomes. In fact, they may force voters to form second and third order preferences. Looked at in this way list PR and single member simple plurality (SMSP) share what might seem a surprising degree of similarity in that they restrict voters to a relatively limited number of preferences. The major difference between list PR and SMSP occurs when the number of parties multiplies to the point where the number of feasible coalitions becomes large, supporting a large number of strategic conjectures by the voter. Even here, however, voters are typically only allowed to express one preference.

But multi-partyism may complicate voters' use of decision rules in other ways too, such as, for example, under the Key-Fiorina hypothesis of the retrospective voter who votes against a government they do not like (Key, 1966; Fiorina, 1981). Again, in a two-party system this is a straightforward case to make. If the Republicans have not performed well, replace them with Democrats. But consider the problem of the German voter. Take an example where the government is a coalition of the CDU/FDP and the opposition parties are the Social Democrats (SPD), the Fascists (Republikan), the Greens, and a small Communist party. I may be dissatisfied with the current government, in that case I can vote for an opposition party; but which one? For the two party case the answer is clear, in a multi-party system, however, it is much less clear. A theory of 'voting the rascals out' requires some amendment to help establish whom to vote in. The need to amend this hypothesis does not stop there, since it is not automatically clear which 'rascal' should be thrown out. Should a person who voted for the FDP last time, and who currently is unhappy with the performance and personality of the CDU Chancellor, switch away from the FDP to, say, the Socialists, or not?

Of the set of strategies available to voters, a wider one is seen when we examine sequential elections. In US presidential primaries, or run-off elections, sequence introduces ways in which voter strategies become more complex, in part either because voters are allowed to express at least two preferences (run-off elections) or because they need to know where they are in the sequence of elections (presidential primaries). Voters at the first stage – or early in the primary season – can begin to vote sincerely or strategically in the hope of influencing later stages; by the second round (in France) or when the presidential field has narrowed to two candidates, the dominant strategy becomes that of voting sincerely. In either event, the voter may be forced to both consider and express a preference for alternatives other than the most preferred one.

A more pronounced widening of possible strategies occurs under preferential or other ordinal systems. Indeed, whether or not strategic behaviour can exist at the level of mass publics can only really be examined by looking at such systems. Deciding whether or not to vote for a third party candidate in the USA or UK is, as we know, a clear cut case of strategic voting which has been fully explored by both aggregate and individual studies. The extent to which voters can engage in more subtle strategizing under more complex conditions is, however, an unknown. It may well be the case, for example, that the complexities involved in making strategic calculations under, say, STV, are so great as to force voters to vote sincerely. Thus, despite their scope for sophisticated voting, systems such as STV may well induce sincere revelation of preferences.

TABLE 4
A CATEGORIZATION OF THE COMPLEXITY OF ELECTORAL SYSTEMS
FROM THE VOTERS' POINT OF VIEW

Complexity	System	Example
Highest	Single Transferable Vote Alternative Vote/Cumulative Vote	Australian Senate, Ireland Australian, a few US local elections
Medium	Sequential elections Categorical, multi-candidate/list	France, US presidential primaries UK, Canada, list PR systems
Lowest	Categorical, two candidate	US Congress

If we consider the scope for strategizing allowed to voters, this implies that we are beginning to think of electoral systems not so much from the parties' point of view, but from that of the voters. Table 4 presents a simple categorization which ranks electoral systems according to the degree of complexity they impose upon voters as measured by the number of preferences voters are asked to express. This is hardly a complete or even a very subtle breakdown of electoral systems. The lumping together of the single member simple plurality system (SMSP) and list PR may strike some as being particularly unwarranted, as indeed might also be the case with the treatment of the alternative vote (single member ordinal system) with the cumulative vote system (multi-member simple plurality systems). Given the range of options considered by Lijphart, Taagepera, Shugart and Rae this may seem a wilfully ignorant categorization. When looked at, however, from the demands made upon the voter the categorization does make at least some sense. List PR and SMSP typically share the attribute of being categorical ballots; voters typically express one preference, or one preference twice in the case of some sequential elections. True enough, list PR may offer voters a wider range of choices from which to choose – and hence may affect preference formation – but voters are only allowed to make one choice. Ordinal ballots, however, open up a much greater range of strategies and choices and thereby invoke a wider range of preferences than categorical systems, especially when it comes time to examine the extent to which ordinary voters can engage in strategic behaviour.

Decision Dependence and Reasoning Voters in Australia and Germany

So far it has been argued that a micro-level understanding of institutions might involve focusing upon a different set of effects and consequences than those identified by the aggregate-level literature. Institutional effects at the level of voters may be seen in terms of their impact on the menu-dependence of preference and the strategic dependence of choice. Putting these arguments together suggests that institutions frame the decisions voters are asked to make. Under different institutional settings voters may be asked to make very different sorts of decisions. Because of this, different institutional settings require different things of voters: they may require either more or less information and can demand or invoke quite different patterns of reasoning among voters. Some very simple examples help to illustrate this. While voters in most US elections rely on party cues, this is not at all relevant in primary contests where voters choose between competing candidates from the same party. In contrast to unitary states, elections in federal states allow voters to use information about parties gained from one level in the system to arrive at conclusions of how to vote at the other level (Bowler, 1990). Each sort of election, then, requires voters to reason over different pieces of information and in different ways and so we may expect voting to be dependent upon the kind of decision voters are being asked to reach.

The example of primary versus general elections will strike some as too obvious an example to allow us to use the suggestion, made above, that party identification may be a useful indicator of the presence of institutional effects, an indicator which will help cast light on the impact of institutions on the way voters reason about the choice they are making. Some empirical examples from Australia and Germany help to illustrate this part of the argument.

The Australian and German systems have the interesting feature of combining two electoral systems in one election. Australian voters simultaneously vote for two houses of the legislature: elections to the upper house use STV, while elections to the lower house use AV. German voters, on the other hand, face the relatively well-known, but not necessarily well-understood, system of having two votes: one for individual candidates, the other for party lists. We can exploit these differences to explore the impact of institutions upon how voters make decisions.

Germany

Germany's two ballot system is well known, but not well understood; least of all, it seems, by German voters themselves. A 1983 election survey showed, for example, that the electorate was divided into three parts: those who thought the first (candidate) vote mattered most, those who thought the second (party) vote mattered most, and those who thought both votes were of equal importance. A simple argument to advance at this point is that if institutions do provide incentives to voters then German voters ought to shift their behaviour in response to how they think the electoral system works.

If a voter believes the second (party) vote to be the most consequential then they should take it more seriously. One indication of how seriously voters will take this act lies in the relationship of party identification to vote choice, since that voter is unlikely to harm the party they support by not taking it seriously. Thus, for voters who believe that the party vote is most important in determining vote choice, their party identification should have a greater impact on choice in the party vote, rather than in the candidate vote. Conversely, if a voter believes the first (candidate) vote is the most important, then their choice of candidate is more likely to be influenced by party identification than the choice of party.

Table 5 presents gamma values from a very basic model which seeks to test these hypotheses for the three main German parties using data from the 1983 election survey. The columns of the 2x2 cell in the top left of that table break down voters into those who think the first vote is more important and those who think the second vote is more important. The rows reflect which vote is being cast (for the party or the candidate), and the cells are gamma values.[11]

By and large the hypotheses conform to the predictions made above and listed at the foot of Table 5. Five of the six hypothesized relationships are in the right direction (although in one case only just). Of course, a fuller model of vote choice would be a better way of exploring the way that party identification, and similar factors, may shift in importance according to the decision presented to voters. Australia's parliamentary elections provide such an opportunity.

TABLE 5
IMPACT OF PARTY IDENTIFICATION ON VOTER CHOICE BY ELECTORAL SYSTEM:
GAMMA VALUES FOR GERMANY, 1983

	First	Second
Party	a	b
Candidate	c	d
CDU		
Party	.948	.962
Candidate	.972	.969
SPD		
Party	.975	.967
Candidate	.948	.962
FDP		
Party	.983	.985
Candidate	1.000	.970
Hypotheses:	b > a	
	c > d	

Notes: Cell entries are gamma values. The original cross-tab is between vote for [named] party (0,1) and strength of party attachment for [named party].

Australia

Despite the importance of the Australian Senate to that country's system, it is the lower house which is clearly the main seat of the government and of the prime minister. We should therefore expect party identification to be more important in determining the vote for the House than for the Senate – notwithstanding the fact that the Alternative Vote system (used for House elections) can produce incentives to vote tactically and hence attenuate the impact of party identification. Moreover, we should also expect evaluations of government performance to be more important in determining the vote for the House than for the Senate.

TABLE 6
VOTE CHOICE FOR HOUSE AND SENATE ELECTIONS BY PARTY: AUSTRALIA 1993
(LOGIT ESTIMATES)

	Labor		Liberal		National	
	House	Senate	House	Senate	House	Senate
Constant	2.18	0.71	-4.46	-4.08	-6.9	-7.1
Middle class	-0.25*	-0.33**	0.07	0.20	0.02	-0.27
	(.16)	(.15)	(.16)	(.15)	(.30)	(.29)
Age	-0.01**	-0.01**	0.007	0.004	0.006	0.01**
	(.004)	(.104)	(.004)	(.004)	(.009)	(.008)
Female	0.01	0.15	-0.05	-0.0008	0.16	0.23
	(.14)	(.13)	(.14)	(.13)	(.28)	(.27)
Income	-0.15*	-0.01	-0.01	0.03	0.31	0.32*
	(.10)	(.10)	(.10)	(.09)	(.20)	(.19)
College	0.04	-0.57**	0.25	0.23	-0.10	-0.55
	(.18)	(.18)	(.18)	(.17)	(.38)	(.41)
Party ID	3.98**	3.62**	3.98**	3.63**	5.00**	4.43**
	(.15)	(.14)	(.15)	(.14)	(.33)	(.31)
Economy	-0.75**	-0.49**	0.55**	0.44**	0.54**	0.45**
	(.07)	(.06)	(.06)	(.06)	(.15)	(.14)
N	2191	2165	2191	2165	2095	2165
% Correct	89	88	89	88	97	97

Note: Figures in parentheses are standard errors
Source: 1993 Australian National Election Study

Table 6 shows evidence consistent with these hypotheses. The last two variables – Party ID and Economy – can be compared across votes for the two houses. Party ID is a simple dummy (1=identification of named party, 0=not) while Economy is a five-point scale asking voters to rank how the economy has improved over the last year (1=a lot better, ...5=a lot worse).[12] While logit estimations typically involve transforming the equations into probabilities, here the parameters can be compared directly since metrics are identical. Comparing across we see that for each of the three parties, party identification and economic assessments are larger for the House vote than for the Senate vote.

What do voters think they are doing when they vote?

The examples of Germany and Australia are intended as partial illustrations of a general argument. The general argument is that the decision voters are required to make is shaped by electoral institutions – either by shaping preferences, or strategies, or both. Different electoral systems require different information of voters, and demand different reasoning processes. Uncovering these requirements demands some sensitivity to the setting itself. What voters think they are doing when they vote should vary by institutional setting, and party identification may well be useful not so much as a tool with which to understand such differences across systems, but more as a convenient measure of their effects.

It is far from clear whether, how much, and in what ways voters understand the electoral process itself. In principle, that understanding should vary both in accord with individual-level attributes as well as with the demands imposed by the electoral system itself. How little we know of how voters approach the act of voting can be illustrated by a further example which looks at differences between the ways supporters of large and small parties approach the ballot.

In June 1994 London voters at the European elections were asked to complete a mock ballot in which they pretended the election was held under STV rules, rather than the current SMSP system. Results from this survey have been examined in greater depth elsewhere (Bowler and Farrell, 1995, 1996), but here it is worth reviewing a couple of smaller effects not really developed in those earlier pieces. In briefly recapping what voters were asked to do, we may note that voters were completely free to fill in as many preferences as they liked for as many parties as they liked.

In an institution-free and/or social psychological-free environment there seems little reason to expect, a priori, that voters will vary by party in the way they approach such a survey. That is, there is little or no reason to expect ahead of time that voters from party A will fill in more of the ballot than, say, Labour voters. However, survey evidence shows that, in this case, voters for the minor parties did, in fact, express more preferences and for more parties than did voters for the two larger parties.

There would seem to be two main arguments which may be advanced in order to explain these patterns. First, voters are responding to institutional incentives. Second, there is a social psychological explanation which lies in the fact that, as Table 7 shows, Liberal Democrat and Green voters have generally weaker attachments to their party than do Labour or Conservative voters and, as evidence presented elsewhere indicates, weak affiliations prompt voters to vote across party lines.

A number of rejoinders are possible which weaken the argument that this is a party identification effect. Weak affiliations may lead to more parties being voted for, but they are also associated with marking less of the ballot (Bowler and Farrell, 1995, 1996). As Table 8 shows, even when controlling for strength of affiliation and comparing, for example, weak Liberal Democrat identifiers to weak Conservative and Labour voters, Liberal

Democrats vote for more parties and mark more preferences. On their own, then, weak identifications cannot explain the patterns of Table 7.

TABLE 7
MEASURES OF PARTY LOYALTY BY PARTY: LONDON 1994

	Cons.	Labour	LibDem	Green
North London				
No. of parties voted for	1.54	1.55	1.92	2.05
	(.95)	(.88)	(1.0)	(1.1)
Total preferences	4.31	4.79	4.62	5.17
	(2.49)	(3.1)	(3.1)	(2.7)
Average party ID	1.9	1.66	2.2	2.13
	(.71)	(.7)	(.64)	(.65)
N	527	964	235	40
South London				
No. of parties voted for	1.75	1.62	2.03	1.91
	(1.0)	(1.0)	(1.06)	(1.16)
Total preferences	3.67	4.19	4.44	5.0
	(2.03)	(2.7)	(3.1)	(3.2)
Average party ID	2.03	1.70	2.14	1.78
	(.7)	(.69)	(.69)	(.69)
N	404	558	237	23

Note: Standard deviations in parentheses
Source: Electoral Reform Society/MORI Euro election survey, June 1994

TABLE 8
THE IMPACT OF STRENGTH OF PARTY IDENTIFICATION UPON THE EXPRESSION
OF PREFERENCES

	No. parties	Total prefs	N	No. parties	Total prefs	N
Conservative						
Very strong ID	1.33	4.64	162	1.37	3.55	93
Fairly strong ID	1.57	4.27	256	1.65	3.76	207
Not very strong ID	1.78	3.89	109	2.33	3.62	104
Labour						
Very strong ID	1.45	4.67	450	1.42	4.22	240
Fairly strong ID	1.62	5.07	388	1.77	4.15	243
Not very strong ID	1.71	4.18	126	1.79	4.25	75
Liberal Democrats						
Very strong ID	1.53	4.87	30	1.69	4.74	42
Fairly strong ID	2.01	4.50	131	2.06	4.14	121
Not very strong ID	1.92	4.70	77	2.19	4.69	74

Source: Electoral Reform Society/MORI Euro election survey, June 1994

More important still, the hypothesis of weak identification simply begs the question of why adherents to small parties should have weaker identifications to begin with. One possible explanation is that they realize their first preferences – even under preferential systems – are unlikely to shape the eventual outcome. As a consequence they do not invest so much as others in a sense of 'belonging' to that party, and are more willing to express more preferences. Such asymmetry – supporters of small parties willing to transfer preferences to large parties, but not vice versa (the 'Jesse effect') – is also found in Irish general election data (Jesse, 1995) and may have a similar explanation there.

The evidence of Tables 7 and 8 may indicate that patterns of identification cannot be the cause of differing patterns of response between the large and smaller parties and that the explanation for party differences must lie elsewhere, but it hardly supports the view that there are institutional effects. Rather it helps pose the questions: do Liberal Democrats see the act of voting differently from Labour or Conservative voters, and if so is that difference related to system effects or individual-level ones? Unfortunately, at this point, the trail goes cold since we know very little about what voters think they are up to once they reach the ballot box. The patterns are highly suggestive of institutional effects acting differently upon different party supporters – but very far from conclusive.

Conclusion

The arguments and examples outlined above suggest that establishing institutional effects on voting behaviour may profit from a finer grained analysis than can be revealed only by large N studies. This is not to say there is no place for cross-national research. Far from it. Large N studies form a central component of any research strategy in this field. Having said that, large N studies can be informed and supplemented by narrower studies, especially when institutional effects may be subtle.

Moreover, it may well be the case that elections from outside the USA and the UK become sensible objects of study. The snag, of course, is that there are often serious and well-known problems of inference attached to case studies. Findings may simply represent a thinly disguised national situation dressed up in general language, and cases may be chosen more with an eye to familiarity with the basic material than any theoretical concern. Despite these potential snags it should be the case that interest in institutionally grounded theories of voting behaviour should take us further afield than the US presidential race or a British general election, notwithstanding the substantive national importance of those elections. True enough, 'second order' elections and elections from smaller nations may not help us predict who wields executive power in rich and nuclear-armed states, but they may help us better understand the impact of institutions on voters.

ACKNOWLEDGEMENTS

The author would like to thank David Broughton, David Denemark, Todd Donovan and David Farrell for advice and help on previous stages of this project, and to the Academic Senate UC Riverside for support. Special thanks are due to David Denemark for assistance with the empirical work on Australia. The author remains responsible for all errors and omissions.

NOTES

1. This is the literature which considers the conditions under which a voter would vote for their second most preferred alternative over and above their most preferred alternative. This choice – and these conditions – form at least part of the micro-level motor which drives the aggregate level result where SMSP is associated with two-party systems. For sophisticated individual-level analysis, see Franklin *et al.* (1994), Niemi *et al.* (1992) and attendant debates.

2. In general it seems easier to achieve finer divisions into integers of a larger number than a smaller one and, hence, achieve more proportional results (Rae, 1995: 69).

3. In other words, modelling institutional effects may not mean elaborating a micro-model which is exactly consistent with electoral results. It may be the case that distinctions between, say the d'Hondt and the St. Laguë formulae either (a) are too fine a distinction for voters to care about, or (b) operate more in a way quite insulated from individual voters.

4. For example in New South Wales in 1980, 11.1% of ballot papers were spoiled (63 candidates); in 1993 the figure was 2.55% (66 candidates).

5. On stock markets the big institutional investors have often traded their multi-billion dollar portfolios by computer in a manner which can lead to massive swings in selling and buying in an instant. The sequential avalanche of preferences in Australian Senate elections suggests that the image of 'program trading' seems an appropriate analogy to adopt here. The Australian Democrats, for ideological reasons, typically give their voters a choice between 'How to Vote' cards.

6. One major reason for this is the running of individualized campaigns within personal bailiwicks inside the constituency. Essentially this amounts to the distribution of individualized 'How To Vote' cards which obviously differ over which candidate should receive first preferences.

7. Indeed, the evidence of small shifts in behaviour before and after the introduction of ticket voting suggests that some institutional changes may be quite innocuous.

8. The example from Bonner used in Table 3 can be seen to provide an example of how independence from irrelevant alternatives can be violated. If alternative x is eliminated from all preference profiles, but alternatives y, w and z are left in their relative places, y and w become elected. That is, removal of x not only means that, sensibly, x does not win, it also means that z loses even though preferences over y, w and z are left unchanged (Bonner, 1986: 90).

9. Laver and Schofield (1990: 122) provide a very clear account of what happens once the policy space is enlarged from one dimension to many. One of the major effects is that stability is much harder to achieve and that 'any policy space of more than one dimension is generically prone to voting cycles and chaos'.

10. The fact that over 20% of voters still vote for the Liberal Democrats suggests that some limits to that effect exist even if we allow for the fact that many of this 20% do not live in constituencies where tactical voting makes sense.

11. A couple of practical problems face estimating the relationship with more powerful methods, most pressing of which is the relatively small N for work of this kind which is roughly 200–300. Copies of results of bivariate and multi-variate probit estimations are available to those who are interested.

12. In the 1993 AES this is variable D5CNTRY. The inequality also works with D6CNTRY and for the Australian Democrat party.

BIBLIOGRAPHY

Australian Electoral Commission Statistics: Result of Count (various years).

Bonner, J. (1986) *Introduction to the Theory of Social Choice.* Baltimore, MD: Johns Hopkins University Press.

Bowler, S. (1990) 'Federalism and Mass Behaviour: An Institutional Explanation for Unstable Political Affiliations in Canada', *Electoral Studies* 9: 133–45.

Bowler S. and D. M. Farrell (1995) 'A British STV Election: The Electoral Reform Society's MORI Poll of London Voters During the 1994 Euro Elections', *Representation* 32: 90–94.

Bowler, S. and D. M. Farrell (1996) 'Party, Candidate and Ballot Effects on Voting Behaviour in a Preferential System: An STV Mock Ballot Survey of London Voters', in C. Rallings, D. M. Farrell, D. Denver, D. Broughton (eds), *British Elections and Parties Yearbook, 1995*, pp.14–31. London: Frank Cass.

Fiorina, M. (1981) *Retrospective Voting in American National Elections.* New Haven: Yale University Press.

Franklin, M., M. Marsh and L. McLaren (1994) 'Uncorking the Bottle: Popular Opposition to European Unification in the Wake of Maastricht', *Journal of Common Market Studies* 32: 455–72.

Franklin, M., R. Niemi and G. Whitten (1994) 'The Two Faces of Tactical Voting', *British Journal of Political Science* 24: 549–557.

Gallagher, M. (1993) 'The Election of the 27th Dáil', in M. Gallagher and M. Laver (eds) *How Ireland Voted 1992.* Dublin: Folens/PSAI Press.

Gerber, E. and J. Jackson (1993) 'Endogenous Preferences and the Study of Institutions', *American Political Science Review* 87: 639–56.

Gunther, R. (1989) 'Electoral Laws, Party Systems and Elites: The Case of Spain', *American Political Science Review* 83: 835–58.

Harrop, M. and W. Miller (1987) *Elections and Voters.* Basingstoke: Macmillan.

Jesse, N. (1995) *The Single Transferable Vote and Duverger's Law: Impact on Party Systems and Voting Behavior.* Unpublished Ph.D. dissertation, UCLA.

Key, V. O. (1966) *The Responsible Electorate.* New York: Vintage.

Lakeman, E. (1974) *How Democracies Vote.* London: Faber.

Laver, M. and N. Schofield (1991) *Multi-Party Government.* Oxford: Oxford University Press.

Lijphart, A. (1994) *Electoral Systems and Party Systems: A Study of Twenty-Seven Democracies 1945–1990.* Oxford: Oxford University Press.

Niemi, R., G. Whitten and M. Franklin (1992) 'Constituency Characteristics, Individual Characteristics and Tactical Voting in the 1987 British General Election', *British Journal of Political Science* 22: 229–40.

Ordeshook, P. (1992) *A Political Theory Primer.* London: Routledge.

Rae, D. (1971) *The Political Consequences of Electoral Laws.* New Haven, Yale: Yale University Press.

Rae, D. (1995) 'Using District Magnitude to Regulate Political Party Competition', *Journal of Economic Perspectives* 9: 65–75.

Riker, W. (1982) *Liberalism Against Populism.* New York: W.H. Freeman.

Sen, A. (1995) 'How to Judge Voting Schemes', *Journal of Economic Perspectives* 9: 91–98.

Silva, R. (1964) 'Relation of Representation and the Party System to the Number of Seats Apportioned to a Legislative District', *Western Political Quarterly* XVII: 742–69.

Taagepera, R. and M. Shugart (1989) *Seats and Votes: The Effects and Determinants of Electoral Systems.* New Haven: Yale University Press.

Tsebelis, G. (1995) 'Decision Making in Political Systems: Veto Players in Presidentialism, Parliamentarism, Multi-cameralism and Multi-partyism', *British Journal of Political Science* 25: 289–325.

Television Can Matter: Bias in the 1992 General Election

Anthony Mughan

Introduction

It is rare for the views of practitioners and students of British politics to come to as different conclusions as they do over the question of the political importance of the media, and especially television. Political parties see this medium as having great political importance and go to some lengths to shape the content and tenor of its coverage of their affairs (for example Kavanagh, 1995). When in office, for example, both Conservative and Labour have protested loudly against alleged anti-government bias in the way the publicly-funded BBC reports politics and political affairs. Dissatisfaction and public accusation reached new heights with the criticisms and actions of the Conservative government of the 1980s–1990s:

> Attacking [BBC] television programmes that offended government sensibilities, while not the exclusive propensity of this Government, was one in which it indulged with a growing ruthlessness...What this amounted to was a form of intimidation, of a kind to which broadcasters were quite well accustomed, but accompanied on this occasion by the kind of action at the BBC which would in previous eras have been unthinkable (Young, 1990: 511–12).

The action in question included most notably the appointment of political sympathizers to the BBC's Board of Governors, freezing its licence fee and pressuring it to cancel some programmes deemed critical of government policy. The objective was to ensure that 'proper' messages were conveyed to the public, presumably at least in part because the 'left-wing bias' perceived by the Conservative Party was concluded to influence popular perceptions and behaviour to its disadvantage.[1]

Political scientists, in sharp contrast, have shown little interest in, or concern with, bias, and its effects, in television's coverage of politics.[2] Indeed, the common conception seems to be that television, unlike newspapers, cannot sway the judgment of voters because the medium is itself not allowed to display prejudice in favour of any party in its political programming, including its news broadcasts. The basis of this anodyne view of the electoral role of the single most popular, trusted and believed medium of political communication is the long-held view that television viewing has no implications for voters' party choice (Harrop, 1987). It is required by law, and especially during election campaigns, to be impartial in its political coverage, an obligation that it has traditionally met by giving equal air time to the major parties (Negrine, 1989: 103–7).

In this article, I side with the politicians and take issue with the prevailing orthodoxy in political science. My basic argument is that while the actual content of television news programmes may not display partisan prejudice, the perception of such bias in them can nonetheless be common among voters.[3] Moreover, this perception, whether grounded in objective circumstance or not, has very real electoral consequences, not so much because it directly affects the way people vote as because, independently of their partisanship, it primes them to react in certain ways to short-term campaign stimuli, like issues and the personalities of the party leaders. These stimuli then directly influence their party choice.

The starting point of this argument is rejection of the assumption that non-partisan reporting and equal air time translate, in the public eye at least, into an absence of bias and, hence, of an electoral impact for television. The key point is that bias is largely a subjective perception that can have its roots in sources other than actual news programme content. It might originate, for example, in party propaganda, discussion with family and friends or the reading of partisan newspapers. The truism that prejudice needs to be in the eye of the beholder for it to influence their attitudes and behaviour means that the study of television bias needs to look beyond the legal framework constraining the medium and explore where it comes from and the electoral consequences it might have. This is the tack taken in this argument that television bias had some effect, albeit a small one, on the outcome of the 1992 general election.

The argument is developed in three stages. The first documents that a significant number of voters do perceive that television newscasts are politically biased and this perception is not a simple function of their partisanship or of frequency of exposure to the television news.[4] The second demonstrates that the perception of partisan bias on the television has implications for voters' responses to the parties, specifically to their issue stances and to their leaders vying for the position of prime minister. Finally, it is shown that while perceived bias may have a direct electoral impact, it largely fades into insignificance when the effects of issues and party leaders are taken into account. In other words, these short-term campaign stimuli are essentially the filter through which the perception of bias in television's coverage of politics shapes opinion and behaviour. The general conclusion is that television, and probably any other medium, can be a potent indirect influence at the polls if voters persuade themselves, or are persuaded, that its political coverage is biased.[5]

The Distribution of Bias

News broadcasts are a pervasive feature of television, whether privately or publicly owned. At the time of the 1992 general election, Britain had five television channels providing news programmes for their viewers. Two of them were owned by the BBC (BBC1 and BBC2) and three by commercial operators (ITN, Channel 4 and SkyNews). The two newscasts with the largest audience by some margin were on the air late on weekday evenings, BBC1's *9 o' Clock News* and Independent Television's (ITN) *News at Ten*. Because of their popularity, these programmes form the basis of the analysis to come.

A perennial problem with all studies of media effects is the disentanglement of cause and effect. This problem is particularly acute when the medium is openly partisan in its political advocacy, like most of the British national press. Does the choice of newspaper shape readers' partisan attitudes and behaviour, or do readers choose a newspaper because it echoes their pre-existing partisanship? (Butler and Stokes, 1974: 115–19; Curtice and Semetko, 1994) The legal context of television news broadcasts largely obviates this problem, however, insofar as the medium's obligation to remain impartial makes it most unlikely that viewers will choose the news channel they watch for the party line it follows. Proponents of the nationalization of industry, for example, will not prefer one channel to the other because of its editorial advocacy of public ownership. Equally, the viewer preferring the Labour leader over the Conservative one will not tune into one channel rather than the other because it echoes his prejudice in this regard.

TABLE 1
PERCEIVED BIAS BY NEWS PROGRAMME AND PARTY IDENTIFICATION

	BBC Bias			ITN Bias		
	Con Id %	Lab Id %	LD Id %	Con Id %	Lab Id %	LD Id %
None	68.7	68.3	77.6	82.2	73.7	85.3
Pro-Conservative	13.2	24.4	18.8	9.6	15.7	12.1
Pro-Labour	18.2	7.4	3.6	8.3	10.5	2.6
N of cases	1,108	665	304	920	636	272

Source: British Election Study 1992

The fact of impartiality, though, is no guarantee of the perception of it. Long-standing party loyalties could well predispose viewers, perhaps subconsciously, to interpret the content of news programmes as systematically favouring one or other party. To determine whether partisanship is indeed associated with a systematic pattern of bias perception, Table 1 sets out the relationship between identification with the three major parties and perceiving partisan prejudice in each of BBC's *9 o' Clock News* and ITN's *News at Ten.*[6]

Three findings stand out immediately. First, the perception of bias is reasonably commonplace and is not simply a function of partisanship. Across the two channels, anywhere between about 15 and 32 per cent of each group of partisan identifiers accept that there is bias in the news programme they watch. At the same time, though, there is no agreement on the direction of this bias insofar as all three groups of identifiers are divided over the question of which party is favoured by it. Second, while there is this disagreement, it is also the case that, contrary to Tory conviction, the tendency – manifest in five of the six groups in the table – is to see the news as favouring the Conservatives.[7] Third, BBC news is distinctive in two important respects. On the one hand, it is perceived to be biased by a larger proportion of identifiers with all three parties than is ITN's. On the other, in contrast to ITN viewers who are always more likely to see a pro-Tory bias, BBC viewers are divided over which direction it is biased in. While about one quarter of Labour and one fifth of Liberal Democratic identifiers see it as having, like ITN, a pro-Tory bias, their Conservative counterparts subscribe in similarly large numbers, to their party's allegation of a left-wing prejudice in the BBC's political coverage.

This dissimilarity is striking because fully 83 per cent of those answering the bias questions passed judgment on the content of *both* news programmes so that the different patterns of bias in Table 1 can hardly be explained away as an artefact of different sets of respondents.[8] Rather, the bias difference between the two channels would seem to be the very real product of contrasting perceptions on the part of largely the same people. But, if not in partisanship, where do these different perceptions originate? The answer is unlikely to be found in pro-Labour proselytizing on the part of the BBC. For a start, it strove especially hard in 1992 to be seen to be meeting its impartiality obligation because it 'was in some ways running scared of the [Conservative] government' (Crewe, 1993: 8). Second, if its programming was systematically biased in favour of one party, the expectation would be one largely of consensus, and not disagreement, on the direction of that bias. Finally, if the source of the bias was in the content of the news programme itself, then a reasonable expectation is that individuals who watched the programme more frequently than others should be substantially more likely, other things being equal, to be aware of its partisan bias. Table 2, however, suggests that this is not the case. Combining all identifiers into a single group, it shows that perception of a pro-Conservative or pro-Labour bias stands in virtually no relationship at all to frequency of watching the BBC news.

TABLE 2
PERCEPTION OF BIAS BY FREQUENCY OF WATCHING BBC NEWS

Times per week watched

	3 or less	4 or more
None	70.9%	68.7%
Pro-Conservative	17.3	17.9
Pro-Labour	11.8	13.4
N of cases	1,189	764

Source: British Election Study, 1992

Seen in the light of the inadequacy of these alternative explanations, a plausible account of the origins of bias must start from the premise that it comes from sources other than the partisanship of viewers or the content of the news programmes themselves. Instead, it would seem to be in people's minds before they seat themselves in front of the television set and, in this particular instance, reflects the 'success' of the Conservative government's loud and repeated allegations of a left-wing bias in BBC programming.[9] Relative to ITN viewing patterns, these allegations would seem to have convinced a disproportionate number of Tory identifiers of their party's interpretation of where the public channel's political sympathies lay. At the same time, this campaign appears to have produced a backlash. While Conservative loyalists apparently 'bought' this party line in greater numbers than not, the indications are that Labour loyalists reacted against it in even greater proportion and imputed a pro-Tory bias to the BBC news programmes they watched (see Table 1). In other words, without the Tories' sustained propaganda campaign against it, it is likely that perceptions of partisan prejudice among BBC viewers would not have polarized in the way they did.

But wherever the perception of prejudice may come from, the more important point is that television, at least in 1992, was not seen by all voters as the impartial medium of political communication and information that the law dictates it should be. The perception of bias is not sufficient in itself, however, to influence either attitudes or behaviour. It might just as easily produce indifference or short-term forgetfulness in viewers firm in their party loyalties. What must be addressed next, therefore, is whether the prejudice imputed to television news broadcasts has electoral implications. In particular, does it influence the way voters react, independently of their party identification, to short-term campaign stimuli?

Bias, Issues and Party Leaders

An important finding of newspaper studies is that the often strident partisanship of the press stands in, at best, a weak relationship to the way readers vote. In 1992, for example, 'only 38 per cent of the readers of *The Sun*, supposedly the most stridently pro-Conservative newspaper, voted Conservative' (Curtice and Semetko, 1994: 44). It is most unlikely, therefore, that any bias there might be in television news programmes will be sufficiently strong and persuasive to determine the way people vote. It would be premature, however, to conclude that the perceived direction of television bias has no implications at all for the party they choose at election time. Instead, the notion of media effects has to be reconceptualized and the burden of proof shifted from their taking the form of the direct determination of the vote to a more subtle and *indirect* one, where the medium places stimuli before voters in the course of the campaign and these stimuli are filtered through, and coloured by, prejudices that may or may not be rooted in long-term party loyalties.

It is important here to recognize that it is not television itself that is the principal actor in determining the stimuli presented to viewers. This is largely the preserve of the competing political parties. Where paid political advertising is allowed, parties enjoy relative autonomy in shaping the content of the media messages received by voters. Where it is not allowed and television is obliged to cover the campaign impartially, as in Britain, the parties have to be inventive and, through the campaign strategies they adopt, shape the content of news broadcasts. This way they can relay to voters the kinds of messages and stimuli they anticipate will play on popular conviction and prejudice and enhance their own chances of victory. In other words, they 'prime' voters, a process whereby parties, through their exploitation of the media opportunities available to them, 'seek not so much to change voters' opinions as to change the very basis of their choice' (Johnston *et al.*, 1992: 212; Iyengar and Kinder, 1987). The party's primary goal is not to persuade the voter that issues, say, are or should be important for the vote, but to focus attention on the issues on which the party is advantaged and the opposition disadvantaged.

According to this logic, there should be some relationship between the direction of the bias perceived in the television news and the pattern of issue preferences and leader evaluations. The interpretative lens which viewers have been persuaded to bring to bear on the news programmes they watch should structure to some degree the way they react to the partisan stimuli coming to them via those programmes. The relationship of bias to these short-term campaign stimuli is detailed in Table 3. The leader evaluation scores are the number of positive character traits that respondents see in each party leader. The traits in question are to what extent the leader is moderate, caring, good for all classes and capable of strong leadership, and their summation produces a score ranging between 0–4.[10] For the sake of comparability between the issue and leader variables, issue preferences are measured similarly. Following Heath *et al.* (1991: 32–51), eight issues of perennial importance in British politics were taken and the Conservative and Labour stances on them identified. Two scores were then created for respondents, one summing the number of their own issue stances that coincided with the Conservative Party's position and the other the number coinciding with the Labour Party's. The issues in question are nationalization, trade union power, big business power, welfare spending, defence, disarmament, European Community membership and immigration. Totals ranged between 0–8 on each party's composite issue score.

TABLE 3
PERCEPTION OF BIAS IN BBC AND ITN NEWS BY ISSUE PREFERENCES
AND LEADER EVALUATIONS

	BBC Bias				ITN Bias		
	None	Con.	Lab.		None	Con.	Lab.
Issue Preferences							
Pro-Conservative	2.20	2.11	3.06		2.27	2.16	2.62
Pro-Labour	3.51	3.93	2.87		3.47	3.89	3.32
Leader Evaluations							
Major (positive)	3.00	2.32	3.33		2.99	2.30	2.66
Kinnock (positive)	2.19	2.36	1.84		2.16	2.38	2.20
N of Cases	1,389	353	245		1,458	220	150

Source: British Election Study 1992

The table presents the mean issue preference and leader evaluation scores for BBC and ITN separately and the news programme viewers of each are divided into three groups – those seeing no partisan bias in programme content, those seeing a pro-Tory bias in it and those seeing a pro-Labour bias. The first of these groups is included to serve as a control group so that, broadly speaking, differences between its evaluations and those of the other two groups provide an estimate of the impact of television bias on the two sets of party evaluations.

There is, of course, a greater similarity between the values of these mean scores than there is difference between them. All this means is that issue preferences and leader evaluations come from sources other than perceived bias in the television news and that, collectively, these other sources exercise a stronger formative impact than television. But more to the point, the table also confirms that the mobilization of perceptions of bias is associated with popular reactions to issues and leaders.

It is noticeable that Labour enjoys an advantage in mean issue preference in all but one group in the table, that is, the one accepting the Conservative Party's claim of the BBC's left-wing bias. This group is distinctive for being most Conservative in its issue preferences and least Labour. Moreover, insofar as viewers seeing the same bias in the ITN news show on average a preference for Labour on issues, this Tory advantage would seem to be a function not of seeing a pro-Labour bias in television news programmes in general, but of seeing it in BBC newscasts in particular. It is difficult to avoid the conclusion that BBC viewers reacted in this distinctive way to the perception of left-wing bias because Tory allegations had raised – perhaps, more accurately, manufactured – their consciousness of, and sensitivity to, it.

Moving on to leader evaluations, they seem generally more responsive than issues to the influence of bias.[11] This is most obvious, once again, among viewers attributing a pro-Labour bias to the BBC. This group is the most polarized, evaluating the Conservative leader, Major, highest on average of any group in the table and the Labour leader, Kinnock, lowest. Looking at Table 3 overall, therefore, it is again difficult to avoid the conclusion that the Conservative Party's propaganda campaign against the BBC heightened the political sensitivity of a significant number of that channel's viewers and swayed their issue preferences and leader evaluations in its favour. Allegations, it would seem, can stick and bear fruit for those making them, even if they do not have a strong basis in fact.

Having established that television can be prejudiced in favour of one or other political party in the eyes of many voters and that this perception colours their interpretation of the political world around them, the next question concerns how the perception of bias mediates the relationship between issues and leaders on the one hand and the vote on the other.

Bias and the Vote

The starting point of this analysis of the vote is recognition that television bias has no necessary implications for the way elections turn out. It is perfectly conceivable, for example, that competing perceptions of the partisan direction of, say, the BBC's prejudice cancel each other out in the aggregate so that the phenomenon of bias itself adds little to our understanding of the distribution of party choice overall. Alternatively, it may be that bias, even though present, does not influence behaviour. Perhaps it is not strongly enough felt. A final possibility is that it may influence the vote, but only indirectly through its effect on issue preferences and leader evaluations. The three-way relationship between television bias, issues and leaders and the vote, in other words, is a potentially complex one whose nature needs to be established empirically, not assumed or taken for granted.

TABLE 4
PARTISAN BIAS AND THE VOTE BY BBC AND ITN VIEWERSHIP

| | BBC | | ITN | |
	Con	Lab	Con	Lab
Party identification	4.96***	5.05***	4.98***	4.96***
Age	.01	−.01	.01	−.01
Female	.32	−.18	.23	−.07
Union member	−.45*	.06	−.49*	.08
Share owner	.27	−.76**	.26	−.88***
Private sector	.63**	−.67**	.69**	−.64**
Home owner	.63**	−.35	.49*	−.27
Social class	−.07	.09	−.10	.12
Education	−.06	.14*	−.09	.14*
Conservative bias	−.51*	.76**	−.20	.18
Labour bias	.72**	−.16	−.24	−.39
Log–likelihood	821.17	739.25	813.84	744.07
Chi–squared	1485.28	1444.96	1424.93	1378.85
N of cases	1668		1619	

*p < .05; **p < .01; ***p < .001 (two-tailed test)

Source: British Election Study 1992

Table 4 explores whether television bias is important in its own right insofar as it has a direct effect on the vote. It leaves unexplored for the moment the question of how this effect makes itself felt; it simply asks whether it is there. The table presents four separate logistic regression equations, two each for BBC and ITN. Two equations are needed for each channel because bias can also influence the behaviour of Liberal Democrat identifiers and persuade them to vote for one or other of the major parties. Thus, in the first BBC equation, for example, the Conservative vote (and partisanship) is scored '1' and their Labour and Liberal Democratic equivalents '0'. In the second equation Labour is scored '1' and Conservative and Liberal Democratic '0'. In addition, all four equations in the table control for party identification and a range of other sociodemographic predictor variables that might independently influence the party choice of voters. These predictors are age, gender, class (measured by the five-point Goldthorpe schema), educational qualification, home ownership, share ownership, trade union membership and employment sector (public versus private or other).[12]

Immediately striking about the table is its demonstration, as with the perception of bias (see Table 1), that the effect of bias is not the same across the two television channels. Bias may shape the voting patterns of BBC viewers, but it leaves that of their ITN counterparts untouched. The reason for this difference is not obvious from the table, but it is again most likely to do with the Conservative propaganda campaign against the BBC. This campaign may have intensified perceptions of prejudice or carried them over some kind of threshold beyond which they assumed implications for party choice. Either way it appears to have successfully primed numerous viewers to interpret BBC newscasts in partisan terms and to be moved in their behaviour by this perception. The direction of their movement is also interesting; bias repulses more than it attracts. Voters who see a prejudice in favour of one major party are more likely to vote *for* the other party than they are to vote *against* the party favoured by it. Thus, if the Conservatives intended with their accusations of left-wing bias to attract Labour and Liberal Democratic defectors into their camp rather than to scare them away from Labour's – perhaps into the Liberal Democrat's – then their strategy worked well.

Bias, then, can have electoral consequences, but it appears to do so only when the perception of it, as in the case of the BBC, is mobilized by party propaganda and actions. When, as for ITN, popular sensitivity is not mobilized in this way, however, its electoral potential would seem to remain latent and not translate into an influence on behaviour at the polls. The analysis from this point, therefore, focuses only on viewers of BBC viewers.

Having established in general terms that, albeit only under certain circumstances, television bias can matter for the way people vote, it would now seem appropriate to specify more precisely the nature of its effect. In particular, is it direct or indirect? Table 3 has already shown that the perception of partisan prejudice in BBC news programmes is associated with voters' issue preferences and evaluations of the major party leaders. It may be that once reactions to these short-term campaign stimuli are controlled, then the direct impact of bias apparent in Table 4 will disappear.

Alternatively, its effect may be relatively independent of such stimuli and represent a generalized reaction that suffuses a voter's response to all aspects of the party and, as such, functions to all intents and purposes as an influence on the vote in its own right. Put differently, if a Tory was convinced of the BBC's bias it could lead to one of two types of response. First, he might respond more extremely to specific stimuli seen in the news programmes. The party leaders are a good example. He might come to view John Major more positively and Neil Kinnock more negatively than he might otherwise have done. This being the case, any effect bias has on the vote in Table 3 should disappear once leader evaluations and issue preferences are controlled by including them in the equation. Second, his response might be more undifferentiated and dismissive of the Labour Party generally. Bias, in other words, will suffuse his reaction to an opposition seen to be gaining an unfair advantage from television coverage of politics and make him more likely to vote Conservative regardless of his position on the short-term campaign stimuli included in the equation. Under these circumstances, bias should continue to influence the vote even when the effects of leader evaluations and issue preferences are controlled.

TABLE 5
PARTISAN BIAS, LEADER EVALUATIONS, ISSUE PREFERENCES AND THE VOTE
FOR BBC VIEWERS ONLY

	Con	Lab	Con	Lab
Party identification	4.96***	5.05***	4.00***	4.01***
Age	.01	−.01	−.00	−.01
Female	.32	−.18	.03	−.06
Union member	−.45*	.06	−.37	.03
Share owner	.27	−.76**	.14	−.89***
Private sector	.63**	−.67**	.49**	−.61**
Home owner	.63**	−.35	.46	−.22
Social class	−.07	.09	−.06	.12
Education	−.06	.14*	−.05	.17*
Conservative bias	−.51*	.76**	−.04	.41
Labour bias	.72**	−.16	.85	−.11
Major (positive)	−	−	.90***	−.49***
Kinnock (positive)	−	−	−.50***	.61***
Conservative issues	−	−	.12	−.12
Labour issues	−	−	−.34***	−.01
Log–likelihood	821.17	739.25	652.55	658.10
Chi–squared	1485.28	1444.96	1653.90	1526.11
N of cases	1668	1668		

*p < .05; **p < .01; ***p < .001 (two-tailed test)

Source: British Election Study 1992

Table 5 details the effect of bias once the campaign stimuli of issues and leaders are controlled. For ease of comparison and simplicity of reference, the equations containing the measures of partisan bias alone, and originally presented in Table 4, are reproduced on the left hand side of this table. The results are interesting because they continue the habit of being different for the two parties. The Labour vote is the more straightforward and so the easier to interpret. When issues and leaders are not included in the analysis, it can be seen that a perception of pro-Tory bias in the BBC news is associated, net of the other variables in the equation, with a greater likelihood of voting Labour, but the relationship disappears once leader and issue effects are controlled. Only the leader effects are statistically significant, however. In other words, the perception of a pro-Tory bias does influence the vote, but only indirectly through its limited ability to shape leader evaluations (see Table 3).

The story is different with the Conservative vote though. For a start, the Conservative vote is more sensitive to bias insofar as it is affected by both pro-Tory and pro-Labour prejudices. These prejudices are uneven in their effect, however. The benefit accruing to Labour from a pro-Tory bias is weaker when issues and leaders are not taken into account and disappears altogether once these short-term campaign stimuli are included in the equation. The Conservatives do better from a pro-Labour bias on both counts. Not only is the electoral bonus provided by this bias stronger when issues and leaders are excluded from consideration, but also it persists, albeit somewhat weakened, when they are taken into consideration. Thus, taking account of short-term campaign stimuli weakens the impact of television bias overall, but reduces it to insignificance only when that bias favours the Tories.[13]

In the specific context of the 1992 election, then, the indications are that bias affects the Labour vote only indirectly and the Conservative vote both directly and indirectly. Voters perceiving a pro-Labour bias in the BBC news react against this bias more strongly and, net of other influences including partisanship, they also tend to be moved more in their voting behaviour by it than those seeing a pro-Tory bias in the same news programme. It is difficult to see how this Tory advantage reflects some perennial difference between the parties, for example, a tendency for the electorate to regard prejudice in favour of Labour, as somehow being less acceptable in principle than pro-Conservative bias. Rather, this analysis suggests, although without proving, that the more plausible explanation of the small advantage accruing to the Conservative government from the distribution and effects of television bias lies in its loud and persistent campaign against the BBC. This campaign would seem to have primed many voters to see in BBC news broadcasts, but not ITN ones, an anti-government prejudice that in turn led them to compensate for it by becoming more supportive of its victim than they might otherwise have been. In this sense, consciously intended or not, it was a campaign that paid off for its instigator in terms of votes won.

Conclusion

This analysis has addressed the question of the electoral implications of bias in television news broadcasts. The picture that emerges is complex. In the first place, the fact that, as dictated by law, these broadcasts strenuously seek to show favour to no party does not mean that this is how they are always viewed by voters. In 1992, 30 per cent of Conservative, Labour and Liberal Democratic identifiers combined attributed a partisan prejudice to the BBC's *9 o' Clock News*. The matching figure for ITN's *News at Ten* was 20 per cent. Second, the relationship between television news and partisan bias is dynamic; neither channel is inevitably seen as favouring one party or the other. In the 1987 election, for example, one study concluded: 'On balance, people felt the bias on both channels favoured the Conservative Party and the Conservative Party alone' (Miller, 1991: 129). This observation continued to hold for ITN in 1992, the majority of those alleging bias on the BBC saw it as being left-wing and favouring Labour. Third, the perception of bias was uneven in its effects. Despite both channels being equally committed to norms of political impartiality and equal coverage, bias was more consequential for both issue preferences and leader evaluations on the one hand and the vote on the other among BBC than ITN viewers and among those seeing a pro-Labour bias in the BBC news than those seeing no bias at all or a pro-Conservative one.

The larger conclusion suggested by this analysis is that television does not have political characteristics and effects in and of itself. It makes little sense to assume that it is inconsequential for election outcomes just because it is bound by law to be impartial in its political coverage. Rather, it is a medium of communication that conveys information to voters and it is not to be forgotten that their reception of this information is to some extent determined by the mind sets they bring to the processing of this information. This is where politics enters the picture. The practitioners of this art can relate to television in one or both of two ways. They can seek to influence the content of the images and messages that reach the voting public through this medium and they can seek pre-emptively to shape the mind sets through which voters process campaign communications. The usual perspective on campaign communications is on the message conveyed by the media. Parties make use of press conferences, negative as opposed to positive advertising, highly sophisticated visual imagery, and the like to convince voters that their leader is competent and has integrity. Their opponents respond by attempting to convince voters otherwise. Perhaps the lesson of this article is that, especially when, as in Britain, the media are predominantly national in both political content and reach, an alternative, more parsimonious campaign strategy for the parties is to undermine the credibility not of the message, but of the messenger.

ACKNOWLEDGEMENT

I would like to thank Roger Scully for his comments and suggestions.

NOTES

1. The Conservative Party continued to accuse the BBC of such bias after the 1992 election. In January 1996, for example, the backbench Conservative parliamentary media committee 'grilled' the BBC's Director of Radio and TV News and Current Affairs over allegations of bias against the government. See the *Guardian*, 24 January 1996, p.9.
2. This observation excludes, of course, the substantial left-wing literature dealing with the role of media bias in supporting a capitalist social, economic and political order (for example, Miliband, 1969).
3. There is some evidence speaking to the question of partisan bias in news content. There may be some, but it does not seem to be great. Miller (1991: 129), for example, concludes tentatively of the 1987 election: 'Our content analysis of television during the election campaign seems to suggest that television was biased towards the right wing and, separately, towards the government of the day.'
4. Bias is measured in the 1992 British Election Study (BES), the weighted version of which provides the data used in this analysis, by a question asking which political party, if any, was 'favoured' by the particular news programme the respondent watched.
5. Television bias may also have a direct effect on the vote insofar as a BBC Labour viewer who comes to see an anti-Conservative bias in 'their' station's political programming may switch their vote to the Tories in protest. Under ideal conditions, this hypothesis could be tested using a panel study monitoring media perceptions and voting choice over two or more elections. Unfortunately, however, the 1987 wave of the 1987-92 BES panel did not ask the bias question of television news programmes. It might also be noted that this kind of conversion is unlikely since it does not even appear to be common even when voters move between highly and openly partisan newspapers (see Curtice and Semetko, 1994).
6. The analysis to follow is based on two BES questions, one asking how often (days per week) the respondent watched the news programme in question and the second whether the news programme favoured a political party. Since very few viewers of either BBC or ITN news (8 for the BBC and 11 for ITN) see a pro-Liberal Democratic bias in these programmes, they are excluded from further consideration in the analysis.
7. For stylistic reasons, the terms 'Conservative' and 'Tory' are used interchangeably in the text.
8. This figure is derived from cross-tabulating those Conservative, Labour and Liberal democratic identifiers who claim to see no favouritism in the BBC news, to see a pro-Conservative bias in it, or to see a pro-Labour bias with the same categories of responses for the ITN news. The total number of respondents in the table is 1,986; 1,654 of them claim to see some or no favouritism in both news programmes.
9. The very fact that ITN news is also seen as being biased by a non-trivial number of its viewers is a clear indication that there are other sources of the perception of bias than political party pronouncements. Long-standing prejudice independent of partisanship, discussion with friends and relatives and reading newspapers are examples that spring to mind. Being concerned more with the effects of bias, however, does not go beyond the Conservative propaganda campaign against the BBC in trying to understand its sources.
10. This is not an ideal measure of popular affect for the party leader because of its restricted variance. Much of its validity depends on the importance that individual respondents attach to these specific traits. It is conceivable, for example, that somebody might recognize a particular party leader as having all these traits but still not be very well disposed towards the leader because they consider other traits more important for a potential prime minister and that the party leader in question does not possess those. Thermometer scales are better suited to measuring this kind of overall effect, but they were not used in the 1992 BES.
11. Remember here that issue preferences ranged between a minimum of 0 and a maximum of

8, whereas the range for leader evaluations stretches only from 0–4. Thus, in any one group, the difference between scores for Major and Kinnock may be smaller in absolute terms than that for issue preferences, but could be greater in relative ones.

12. For comparability's sake, these control variables are the same as those in Curtice and Semetko (1994).

13. This is not to argue that the Tory advantage is altogether impervious to short-term forces. If the analysis is extended to include, in addition to issue preferences and leader evaluations, perceptions of change in individual and national living standards since the last general election, the effect of a pro-Labour bias recedes into insignificance. This finding strengthens my general argument that bias makes its effect felt through shaping viewers' interpretations of short-term campaign stimuli.

BIBLIOGRAPHY

Butler, David and Donald Stokes (1974) *Political Change in Britain*. (2nd edn) London: Macmillan.

Crewe, Ivor (1993) 'The Thatcher Legacy', in Anthony King (ed.) *Britain at the Polls 1992*. pp.1–28. Chatham, NJ: Chatham House.

Curtice, John and Holli Semetko (1994) 'Does It Matter What the Papers Say', in Anthony Heath, Roger Jowell and John Curtice with Bridget Taylor *Labour's Last Chance: The 1992 Election and Beyond*. pp.43–63. Aldershot: Dartmouth.

Harrop, Martin (1987) 'Voters', in Jean Seaton and Ben Pimlott (eds) *The Media in British Politics*. pp.45-63. Aldershot: Avebury.

Heath, Anthony, Roger Jowell, John Curtice, Geoff Evans, Julia Feld and Sharon Witherspoon (1991) *Understanding Political Change: The British Voter 1964–1987*. Oxford: Pergamon Press.

Iyengar, Shanto and Donald Kinder (1987) *News that Matters*. Chicago: University of Chicago Press.

Johnston, Richard, André Blais, Henry E. Brady and Jean Crête (1992) *Letting the People Decide*. Stanford, CA: Stanford University Press.

Kavanagh, Dennis (1995) *Election Campaigning: The New Marketing of Politics*. Oxford: Blackwell.

Miliband, Ralph (1969) *The State in Capitalist Society*. London: Weidenfeld & Nicolson.

Miller, William L. (1991) *Media and Voters*. Oxford: Clarendon Press.

Negrine, Ralph (1989) *Politics and the Mass Media in Britain*. London: Routledge.

Young, Hugo (1990) *One of Us. A Biography of Margaret Thatcher*. London: Pan Books.

Political Outcomes, Women's Legislative Rights and Devolution in Scotland

Bernadette C. Hayes and Ian McAllister

By any standards, the legislative representation of women is extremely low in Scotland (Brown, 1995, 1991; Brown and Galligan, 1993; Sharp, 1991). Even in the 1992 general election, which must be considered a significant improvement in relation to female political representation in Britain (Studlar and Welch, 1993), only five women (or 6.9 per cent of the Scottish total) were elected to represent Scottish constituencies at Westminster (see Table 1). Three of the women MPs were members of the Labour Party, one a Liberal Democrat, and one a Scottish Nationalist. This is in direct contrast to England, where 54 female members (or 10.3 per cent of the English total) were elected to the House of Commons, more among Labour (16.9 per cent) than among the Conservatives (6.3 per cent). Only in Wales is female electoral representation much lower than in Scotland; only one women (a Labour candidate), or 3.7 per cent of the Welsh total, was elected to the House of Commons in 1992. Despite these electoral successes, however, there has been comparatively little improvement in the representation of women during the post-war period (Levy, 1992).

A similar pattern emerges when the selection of women candidates is considered, as opposed to those who are actually elected. Fewer women were selected to stand for the House of Commons in both Scotland and Wales than in England. Furthermore, of the 64 selected Scottish women candidates, the vast majority were proposed by minor fringe parties (21 per cent) who won no seats, the Nationalists (21 per cent) who won only three seats, or the Liberal Democrats (29 per cent) who elected nine members to Westminster. This is in direct contrast to the Labour Party which, despite gaining 49 of the 72 parliamentary seats available, selected only six female candidates. Thus, as is also the case among Conservatives in England and Wales, it is the party which is the most likely to be elected which has the poorest record in relation to the number of women candidates fielded in Scotland.[1]

What accounts for this greater under-representation of women in Scotland? One explanation is that the question of female representation has been slow to emerge as a political issue in Scotland. Nationalism, rather than equal rights for women, has long dominated the Scottish political agenda. Even during the highly controversial and unsuccessful devolution referendum in 1979, the question of female legislative rights failed to emerge as a political issue (Lindsay, 1991; Breitenback, 1990). Although the question of women's representation did arise during the period of the Scottish Constitutional Convention in 1989, even then, there was little consensus on the reasons for their lack of achievement as well as corrective mechanisms to remedy the low levels of female political representation. In contrast to England and Wales, the question of women's representation in Scotland remains mediated within a highly contested and controversial constitutional framework (see Brown and Galligan, 1993).

TABLE 1
CANDIDATES AND MPs BY GENDER, PARTY AND REGION, 1992

	Scotland			Wales			England		
	Male	Female	(%)	Male	Female	(%)	Male	Female	(%)
(Candidates)									
Conservative	61	11	(15)	36	2	(5)	474	50	(10)
Labour	66	6	(8)	34	4	(11)	396	128	(24)
Lib-Dem	51	21	(29)	30	8	(21)	408	114	(22)
Nationalist	57	15	(21)	28	7	(20)	na	na	na
Other	42	11	(21)	25	6	(19)	572	185	(24)
Total	277	64	(19)	153	27	(15)	1850	477	(20)
(Members of Parliament)									
Conservative	11	0	(0)	6	0	(0)	299	20	(6)
Labour	46	3	(6)	26	1	(4)	162	33	(17)
Lib-Dem	8	1	(11)	1	0	(0)	9	1	(10)
Nationalist	2	1	(33)	4	0	(0)	na	na	na
Other	0	0	(0)	0	0	(0)	0	0	(0)
Total	67	5	(7)	37	1	(3)	470	54	(10)

Source: Brown and Galligan, 1993: 170; Norris and Lovenduski, 1993: 45–46; *Times Guide to the House of Commons*, April 1992.

To what extent, is this explanation for the lack of female representation in Scotland supported by the evidence? In other words, does attitudes towards constitutional change and electoral reform and not the political representation of women continue to divide the Scottish electorate? This article addresses this question, using survey data collected in Scotland immediately after the 1992 general election.

Constitutional Reform and Women's Political Rights in the 1992 Election

The question of independence and the lack of women's political representation have become two key and divisive issues among the Scottish political parties. This was particularly the case during the 1992 general election campaign, where not only did all the main political parties adopt a range of competing positions in relation to constitutional reform but this was also the case in terms of corrective strategies for the under-representation of women in politics. Women's representation as well as constitutional reform were heavily influenced both by party ideology and political pragmatism, as the differing positions of the main political parties on the question of Scottish nationalism and gender equality immediately prior to the 1992 election attests (see Brown and Galligan, 1993: 181–4).

In terms of both Scottish nationalism and gender equality, the Scottish Conservatives epitomized the party of the status quo. Not only did the Conservatives strenuously oppose electoral reform or any constitutional change which would have granted greater devolution to Scotland, but this was also the case when positive action for women was considered. Arguing that Scotland was an integral part of the United Kingdom and that all those who were qualified could aspire to elected office regardless of gender, no special concessions were made either in terms of electoral reform or in the representation of women. Thus, at least as far as Conservative policies were concerned, explanations for the lack of female representation rested with women themselves; it was women's own failure to come forward as candidates for election as well as their general political apathy which resulted in their lesser legislative representation.

The constitutional issue and the question of women's political participation, however, were two central issues discussed during Labour's 1992 election campaign. In contrast to the Conservatives, not only did the Scottish Labour Party advocate a separate Scottish parliament elected by a system of proportional representation, but it also introduced a series of specific measures to deal with the question of women's legislative rights. Arguing that the lack of female representation had its roots in a series of social and political barriers, Labour introduced the compulsory selection of at least one female candidate on all shortlists, the inclusion of a quota of 50 per cent representation for women at different levels of the party,[2] and the establishment of a Ministry for Women in any future Labour government.

Like the Scottish Labour Party, the Scottish Liberal Democrats also have a long-standing commitment to devolution and equal access for women in Scotland (see Grieve, 1991). In fact, since their foundation in 1988, the Scottish Liberal Democrats have systematically advocated devolution, or the establishment of a separate Scottish assembly, as the cornerstone of their constitutional agenda.[3] In contrast to Scottish Labour, however, the Scottish Liberal Democrats were initially opposed to quotas as a means of guaranteeing equal representation for women, despite being strong advocates of gender equality in legislative outcomes.[4] This position was justified on the grounds that quotas prevented freedom of choice for individual women, deprived voters of choice, and was essentially undemocratic and could lead to tokenism. Electoral reform – the single transferable vote plus additional member system – was proposed as the primary mechanism to redress unequal female representation. Although a compromise position was eventually reached, whereby Labour agreed to an additional member system of election to a future Scottish parliament and the Liberal Democrats to a statutory obligation on parties to select women candidates, support for the quota policy was only achieved as part of a negotiated settlement.[5]

In contrast to Scottish Liberal Democrats and Labour, the Scottish Nationalists have never been active on behalf of women. Since its foundation in 1934, constitutional reform has dominated the policies and agenda of the Scottish National Party (see Harvie, 1994; Brand, 1992; McCrone, 1992). In fact, not only is the SNP unique in its single-issue perspective, but this is also the case in relation to its current constitutional policies. Contrary to all other Scottish political parties, the SNP seeks an independent nation within the European Community. Unlike both Scottish Labour and the Liberal Democrats, not only do the nationalists seek an end to the union with England, but they also seek direct representation as a sovereign nation within Europe. As the current slogan of the SNP succinctly explains: 'Scotland's Future: Independence in Europe' (Macartney, 1990).

The SNP's emphasis on constitutional change is not to deny the importance it places on electoral reform. Concurrent with Labour and Liberal Democrat policies for Scotland, the Scottish Nationalist Party also supports the introduction of proportional representation through an additional vote combined with the additional member system. It is important to note, however, that while these reforms (combined with a quota system) are considered key mechanisms to redress gender imbalances in legislative outcomes for the Liberal Democrats and Scottish Labour, for nationalists any efforts to increase female participation is not a major issue. The priorities of the party remain independence and electoral reform, through which, it is assumed, the women's representation issue will eventually be resolved; at best, the question of gender equality remains on the fringe of their political agenda (Brown and Galligan, 1993).

Constitutional reform and female legislative rights have therefore become two of the most controversial issues in Scottish society. This was particularly the case during the 1992 general election when not only did significant party differences emerge on both these issues, but also on the means by which they could be resolved. The Conservatives adamantly rejected any change to the constitutional position of Scotland, while all of the other main political parties strongly endorsed such an initiative either in terms of a devolved assembly within the United Kingdom (Labour and Liberal Democrats), or as an independent parliament in Europe (SNP).

A different division occurred in relation to the legislative position of women. The Conservatives showed little concern and no policy initiatives to redress the absence of women in elected office and the SNP was equally unconcerned about the issue. By contrast, the Scottish Labour Party and the Liberal Democrats both placed the question of women's political rights centre-stage in their election campaign, and proposed a series of radical reforms to remedy the perceived structural barriers to female opportunity. To what extent did these differing party responses affect electoral outcomes or party choice in Scotland? Did the priority placed on both the constitutional and female representation issues by Labour mirror the views of the general public at large? Or was the single-issue, exclusively constitutional response of the SNP more likely to attract more support than their leading competitors? We address these questions in the remainder of the article using the Scottish sample of the 1992 British Election Study.

Data and Methods

Data

The data are the 1992 British Election Study (n=3,534), which was a random sample of the British electorate conducted between April and July 1992, yielding a response rate of 73 per cent. The analyses conducted herein are restricted to the 950 respondents who formed the Scottish 'booster' sample (see Taylor *et al.*, 1994, Appendix). The survey contained a number of statements on attitudes towards Scottish independence and competing explanations for the lack of political representation among women; these data provide a unique opportunity to assess party differences in relation to these issues, as well as their consequences for electoral outcomes.

Questions

As noted above, the political parties differ in their explanations for the lack of female political representation in Scotland. Thus, while the Conservatives stress personalized factors such as the lack of self-selection by female candidates or political apathy among women generally, Labour and the Liberal Democrats identify political and social barriers to female legislative opportunity in Scotland. In fact, it was this perceived recognition of discriminatory practices by party organizations and selection committees that initiated current Labour policies on quotas for female candidates. To examine this issue, attitudes toward women's political rights were measured by six questions, five dealing with competing explanations for the under-representation of women in parliament and one with policies to promote equal opportunities for women in society.

On the under-representation of women, the respondents were asked to give their opinion on five statements: 'Women don't come forward as candidates'; 'Women lose votes'; 'Women are not given the opportunities by political parties'; 'Women are not suited to the job of MP'; and 'Women are not interested in politics'. For each question the response categories were strongly agree, agree, neither agree nor disagree, disagree, and strongly disagree. Attitudes towards the promotion of opportunities for women were measured by the question: 'How about attempts to give equal opportunities to women in Britain?' The response categories were: 'gone much too far', 'gone too far', 'about right', 'not gone far enough', and 'not gone nearly far enough'.

Attitudes towards Scottish nationalism were assessed by four questions, two dealing with the advantages of an independent Scottish assembly, one with electoral reform, and one with changes to the constitutional position of Scotland. On an independent Scottish assembly, respondents were asked to indicate their views on two questions: 'Would independence make Scotland better off than now, worse off, or would it make no difference?'; and 'Would independence for Scotland make you personally better off than now, worse off than now, or would it make no difference?' Attitudes towards electoral reform were based on a single question: 'Britain should introduce proportional representation so that the number of MPs each party gets matches more closely the number of votes each party gets.' The response categories were: 'strongly agree', 'agree', 'neither agree nor disagree', 'disagree', 'strongly disagree'.

Finally, change to the constitutional position of Scotland was measured by the statement: 'An issue in Scotland is the question of an elected Assembly – a special parliament for Scotland dealing with Scottish affairs. Which of these statements come closest to your view: Scotland should become independent, separate from the UK and the European Community?; Scotland should become independent, separate from the UK but part of the European Community?; Scotland should remain part of the UK but with its own elected Assembly that should have some taxation and spending power?; There should be no change from the present system?'

Public Opinion on Women and the Constitution

The question of independence and the lack of women's political representation have become two key and divisive issues among the Scottish political parties. To what extent are these party differences reflected in the beliefs held by the Scottish electorate? Tables 2 and 3 address this question. Although there is some support for the Conservative view that part of the explanation for the lack of female political representation can be traced to women choosing not to stand – 50 per cent agreed with this view – there is little support for the accompanying view that the explanation rests with a lack of political interest among women – 80 per cent reject this view. There is equally little support for the view that women candidates lose votes, or that women are unsuitable to be MPs. Overall, Scottish voters are more likely to blame the political parties for the under-representation of women; 59 per cent agree that it is 'lack of opportunities by political parties' that has created the problem.

Scottish voters are equally clear in their opinions about constitutional change. A narrow majority, 51 per cent, support devolution, which is about twice the proportion who favour either independence (24 per cent) or the status quo (25 per cent), and a slightly larger majority, 60 per cent, support the introduction of a PR electoral system. In line with the comparatively small group who support independence, 47 per cent believe that Scotland would be worse off under independence, while 56 per cent consider that it would leave their own situation unchanged. As a wide range of other research has found, Scottish independence is the least popular of the major constitutional options facing Scotland (Brand, 1992), although there is widespread support for the introduction of a PR electoral system.

TABLE 2
ATTITUDES TOWARDS THE POLITICAL REPRESENTATION OF WOMEN IN SCOTLAND (%)

Agree	Neutral	Disagree	Total	(N)
Lack of candidate self-selection				
50	25	25	100	(850)
Lose votes				
18	22	60	100	(845)
Not suitable as MPs				
6	12	82	100	(856)
Uninterested in politics				
8	12	82	100	(852)
Lack of opportunities by political parties				
59	19	22	100	(844)
Promotion of female equality in Britain				
60	36	4	100	(935)

Source: Scottish Election Survey, 1992

TABLE 3
ATTITUDES TOWARDS CONSTITUTIONAL REFORM AND SCOTTISH INDEPENDENCE (%)

Constitutional reform		Introduction of proportional representation	
Independence	24	Agree	60
Devolution	51	Neutral	20
No change	25	Disagree	20
Total	100	Total	100
(N)	(924)	(N)	(875)

Independence advantageous for Scotland		Independence advantageous for you	
Better off	34	Better off	15
No difference	19	No difference	56
Worse off	47	Worse off	29
Total	100	Total	100
(N)	(868)	(N)	(844)

Source: Scottish Election Survey, 1992.

The extent of differences in these opinions among voters is shown in Table 4. As we would expect, the constitutional issues generate the largest divisions between voters of the four major Scottish parties, as reflected in attitudes towards independence and whether or not independence would benefit Scotland as a whole. Not surprisingly, SNP voters are most supportive of independence, with Conservative voters being most opposed; however, it is notable that there is also substantial support for independence among Labour voters, more so than is found among Liberal Democrats. By contrast, the issue of PR creates fewer divisions, at least among supporters of the non-Conservative parties. In comparison with the constitutional issues, voter differences on the issue of women's political representation are negligible. What differences exist are concerned mainly with the issue of female equality, with supporters of the non-Conservative parties believing that it has not gone far enough.

In summary, then, although the issues of independence and the lack of women's political representation have become two key and divisive issues among the political parties, this is not the case among the Scottish electorate as a whole. As a group, Scottish voters, hold similar, though moderate, views in relation to the question of women's rights as well as electoral reform in Scotland. In other words, irrespective of party preferences, not only do the majority of Scots tend to blame women and parties for the lack of female representation, but a clear majority also support the introduction of proportional representation. Even in the case of major political differences among voters, such as constitutional reform, only a small minority of the population supports this position.

TABLE 4
VOTING, WOMEN'S POLITICAL REPRESENTATION AND SCOTTISH INDEPENDENCE

	Con	(Means, zero to 10) Lab	Lib- Dem	SNP	(F-ratio)
Women's political representation					
Self-selection as candidate	3.9	4.2	4.4	4.5	(1.85)
Not lose votes	6.2	6.0	6.8	6.5	(2.86*)
Suitable as MPs	7.3	7.7	7.5	7.8	(1.39)
Interested in politics	7.3	7.5	7.8	7.4	(0.83)
Lack of opportunities by parties	5.7	6.3	6.3	6.5	(2.82*)
Promotion of female equality	6.1	6.8	6.7	6.8	(8.63*)
Scottish independence					
Support Scottish independence	1.6	3.7	2.9	5.6	(101.25*)
Support PR	4.8	6.4	7.9	7.4	(46.67*)
Independence better for Scotland	1.4	4.7	2.4	8.1	(108.65*)
Independence better for you	2.6	4.6	3.1	6.0	(40.48*)

* statistically significant at the 0.05 level.

Source: Scottish Election Survey, 1992.

A similar pattern is echoed in relation to the rest of Great Britain. Regardless of whether England or Wales is considered, constitutional differences again emerged as the major source of division although among only a minority of voters, with Liberal Democrat voters being most supportive of independence, and the Conservatives most opposed. Although the issue of PR created fewer divisions, Conservative supporters still rank well below the other two main political parties in their support for this issue. In contrast to Scotland, voter differences in relation to women's rights did emerge as a distinguishing political issue, at least as far as England is concerned.[6] As a group, not only do Conservative English voters hold women themselves overwhelmingly responsible for their lack of representation in politics, but there is some evidence to suggest that this is even more the case among their Labour colleagues. In other words, contrary to Labour voters in Scotland, it is both the perceived characteristics of women themselves (their believed greater unattractiveness to voters, lesser suitability as MPs, and lack of political interest) as well as their lack of political opportunities which distinguishes Labour voters from Conservative voters in England.

The Electoral Impact

It remains to examine the influence of attitudes towards women's political representation and Scottish independence on the vote, net of a wide variety of other factors. Table 5 presents the results of a multinomial logistic regression analysis, which shows the influence of these attitudes on the 1992 vote.[7] Since the bivariate analyses demonstrated that Conservative voters were the group most distant from supporters of the other three parties, they are used as the basis for the contrast. A wide range of socio-demographic control variables are included.[8] The figures in each equation are the parameter estimates, while the standard error for each estimate is shown in parentheses. These parameter estimates are the logistic regression coefficients for the effects of the independent variables and are expressed on a log odds scale. The coefficients may be used to determine the direction of the effects of the independent variables, and the magnitude may be assessed by converting these coefficients into conditional odds ratios by taking the natural antilogarithm of each coefficient.

Once again, attitudes towards Scottish independence provide the most substantial influences on the vote. Labour, Liberal Democrat and SNP voters all differ from Conservative voters in their greater support for independence. For example, whereas SNP voters are 376 times more likely to support Scottish independence than Conservative voters (the exponential of 5.93), Labour voters are about 86 times more likely to do so.[9] A similar, though less consistent, pattern is echoed in relation to proportional representation. That is to say, although there are no notable differences between Conservative and Labour voters on this issue, both Liberal Democrat and SNP voters are significantly more supportive of PR than their Conservative colleagues. More specifically, whereas Liberal Democrat voters are approximately 65 times more likely to support the introduction of PR than Conservative voters (the exponential of 4.17), SNP voters are about seven times more likely to do so. Finally, only among SNP supporters is independence seen of benefit to Scotland, and there are no notable voting differences among the parties when the effect of independence on personal circumstances is considered.

TABLE 5
VOTE AND POLITICAL ATTITUDES (MULTINOMIAL LOGISTIC REGRESSION ESTIMATES)

Variables	Lab vs Cons		Lib-Dem vs Cons		SNP vs Cons	
	Est	(SE)	Est	(SE)	Est	(SE)
Socio-demographic controls						
Gender (male)	0.95*	(0.38)	1.48**	(0.50)	0.83	(0.44)
Marital status (married)	0.08	(0.38)	-0.17	(0.50)	-0.05	(0.45)
Ethnicity (Scottish)	0.78*	(0.35)	-0.10	(0.48)	1.15*	(0.45)
Age (years)	-0.02	(0.01)	0.01	(0.02)	-0.02	(0.02)
Religion (catholic)	2.51**	(0.75)	1.28	(0.93)	1.65*	(0.83)
Church attendance (attends)	-0.29	(0.47)	-0.56	(0.65)	0.29	(0.54)
Education:						
Tertiary	-0.36	(0.41)	1.04	(0.63)	0.28	(0.49)
Secondary	0.02	(0.50)	0.71	(0.77)	-0.36	(0.60)
No qualifications	–		–		–	
Housing occupancy (owner)	-0.92*	(0.39)	-1.18*	(0.54)	-0.68	(0.44)
Union membership (member)	0.93*	(0.40)	-0.38	(0.55)	0.70	(0.45)
Subjective class (middle)	-1.08**	(0.42)	-0.19	(0.52)	-1.52**	(0.49)
Employment sector (public)	0.85*	(0.36)	0.57	(0.53)	0.28	(0.43)
Occupation status (non-man)	-0.43	(0.38)	0.17	(0.53)	0.01	(0.45)
Employment status (labour active)	-0.73	(0.47)	1.25	(0.70)	0.24	(0.57)
Women's political representation						
Lack of female opportunities	1.02	(1.01)	3.35*	(1.45)	1.74	(1.17)
Support women in politics	2.48*	(1.10)	3.13*	(1.58)	1.96	(1.25)
Scottish independence						
Pro-Scottish independence	4.46**	(0.94)	4.04**	(1.23)	5.93**	(1.04)
Pro-PR	0.92	(0.64)	4.17**	(0.96)	1.96*	(0.76)
Independence better for Scot.	0.28	(0.52)	-0.49	(0.72)	2.12**	(0.58)
Independence better for you	0.44	(0.66)	-0.96	(0.89)	0.49	(0.75)
Constant	-2.70		-9.84**		-6.73***	
% of cases correctly predicted	63.49					
N of cases	430					

** statistically significant at the 0.01 level; * 0.05 level.; standard errors are in parentheses
Source: Scottish Election Survey, 1992

In contrast to the constitutional issue, there are only minor party variations in views of women's political representation, and these are significant only for the three Britain-wide parties, not the SNP. Whereas Liberal Democrat voters are approximately 23 times more likely to support women in politics than their Conservative counterparts (the exponential of 3.13), the equivalent conditional odds among Labour voters is 2.48, or 12 times that of the Conservatives. Furthermore, only for one group of voters is there any significant differences between Conservative voters and supporters of the other three political parties in relation to the responsibility of parties for the lack of female representation. Here, it is Liberal Democrat voters who are approximately 29 times more likely than Conservatives to stress this interpretation for the lack of female political representation in Scotland (exponential of 3.35). These results, then, largely confirm the pre-eminent role of the constitution in party voting, and confirm the results of the bivariate analyses, even after a wide range of other socio-economic factors have been taken into account.

Conclusion

Over the last ten years, the political representation of women has emerged as a key issue in Scottish politics. Nearly all the main political parties have now adopted a series of electoral strategies to encourage the promotion of female candidates and greater gender equality in legislative outcomes, a change that is particularly notable in relation to the Scottish Labour Party and the Scottish Liberal Democrats. Despite the best efforts of the political elites, however, the constitutional issue still overshadows the question of female representation in Scotland. It is attitudes towards constitution change and electoral reform, not concerns about the legislative rights of women, which continues to determine electoral support within the society. In contrast to the primacy of the constitutional issue, for the vast majority of the Scottish public the question of women's representation still remains, at best, on the fringe of their voting agendas.

Why does women's representation not have a larger influence on the vote? After all, the issue was widely discussed in Scotland among the political parties during the 1992 election campaign and before, and it is linked to constitutional change. One explanation is that while the issue is salient at the elite level, it has yet to be fully articulated among the mass electorate. Voters are only gradually becoming aware of the issue, mainly through Labour's introduction of quotas; after the next general election, we might expect to find more popular awareness of women's representation. A second, related, explanation is that two of the four Scottish parties – the Conservatives and the SNP – have not addressed the issue directly. While the Conservatives' electoral position in Scotland is fragile, they are the governing party at Westminster, and exercise considerable influence in setting the political agenda. Finally, Scottish political culture is likely to play a role in suppressing debate: since the late 1960s the constitutional question has been paramount, and has eclipsed all other issues, with the possible exception of the poll tax during the 1980s.

This is not to deny the potential importance of this issue in the future. In this article we have shown that there is general popular support in Scotland for the increased representation of women and that a majority of voters tend to blame the political parties for the paucity of women in political life. Although the issue has not generated the party political divisions that have marked the constitutional question, and it did not contribute significantly to the 1992 election outcome in Scotland, women's representation has considerable electoral potential in the future. Unique in the UK, the prospect of devolution creates opportunities to redress the legislative under-representation of women, through establishing institutional procedures and practices which would ensure fair and equal representation. What is the likelihood that the significant expectations this debate has raised will be fulfilled?

If the issue of women's political representation is to form a significant part of the discussions about the institutional form of Scottish devolution, three conditions need to be met. The first is that the issue of women's representation has to be linked to the constitutional question. There has to be an awareness that devolution provides an unprecedented opportunity to deal with fundamental political problems. Although this has happened with the Labour Party political elite, and to a lesser extent among the Liberal Democrats, it is not a view shared by either the SNP or the Conservatives. Second, there has to be concerted, informed discussion of the issue within the elite. Third, if elite discussion takes place, then this has to be translated into a popular awareness of the issues that are involved, and the alternatives that exist. Only when these three conditions are met are we likely to see any serious institutional attempt to remedy the legislative under-representation of women in Scotland.

ACKNOWLEDGEMENTS

The data used in this article are from the 1992 British Election Study, which was collected by Anthony Heath, Roger Jowell, John Curtice, Jack Brand and James Mitchell and funded by the Economic and Social Research Council. The data were made available by the ESRC Data Archive at the University of Essex. An earlier version of this paper was presented at the Elections, Public Opinion and Parties conference, London, September 1995. Our thanks to members of the group, and to David Farrell, for their comments on an earlier draft. The usual disclaimer applies.

NOTES

1. The situation at other levels of government is broadly similar. Although women do somewhat better in local government, female representation still significantly lags behind that of their male colleagues. For example, only 251 women were elected as Councillors (22.0 per cent) in the 1992 Scottish district elections, and the equivalent figure for the earlier 1990 regional council elections was even lower at only 16.2 per cent (see Brown and Galligan, 1993).
2. As compared to 40 per cent in England and Wales (see Norris and Lovenduski, 1993:52).
3. The Scottish Liberal Democratic Party is the product of a merger between the Scottish Liberal Party and the Social Democratic Party.
4. This is in contrast to Liberal Democrats in England and Wales, where compulsory short-listing of female candidates dates back to the mid-1980s (Studlar *et al.*, 1988). In fact, during the 1987 British election, the SDP was the only political party which specified the short-listing of female candidates.
5. The opposition of the Liberal Democrats to quotas was evident throughout the period of the Scottish Constitutional Convention. Liberal Democrats were suspicious of Labour's support

for the 50:50 quota option on the grounds that it could be used as a means of side-stepping electoral reform, which the Democrats have always regarded as central to any fundamental constitutional change.

6. Contrary to the results in England, no voter differences emerged in relation to the issue of women's political representation in Wales.

7. Contrary to our immediately previous results in Table 4, for these analyses, the six items measuring attitudes towards women's political participation have been summed into the following two composite variables: (a) lack of female opportunities (measured in terms of the lack of opportunities by political parties plus the promotion of female equality); and (b) support for women in politics (measured in terms of self-selection as candidates, not lose votes, suitable as MPs, and political interest).

8. The socio-demographic control variables are: gender (coded 1 for male and 0 for female), marital status (coded 1 for married and 0 for other), ethnicity (coded 1 for Scottish and 0 for other), age (measured in number of years), religious affiliation (coded 1 for Catholic and 0 for other), church attendance (a six point scale ranging from 0 for never attended to 1 for attends every day), education (a three-category dummy variable distinguishing between degree-holders or the professionally qualified and secondary school graduates versus the unqualified as the omitted category of comparison), housing occupancy (coded 1 for house ownership versus 0 for other), union membership (coded 1 for members and 0 for non-members), subjective class (coded 1 for middle class and 0 for working class), employment sector (coded 1 for public versus 0 for private or self-employed), occupational status (coded 1 for nonmanual versus 0 for manual), and employment status (coded 1 for labour active versus 0 for other).

9. It is important to note, however, this dramatic division between Conservative and SNP voters in relation to this issue may be explained by the overwhelming tendency of SNP voter to also endorse either devolution or independence in Scotland. For example, of the 190 individuals (or 19 per cent of the total sample) who voted for the SNP in the 1992 election, over 90 per cent, also supported either the introduction of a separate assembly (38.4) or complete independence for Scotland (56.8). Thus, for Scotland at least, support for its nationalist party is, in effect, almost tantamount to a vote for either a devolved assembly or independence for Scotland.

BIBLIOGRAPHY

Brand, Jack (1992) 'SNP Members: The Way of the Faithful', in Pippa Norris, Ivor Crewe, David Denver and David Broughton (eds) *British Elections and Parties Yearbook 1992*, pp.79–91. Hemel Hempstead: Harvester Wheatsheaf.

Breitenback, Esther (1990) 'Sisters are Doing it for Themselves. The Women's Movement In Scotland', in Alice Brown and Richard Parry (eds) *The Scottish Government Yearbook 1990*, pp.209–25. Edinburgh: Unit for the Study of Government in Scotland.

Brown, Alice (1995) 'Legislative Recruitment in Scotland: The Implications for Women of a New Parliament', Paper delivered at the ECPR Joint Workshops, Bordeaux, 27 April–2 May.

Brown, Alice (ed.) (1991) *Women in Scottish Politics*. Edinburgh: Unit for the Study of Government in Scotland.

Brown, Alice and Yvonne Galligan (1993) 'Views from the Periphery: Changing the Political Agenda for Women in the Republic of Ireland and in Scotland', *West European Politics* 16: 165–89.

Grieve, Sandra (1991) 'Women in the Scottish Liberal Democrats', in *A Woman's Claim of Right in Scotland*, pp.60–65. Edinburgh: Polygon.

Harvie, Christopher (1994) *Scotland and Nationalism*. London: Routledge.

Levy, Catriona (1992) 'A Woman's Place? The Future Scottish Parliament', in Lindsay Paterson and David McCrone (eds) *The Scottish Government Yearbook 1992*, pp.59–73. Edinburgh: Unit for the Study of Government in Scotland.

Lindsay, Isobel (1991) 'Constitutional Change and the Gender Deficit', in *A Woman's Claim Of Right In Scotland*, pp.7–13. Edinburgh: Polygon.

Macartney, Allan (1990) 'Independence in Europe', in Alice Brown and Richard Parry (eds) *The*

Scottish Government Yearbook 1990, pp.35–48. Edinburgh: Unit for the Study of Government in Scotland.

McCrone, David (1992) *Understanding Scotland*. London: Routledge.

Norris, Pippa and Joni Lovenduski (1993) 'Gender and Party Politics in Britain', in Joni Lovenduski and Pippa Norris (eds) *Gender and Party Politics*, pp.35–59. London: Sage.

Sharp, Carol (1991) 'Women Councillors.' in *A Woman's Claim of Right in Scotland*, pp.34–46. Edinburgh: Polygon.

Studlar, Donley T. and Susan Welch (1993) 'A Giant Step for Womankind? Women Candidates and the 1992 General Election', In David Denver, Pippa Norris, David Broughton and Colin Rallings (eds) *British Elections and Parties Yearbook 1993*, pp.216–28. Hemel Hempstead: Harvester Wheatsheaf.

Studlar, Donley T., Ian McAllister and Alvaro Ascui (1988) 'Electing Women to the British Commons: Breakout from The Beleaguered Beachhead?', *Legislative Studies Quarterly* 13: 515–28.

Taylor, Bridget, Lindsay Brook and Gillian Prior (1994) 'The 1992 Cross-Section and Panel Surveys', in Anthony Heath, Roger Jowell, and John Curtice, with Bridget Taylor (eds) *Labour's Last Chance? The 1992 Election and Beyond*, pp.301–8. Aldershot: Dartmouth.

'The Death of the Past': Symbolic Politics and the Changing of Clause IV

Tim Bale

Introduction

Tony Blair's successful attempt to change Clause IV of the Labour Party's constitution is testimony to the important role that symbols and symbolism still play in modern party politics. Yet they are not something into which most academic analysts of politics tend to delve too deeply. Possibly such reluctance owes something to the widespread assumption that symbols and symbolism operate at a level which, if not unconscious, are at least subliminal, impacting on the visceral or the emotional rather than the intellectual. It may also have something to do with the fact that when the notion of a symbol is subjected to closer scrutiny it becomes highly – almost off-puttingly – problematic: even finding a commonly agreed definition, for instance, is difficult.[1] Of course none of this would matter if we could omit all consideration of symbols from our work, be it on parties or other aspects of politics. The problem is we cannot. On the one hand, like all good social scientists, we shy away from anything which smacks of the metaphysical: symbols are after all literally insubstantial, floating above and perhaps disguising what most of us are content to think of as reality. On the other, we are loath to dismiss something which, after a moment's reflection, we realize plays a part in so many aspects of our lives. Consequently, if most of us have been reluctant to thoroughly explore the topic in our work, we find it impossible to ignore altogether – not a particularly happy or informative combination.

Our dilemma is not a recent one. Indeed it was well summed up over seventy years ago by the Cambridge philosopher A. N. Whitehead:

> The attitude of mankind towards symbolism exhibits an unstable mixture of attraction and repulsion....Hard headed men want facts and not symbols. A clear theoretic intellect, with its generous enthusiasm for the exact truth at all costs and hazards, pushes aside symbols as make-believes, veiling and distorting that inner sanctuary of simple truth which reason claims as its own....There is, however, a Latin proverb....In English, it reads thus: Nature, expelled with a pitchfork, ever returns. This proverb is exemplified by the history of symbolism. However you

may endeavour to expel it, it ever returns. Symbolism is no mere idle fancy or corrupt degradation: it is inherent in the very texture of human life... (Whitehead, 1928: 71–4; see also Cohen, 1974)

This being so, political scientists need to be more systematic in their approach (see Elder and Cobb, 1983). Brief asides accompanied by a ritualistic reference to the one book on the subject everybody has heard of, Murray Edelman's *The Symbolic Uses of Politics*, are not enough. True, a handful of political scientists interested in British government and party politics are beginning to go beyond this (see Dunleavy, 1995), while those involved in the study of manifestos and in the emerging sub field of 'political marketing' are especially likely to recognize the importance of symbols in party images. For the latter, however, the focus is likely to be limited to their role in selling the party. But what about the role of symbols in the internal life as well as the external image of the party? If we really want to get inside parties (see Mair, 1983) we also need, despite the difficulties, to 'get into' symbols more thoroughly than we have yet done. In any case, these difficulties can be easily overstated: there are a number of mapped routes already available. These are pursued in more detail throughout the article and, for the purpose of illustration, applied to a consideration of earlier and more recent arguments over Clause IV. However, an overview at the outset may be useful.

Four Possible Routes

Broadly speaking, there are four ways we might profitably think about the role of symbols and symbolism when it comes to political parties: they can be conveniently labelled *instrumental, functional, interpretative and new institutional*. The first route, the instrumental, concentrates on the way leaders who lack the capacity to deliver more material incentives use symbols to get what they want out of followers. The second route, the functional, argues that to see symbols merely as one small and possibly shady part of an exchange relationship between leaders and led is too limiting: symbols, and culture in general, are a far more important facet of political life than they are generally given credit for, and acting upon them represents a profound attempt to shape the identity and destiny of any organization. The third route, the interpretative, goes further still: since symbols are an inevitable and ubiquitous feature of all social practice, it is argued, it cannot be useful to maintain a distinction between what is 'substantial' and what is 'symbolic' or to focus, for example, on how the latter may be manipulated to attain the former. The fourth route, the new institutional, seeks to hold on to this heightened sensitivity to the inherently symbolic nature of social practice, but refuses to abandon the notion that actors are able to turn that fact to their advantage. None of these routes is a complete blind alley; but if each approach is applied in turn (see Dunleavy, 1995) to the same case study – past and recent debates over changing Clause IV of the Labour Party's constitution – we may find some more useful than others.

The first three routes are not without their merits, but they also have their drawbacks. Seeing attempts to change Clause IV in instrumental terms is not unhelpful: it concentrates the analyst's mind on the potential trade-off that, arguably, all party leaders face between room to manoeuvre and committed support. On the other hand it relies on possibly unsustainable distinctions, first, between what is symbolic and what is substantial and, second, between leaders as sophisticated symbol manipulators and followers as consumers irrationally attached to what they know and love. Though the second route, which emphasizes the functionality of certain symbols within a party's culture, raises the profile of the symbolic aspect of political action, it is not altogether clear that it entirely escapes the same dubious distinctions. Thus it makes it easy to appreciate why a party leader anxious for change might in theory be well-advised to act in the symbolic mode (that is, on Clause IV), but difficult to understand why in practice his followers might go along with him. The third route also has its merits, but is ultimately even more problematic: it forces us to think creatively about the symbolic resonance of everything to everybody in the party – leader as well as led; however, it also makes it difficult not only to justify focusing on one particular symbol (like Clause IV), but also to pursue answers to the cause and effect questions that many of us still think are worth asking.

The fourth route is the most promising because it continues to ask the cause and effect questions of the first two routes but admits that some of the answers to them may be found in the realm of the third. Routes one and two would probably proceed by a) acknowledging the importance of symbols to a greater or lesser degree, b) identifying one – Clause IV – as particularly significant to the membership but politically problematic for the leadership and then c) going on to show how by very material means (backstage manoeuvres, agenda and media manipulation, etc.) its transformation was achieved in 1994–5, but not in 1959–60. Route four, however, aims at a richer account of the motivations of the leadership and the reactions of its followers. It locates Blair's recent success not in the fact that he was necessarily cleverer than Gaitskell, nor in the fact that party members under Blair were more desperate for victory than their predecessors. Instead it explores the extent to which both leader and led were enabled by their shared symbolic understanding of a range of social developments to demand and welcome change. Before undertaking such an exploration, however, it is useful, indeed necessary, to travel the other available routes.

The Prevailing Trend to Instrumentalism

Despite Whitehead's warning plea, it may well be the case that most analysts of British party politics, even if they drop the 'idle', still see symbols as essentially an exercise in masquerade (though see Mount, 1972). If one's interest lies primarily in government then it is perhaps all too easy to fall prey to the idea that, if indeed symbols are important, then such importance rests in their ability to hide or at least facilitate what is 'really' going on. After all the traditional task of the analyst in this field, as conceived for example by pioneers like Marx and Bagehot, is to penetrate beyond what is more or less *dignified* to what is actually *efficient*, 'to pry behind the facade and observe the technique of power' (Crossman, 1963: 38). Little wonder, then, that symbols – for example the 'popular capitalism' that glossed the sell-offs and de-regulation of the 1980s – are seen as the ultimately empty words of what Vance Packard famously called the 'symbol manipulators', those who exploit the rest of us who are 'bundles of day dreams, misty hidden yearnings, guilt complexes, irrational emotional blockages...image lovers given to impulsive and compulsive acts' (Packard, 1957: 7).

Unfortunately this tendency to view symbols instrumentally – as manipulative means to ultimately material ends – can be reinforced by references to probably the first and best-known work in political science on the subject, Murray Edelman's *The Symbolic Uses of Politics*. In fact, as we shall see, the book is more complex than many give it credit for; but it is all too easily read as an exposé of how organized pressure groups and wire-pulling politicians can exploit the irrationality to which the public (though not they themselves) are supposedly so prone.

The idea that symbols do matter, but that they are interesting mainly because they are useful to those clever enough to use them, arguably dominates the way they are treated in theoretically informed studies of British political parties. It dovetails especially neatly, for instance, with recent attempts to improve upon the arguably narrow materialism of the rational choice approach to politics in general and parties in particular, proving particularly relevant for those seeking to explore how leaderships strive to reconcile their need, on the one hand, for active party members and, on the other, their room for manoeuvre. Alan Ware (1992: 79), for instance, has argued that British party leaders, denied sufficient opportunity to provide purposive or material incentives to supporters by the characteristics of the political culture in which they operate, have always stressed 'shared symbols and values'. These symbols need to be 'expressive' enough to inspire what are often *affectively* motivated memberships (see Seyd and Whiteley, 1992; Whiteley *et al.*, 1994), but at the same time sufficiently nebulous to afford flexibility to their leaders. Symbols have thus become incorporated into a larger attempt – typified perhaps by Dunleavy (1991) – not to break completely from economic approaches, but to enhance their already considerable explanatory power by rounding or fleshing them out.

Seeing symbols as something strong enough to enlist membership support, yet vague enough to minimize the constraints or grounds for criticism that more specific or concrete promises might entail, also fits in well with what many possibly less objective analysts have been saying about the British Labour Party over the last thirty years or so. True, back in the mid-1960s John Saville (1967: 44) temporarily turned aside from one of his tirades to muse briefly upon the fact that '[m]yths and illusions form an interesting and often extraordinary part of the political behaviour of many individuals who make up the labour movement.'[2] But further exploration of the subject by the critics of Labourism seems to have been strangled at birth by partisan distrust. To those most censorious of the party, its symbols have remained objects of derision and suspicion in equal measure – not least perhaps because their supposed manipulation was a technique especially associated with a leader whose poor reputation, until recent rehabilitation, assumed almost Nixonian proportions. The ultimate failure of that leader, Harold Wilson, to live up to his rhetorical promise, in other words, served to encourage a pre-existing tendency to treat symbols as if they were somehow unreal, part of a trick played on the anonymously heroic rank and file by leaders programmed or predestined to repeat a history of betrayal.[3]

Wilson, of course, is best remembered by popular commentators for his lashing together of science and socialism – a move which supposedly differentiated Labour from its own past, as well as from Douglas-Home's grouse-moor Toryism, in order to attract the frustrated meritocrats of middle Britain into the socialist fold. Often remarked on too is his stance in the first attempt to change Clause IV by Hugh Gaitskell in 1959. To Wilson, and many others, this was simply not a debate worth having: if Clause IV was what the party wanted, then so be it; it was, after all, only 'theology' – neither a great concern to the electorate, nor a specific commitment which any future Labour government would be pledged to or judged on. In so saying, Wilson was in effect both confirming the suspicions of the *Milibandetti* and conforming to the models with which political scientists interested in parties tend to operate when it comes to symbols.

But if this instrumental model explains Wilson's position and Clause IV's function perfectly, can it really shed much light on the motives of those in the party who have attempted to do away with Labour's chief symbol of its class-based socialism (Drucker, 1979: 38)? Surely, such attempts are irrational? If activists are – to borrow a phrase from Robert Goodin (1977) – 'being bought off cheaply' by an emotionally appealing symbol at little demonstrable cost in terms of inescapable policy commitments or direct electoral damage, why bother to change things? This is an even tougher question for the analyst who is habitually critical of Labour leaders – any such overt attack on the party's 'ark of the covenant' (see Williams, 1982: 333), after all, challenges the premise that the entire bunch are duplicitous promisers of the earth who will deliver nothing like it when helped into office by those whom they have duped.

This perhaps explains the confusion evident in many historical accounts of Gaitskell's first failed attempt at change.[4] David Howell, for example, in what is otherwise one of the most lucid and shrewd political science histories of the party, ties himself up in knots on the issue. His general awareness of the importance of party symbols is obvious throughout his text, but it always exists alongside a suspicion that they are essentially a means of fooling the faithful – a doublethink exposed most glaringly in his account of the Clause IV debate in 1959. On the one hand, we are told that the clause was so important that any attack on it would prove 'costly' because it risked 'endangering the stability of the moderate alliance' between the industrial and political leaderships. On the other, we are told that the attack was 'a bizarre episode' on 'an issue that was...irrelevant'. All in all, Howell (1976: 222) concludes, the affair was 'the best example of [Gaitskell's] readiness to seek total victory without apparently attaching any importance to the emotional appeal of traditional symbols'.

Howell is by no means alone in his confusion. In his detailed account of the affair Philip Williams, a political scientist as well as Gaitskell's biographer, wavers between full recognition of his subject's appreciation of the importance of symbols like Clause IV and the feeling that his 'commitment to rational discourse...blinded him to the emotional reactions of his followers' (Williams, 1982: 333). This mirrors the interpretation of Henry Drucker (1979: 38), who, despite being the most perceptive of all analysts of the party when it comes to symbols, feels forced to conclude that 'Gaitskell was overlooking the immense symbolic value which a continuous tradition of capitalism had for Labour' and 'forgetting the strength of the ethos of the party'. In other words, Gaitskell's doomed attempt to rewrite Clause IV owed much either to his intellectual style or his lack of sensitivity, both of which made him (unlike, presumably, those writing about it!) incapable of understanding 'this great movement of ours'.

What happens, however, if we discount such judgements and instead run with the argument put, for instance, by David Marquand (1992: 134) that Gaitskell, rather than misunderstanding the Labour movement, 'understood it only too well' and embarked upon his course in 1959 well aware of what he was doing and the difficulties involved? This opens up three possible routes, the first two being fairly smooth, the third rather less so. All have something useful to say about the attempts to change Clause IV in 1959–60 and 1994–5 but progressively challenge our commonly held notions of the role of symbols in politics.

To take the first route is to return to the model outlined above, in which the leadership consciously recognizes the trade-off between, on the one hand, the extent to which a symbol constrains leadership control of policy and presentation, and on the other, the extent to which it helps to keep the party's activists 'at their task' and to 'bind the organization together' (Drucker, 1979: 30).[5] On this view what the 1959 election drubbing, and the presumed need to respond to it, did for some in the Labour leadership was to change the terms of the trade-off: put baldly, they were prepared to sacrifice some support for more room to manoeuvre. This is classic rational choice, as that term is commonly understood: the ends remain the same; it is the situation which changes, and with it the mix of the means employed. As such it is still within what we have called the instrumental approach.

The 'Functionality' of 'Organizational Culture'

The second route – and surely the one implied by Marquand's comment – is to suggest that a model which focuses on a trade-off is just too limited to do justice to the ends, means and situation as historically observed. Instead it considers the action of Gaitskell and Blair not so much as an attempt to trade-off between the two implications of a symbol (constraint vs. ideological glue), but instead as an effort to effect profound change in the organization at what both recognized is the crucially important level of culture. Support, in other words, is not to be sacrificed, it is to be transformed. The project of the leadership is less a re-calculation of its opportunities than a wholesale and historic re-education of its followers. Going down this route lends action in the symbolic rather than the material mode a relative importance than it is not normally afforded, even by those who are prepared to factor it in to models that are otherwise materialistic. But it is not too much of a departure for most of us to make. Essentially, after all, it is rooted in Drucker's well-taken point that ethos matters as much as doctrine. It is also very much in line with what many of us, possibly in our recent professional lives, have come to realize is the stress placed on 'culture' by those who run organizations in the late twentieth century.

Much of the contemporary attention paid to 'organizational culture' owes its origins to the work of academic social scientists (particularly in management schools) in the 1960s–1970s. It became common wisdom that enterprises which do well owe their performance not only to their technical systems but also to the ethos with which they operate: any attempt to improve things, therefore, needs to be directed at the level of culture as much as at the bottom line and the organogram. Symbols are constitutive of culture, and therefore everything is potentially 'functional' in the sense of contributing towards the desired atmosphere, which in turn contributes to the capacity of the organization to fulfil its goals – right up from the colour of an office door, through the dining arrangements and on up to the ultimate symbol, the mission statement.[6]

If this is accepted, then symbols, while still supposedly separable in analytic terms from practice or behaviour, have to play a more fundamental role in our analysis than is envisaged in instrumentalist accounts. Instead of floating or sitting on top of practice or behaviour they are seen to underlie it, thereby setting, to quote political theorist Michael Walzer (1967: 196), '(rough) limits to thought, supporting certain ideas making others almost inconceivable'. In short, symbols go as deep as language; they are constitutive of thought and feeling and therefore action. To change a fundamental symbol is to ban the use of certain words (or possibly even dialects) and encourage the use of others in the knowledge, or at least the hope, that this will narrow and/or open up options as appropriate.[7] As far as Clause IV is concerned, a Labour leader can achieve a great deal more by acting on this symbolic level ('ethos') rather than at the level of say a policy review ('doctrine'): he can not only remove the one sure way in which all actions of a future Labour government can be measured and inevitably found wanting; he can also greatly widen the extent to which policies that 'manage capitalism' rather than undermine it can be explicitly and legitimately considered.

Anyone familiar with the linguistic aspect of the struggles of, for example, the Basque and Catalonian regions against the centralizing ambitions of Franco's regime in post-war Spain can quite easily appreciate that any attempt to achieve change at the symbolic level will encounter stiff resistance. Losing a symbol, as Walzer (1967: 196, 198) reminds us, 'is like losing a language, a loss which surely would be terrifying if we could properly imagine it'. Not only do symbols create 'units of discourse which are fundamental to all thinking and doing'; they also create 'units of feeling around which emotions of loyalty and assurance can cluster'. In other words, because they 'are matters of feeling as well', because 'they shape our whole sensibility[,]...guarantee a sure place in a known world [and] tell us more than we can easily repeat', any attempt at transforming them risks encountering 'a resistance which logical demonstration does not or ought not to meet'. This, as Drucker and Williams attest, was certainly true of Gaitskell's first, failed attempt to jettison Clause IV; but it is hardly an accurate prediction for the events of 1994–5. Before going on to suggest why this might be so, however, it is profitable to trace the third of the three routes mentioned above.

The Wholly Interpretative Approach

Just as the importance of culture and symbols, in the convenient formulas of management gurus, was being picked up on by the organizational practitioners, the organizational theorists were moving onwards to more elaborate and less immediately or clearly usable approaches. From a recognition that such things mattered, many began suggesting that the ultimate significance of symbolic activity, rather than being instrumental or (less Machiavellian) 'functional', may in the end actually transcend both (for example, Pettigrew, 1979; Dandridge *et al.*, 1980; Meyer, 1982).[8] In the words of one organizational theorist, there began a move away from seeing symbolically constituted culture as something the organization *has*, to something the organization *is* (Riley, 1983; Smircich, 1983). This was rooted in increasing dissatisfaction with 'harder' or more positivistic social science approaches and its correlative, a turn to what might be called interpretative approaches. The latter were exemplified in a range of writing in linguistics and sociology located in what might be called the humanistic tradition, which holds that since the social world is constituted by the meanings and purposes of human agents, the function of social science is to interpret meaning and render it intelligible, not to tease out causation.[9] According to this tradition, man is nothing if not a producer and consumer of symbols, the sharing of which creates and reproduces culture – a reality which is not independent of the material world and which, if not objective, is sufficiently intersubjective to allow meaningful and concerted social action to take place. As such, there is no useful distinction to be made in any social activity between process or outcome, between what is real and what is symbolic.

Ironically, Edelman had attempted in the mid 1960s to bring some of these points to bear on his own analysis and thus to introduce political scientists to a range of approaches to politics which operated largely outside the methodological current with which many at that time had chosen or been forced to swim. Indeed as he continued his work, he moved more openly towards an interpretative stance. A later study, for example, contained what amounted to a manifesto for the symbolic interactionist approach (see note 11), an approach which:

> places at the center of attention the symbolizing ability with which man adapts his world to his behavior and his behavior to his world. Only man among living things reconstructs his past, perceives his present condition, and anticipates his future through symbols that abstract, screen, condense, distort, displace, and even create what the senses bring to his attention....To explain political behavior as a response to fairly stable individual wants, reasoning, attitudes, and empirically based perceptions is therefore simplistic and misleading. Adequate explanation must focus on the complex element that intervenes between the environment and the behavior of human beings: creation and change in common meanings through symbolic apprehension in groups of people of interests, pressures, threats, and possibilities (Edelman, 1971: 2).

Edelman still finds himself, however, located in the conventional, instrumentalist tradition – despite his later claim (in the Afterward to Edelman, 1985) that even his first and best-known work was predicated on the denial of 'an objective political "reality" from which symbols can divert attention [since] interpretations and meanings shape behavior (and vice versa)'.[10] The fact that he is so located is due not only to the tendency of political scientists to see in his work only what they wanted to see, namely a sophisticated exposé of the use of symbols to obtain concrete ends. It is also because it is redolent with an ambiguity which arises not just from its author's admitted intention to provide just such an exposé, but also from his wholly understandable concern to study politics as human interaction – and as dramaturgy, language and style – without disappearing into a world where such things, rather than being determined by socio-economic structures and interests, are utterly unrelated to them.[11]

Edelman, then, implicitly understood that the interpretative route is one that potentially leads just a little too far off the beaten track for those of us who are still interested in being able to trace cause and effect. We can cope with moving away from the simplicities and the suspicions of the instrumental route towards the more complex 'functional' or 'organizational culture' perspective, but thus far and no further. After all if 'symbolism is a generic process rather than a narrowly defined and specialized activity', meaning that '[a]ny object, action, event, utterance, concept or image offers itself as raw material for symbolic creation, at any place and at any time' (Morgan *et al.*, 1983: 5), it is difficult to see how we might hope to pin down or delimit our studies: such an approach seems to promise adventures through the looking glass rather than provide a solid basis for substantive research. In addition, 'the very existence of symbolism as a generic human process questions the adequacy of metaphors drawn from the natural sciences as frames of inquiry in the human sciences....[T]he more complex conscious and unconscious sets of symbols which manifest themselves throughout organizational life in the most intricate and subtle of ways...do not lend themselves for treatment as variables which can be plugged into traditional modes of analysis' (Morgan *et al.*, 1983: 31–2). Those 'traditional modes' are what most of us studying parties, without feeling we need to apologize for it, still work within and find generally productive.

A Fourth Route: the 'New Institutionalism'

Going down the third route would seem to involve pursuing the management scientists into a world where a concept arguably becomes so ubiquitous that it begins to lose what (possibly limited) use it had in the first place. The interpretative approach counsels against concentrating on commonly acknowledged symbols lest we forget that everything is symbolic. Surely this would force us to look beyond a particular entity, issue or controversy into every area of party life, every action of the party leader and led – a potentially infinite and therefore impossible task? Fortunately, this is not necessarily so. This is particularly the case if we follow those political scientists who reject the claim that a concern with the centrality of symbols means isolating oneself from what is, after all, really a straw-man, namely the supposedly positivistic mainstream of the discipline. This open-mindedness applies in particular to the so-called 'new institutionalist' work of James March and colleagues, political scientists with (perhaps significantly) a strong grounding in organizational science.[12]

The work of the new institutionalists is wide ranging and is of course concerned with more than symbolism. However, some seminal examples give a flavour of its desire to reconcile interpretative, functional and instrumental approaches to symbols. For example, after examining information-gathering and use in organizations with a view to understanding why so much is called for but so little is actually useful, Feldman and March conclude that the key to the process is its capacity to symbolize commitment to the (rational) decision models that legitimize organizations not just in the eyes of wider society, but also among the participants themselves (who are in any case part of that society). Process in politics is at least as important as its outcomes because it is process that makes organizations and life in general not just 'acceptable', but 'meaningful' as well (Feldman and March, 1981: 178; see also Meyer and Rowan, 1977). March and Olsen's study of administrative reorganization reaches similar conclusions. It stresses that organizations are 'cultural systems'.[13] Actions within them are 'tied to the discovery, clarification, and elaboration of meaning as well as to immediate action or decision making' and 'have symbolic meaning that is independent of their instrumental consequences' (March and Olsen, 1983: 289–90). The stress is on the fact that symbols 'are important to politicians, not only as ways to fool voters but also as reflections of their own beliefs', proofs of their capacity as human agents to direct and control the environment. The perceptual distance between leaders and led, so crucial to the instrumental and the functional view of symbols – and indeed to the way most of us think and write about political parties – is thus collapsed. 'Leaders', March and Olsen (1983: 290–1) remind us, 'need reassurance too'. The new institutionalism, then, encourages us to move away from the fallacy that leaders who operate skilfully in the symbolic mode somehow manage to isolate themselves from its claims and influence.

The new institutionalism's interest in symbols is part of its wider rejection of purely economic approaches to political science and the claim that such approaches have proved more useful than any previous methods – a rejection based on the belief that their findings often clash with what is observed by empirical research, as well as what is experienced and understood by participants. This clash is particularly evident, claim March and Olsen, when it comes to discussions of symbols, which are dominated by an instrumentalist view. While 'symbolic behaviour', they point out, can indeed be 'a strategic element in political competition', we must never forget that 'politics is only partly – and often almost incidentally – concerned with producing outcomes' and that it is also 'a place for discovering, elaborating, and expressing meanings, establishing shared (or opposing) conceptions of experience, values, and the nature of existence' (March and Olsen, 1989: 48–9; see also Swidler, 1986). Exclusive concentration on outcomes, combined with a view that symbols merely obfuscate them, mistakes the rationalization of political behaviour for its reality and tends 'to underestimate the diffuse, interactive way in which meaning, intentions, and action are woven together' (March and Olsen, 1989: 52). In short, the process of politics 'gives meaning to life, and meaning is a major part of life. The reason that people involved in politics devote so much time to symbols, myths, and rituals is that they (appropriately) care about them' (March and Olsen, 1989: 51).

The new institutionalism's focus on the interpretative world of political actors would obviously support a focus on party elites; but this does not prevent its being useful in the study of symbols and sense-making in political parties as a whole. After all, it would seem to provide an approach – a fourth route, if you like – which is at once interpretative and instrumental, which emphasizes the internal history and structure of the organization, but also stresses how they are inevitably influenced and in part constituted by developments in the wider environment. This last point is important. Writing about the decay and replacement of old symbols (in words which cannot help but call to mind Labour's ideological and policy contortions in the post-war period and Blair's attempt to resolve them), Michael Walzer (1967: 198) concludes:

> The process of destruction is very complex. What occurs is a slow erosion of the old symbols, a wasting away of the feelings they once evoked, an increasingly disjointed and inconsistent expression of political ideas, a nervous insistence upon the old units and references – all this accompanied, willy nilly, by a more and more arbitrary manipulation of them – until finally the units cease to be accepted as intellectual givens and the references cease to be meaningful. But since men cannot orient themselves in the political world without...symbols, the systems are replaced even as they are called into question....The precise nature of the new symbols is by no means determined; it depends on the availability of new reference-worlds and on the artistic and intellectual sense with which these are appropriated and the new references worked out.

All this can lead us on to questions which may not be those we would initially think of asking. But they are worthwhile because they encourage us to think about how a political party, and all within it, interact – just as all organizations and their members interact – with common-sense notions that do indeed change over time, but which are always reflective and constitutive of the wider society (see Dobbin, 1994).

What would following the fourth route involve us in if we were to apply it to Clause IV? Firstly, it would encourage us to ask what the change meant to those engaged in it, rather than simply speculate on its intended effect on the electorate or the membership: we might ask, for example, what was the 'message' that Tony Blair was sending not just to the electorate or his party, but to himself? Did his decision have something to do with how 'strong leadership' has come historically to be understood in the Labour Party over the years – to the notion, possibly prevalent in all modern social democratic parties, that such leadership is defined as much by denying one's supporters what (supposedly) they want as by the ability to wring concessions for them from the prevailing liberal capitalist system? Secondly, the fourth route would encourage us to concentrate on the way in which the change was achieved, on the way both leaders and led participated in a process by which the party – in order to retain legitimacy – adjusted its practices and language in order to fit with prevailing ideas of what the world is and the way organizations in that world should work. This, in turn, might help us to address the most obvious question raised by recent events, namely why did Gaitskell fail so miserably but Blair succeed so easily?

There are of course myriad factors involved in any full answer to that historical question. It would be foolish to ignore the obvious fact that a newly elected leader with a winnable election around the corner is in a far better position than one who has just presided over an unexpectedly bad defeat at the hands of voters who've never had it so good. Blair's success may also have owed much to his skilful exploitation of the new populism, in which the distinction between 'the few and the many' has been leant a new lease of life by symbolic stories of 'fat cats' lapping up their 'executive share options' while the 'average man or woman in the street' can only struggle along. But another important factor may have been the way in which Blair's attempt both emanated and was legitimized – in the active as well as the passive sense – by symbols which reflected long and short term material and political changes. Many of these owed much to the Thatcher governments of the 1980s and, as such, were simply not available, let alone shared, in the society or the organization in which Gaitskell operated.

Comparing 1994 to 1959, Labour is a changed party operating in a changed society. Its membership, as Seyd and Whiteley stress, has not only seen four elections lost but is now more middle-class and more public sector oriented.[14] Its trade union wing has largely set aside vanguardism in favour of the sort of responsive service provision that in theory will help it both to hang on to the subscriptions and better represent the interests of its dwindling rank and file. The party today, then, is more prone than the party of Gaitskell's era to believe in the literal truth and electoral consequences of the symbolic 'affluent worker', now leant more spurious legitimacy by the 'scientific' yet equally symbolic label 'C2'. The current membership's occupational experience and cognitive world is peopled, in a way that the worlds of the old membership never were, by women, ethnic and other minorities whose claims are recognized as every bit as pressing, and indeed intertwined, with those of the working class. Just as importantly, that same world has also been dominated, rhetorically and in reality, by 'restructuring', 'performance review', 'objective setting', the 'permanency of change', and by 'consultation exercises' which once complete legitimize 'the right to manage'.[15] All this has gradually been accepted, however grudgingly, as an inevitable part of working in an organization in 'the modern world', a world in which economic sectors once considered separate are now increasingly blurred. It is no coincidence that similar ideas suffused the language employed by those who succeeded in changing Clause IV in 1995 – even by those who were initially sceptical.[16]

This is to say that the attempt in 1994–5 succeeded where the attempt in 1959–60 failed because it could count on the fact that the images and symbols necessary for success – images and symbols which communicate an understanding of how the world is and what organizations are about – were more deeply rooted in the later than in the earlier period. Gaitskell attempted to appeal to his party to consider new developments, but could not hang that appeal on symbols that truly made grounded sense to those to whom he was appealing. To have succeeded then would surely have been an exercise in what James Macgregor Burns calls 'transformational' leadership.[17] Blair, on the other hand, was telling people what they already knew – even if it took something to admit it – in a language they had already come to understand and even begin to speak. In the terms employed by Michael Walzer (see above), Blair was able to escape from the Wilsonesque 'arbitrary and extravagant manipulation' of the old Clause IV not only because its sentiments had lost or at least changed their meaning in the contemporary lives of his members, but also because of the ready 'availability of new reference-worlds' which had themselves contributed to this loss of meaning in the first place.

Conclusion

There is a case, then, for arguing that because Blair exploited existing (albeit latent) needs and knowledge, his leadership even on Clause IV was, in

Burns's categorization, less 'transformational' than 'transactional' (Burns, 1978: 118).[18] On the other hand, though, it would be unwise to underestimate Blair's skill or his achievement. Blair's success owed much to his willingness to honour the party's past: the old Clause IV had not been wrong *per se*, he stressed, it was just that circumstances had changed. This was not necessarily an unconvincing argument to many on the left (Marxist and non-Marxist alike) who have recognized the need to adjust to changes wrought not only by Thatcherism but, among other things, the increasing globalization of capital. And as long ago as 1952 Aneurin Bevan ([1952] 1978: 34), long-time hero of the Labour left, was warning it not to be too fond of 'the old words, for the words persist when the reality that lay behind them has changed'. Their 'Holy Grail' must be 'the living truth, knowing that being alive the truth must change'. If this was not recognized, he claimed, 'our ideas degenerate into a kind of folklore which we pass to each other fondly thinking we are still talking of the reality around us'. He continued:

> If this is not understood, we become symbol worshippers. The categories we once evolved and which were the tools we used in our intercourse with reality become hopelessly blunted. In these circumstances the social and political realities we are supposed to be grappling with change and reshape themselves independently of the collective impact of our ideas. We become the creature and no longer the partner of social realities. As we fumble with outworn categories our political vitality is sucked away and we stumble from one situation to another, without chart, without compass, and with the steering wheel lashed to a course we are no longer following (Bevan [1952] 1978: 34).

Blair's decent burial of Clause IV also had the effect of 'historicizing' the past he was prepared to honour. This, arguably, is the crux of his achievement. To use Henry Drucker's terms, the Labour Party has hitherto been unable to escape from 'a living past', from being a party which lives on 'cyclical' rather than on 'clock' time, a party which truncates time so that the heroes and deeds of old seem as relevant as the challenges of the present and the future. This quality was, as Drucker observed, a useful source of solidarity; but it was also one which prevented Labour from ever becoming '*simpliciter* a party of the future...a radical social democratic party' of the sort more familiar in continental Europe. This for some, including Drucker, was a good thing because it tied the party to a socialist (though incrementalist) project. For others, however, including for example David Marquand, it has been the root of the party's inability to pass properly into the progressive inheritance that would have transformed Britain and made Labour the natural party of government. By dispensing with the old Clause IV, it can be argued, Blair has done far more than dump an electorally embarrassing commitment to state ownership; rather he has achieved inside the Labour Party what the historian J.H. Plumb called 'the death of the past' (see Drucker, 1979: ch. 2; Marquand, 1992).

On the other hand, Labour's modernizers should not overstate their victory or misunderstand its nature. They have replaced one symbol with another, and they have certainly not rid the party of all its other symbols. Although disputable, the distinction between 'transformation' and 'transaction' is useful because it prompts us to think about those symbolic issues which would have to be tackled to justify Tony Blair's inclusion in the more demanding of the two categories – what price private health insurance replacing the cherished NHS under a Labour government, for example? This is not to dismiss out of hand the possibility that what we are witnessing is the beginning of a transformative process that may make such things possible. New Labour's leaders may indeed be involved in micropolitics, waging an ultimately successful war of position wherein victory in one battle creates the conditions for success in battles yet to come – it is hard to envisage the concept of the 'stakeholder economy' being bandied about quite so easily before the rewriting of Clause IV, for example. Yet it still seems unlikely that the exercise will be able to undermine internal opposition in all areas. If the party is indeed a cultural system, it is inevitably constituted and given boundaries by myriad symbols; it cannot therefore simply be evacuated at the convenience of the leadership. As the increasing significance placed on the social chapter and the national minimum wage shows – and as Bevan should have realized – Labour Party members, like all human beings, cannot help but be 'symbol worshippers': if one symbol is taken away, they will always find others to revere.[19]

It is also important to remember that because symbols are not just the fictions of leaders, but are also the means through which all those in organizations like parties understand and act, they can also be appropriated by the led. In his useful study of the Labour Party, Alan Warde (1982: 19) stresses the fact that 'differing orientations within the one tradition invariably legitimate themselves by the use of the same symbols'. As James Scott (1992) has pointed out in another context, acceptance of shared symbols may not reflect the pitifully genuine consent of the supposedly 'hegemonized'; it may instead be a strategic choice, based on the knowledge that hoisting those in authority on their own petard can often be the most effective way of keeping up the pressure to get what you want – 'saying what we mean and meaning what we say' makes hypocrisy on the part of Shadow Cabinet members, for example, rather harder to justify. Quite possibly, and especially if he ever does get into office, Mr Blair may yearn for the day when the only explicit yardstick (beyond the manifesto) by which Labour leaders were judged was an atavistic aspiration rather than a modern, wide-ranging and (relatively speaking) more specific list of 'performance indicators'.

NOTES

1. One student of political symbolism, in a useful though at times impenetrable article (Dittmer, 1971), notes that: 'It is difficult to define the term either synthetically (that is, by distinguishing it from related concepts) or analytically (that is by specifying its characteristics)'. On the grounds that, on the one hand, not to proffer a definition would be a dereliction of duty and, on the other, a desire not to render the foregoing pointless by providing one which is so narrow or specialized as to provoke disagreement or (worse) lack of interest, it may be best to indicate rather than pontificate and over-specify. Hence etymology may be a helpful place to start: the word symbol derives from the Greek and combines the idea of a token with the idea of throwing or putting together. Another useful way of understanding what is meant is by concentrating on the fact that a symbol is a sign which invokes more than it is designed to resemble or refer to; in short it is invested with meaning above and beyond what it indicates at the most basic level. The problem is, of course, that, depending on circumstances, this could apply to almost anything: if I am on time for an appointment the 30 mph sign is a reminder for me not to drive any faster; if I am late, it is a frustrating infringement on my liberty! Thirdly, the borrowed definition of 'condensation symbols' supplied by Murray Edelman ([1964] 1985: 6) is at least generally intelligible and serviceable: such symbols, he writes, 'evoke the emotions associated with the situation. They condense into one symbolic event, sign or act patriotic pride, anxieties, remembrances of past glories or humiliations, promises or future greatness: some of these or all of them.' In the end, rather ironically perhaps, the very term symbol is like a symbol, both in the sense of conveying more than what is there and being interpreted differently (as well as possibly similarly) by various groups and individuals.

2. Perhaps symptomatic of a general failure to develop the point is the fact that it is repeated verbatim in Saville (1988).

3. Miliband (1972) provides the paradigm text.

4. The move was widely understood as an unintelligible own goal, even by Labour's opponents. The acid-tongued Iain Macleod noted that Labour had 'provided us with a mine so inexhaustible but so rich that every Tory candidate can dig with profit in it forever. I do not understand why they should load us with such golden gifts' (*Daily Telegraph*, 22 March 1960).

5. Drucker recognizes these two functions and the dilemma they pose, but insists that Gaitskell tried to solve it by pretending that 'the second horn' (the affective motivating function) 'does not exist'.

6. A telling pastiche on American corporate symbolism – an acute *reductio ad absurdum* in which door colour and even sofa size play a vital part – is Don DeLillo's novel *Americana* (published in England by Penguin in 1990); as for dining arrangements, witness the naive but sneakingly popular suspicion that the relatively superior performance of Japanese companies has something to do with the bosses and the shop-floor workers all eating in the same canteen. A more rigorous, academic examination of this functional aspect of organizational symbols and culture can be found in the work of Jeffrey Pfeffer (e.g. 1984).

7. This is George Orwell's point in both *Homage to Catalonia* and, even more explicitly, in *Nineteen Eighty Four*. Quite the most brilliant and sustained academic analysis of both the constraining and enabling potential of language is contained in the essays of J.G.A. Pocock (1989).

8. A useful overview of a decade and a half of developments in organizational culture research is provided by Alvesson (1993). See also W. R. Scott (1990).

9. The main 'schools' in this tradition are phenomenology (see Husserl, 1994; Schutz, 1970), symbolic interactionism (see Blumer, 1969) and hermeneutics (see Habermas, 1989).

10. This does not seem to have convinced everybody: see Eriksen (1987: 259). Perhaps significantly, the majority of contributions to a recent collection published in Edelman's honour (Merelman, 1992) tend toward the instrumental.

11. This is also the concern of Pierre Bourdieu, whose work on symbolic power is as richly ambiguous as Edelman's: see Bourdieu (1991), especially Part III, 'Symbolic Power and the Political Field'.

12. The new institutionalism covers a multitude of subtly different approaches, united mostly by the belief that institutions, or more specifically the grounded and peculiar rules and roles which they create, sustain and perpetuate, are just as important in explaining (political) behaviour as supposedly universal rationality or classic ideologies – an idea which obviously fits well with many approaches to political parties, particularly, for example, that of Panebianco (1988). A useful overview is provided by Robertson (1993); see also Koelble (1995).

13. The phrase is originally anthropologist Clifford Geertz's, who (1964) challenged prevalent materialist and pseudo-psychological notions of ideologies by arguing they are not so much 'projections of unacknowledged fears, disguises for ulterior motives, phatic expressions of group solidarity' as 'ordered system[s] of cultural symbols' which 'make an autonomous politics possible by providing the authoritative concepts that render it meaningful, the suasive images by means of which it can sensibly be grasped'.

14. Few students of the party have sought explicitly to explore the implications of changing class differences or similarities between the leadership and its membership – possibly because of the flack suffered by an early attempt, which sought to explain the failure of the Labour leaders to promote the interests of its traditional constituency by pointing to the increasing social gulf between the leadership and its traditional constituency: see Hindess (1990), but also Hine (1986). One possible effect of work by Seyd and Whiteley may be to encourage more empirically sound attempts in this area.

15. Acceptance of the right to manage probably still depends, as far as trade unions are concerned, on what precisely is being managed. The separate spheres stressed by Minkin (1991) are still very much in force; indeed, to judge from recent pronouncements from both wings of the Labour movement, they are possibly even stronger now than ever before.

16. For example, by Deputy Leader John Prescott on BBC Radio's *Today* programme, 21 August 1995.

17. Transformational leadership goes beyond some kind of exchange relationship between leader and led, based largely on existing and predictable needs – in other words the 'transactional' leadership which is arguably the norm for party leadership. Instead it is a mutual process of discovery of and dedication to meeting new needs which may eventually 'convert leaders into moral agents'. See Burns (1978: 4).

18. On the other hand, it might be argued (as Burns does) that this is to set the criteria for transformational leadership so impossibly high that few democratic politicians of the modern age, including even Margaret Thatcher, are ever likely to achieve it.

19. Arguably, the belief that symbols are some sort of primitive constraint that modern societies and organizations can somehow transcend remains deeply ingrained even in those of us trained to avoid the Whig interpretation of history; see the comments of Mary Douglas (1970) on the damaging 'anti-ritualism' of (middle class) academics and politicians who refuse to acknowledge the still symbolic nature of modern group communication and identification. In fact, this tendency to see symbols as primitive mystifications which once exposed will become unnecessary is much older. Writing about sixteenth and seventeenth century England, Michael Walzer (1967: 198–9) notes that, despite their belief that they were calling into doubt 'the very process of symbolisation itself', those who sought to criticize traditional conceptions of the state by undermining the symbols that supported them inevitably ended up replacing one set of symbols (e.g. the body politic) by another (e.g. the body in motion).

BIBLIOGRAPHY

Alvesson, Mats (1993) *Cultural Perspectives on Organizations.* Cambridge: Cambridge University Press.

Blumer, Herbert (1969) *Symbolic Interactionism, Perspective and Method.* Englewood Cliffs, NJ: Prentice Hall.

Bourdieu, Pierre (1991) *Language and Symbolic Power.* Cambridge: Polity Press.

Burns, James Macgregor (1978) *Leadership.* New York: Harper and Row.

Cohen, Abner (1974) *Two Dimensional Man: an Essay on the Anthropology of Power and Symbolism in Complex Society*. London: Routledge and Kegan Paul.

Crossman, Richard (1963) 'Introduction', in Walter Bagehot, *The English Constitution*. London: Fontana.

Dandridge, Thomas, Ian Mitroff, and William Joyce (1980) 'Organizational Symbolism: a Topic to Expand Organizational Analysis', *Academy of Management Review* 5: 77–82.

Dittmer, Lowell (1971) 'Political Culture and Political Symbolism: Toward a Theoretical Synthesis', *World Politics* 29: 552–83.

Dobbin, Frank R. (1994) 'Cultural Models of Organization: the Social Construction of Rational Organizing Principles', in Diana Crane (ed.) *The Sociology of Culture: Emerging Theoretical Perspectives*. Oxford: Blackwell.

Douglas, Mary (1970) *Natural Symbols: Explanations in Cosmology*. London: Barrie and Rockliffe/Crescent Press.

Drucker, Henry (1979) *Doctrine and Ethos in the British Labour Party*. London: George Allen and Unwin.

Dunleavy, Patrick (1991) *Democracy, Bureaucracy and Public Choice: Economic Explanations in Political Science*. Hemel Hempstead: Harvester Press.

Dunleavy, Patrick (1995) 'Reinterpreting the Westland Affair: Theories of the State and Core Executive Decision Making', in Rod Rhodes and Patrick Dunleavy (eds) *Cabinet and Core Executive*, pp. 181–218. London: Macmillan.

Edelman, Murray ([1964] 1985) *The Symbolic Uses of Politics*. Chicago: University of Illinois Press.

Edelman, Murray (1971) *Politics as Symbolic Action: Mass Arousal and Quiescence*. Chicago: Markham.

Elder, Charles and Roger Cobb (1983) *The Political Uses of Symbols*. New York: Longman.

Eriksen, E.O. (1987) 'Symbols, Strategy and Legitimacy in Political Analysis', *Scandinavian Political Studies* 10: 259–78.

Feldman, M. and J. G. March (1981) 'Information in Organizations as Signal and Symbol', *Administrative Science Quarterly* 26: 171–86.

Geertz, Clifford (1964) 'Ideology as a Cultural System', in David Apter (ed) *Ideology and Discontent*, pp.47–76. London: Collier Macmillan.

Goodin, Robert (1977) 'Symbolic Rewards: Being Bought off Cheaply', *Political Studies* 25: 383–96.

Habermas, Jurgen (1989) *On the Logic of the Social Sciences*. Cambridge: Polity Press.

Hindess, Barry (1990) '" The Decline of Working-Class Politics": a Reappraisal', in Ben Pimlott and Chris Cook (eds) *Trade Unions in British Politics: the First 250 Years*, pp. 223–42. London: Longman.

Hine, David (1986) 'Leaders and Followers: Democracy and Manageability in the Social Democratic Parties of Western Europe', in William E. Paterson and Alastair H. Thomas (eds) *The Future of Social Democracy, Problems and Prospects of Social Democratic Parties*, pp. 261–90. Oxford: Clarendon.

Howell, David (1976) *British Social Democracy: a Study in Development and Decay*. London: Croom Helm.

Husserl, Edmund (1994) *The Idea of Phenomenology*. Dordrecht: Kluwer.

Koelble, Thomas A. (1995) 'The New Institutionalism in Political Science and Sociology', *Comparative Politics* 27: 231–43.

Mair, Peter (1983) 'Adaptation and Control: Toward an Understanding of Party and Party System Change', in Peter Mair and Hans Daalder (eds) *Western European Party Systems: Continuity and Change*, pp. 405–29. London: Sage.

March, James G. and Johan P. Olsen (1983) 'Organizing Political Life: What Administrative Reorganization Tells Us About Government', *American Political Science Review* 77: 281–96.

March, James G. and Johan P. Olsen (1989) *Rediscovering Institutions: the Organizational Basis of Politics*. London: Free Press.

Marquand, David (1992) *The Progressive Dilemma*. London: William Heinemann.

Merelman, Richard (ed.) (1992) *Language, Symbolism and Politics*. Oxford: Westview.

Meyer, A. (1982) 'How Ideologies Supplant Formal Structures and Shape Responses to Environments', *Journal of Management Studies* 19: 45–61.

Meyer, John and Brian Rowan (1977) 'Institutionalized Organizations: Formal Structure as Myth and Ceremony', *American Journal of Sociology*, 83: 340–63.

Miliband, Ralph (1972) *Parliamentary Socialism*. London: Merlin Press.

Minkin, Lewis (1991) *The Contentious Alliance: Trade Unions and the Labour Party*. Edinburgh: Edinburgh University Press.

Morgan, Gareth, Peter Frost and Louis Pondy (1983) 'Organizational Symbolism' in Louis Pondy *et al.* (eds) *Organizational Symbolism*. London: JAI Press.

Mount, Ferdinand (1972) *The Theatre of Politics*. London: Weidenfeld and Nicolson.

Packard, Vance (1957) *The Hidden Persuaders*. London: Longmans, Green & Co.

Panebianco, Angelo (1988) *Political Parties: Organization and Power*. Cambridge: Cambridge University Press.

Pettigrew, Andrew (1979) 'On Studying Organizational Cultures', *Administrative Science Quarterly* 24: 570–81.

Pfeffer, Jeffrey (1984) *Power in Organisations*. London: Pitman.

Pocock, J.G.A. (1989) *Politics, Language and Time*. London: University of Chicago Press.

Riley, Patricia (1983) 'A Structurationist Account of Political Culture', *Administrative Science Quarterly* 28: 414–37.

Robertson, D. B. (1993) 'The Return to History and the New Institutionalism in American Political Science', *Social Science History* 17: 1–36.

Saville, John (1967) 'Labourism and the Labour Government', *Socialist Register*.

Saville, John (1988) *The Labour Movement in Britain*. London: Faber and Faber.

Schutz, Alfred (1970) *Alfred Schutz on Phenomenology and Social Relations*. London: University of Chicago Press.

Scott, James (1992) 'False Consciousness, or Laying It On Thick', in Richard Merelman (ed.) *Language, Symbolism and Politics*. Oxford: Westview.

Scott, W. Richard (1990) 'Symbols and Organisations: from Barnard to the Institutionalists', in Oliver Williamson (ed.) *Organizational Theory from Chester Barnard to the Present and Beyond*, pp. 38–55. New York: Oxford University Press.

Seyd, Patrick and Whiteley, Paul (1992) *Labour's Grass Roots: the Politics of Party Membership*. Oxford: Clarendon Press.

Smircich, Linda (1983) 'Concepts of Culture and Organisational Analysis', *Administrative Science Quarterly* 28: 339–58.

Swidler, Anne (1986) 'Culture in Action: Symbols and Strategy', *American Sociological Review* 51: 273–86.

Walzer, Michael (1967) 'On the Role of Symbolism in Political Thought', *Political Science Quarterly* 82: 191–204.

Warde, Alan (1982) *Consensus and Beyond: the Development of Labour Party Strategy Since the Second World War*. Manchester: Manchester University Press.

Ware, Alan (1992) 'Activist-Leader Relations and the Structure of Political Parties: "Exchange" Models and Vote Seeking Behaviour in Parties', *British Journal of Political Science*, 22: 71–92.

Whitehead, A. N. (1928) *Symbolism: Its Meaning and Effect*. Cambridge: Cambridge University Press.

Whiteley, Paul, Seyd, Patrick and Richardson, Jeremy (1994) *True Blues: the Politics of Conservative Party Membership*. Oxford: Oxford University Press.

Williams, Philip M. (1982) *Hugh Gaitskell*. Oxford: Oxford University Press.

Modernization and Clause IV Reform: The Attitudes of Labour Backbench MPs

Michael Levy

> If the leader jumps off a cliff, you have no alternative but to catch him. You just don't discredit your leader if he puts himself on the line...we're not like the Tory Party. (Northern Labour MP referring to the Clause IV debate)

The above reflects the grudging, yet overwhelming, support for modernization among Labour MPs. Most of them support changes in the party's constitution and programme over the last decade; however, that support does not appear very deep and it is not exactly enthusiastic. MPs may be more willing to remain silent while in opposition, especially after four elections in the electoral wilderness; but what should we expect from the Labour Party in the future, either in government or if it continues to lose elections? Is support for Labour's policy and institutional changes genuine or a self-imposed discipline of MPs seeking government? This article addresses these questions, analysing the attitudes of Labour MPs to determine whether the Labour Party really is Tony Blair's 'New Labour Party' or whether 'Old Labour', however defined, lurks in the shadows waiting to reappear.

The modernization agenda of the Kinnock, Smith, and Blair eras has been seen as essential by most people within and outside the party – especially among the Parliamentary Labour Party's (PLP) centre-right – if it is to wrest control of government away from the Conservatives and govern 'in the way Britain needs' (Blair, 1995). Previous works (such as Kogan and Kogan, 1982; Hughes and Wintour, 1990; Shaw, 1994; Smith and Spear, 1992) have provided valuable insight into how the battle over modernization was waged and why the various changes were set in motion at particular junctures. Seyd and Whiteley (1992) allow observers a glimpse into the psyche of Labour members and how they viewed the Policy Review following the 1987 election defeat. These studies provide useful contextual detail of the changes; however, apart from a few exceptions (for example, Norris, 1994), they have tended to leave one area of the modernization puzzle unstudied – Labour's MPs. This article supplements the personal interview section of Norris's British Candidate Study by examining the attitudes of 45 Labour backbench MPs[1] towards the modernization process and Clause IV reform, and looking at general impressions of the changes in the party over the past dozen years. The attitudes of Labour MPs towards these changes, and the attempt to capture middle England, are examined in order to determine: the relative level of support for modernization, especially as it relates to the 1995 version embodied in Clause IV reform; whether MPs' attitudes towards modernization and Clause IV reform differ by region, tenure in office, and ideological self-placement (or other characteristics); and what might be expected after the next general election.

Framework for Gauging Attitudes of Labour MPs

Interviews and surveys were conducted to examine the attitudes of Labour MPs to the changing political landscape in Britain and to Labour Party reforms in the light of this. The starting point is Norris' claim (1994: 185) that the aims of the Labour leadership, in producing a party supportive of reforms, have been achieved. Her data suggest that Labour 'is just as much, if not more, moderate and united than the Conservatives' (Norris, 1994: 186).

Assuming that front-bench spokespeople are loyal to the party's modernization efforts and the leadership, this article focuses (with minor exceptions) on backbench MPs. Letters were sent to 200 (190 backbench; 10 frontbench) Labour MPs in November 1994 inviting their participation either in a survey or interview. Ninety MPs responded, 55 affirmatively. Twelve agreed to complete a questionnaire, the remainder to a sit-down interview. Due to scheduling difficulties and time constraints, nine surveys were completed and a further 36 MPs participated in interviews, representing 22.5 per cent of the MPs targeted and 17 per cent of the total PLP. The interviews were carried out in two waves, the first in March 1995 (coinciding with the unveiling of the new Clause IV). The second wave took place during the Conservative Party leadership contest in the last week of June and the first week of July 1995.

In social scientific research, especially where predictions are being generated, it is important to have a random sample. Clearly this is not the case here; however, I argue, following Devine (1992), that tentative conclusions can be drawn about the attitudes of a grouping of individuals from a small non-random set. Since the total pool of possible backbench MPs numbers only 200, and given various constraints, it was impossible to randomly sample the population. Despite this, the group of MPs who participated turned out to be fairly representative of the PLP.

Though not random in terms of region, gender, and marginality,[2] the sample does approach representativeness. Table 1 provides a demographic comparison of the sample and the entire PLP. While the sample is biased, including a slightly higher percentage of women than the PLP, this difference is only marginal and should not affect the outcome of the results significantly. Additionally, two regions are misrepresented, with a slight skew against the

North and in favour of the Midlands, which, if the regional hypothesis is valid, may result in some over-statement of support for modernization. The sample also over-represents MPs in marginal seats. The focus on backbenchers played a role in skewing the marginality figures, as recently elected MPs who took seats away from Conservatives (as opposed to inheriting the seat from a retiring Labour MP) are more likely to have won with comparatively smaller margins.

TABLE 1

DEMOGRAPHIC CHARACTERISTICS OF THE SAMPLE AND THE PLP

	Sample		PLP	
	No.	%	No.	%
Gender				
Male	36	80.0	234	86.4
Female	9	20.0	37	13.7
Region[a]				
South	2	4.4	10	3.7
London	6	13.3	35	12.9
Midlands	10	22.2	43	15.9
Wales	4	8.9	27	10.0
North	15	33.3	107	39.5
Scotland	8	17.8	49	18.1
Majority[b]				
0.0–5.0	11	24.4	33	12.2
5.1–10.0	4	8.9	29	10.7
10.1–15.0	5	11.1	27	10.0
15.1–20.0	10	22.2	35	12.9
20.0+	15	33.3	147	54.2

a   Uses an amalgamation of the standard regions by the OPCS: South comprises East Anglia, the Southeast, and the Southwest; Midlands is the East and West Midlands; and North is Yorkshire and Humberside, the North and Northwest. The other regions are not amalgamated.

b   In per cent. Refers to the margin of victory over the second place party within a constituency.

Tapping Attitudes Towards Modernization

Drawing upon the Seyd and Whiteley (1992) study of party members, support for modernization and Clause IV reform is measured in two stages. First, interview responses were coded, utilizing the answers to the following themes:

* Do you support the modernization process, embodied in such concepts as Meet the Challenge, Make the Change, the Policy Review, and One Member One Vote?

- Do you support the leadership's attempt to reform Clause IV?
- Please comment on the following statement: unilateral nuclear disarmament was a policy which cost the party many votes and was rightly abandoned.
- Is greater European integration necessary to either or both the long-term economic competitiveness of Britain and to ensuring good conditions at the work and a clean environment?
- What type of voter do you think the party should target? Should it target the centre voter who may have voted Alliance or Conservative in the 1980s and 1992, or should it aim its core message at traditional working class supporters?

The questions tap underlying levels of support for or opposition to modernization, since the party has radically changed direction on each issue. Recalling the 1983 manifesto, one notes that Labour was committed to a radical 'redistribution of wealth', withdrawal from the EC, unilateral nuclear disarmament, a class-oriented politics, and increased nationalization of industry. Clause IV, the party's previous commitment to public ownership of the means of production, is utilized as a surrogate for support/opposition to increasing nationalization and indicates how wedded that MP is to 'Old Labour' ideals.

The second stage in the analytic process was to examine the responses contextually and qualitatively. For example, in coding a response as positive or negative, linguistic nuances may indicate a feeling deeper than simply opposition or support. Thus, I take the core questions relating to modernization and Clause IV reform and then utilize the more in-depth responses to disentangle the meanings behind the coding. This quantitative and qualitative mix provides a rich depiction of how MPs are responding to Labour's changes.

Two main research questions guide this article. The first of these is the suggestion that there are two separate Labour parties (Seyd and Whiteley, 1992): traditional Labour, with lukewarm support for or opposition to the changes since 1983; and another Labour Party comprised of modernizers supportive of the post-1983 changes. While the 'hard left' has diminished in strength, it remains an important intellectual force capable of causing severe strain, or toppling a future Labour government. Second, Seyd and Whiteley (1992) suggest that we should expect opponents to be a demographically distinct subgroup. Thus, I suggest that opponents of modernization are more likely to fit the following profile: recently elected, more likely to represent a constituency in the Labour heartlands and to locate themselves on the ideological left.

In disaggregating the two main guiding principles, three hypotheses are generated. The first proposes that a major determinant of views towards modernization is ideological self-placement. It is expected that MPs who place themselves on the left of the party are more likely to oppose modernization while MPs on the centre or right will be more supportive. This ideological polarization has resulted in the formation of the two internal parties, one disciplined and committed to the reforms, the other comprising 'Old Labour', viewing these changes with great suspicion and opposition. By and large 'New Labour' has supplanted 'Old Labour'; however, the strength of 'Old Labour' will determine the future of the party (discipline versus discord, fractious versus united, and so on).The second hypothesis is that we are seeing a generational division. The literature on party elites suggests that MPs should moderate their views during their tenure in office. We should expect those elected recently to be more hostile towards modernization than the party's most senior MPs. The third hypothesis proposes a regional division. We can expect MPs from traditional heartland areas (that is, northern England and Scotland) to be more likely to oppose modernization than those representing other regions. As discussed in the literature on electoral geography (for example, Johnston *et al.*, 1988; Curtice and Steed, 1982), during the 1980s, there was a regional polarization in British elections. At issue here is whether the regional polarization has made its way into Labour.

Quantitative Analysis of MPs' Attitudes

In the aggregate, MPs express overwhelming support for modernization. Significantly, though, on most issues, a core 20 per cent remain committed to old Labour Party ideals. This section analyses the results in two stages. First, what are the levels of support for and opposition to the modernization process? Second, a cross-sectional analysis provides insight into the demographics of the opponents of modernization, to test the three hypotheses. After discussing the results of the quantitative analysis, I examine the meanings behind the codes, to determine the depth of support for modernization.

Aggregate Results

An overwhelming majority express support for modernization, though it is clear from Table 2 that major divisions remain; the opponents are a small but potentially significant factor. For example, although 80 per cent support Clause IV reform, on most issues 20 per cent remain opposed to reform.

TABLE 2
ISSUE SUPPORT FOR MODERNIZATION

	Support		Opposition	
	No.	%	No.	%
Pro-modernization (general)	36	80.0	9	20.0
Clause IV reform	36	81.9	8	18.2
Anti-unilateralism[a]	24	64.9	13	35.1
Pro-Europe	40	88.9	5	11.1
Target group[b]	32	80.0	8	20.0

a   Refers to unilateral nuclear disarmament, where 'support' means that the MP favoured scrapping the unilateralist pledge of 1983.
b   'Support' means that the MP wanted the party to aim the core message at either the political centre or at all voters; 'opposition' means that the MP wanted to target the party's traditional base.

Unilateral nuclear disarmament – a key policy costing significant numbers of votes in the 1983 election (McAllister and Mughan, 1986) – was abandoned dramatically during the Policy Review. Significantly, 35 per cent indicated dissatisfaction with the way the party reversed position after the 1987 election, many arguing that the policy cost few votes and was fundamentally sound.The goal of modernization has been to target the middle classes and the affluent working class who abandoned Labour in droves during the 1980s. MPs were asked whether they felt Labour should aim at the political centre and the middle classes, or at the party's traditional heartlands and core working-class supporters. Twenty per cent responded that the party should aim for its traditional core, while 45 per cent thought the party should adjust its policies and message to aim at the centre (35 per cent thought the party should aim to reach all voters). Again, the anti-modernization position was advocated by 20 per cent of MPs, which should cause the leadership some pause.

Cross-Sectional Analysis

It is of interest to explore whether the opponents of modernization form a distinctive subgrouping. This section examines whether attitudes about modernization differ in terms of ideology, tenure in office, and region.

Ideological polarization. Attitudes towards modernization are highly correlated with ideological self-placement. MPs were given an 11-point left–right scale (0–10), where 5 represents centre-placement; 0 is the far left, 10 the far right. While this scale is problematic, given the reality that political attitudes cannot necessarily be broken down into a uni-dimensional scale, it does at least provide a useful heuristic device for understanding and classifying the attitudes of Labour's MPs. Table 3 shows that 13 MPs classified themselves in the centre or centre-right (5–7) while 21 placed themselves as left of centre (0–4). None of the MPs placed themselves at 1 or to the right of 7.

TABLE 3
IDEOLOGICAL SELF-PLACEMENT AND SUPPORT FOR MODERNIZATION

	Left			Centre[a]			Right
	0	2	3	4	5	6	7	Total
Support modernization?								
Yes	0	1	5	8	6	5	2	27
No	1	3	4	0	0	0	0	8
Support Clause IV reform?								
Yes	0	2	4	7	6	5	2	26
No	1	1	5	1	0	0	0	8
Unilateralism was rightly abandoned?								
Yes	0	0	1	5	4	5	2	17
No	1	3	5	2	1	0	0	12
Support deepening European integration?								
Yes	1	4	7	8	6	4	2	32
No	0	0	2	0	0	1	0	3
Target which voters?								
All voters	1	1	1	3	2	1	1	10
Political centre	0	1	3	4	2	4	1	15
Traditional supporters	0	2	5	1	0	0	0	8

a   Scale of 0–10, where 0=left; 5=centre; 10=right; categories with no entries are ignored

There is a clear division in Table 3 between those placing themselves on the ideological centre and right, and those on the left. For the purposes of interpretation, the MPs are broken down into three categories: the left (0–3), the centre (4–6), and the right (7–10). As is apparent in Table 3, the centre and the right express attitudes consistent with support for modernization, while the left remains largely unconvinced, and therefore opposed to modernization. On unilateral nuclear disarmament, the left was more likely than the centre-right to argue that the policy should not have been changed. While accepting that the issue was now irrelevant, given the collapse of the Soviet Union, left MPs opposed the abandonment of unilateralism by a margin of 9:1, while the right (2:0) and centre (14:3) supported the change in policy. The issue of European integration was not divisive, at least in terms of the general notion of the future of Britain in Europe as raised here. Each of the ideological groupings supported increased integration: the left by a margin of 12:2, the right by 2:0, and the centre most enthusiastically by a margin of 18:1. A caveat should be mentioned. As in the Conservative Party, it is clear that the issue of a single currency would present enormous political problems for a Labour government; although, one MP hastened to add that in '200 years it [the single currency] will be an argument that people will laugh and say "what was all the big fuss about?".'In defining how the party should target its core message, the left's focus remains on the party's traditional working-class supporters, while the right is more likely to support appealing to the centre voter.[3] Seven left MPs supported targeting the party's base, while four wanted to woo the centre voter. Among the centre-right, more favoured targeting the centre voter.

Generational division. As was suggested above, recently elected MPs are more likely to oppose modernization. As Table 4 shows, those elected before 1987 supported modernization unanimously (10:0), while those MPs elected between 1987–1992 were somewhat less supportive. This suggests that longer serving MPs are hungrier for power, even if it means sacrificing ideological principles. Conversely, more recently elected MPs may be less willing to sacrifice some of their principles to achieve power, echoing the view of one MP elected in 1987 who expressed major concern that the party's 'luvvies' were selling out its base and that he was not one who wanted 'power at any cost'.

TABLE 4
SUPPORT FOR MODERNIZATION BY WHEN FIRST ELECTED AS MP

| | When First Elected | | | | | |
	1974 or before	75–79	80–86	87–88	89–92[a]	Total
Support modernization?						
Yes	3	2	5	12	14	36
No	0	0	0	11	5	9
Support Clause IV reform?						
Yes	2	2	4	14	14	36
No	1	0	0	1	6	8
Unilateralism was rightly abandoned?						
Yes	1	2	3	10	8	24
No	1	0	1	3	8	13
Support deepening European integration?						
Yes	2	0	4	15	19	40
No	1	2	0	1	1	5
Target which voters?						
All voters	2	1	1	4	6	14
Political centre	1	0	2	8	7	18
Traditional supporters	0	1	1	2	4	8

a   post-Policy Review

This same pattern continues on the other issues. Those elected up to and including the 1987 general election favoured Clause IV reform overwhelmingly (22:2), compared with the figure of 70 per cent for these MPs elected in 1992. Pre-Policy Review MPs (those elected before 1989) favoured the change on unilateral nuclear disarmament (16:5), while post-Policy Review MPs were evenly split (8:8). European integration yields an interesting result. All groups, except those elected in 1979 or before, were supportive of increased integration.

Given the higher level of opposition to modernization and Clause IV reform among newly elected MPs, it is surprising to find that they are almost as likely to support the notion of capturing the middle ground in British politics. Pre-Policy Review MPs supported either targeting the party's traditional working class base or else all voters (11:4, with 8 saying to target all voters). By a seven-to-four margin, MPs elected in 1992 supported targeting the political centre (6 said to target all voters).

The party leadership is clearly aware of the need for future freshman classes to be ideologically supportive of modernization. During the party conference in October 1995, the party exerted control over the selection of local candidates and nullification of some 'hard-left' parliamentary candidates. During the conference, Liz Davies' selection as the parliamentary candidate for Leeds North East was rejected by the party's National Executive Committee since she was, according to Clare Short (party spokesperson on women), a Trotskyist who was likely to break the party's whip in parliament (Copley, 1995).

Regionalism. During the Thatcher era, Labour's support dramatically dropped in southern England, the Midlands, and London while it remained stable or increased in the party's traditional heartlands in the north, Scotland, and Wales. Table 5 shows a clear intra-party regional divide within the PLP. Scottish MPs are most sceptical about modernization; northern MPs are only slightly less favourable towards modernization than are those from other regions. On modernization and Clause IV reform, MPs from southern England, London, the Midlands, and Wales are highly favourable (19:3 for both); northern English MPs, while favourable, are a bit less supportive; in Scotland there is a split (5:3 against the changes). Only on European integration do regional differences disappear. All eight Scottish MPs expressed support for continuing integration, reflective of their support for subsidiarity. European integration is viewed as a vehicle to enhance decision-making authority at the local and Scottish levels.

TABLE 5
SUPPORT FOR MODERNIZATION BY REGION

Region

	South	London	Midlands	Wales	North	Scotland	Total
Support modernization?							
Yes	1	5	9	4	12	5	36
No	1	1	1	0	3	3	9
Support Clause IV reform?							
Yes	1	5	9	4	13	4	36
No	1	1	1	0	2	3	8
Unilateralism was rightly abandoned?							
Yes	1	2	7	1	9	4	24
No	0	1	3	1	5	3	13
Support deepening European integration?							
Yes	2	6	9	4	11	8	40
No	0	0	1	0	4	0	5
Target which voters?							
All voters	0	1	4	2	6	1	14
Political centre	2	3	5	2	3	3	18
Traditional supporters	0	1	0	0	3	4	8

It is clear that two Labour parties exist, one in Scotland, and another in England and Wales. In every category, except Europe, Scottish MPs expressed attitudes very different from their English and Welsh counterparts. They are more favourable to targeting the party's traditional base, less likely to support modernization and Clause IV reform, and more likely to argue that the removal of the unilateralist pledge was wrong (or done for the wrong reasons). This regional difference has important implications. Scottish MPs represent almost one-fifth of all Labour MPs (though the percentage is likely to drop if Labour makes significant electoral gains in London, the Midlands, and southern England). If their concerns go unheeded the party risks intra-party rows or losses of Scottish votes to the SNP. Further, a potential of twenty Scottish opponents of modernization could threaten the stability of a Labour government on controversial issues (such as devolution) if the majority is slender.

Modernizers and Traditionalists

By utilizing the Seyd and Whiteley (1992) traditionalist-modernizer dichotomy (with the addition of an intermediate category), it is possible to construct an index of modernization from the above data. Traditionalists are defined as opponents of modernization, while modernizers are supportive (Seyd and Whiteley, 1992: 146–47). MPs were placed in one of three categories, utilizing ideological self-placement, support for modernization generally, support for Clause IV reform, unilateralism, and the target voter group.[4] Taking these five indicators, if a respondent gave at least four responses (or three if one value is missing) in favour of the modernization position, that person is labeled a modernizer. A respondent giving the opposite number of anti-modernization answers is a traditionalist, while those split in their attitudes (either 2:2 or 3:2) are labelled intermediates.

Table 6 shows that most MPs can be placed squarely in the modernization camp. Two-thirds are modernizers; most (22 of 28) provided answers entirely consistent with support for modernization. Conversely, 19 per cent (n=8) are traditionalists; however, of this group, only three gave responses entirely consistent with opposition to the modernization process. Comparing this with Seyd and Whiteley's (1992) finding that 18 per cent of party members could be labelled traditionalists, suggests that the party in parliament to a large degree reflects the ideological make-up of the membership.

This split produces two ideological camps; the traditionalists (or 'Old Labour') representing 20 per cent of MPs, and 'New Labour' modernizers encompassing almost 70 per cent. Generalizing, it can be estimated that if the ideological breakdown of the PLP is similar to that of the sample (and there is, of course, the possibility that it is not), approximately 50 MPs in the post-1992 parliament fall into the traditionalist category, representing a potential obstacle to the modernizing agenda should the party win the next election.

TABLE 6
DISTRIBUTION OF MODERNIZERS AND TRADITIONALISTS

Label	Number	%
Modernizer	28	66.7
Intermediate	6	14.3
Traditionalist	8	19.1

Note: Due to rounding, numbers do not total 100 per cent.

Traditionalists and modernizers differ along regional lines, tenure in office, and ideological self-placement. As Table 7 shows, modernizers predominate among every regional grouping except Scotland. Whereas English and Welsh MPs combined produce 24 modernizers, five traditionalists, and five intermediates, the Scottish MPs are more likely to be traditionalists. Of the eight Scottish MPs, one is classified as intermediate, four as modernizers, and three as traditionalists.

TABLE 7
DEMOGRAPHIC CHARACTERISTICS OF TRADITIONALISTS, INTERMEDIATES,
AND MODERNIZERS

	Modernizer	Intermediate	Traditionalist
Region			
South	1	–	1
London	5	–	1
Midlands	7	–	1
Wales	3	–	–
North	8	4	2
Scotland	4	1	3
First Elected			
1974 or before	1	1	–
1975–79	1	1	–
1980–86	3	1	–
1987–88	12	1	2
1989–92	11	2	6
Ideological Self-Placement			
0 (Left)	–	–	1
2	1	–	3
3	1	4	4
4	6	2	–
5 (Centre)	6	–	–
6	5	–	–
7 (Right)	2	–	–

In terms of tenure in office, those elected in 1992 are much more likely to be traditionalists than any other grouping. Six of the nineteen MPs elected after the policy review of 1992 were categorized as traditionalists, in contrast to only two before. Further, all MPs placing themselves in the centre or centre-right (5–7) were modernizers (13:0). Of those placing themselves between 0–3, two were modernizers, four intermediates, and eight traditionalists. This suggests that 'Old Labour' is, indeed, demographically distinct from 'New Labour'.

The level of enthusiasm for the modernizing agenda is not very high even among its supporters. The next section explores the language used to express support for or opposition to modernization, to determine whether the party is highly unified and disciplined or still subject to the factional strife which has historically plagued it.

Qualitative Analysis of MPs' Attitudes

At the aggregate level, MPs are highly supportive of modernization. Most agree it was necessary to moderate party policies and change Clause IV (at least for symbolic reasons) so as to be more attuned to voters' aspirations. Even opponents admit the process has enabled the party to appeal to a broader cross-section of the public and should win votes. However, many supporters seem a bit sceptical about the motives of the modernizers and feel the reforms were pursued for symbolic reasons. The qualitative analysis proceeds in two stages. First we examine MPs' general statements on whether reforms have made the party little more than 'Conservative-light' or SDP mark 2 (Heffer, 1986). The second stage is limited to a few central issues: MP attitudes towards modernization and Clause IV reform generally; the importance of the reform; and its regional effect.

An examination of the words behind the opinions shows that, while a significant number of MPs are strongly supportive of party reform, a number expressed support in pragmatic terms, suggesting their support was because of the negative public relations which would have resulted from the changes not being implemented once initiated. By focusing on this contextual analysis, we can classify MPs into one of three categories (beyond the traditionalist–modernizer dichotomy): enthusiastic supporters, pragmatic supporters, and opponents.

Some MPs fear, others hail, Labour's move to the centre of the political spectrum. When reflecting on whether party reforms make the party too much like the Liberal Democrats (or even the Conservatives), MPs are split. Despite the claim by one MP that she couldn't compare the policies of the two parties because the Liberals 'don't have any', most supporters of modernization could distinguish Liberal Democrat and Labour policy positions. However, the differences highlighted by MPs show a definite convergence. One southern supporter of modernization distinguished the parties only along the lines of the single currency; the acute fear was that Labour's policies could fairly be described on public spending, taxation, and public ownership as the 'Liberal Democrat position', undermining credibility in its traditional heartlands. Opponents concur in the view that the positions of Labour and the Liberal Democrats have blurred, but express their attitudes more vehemently, claiming that the party has failed to enunciate clearly any policies, and/or to adopt policies which offer any positive reason to vote Labour.

In general, the supporters of modernization claimed that comparisons between Labour and the Liberal Democrats were unfair. One northern modernizer argued that parties always adjust policies and that when Labour 'goes right-wing' as in 1945 and the 1960s, it does well. In the past, for Labour to perform well, especially in southern England, the party needed to have a strong defence policy. Now, however, with the end of the Cold War and the demise of the defence industry, the advent of unemployment in the south, coupled with declining health and education services, makes the area one where Labour can do well if it crafts its message carefully. In fact, Labour, he maintained, benefits from the Conservative destruction of the unions in the 1980s:

> there's an old saying in politics that you should never shoot your fox and they did. They could blame the unions for inflation, pay rises, damaging strikes, irresponsibility, controlling the Labour party, everything. It was always the unions crippling Britain and tearing Britain down and destroying it. Then they destroyed the unions 10 years ago.

Now with union power diminished and the reform of the conference bloc vote, Labour has been able to rid itself of some weapons previously available for the Conservatives to use against them. Ultimately, then, it was 'essential to shift the party and modernize the party like Blair [did]'. These views were echoed by avid supporters of modernization who believe the party has created positive centrist policies. However, even among these supporters of modernization, some are wary that the party has no policies, that it has been too concerned with the elimination of unpopular policies at the expense of the creation of positive policies. Traditionalists argue that Labour runs enormous risks of losing traditional supporters by moving too close to the Liberal Democrats.

This fear is particularly acute in Scotland where socialism is not viewed as negatively as elsewhere and given that the Scottish National Party stands to benefit from Labour's centrist move. One Scottish MP, reflecting on modernization and its potential negative influence in his constituency, argued that 'in the north of England, they really don't have anywhere else to go, ...[but] in Scotland you can vote SNP'. Thus, centrist policies could have a positive impact on the party's share of the vote in the Midlands and southern England, but it could be harmful in traditional heartlands. However, from the perspective of seat-maximization, the reforms are understandable since most Labour seats in Scotland are highly safe; even a major swing away from Labour (which is unlikely) and vote share gains for the SNP, Liberal Democrats, or Conservatives would put relatively few Labour seats at risk.

It is clear that some supporters were very positive about the changes, while some were more lukewarm. It is important to examine the comments of this latter group, since their continued support is crucial for the Labour leadership. Of the 36 MPs interviewed, seven opposed party reforms, fourteen expressed extremely positive support, while fifteen were pragmatically supportive. Those expressing strong support for Clause IV reform maintained they never supported the original clause and were happy to see the party restating its aims and commitments.

Party unity is of paramount importance: minimal support for modernization should cause concern for the Labour leadership since the party will need the support of nearly all its MPs to pass important and controversial legislation should Labour be returned to office with a slender majority. To vote against the leadership on a major policy decision in a parliamentary system is tantamount to suicide; even if they disagreed strongly with the party leadership, most MPs would not vote against the party and risk a general election unless a major issue of principle should arise. An issue such as Europe, the NHS, privatization of the utilities, or grant-maintained schools, could force some MPs to vote against the party whip. In these instances, the size of the pragmatic supporters for and opponents of modernization becomes important since they could be sizeable enough to topple a Labour government.

It was something of a surprise in September 1995 that newspaper reports on the eve of the Liberal Democrat conference suggested a potential Liberal-Labour pact. Perhaps anticipating the potential for an important hard-left bloc in a future Labour government, Blair showed a willingness to court the Liberal Democrats. Reminiscent of the Lib-Lab pact which ensured Labour's survival in office from 1975 to 1979, Labour could depend on Liberal support, especially on a contentious issue. The policy and intra-party implications are important and could lead to a change in the electoral system, and/or a split which could result in a walkout of the Labour left reminiscent of the right's departure due to the increasing control by the hard left over the party's policymaking institutions.

Enthusiastic Supporters: (n=14; 39 per cent of MPs)

Fourteen MPs (39 per cent) were extremely positive about party reforms; their responses were entirely consistent with modernization, arguing, further, that the changes were necessary, beneficial, and fundamental. The following are a cross-section of these views.

> I was delighted that Tony put it [Clause IV] centre stage because...I've never supported it. It was all about central control...[and] the nationalization of everything...The only person who opposed the rewriting of Clause IV has been a former member who was expelled. (northern English MP)

> I think it should be changed because we are not about owning everything as a government... It [maintaining Clause IV] is really perpetrating a mistruth on the electorate. So I've been supportive of change because we should be saying for the twenty-first century what we believe. (Welsh MP)

> They [the public] will see that [getting Clause IV reformed] as skilled leadership... Gaitskell tried, Harold Wilson tried, Neil Kinnock launched the philosophy that we needed to change it but obviously didn't have the time to do it. So I think people will view that as the most significant part of the changes in our constitution. (Northern MP)

It's about a new leader initiating change... It has been an honest debate... and is going to have a positive impact since it can give us clear aims and values... [and] should make the party stronger and united. (elected 1987)

[Kinnock's] strength was that he changed the rules of the party and the outlook of the party and stopped the tail wagging the dog, whereas previous leaders, like Michael Foot, had their philosophical head in the clouds... It was very important that John Smith and Tony Blair got a grip on it; and then when Blair was elected and took the main ten commandments of the party, Clause IV, which nobody had bothered with for years, but which the Tories had used against us, by creating a commanding win on that, it stopped the Tories from using it and jibing us. (MP elected before 1974)

It [modernization] is essential to us winning... Only after the process had gotten under way with Neil Kinnock, gathering strength with John Smith and now with Tony Blair, are we starting to see the dividends in terms of electoral support... We have to win the next election not just because the Tories are unpopular, but so that people are thinking positively about Labour. Modernization provides us with this. (MP elected in 1992)

Pragmatic Supporters: (n=15; 42 per cent)

There was a significant proportion of MPs who, while supportive of changes in the party's constitution and policies, implied that their support was pragmatic rather than deeply ingrained. For example, many recognized that if Blair lost the Clause IV debate, the party (and Blair's legitimacy as leader) would be, potentially, fatally damaged for the next election, letting the Conservatives in for yet another term. For negative supporters, this result is to be avoided at all costs. The following is a sample of the types of sentiments expressed by these fifteen MPs.

I don't think it is very important [Clause IV reform]... I think that Blair is just trying to prove that he can run the party since...how they [the electorate] perceive the party is extremely important. (Midlands MP)

Clause IV is not an albatross to the party... Nobody on the ground has ever complained about Clause IV to me and people don't even know what it is... I wouldn't have started the debate over Clause IV because I didn't think it needed to be opened, ...[but] it is a debate that Tony has to win. (Northern MP)

The Policy Review was very positive... My worry about the process was that it was only concerned with eliminating negative images rather than trying to put forward positive images... Someone said in a taxi to me that 'if Clause IV was that important, why wasn't it Clause I?' I think that sums up what a lot of people feel... I never had people on the doorstep say 'well I would vote for Labour except for this bit in your constitution'... The debate is distorted since it gets into an argument about what you're not. (Highly marginal MP elected in 1992)

I don't think it makes any difference [changing Clause IV]... It's just a symbolic change... In that sense [it] will strengthen Blair rather than the party... It's like the 39 articles of the Church of England, something... distant that nobody takes any notice of and which is more trouble to get rid of than is worth the effort. So, it's not something I would have done but it is clearly something that he had to win... It was carried through skillfully because it had no possibility of failing since the questions were so loaded. (Northern MP)

I come from a trade union background...and my first loyalty is to the people it represents, who tend to be from the lower working class... I feel the debate [over Clause IV] just feeds into all of the old public perceptions of what the Labour party is like... I have come to the reluctant conclusion that Blair's got to win if we are to have any chance of winning the election. (Scottish MP)

Modernization's Opponents: (n=7; 19 per cent)

While most MPs supported, in some form or another, the changes in the party over the last dozen years, a significant percentage remain wary, fearful that the party has abandoned its traditional base and mission. Importantly, among this group, three represent Scotland which could foreshadow a future disaster for Labour after the next general election if the party loses or if Blair does not deliver relief to the party's traditional heartlands. The following are a reflection of the anger and apprehension of this group. Though small in number, they could present a challenge to Blair if Labour wins with a narrow majority at the next election: combined with the negative supporters, they represent a potential constraint on the Labour leadership.

It was an unproductive debate for six months when we should have been debating policy... The real danger is not that soundbites won't win us the next election, it is that it won't actually reflect a policy that will sustain us afterwards... I would argue that Labour has yet to spell out the policy difference between us and the Tories and Liberal Democrats. (Southern MP)

I view the changes with great suspicion and apprehension... I've known Tony for many, many years, ...but I think he is going too far and too quickly and this is being done without any degree of humility whatsoever. (Northern MP)

I am very much afraid that when people talk about presentation and public relations exercises they are often hiding a philosophy of intent... Don't get me wrong, I am not concerned that we are 40 per cent ahead in the polls, the only trouble is that when we build up expectations and you're a little bit thin on political philosophy, ...there is a danger... I've been campaigning for the retention of Clause IV... I don't think we need to be afraid of common ownership... It has stood the test of time and I think it stands very favourably to an unbridled market economy. (Northern MP)

I have been on the side of the traditionalists... [Clause IV reform] is aimed essentially at the electorate in southern England... The problem is that it is damaging our electoral credibility in Scotland and the north of England where Clause IV isn't seen as bad and the fact that the Labour Party is seen as a socialist party is a plus. (Scottish MP)

[I]t was an American politician that said that absolute power corrupts but absolute powerlessness corrupts even more... We have been out of office for so long that we... would pick up dog dirt with our hands and eat it if we thought we would get elected... The leadership of the party has decided that the way of getting in is to say nothing... on policy. (Midlands MP)

Although modernization is supported by most, this is not in all cases with much emotion or enthusiasm. A significant proportion opposed the changes and resist further change. Parties may adapt in the name of electability, but they do not necessarily convince all party elites as to the necessity or correctness of the changes.

Conclusion

This article tested three hypotheses over the determinants of support for Labour's modernization: regionalism, ideological polarization, and tenure in office. The generational findings suggest that Labour is recruiting MPs who are more suspicious of modernization than are veterans. It is possible (and, indeed, likely) that longer service in Parliament has a moderating influence and that, in time, the 'classes' of 1987 and 1992 will express similar attitudes to those MPs elected before 1987;[5] however, at the very least, the newly elected MPs represent a significant potential obstacle for the modernizers.

The region which an MP represents is a good indicator of the likelihood of support for modernization. Whether the tendency of Scottish MPs to be more suspicious of modernization is caused by their representing a more working class region or vice-versa is undetermined. But it is clear that the regional polarization ushered in by Thatcherism made its way into the PLP. Further, the ideology of an MP is highly correlated with attitudes towards modernization.

Although it would not be prudent to overplay the power of the traditionalists, given the 20 per cent opposition to modernization and the 40 per cent pragmatic supporters, it can be expected that a Labour government with a small majority will be riven with factional fighting. A slender majority would pose the potential for a successful vote of no confidence on a controversial and socialist touchstone issue, especially if the aid of the Liberal Democrats was unavailable. The overtures made towards Paddy Ashdown and the Liberal Democrats by Tony Blair suggest that the leadership is aware of this possibility. Such close contacts could potentially lead to another claim of betrayal by the Labour Left and a second Labour split if Blair is seen as acceding to the demands of the Liberals rather than the traditionalists.

ACKNOWLEDGEMENTS

I would like to thank Barry Sheerman, MP for Huddersfield, and his parliamentary research assistant Alex Chandler for aiding me in the completion of this research. They, however, bear no responsibility for the gathering or interpretation of the results. Further, I would like to thank Patrick Seyd for suggestions on the drafting of questions and the original letter to MPs as well as advice in conducting the interviews. I would also like to thank David Farrell, Karen Mingst, and Derek Agard for comments on earlier drafts of this article. Finally, I would like to thank sincerely all those MPs who participated in this project since, without them, there would be no article.

NOTES

1. Thirty-six interviews were conducted utilizing interviews, while nine filled out survey questionnaires. Forty-two of the MPs were backbenchers, and three were front-benchers.
2. Tenure in office is omitted due to the focus on backbenchers, as the backbenchers sampled are expected to be more likely to have been elected in 1987 and 1992.
3. Significant numbers offer that Thatcherism damaged all segments of society and that the party should aim at all groups.
4. Those expressing a desire to target all voters or to target the centre were coded as pro-modernization.
5. Traditionally, service in Parliament and in government has been viewed as having a moderating influence on MPs, though Tony Benn is an exception (see Seyd, 1987).

BIBLIOGRAPHY

Blair, Tony (1995) Speech to the Labour Party Conference.

Copley, Joy (1995) 'Left Wing Defeated: Davies Weeps at Bid Reject', *Electronic Telegraph,* 4 October.

Curtice, John and Michael Steed (1982) 'Electoral Choice and the Production of Government', *British Journal of Political Science* 12: 249–88.

Devine, Fiona (1992) 'Working-class evaluations of the Labour Party', in Ivor Crewe, Pippa Norris, David Denver, David Broughton (eds) *British Elections and Parties Yearbook 1991*, pp.161–73, Hemel Hempstead: Harvester Wheatsheaf.

Heffer, Eric (1986) *Labour's Future: Socialist or SDP Mark 2?* London: Verso.

Hughes, Colin and Patrick Wintour (1990) *Labour Rebuilt.* London: Fourth Estate.

Johnston, Ron J. *et al.* (1988) *A Nation Dividing?* New York: John Wiley and Sons.

Kogan, David and Maurice Kogan (1982) *The Battle for the Labour Party.* New York: St. Martin's Press.

McAllister, Ian and Anthony Mughan (1986) 'The nuclear weapons issue in the 1983 British General Election', *European Journal of Political Research* 14: 651–8.

Norris, Pippa (1994) 'Labour Party Factionalism and Extremism', in Anthony Heath *et al.* (eds) *Labour's Last Chance*, Aldershot: Dartmouth.

Seyd, Patrick (1987) *The Rise and Fall of the Labour Left.* New York: St. Martin's Press.

Seyd, Patrick and Paul Whiteley (1992) *Labour's Grass Roots.* Oxford: Clarendon Press.

Shaw, Eric (1994) *The Labour Party Since 1979.* New York: Routledge.

Smith, Martin and Joanna Spear (eds) (1992) *The Changing Labour Party.* New York: Routledge.

How Did He Do That? The Second Round of the 1990 Conservative Leadership Election

Philip Cowley

Introduction

The transformation of Britain into a 'dominant' party system (King, 1993) has increased the importance of Conservative leadership elections. General elections remain important: the electorate can still choose to 'turn the rascals out'. But if they choose not to – if general elections become merely confirmations of one-party dominance – then elections to decide which faction dominates the dominant party become vital. This article concentrates on one such contest: the second round of the 1990 leadership election, which saw John Major emerge victorious. Explanations of Major's victory have been numerous and have focused on a vast array of potential factors (Anderson, 1992; Ellis, 1991; Foley, 1993; Jenkin, 1990: 149–67; Junor, 1993; Norton, 1993; Pearce, 1991; Shepherd, 1991; Watkins, 1992). However, although often stunningly detailed – and very entertaining – these accounts are mostly anecdotal. (The one exception – though based on a small number of cases – is Garry, 1995). In part, this is because it is difficult to carry out a systematic examination of a secret ballot. However, although difficult, it is not impossible – with a little work and the right information – to estimate the individual voting behaviour of all 372 MPs.

Using these data, and constructing a data-base of ideological, socio-economic and political variables for all 372 Conservative MPs, this article attempts the first systematic explanation of the candidates' support. Were those in safer seats more likely to vote for Hurd, being less worried about the effect that the least 'popular' candidate might have on their own seats? And what was the effect of education? Did those who had come from private schools and Oxbridge eschew the alumnus of Rutlish Grammar? Or were all of these various factors overwhelmed by the pull of ideology?

Existing Explanations

Many of the accounts of Major's rise detail the effect that ideology had on the contest.[1] Major (supposedly to the 'right' on economic matters but to the 'left' on social matters) is said to have been able to draw his support from the 'right' of the party (helped by Mrs Thatcher's vocal backing), as well as from the centre. Hurd and Heseltine are said to have been stuck with those on the 'left' of the party (often said to have been a small number). But we need to be clear exactly what we mean by 'ideology'. Authors frequently throw phrases like 'wet', 'dry', 'Thatcherite', or 'one-nation Tory' around without prior definition. One exception is Philip Norton who used a series of ideological categories to examine the 1989 challenge to Mrs Thatcher and to detail the flows of the votes between the first and second round ballots in 1990 (Norton, 1990, 1993).[2] Norton's typology has been criticized for being, *inter alia*, two-dimensional (Dunleavy, 1993). More significantly, it is time-bound, an accusation its author accepts: it is a 'snapshot of the parliamentary party, albeit one with a slow ten-year exposure' (Norton, 1990: 52). It thus fails to cope with some of the more recent cleavages in the Conservative Party (Baker *et al.*, 1994). However, for an examination of the events of November 1990 – before these splits became quite so manifest – the typology is ideal.

The Norton categories can be summarized as follows: *Neoliberals* believe in the rigorous application of market forces; the *Tory Right* stress moral issues, especially law and order; *Pure Thatcherites* combine market forces with law and order; *Wets* believe in a role for government intervention in social and economic affairs; *Damps* believe in the same as Wets but not as intensely; *Populists* reflect popular attitudes, being left wing on social issues but right wing on law and order; and the *Party Faithful* (the largest group) support the party rather than ideological strands of thought. The Pure Thatcherites, Tory Right, and Neoliberals are sometimes grouped together and called *Thatcherites*, and the Wets and Damps are similarly collectively known as *Critics*.

In November 1990, there were 67 Critics (18 per cent of the parliamentary party), made up of 27 Wets and 40 Damps. There were 71 Thatcherites (19 per cent of the party), consisting of 15 Neoliberals, 30 Pure Thatcherites, and 26 members of the Tory Right. There were just 17 Populists (5 per cent). The majority of the party consisted of members of the Party Faithful (217 MPs or 58 per cent of the party).[3] Norton classes both Hurd and Heseltine as Damps. Major is a member of the Party Faithful: 'He could thus appeal to all parts of the party. Thatcherites saw him as fiscally conservative. Thatcher herself supported him and lobbied on his behalf. Wets and damps were attracted by his reputation for being liberal on social issues and by his advocacy of membership of the ERM' (Norton, 1993: 59). Heseltine and Hurd, by contrast, 'were basically competing for the same constituency'.

Even a casual reading of the extant literature on the leadership election soon raises the suspicion that ideology will not explain all (for example, Anderson, 1992: 336–40). One other important political factor could be the career status of the voting MP. This article uses a three-fold typology memorably made famous by John Major himself in a later off-the-record conversation.[4] Major referred to the 'dispossessed and the never possessed' as those MPs who were causing him trouble. The dispossessed were those who had once held office, but had since had it removed from them. The never possessed were those who had never even begun to climb the career ladder. (It is of some interest – and slightly unfortunate – that using Major's own typology, those who serve in his government are known as 'possessed'.) Major's proposition was simple: these people cause trouble because they are bitter. Although empirical analysis makes the validity of Major's claims seem suspect in relation to his own bothersome backbenchers (Hague and Berrington, 1995), it is possible that a similar effect occurred under Mrs Thatcher: the dispossessed and the never possessed might be hypothesized, *ceteris paribus*, more likely to vote for Heseltine (as the man responsible for bringing down Mrs Thatcher) or at least to be more likely to vote against John Major (as Mrs Thatcher's anointed successor). Similarly, there could be an insider/outsider effect. Foley has traced the rise of 'spatial leadership', and the attractiveness of 'outsiders' in both American and British politics. He claims that Heseltine used his outsider status during the 1990 leadership campaign: 'As an "outsider", he was offering what an "outsider" can only ever offer – namely himself, his individual leadership, his private licence for political vision and his own personal popularity with a public encouraged to want and to expect change' (Foley, 1993: 187).

If Foley is right, we could expect Heseltine to have drawn support disproportionately from other 'outsiders'. Overall, we might assume that Major would do least well among outsiders; and Heseltine might do disproportionately well. The effect of career status on Hurd's support might be neutral: he may gain some votes from outsiders for not being Mrs Thatcher's chosen successor, but lose some by not being an outsider.

The importance of a social dimension has been stressed in many previous accounts of the 1990 contest. Indeed, class was first raised by Major himself at the launch of his campaign:

> It was an inspired idea... The media loved it, and the spotlight immediately fell on the other two in terms of class. Heseltine was unashamedly and ostentatiously rich, money he had made himself in the best Thatcherite tradition... Hurd was an old Etonian and found himself on the defensive about it, explaining that there would have been no question of his father, a tenant farmer, sending him to Eton had he not won a scholarship (Junor, 1993: 202).

Major, by contrast, represented a growing breed of middle-class, self-made men and women in the parliamentary party. Such men and women, claims Norton, 'voted for one of their own' (Norton, 1993: 59). Foley again argues that this was evidence of an 'outsider' effect: 'Major's political status as a social "outsider" also cut into Heseltine's reputation as a political "outsider"' (Foley, 1993: 201). However, Anderson claims that there was also a significant 'toffs for Major' movement (Anderson, 1992: 343). We might therefore expect socio-economic factors to be important. Major should disproportionately gain the support of the more middle class sections of the party.

The existing studies suggest that the size of an MP's majority might also be important. Although the electorate in the leadership election was that 'somewhat select constituency, the Conservative Parliamentary Party' (Ellis, 1991: 3), the MPs were said to be aware of the appeal that the candidates had to the wider electorate. Alan Clark claimed that: 'Not so many in the Party really want to vote Heseltine, for himself....the bulk of Michael's support comes from his so-called Election winning powers... Once they have a real reason to do so, they'll abandon him' (Clark, 1994: 369).

Despite being practically unknown before the election started, in terms of his positive effect on the electoral fortunes of the Conservative Party, opinion polls showed that Major had drawn level with Heseltine (and in one poll pulled ahead) by 22 November. In his diaries, Clark claims to have met Heseltine just after these figures had been released. Heseltine had realized how damaging the polls were to his challenge:

> At the last turn in the landing I heard the top door open in a rush and there, quite alone, wild-eyed and head to head stood Heseltine.
> 'Hullo Michael', I said.
> He made no answer, rushed past... he was a zombie, shattered. It was Mates who had brought him the numbers (Clark, 1994: 370).

It is never made clear if the electoral appeal of both Major and Heseltine was an individualistic or a collective phenomena. If it was the former – based on the effect that a candidate could make to an individual MP's seat – then we might expect those in the more marginal seats to have been more likely to support either Heseltine or Major, at the expense of Hurd. Conversely, if the electoral appeal was more collective – not so much a fear of losing one's own seat but of the party ceasing to be in government – then marginality should not have any effect.

There could also be differences depending on age and experience. At 47 Major was much the youngest of the three candidates (Hurd was 60 and Heseltine 57), and was the nearest of the three candidates to the median Conservative MP, who was aged 51. Perhaps more significantly, Major entered the Commons in 1979. Hurd and Heseltine had both been in the House for much longer (entering in 1974 and 1966 respectively). By 1979, when Major entered, both the other candidates were already in the government. Hurd was a minister of state in the Foreign and Commonwealth Office. Heseltine, who had entered government as long ago as June 1970, was in the cabinet. Both were therefore not fully accessible to any new and inexperienced Conservative MPs elected in the three Conservative victories of 1979, 1983 and 1987: Heseltine by virtue of his seniority, Hurd because he spent much of the time outside of the country. Heseltine was, in addition, a notoriously bad 'mixer'. Foley notes that Heseltine was 'an unclubbable individual not given to the sociable dimension of life in the House of Commons' (Foley, 1993: 186). (If this did harm him, then it is evidence of the harmful effects of being an 'outsider' when your electorate is composed mainly of insiders, a fact not appreciated by Foley.) In 1990 over half the Parliamentary Conservative Party had entered with or after John Major. One of the 1983 intake argued that the younger and more inexperienced MPs elected in 1983 or 1987 found Major, in contrast with Hurd and Heseltine, in the House *and* accessible (interview). Major does not list a single foreign trip in any of his entries in the register of members' interests from 1979 onwards. He was never a member of a foreign delegation taking him away from the House for long periods. And he had a very good – meaning high – voting record.[5] In part this was due to the nature of his career. He became a PPS in January 1981, and then entered the Whips' Office in 1983 and served both as a junior and senior whip until September 1985.[6] Because of his career and personality, Major was therefore both in the House and in contact with and accessible to the other MPs.[7] The other two candidates were either not there or were aloof. If this is true, then it will have done Major no harm among candidates of any age, but it might have been a particularly keen effect among the younger and more inexperienced MPs.

All of these explanations focus on the voters: they try to explain why certain people voted for a candidate based on a series of attributes held by the voter. Although the hypothesis may implicitly relate attributes of the voter to attributes of the candidates – say, for example, ideology – any other attributes of the candidates are overlooked. Yet the existing works on the 1990 contest are riddled with candidate-centred explanations, especially explanations which focus on Major.

All the observers, for example, agree that Major was seen by his peers as competent. As Shepherd says: 'At the DHSS, dealing with social security, a potential minefield for ministers where the devil is in the detail, he developed a reputation for mastering his brief and presenting an assured, calming impression at the dispatch box' (Shepherd, 1991: 55). When Major was Chief Secretary to the Treasury, Thatcher is said to have become impressed by his 'mastery of detail and good housekeeping' (Shepherd, 1991: 56). Similar stories are told of Major's time as a Whip (Pearce, 1991). Bruce Anderson (1992: 72) describes Major as a 'natural networker' (also Young, 1993:

564–5). He also comments on Major's capacity for hard work, his warmth and his lack of enemies. Major's campaign team also received praise (Anderson, 1992).

These candidate-centred approaches to the contest do not explain why any of the candidates do particularly well or badly among certain groups of MPs. Major's campaign team may have been important in explaining why he did so well in absolute terms, but if we find that he did particularly well among certain groups in the party that cannot be the product of any candidate effect. Similarly, Major might well be 'warm' and 'competent', but if we find that the more elderly MPs were disproportionately likely to eschew him in favour of the 'unclubbable' Heseltine, then the explanation clearly needs to focus on the voters rather than the candidates.

Analysis

This section provides bivariate breakdowns of the candidates' support by the socio-economic and political variables discussed above, in an attempt to test the hypotheses derived from the existing explanations of the election.[8] Each table contains three different sets of results: a) results derived from confirmed data only; b) results derived from both confirmed and probable data; and c) results derived from confirmed, probable and doubtful data. The Appendix explains what is meant by confirmed, probable or doubtful, as well as providing details of how the data were gathered. For simplicity's sake most of the analysis below focuses on the middle set of data – results derived from both the confirmed and probable data – although as a glance at the tables will confirm, the results are substantially the same whichever set of data is used.

Ideology

Table 1 shows the ideological breakdown of the three candidates' supporters. There are, as expected, clear ideological differences. Heseltine attracted the support of just over 80 per cent of the Wets and of almost 40 per cent of the Damps. Hurd failed to gain the support of many Wets (under 15 per cent supported him) but like Heseltine he received the support of 40 per cent of the Damps. Accordingly, Major's support did not come from this section of the party – the so-called 'Critics'. Of the 64 Critics (whose intentions are either probable or confirmed) Major attracted the support of just eight, or 13 per cent, and of these, only one was a Wet. This is perhaps not altogether surprising, but it is noticeable both how Heseltine (classed by Norton as a Damp) attracted support from those more wet than him, at the expense of Hurd (also a Damp) and how so little of Major's support came from this wing of the party. Norton (1993: 59) claimed that Major could 'appeal to all parts of the party', and that Wets and Damps were 'attracted' to him by his reputation for social liberalism and support for the ERM. They may have been 'attracted', but they were not attracted enough to vote for him. More Thatcherites voted for Michael Heseltine than Critics for John Major.

TABLE 1
IDEOLOGICAL NATURE OF THE CANDIDATES' SUPPORT

	Major		Heseltine		Hurd		Total
	n	%	n	%	n	%	n
With confirmed data only							
Wet	1	5.9	12	70.6	4	23.5	17
Damp	5	18.5	9	33.3	13	48.1	27
Neoliberal	5	50.0	2	20.0	3	30.0	10
Pure Thatch.	17	77.3	2	9.1	3	13.6	22
Tory Right	14	77.8	3	16.7	1	5.6	18
Populist	4	40.0	6	60.0	0	0.0	10
Party Faithful	70	56.0	35	28.0	20	16.0	125
All MPs	116		69		44		229
With probable data included							
Wet	1	3.7	22	81.5	4	14.8	27
Damp	7	18.9	15	40.5	15	40.5	37
Neoliberal	8	53.3	3	20.0	4	26.7	15
Pure Thatch.	23	79.3	3	10.3	3	10.3	29
Tory Right	18	75.0	5	20.8	1	4.2	24
Populist	7	43.8	8	50.0	1	6.2	16
Party Faithful	111	58.4	58	30.5	21	11.1	190
All MPs	175		114		49		338
With doubtful data included							
Wet	1	3.7	22	81.5	4	14.8	27
Damp	9	22.5	15	37.5	16	40.0	40
Neoliberal	8	53.3	3	20.0	4	26.7	15
Pure Thatch.	23	76.7	4	13.3	3	10.0	30
Tory Right	18	69.2	5	19.2	3	11.5	26
Populist	8	47.1	8	47.1	1	5.9	17
Party Faithful	118	54.4	74	34.1	25	11.5	217
All MPs	185		131		56		372

Note: In this and all following tables not all percentages sum to 100 due to rounding.

Also as expected, Major did draw substantial support from the wing of the party collectively known as the Thatcherites (Neoliberals, Pure Thatcherites and the Tory Right): Major won the support of the majority of all three of these ideological groupings. But there are important differences between the Thatcherite factions. Major did least well among the Neoliberals (gaining 53 per cent of their votes), with the remainder splitting fairly evenly between Hurd and Heseltine. However, the Neoliberals are one of the smallest ideological groupings in the Conservative Parliamentary Party, and Major did better among the two larger Thatcherite groupings, gaining 75 per cent of the Tory Right's vote (with those that did not support him eschewing Hurd almost completely in favour of Heseltine), and almost 80 per cent of the Pure Thatcherites. However, Major's support among the Thatcherites was not as firm as his rejection by the Critics. As noted above, only 13 per cent of the Critics supported Major. But of the Thatcherites, 28 per cent voted for one of the other candidates.

Exactly half of the Populists supported Heseltine, a substantial minority (40 per cent) went for Major, and only one voted for Hurd. But the Populists – like the Neoliberals – are a small grouping. Much more important is the largest group of all: the Party Faithful. The majority (some 58 per cent) supported Major, with over 30 per cent backing Heseltine. Hurd attracted just 11 per cent.

As expected, therefore, there were clear ideological dividing lines between the candidates. The Critics supported either Hurd or Heseltine. The Thatcherites – a group of similar size to the Critics – went for Major. But they did not support him as enthusiastically as the Critics rejected him. Major's real success however came in attracting the support of the Party Faithful. Winning a clear majority of the ideologically 'unattached' was more important than the support of the Thatcherites. Using the third set of figures (including the doubtful data) briefly, we see that Major gained the support of 49 Thatcherites (with 22 voting for one of the other candidates). But 118 members of the Party Faithful – almost two and a half times as many – supported him.

Given that under the Norton classification the Party Faithful are the majority of the party, we would be surprised if they did not form a large part of any candidates support. What is important, however, is the extent to which the candidates reached outside of their 'natural' support and into the Conservative Parliamentary Party's floating voters. This point can be illustrated easily by examining column percentages: that is, by seeing how much of each candidate's support came from one grouping or another. (Here, again, the second group of data – probable and confirmed data – is used and although the following figures are not given in the tables they can easily be derived from those that are provided.) Major's support was 5 per cent Critic, 28 per cent Thatcherite, 4 per cent Populist, and 63 per cent Party Faithful. Heseltine's was 32 per cent Critic, 10 per cent Thatcherite, 7 per cent Populist, and 51 per cent Party Faithful. Hurd's support was 39 per cent Critic, 16 per cent Thatcherite, 2 per cent Populist, and 43 per cent Party Faithful. So, whereas the two losing candidates drew just over or noticeably under half their support from the ideologically unattached, Major gathered almost two-thirds of his support from this grouping.

Career Status

Table 2 shows the career status of the candidates' supporters, utilizing the trichotomy discussed above of possessed, dispossessed, and never possessed.

TABLE 2
CANDIDATES' SUPPORTERS BY CAREER STATUS

	Major		Heseltine		Hurd		Total
	n	%	n	%	n	%	n
With confirmed data only							
Possessed	45	54.2	11	13.3	27	32.5	83
Dispossessed	33	43.4	34	44.7	9	11.8	76
Never possessed	38	54.3	24	34.3	8	11.4	70
All MPs	116		69		44		229
With probable data included							
Possessed	61	55.0	21	18.9	29	26.1	111
Dispossessed	55	45.8	54	45.0	11	9.2	120
Never possessed	59	55.1	39	36.4	9	8.4	107
All MPs	175		114		49		338
With doubtful data included							
Possessed	65	53.7	26	21.5	30	24.8	121
Dispossessed	58	44.6	58	44.6	14	10.8	130
Never possessed	62	51.2	47	38.8	12	9.9	121
All MPs	185		131		56		372

There are clear insider/outsider effects. Of those in government (the possessed) Heseltine managed to gain the support of just 21 MPs, or under 19 per cent. Hurd gained more votes from those in government than Heseltine. Those on the inside gave their support to others on the inside. Note however that the percentage of support which Heseltine draws from those in government increases the more unreliable the data becomes. This could simply be a fault with the data, but it is more likely to be evidence that those in government were unwilling to publicly support the man who brought down Mrs Thatcher. This rejection from those on the inside would not have mattered so much to Heseltine if those on the outside – of whom there were almost twice as many – had supported him as a fellow outsider. Unfortunately, for Heseltine, they did not. He does gain a similar share of the votes of the dispossessed as Major, but the never possessed (who, since they have never been in government can be seen as the true outsiders) voted for Major rather than Heseltine. Foley's theory of the 'outsider' may work with the general public, but Conservative MPs – especially Conservative MPs on the inside – seem to have an antipathy towards outsiders.

Education and Occupation
Table 3 shows the pre-parliamentary occupations of the candidates' supporters.

TABLE 3
CANDIDATES' SUPPORT BY OCCUPATION

	Major		Heseltine		Hurd		Total
	n	%	n	%	n	%	n
With confirmed data only							
Lawyer	20	48.8	10	24.4	11	26.8	41
Other professionals	40	51.3	24	30.8	14	17.9	78
Business	36	48.0	25	33.3	14	18.7	75
Other	20	57.1	10	28.6	5	14.3	35
All MPs	116		69		44		229
With probable data included							
Lawyer	30	50.8	18	30.5	11	18.6	59
Other professionals	59	56.2	32	30.5	14	13.3	105
Business	56	48.3	42	36.2	18	15.5	116
Other	30	51.7	22	37.9	6	10.3	58
All MPs	175		114		49		338
With doubtful data included							
Lawyer	32	47.1	24	35.3	12	17.6	68
Other professionals	62	53.9	36	31.3	17	14.8	115
Business	60	46.5	49	38.0	20	15.5	129
Other	31	51.7	22	36.7	7	11.7	60
All MPs	185		131		56		372

Unlike the previous two areas, here there are no noticeable differences between the candidates. Major received the support of around half of all occupational groups. Heseltine receives the support of the second largest amount of each occupational group, with Hurd receiving the smallest share of all three groups. There are some slight variations – Hurd does slightly better among lawyers, and Heseltine does well among those from business or other occupations – but these differences are not great.

Table 4 shows the educational mix of the candidates' supporters. It is split into three groups: (a) showing whether the MPs were state or privately educated; (b) whether they received a university education or not; and (c) whether those educated at university went to Oxbridge or to other universities.

TABLE 4
CANDIDATES' SUPPORT BY EDUCATION

	Major		Heseltine		Hurd		Total
	n	%	n	%	n	%	n
With confirmed data only							
Private	63	43.4	49	33.8	33	22.8	145
State educated	53	63.1	20	23.8	11	13.1	84
Sub-total	116		69		44		229
University	84	48.0	53	30.3	38	21.7	175
Not university	32	59.3	16	29.6	6	11.1	54
Sub-total	116		69		44		229
Oxbridge	45	40.2	37	33.0	30	26.8	112
Other university	39	61.9	16	25.4	8	12.7	63
Sub-total	84		53		38		175
With probable data included							
Private	96	46.6	74	35.9	36	17.5	206
State	79	59.8	40	30.3	13	9.8	132
Sub-total	175		114		49		338
University	122	48.4	88	34.9	42	16.7	252
Not university	53	61.6	26	30.2	7	8.1	86
Sub-total	175		114		49		338
Oxbridge	62	40.0	59	38.1	34	21.9	155
Other university	60	61.9	29	29.9	8	8.2	97
Sub-total	122		88		42		252
With doubtful data included							
Private	103	44.2	88	37.8	42	18.0	233
State	82	59.0	43	30.9	14	10.1	139
Sub-total	185		131		56		372
University	130	46.4	103	36.8	47	16.8	280
Not university	55	59.8	28	30.4	9	9.8	92
Sub-total	185		131		56		372
Oxbridge	68	39.1	68	39.1	38	21.8	174
Other university	62	58.5	35	33.0	9	8.5	106
Sub-total	130		103		47		280

Clear differences emerge, and these are, by and large, in line with the hypotheses derived from the literature. Major's supporters were disproportionately state educated, whereas Hurd's were disproportionately privately educated. Similarly, Major's supporters disproportionately did not receive a university education, while Hurd's supporters were proportionately more likely to. The most striking difference, however, concerns those educated at university: over 60 per cent of those educated at non-Oxbridge universities voted for Major, compared to only 40 per cent of those educated at Oxbridge. Again, Hurd's figures are the reverse: almost 22 per cent of those educated at Oxbridge voted for him, compared to less than 9 per cent of those educated at other universities. Insofar as education is a valid surrogate for 'class' or 'privilege' (a matter discussed further below), the hypotheses advanced above seem to hold true for Hurd (who clearly had a problem reaching those who were not privately educated, did not go to university or went to universities other than Oxbridge). Conversely, as expected, Major did better among those who were state educated, did not go to university or went to non-Oxbridge universities. In Norton's words the supporters of both Hurd and Major clearly did vote for 'one of their own'. But it would be wrong – as is sometimes implied – to suggest that Major's support was all 'new Tory'. Anderson's caveat about the 'Toffs for Major' movement is important. For although Major did well among those who were state educated, he did not do badly among those who were privately educated either. Indeed, in each of the three categories the 'privileged' were in the majority among his supporters (that is, more privately educated MPs voted for him than did state educated MPs; more university educated MPs voted for him than did those without a university education; and more Oxbridge educated MPs voted for him than did those who had received their higher education elsewhere).

What of Heseltine? Most of the focus on the social background of the candidates centres on Hurd (Eton) vs. Major (Brixton). Heseltine (Shrewsbury, Oxford, and very very rich) often gets overlooked. Examining row percentages seems to indicate that Heseltine's support was not drawn from any particular educational category – he appears to draw approximately proportionate support from each of the groupings – but an examination of the column percentages (again, not reproduced in the table, but derived from it) shows that there is indeed a difference between Heseltine and Major. Some 65 per cent of Heseltine's support came from the privately educated, compared to 55 per cent of Major's; 77 per cent of Heseltine's supporters were university educated, compared to 70 per cent of Major's; and of those who were university educated 53 per cent of Major's support came from those educated at Oxbridge compared to 69 per cent for Heseltine.[9]

In their analysis of the political elite, Burch and Moran (1985) noted that examining MPs' socio-economic background was fraught with difficulties. But, despite all the problems, they concluded that 'the alternative to this limited and imperfect information... is often no information at all'. The limited and imperfect information analysed here – education and pre-parliamentary occupation – has found some clear socio-economic differences in the candidates' support. There appears to be little difference in the candidates' support when broken down by pre-parliamentary occupation, but the differences in educational status were both noticeable and pointed in the direction expected.

Majority

Table 5 shows the mean majority of the candidates' supporters.

TABLE 5
MEAN MAJORITY OF CANDIDATES' SUPPORTERS

	Confirmed data only		Probable data included		Doubtful data included	
	n	%	n	%	n	%
Major	10397	19.6	10654	19.9	10600	19.8
Heseltine	11107	20.1	11823	21.5	11857	21.7
Hurd	11944	22.4	11857	22.1	12275	22.7
All MPs	10908	20.3	11223	20.8	11295	20.9

Marginality does appear to matter. In both numerical and percentage terms – and using all three sets of data – Major's supporters sat for the more marginal seats. The difference is not great but at an average of over 1,000 votes it is still noticeable. Heseltine's supporters sat for the next safest, with Hurd's supporters, on average, sitting for the safest seats. However, the hypothesis derived from the literature was that if there was an individualistic marginality effect it would work for *both* Major and Heseltine (since their electoral appeal was equal) at the expense of Hurd. But the difference between Hurd's supporters and Heseltine's was not great. There are three possible explanations. First, there may never have been any marginality effect at all: MPs paid no heed to the effect that different candidates were said to have on the public. But this seems unlikely because it appears that Major benefited from just such an effect. If Major, why not Heseltine, whose 'voter pulling power' was as strong as Major's? Alan Clark may have provided the answer: Heseltine's main appeal lay in his 'so-called election winning powers' (as discussed above). But when it appeared that another candidate (Major) had those powers too, those in marginal seats deserted Heseltine, just as Clark predicted ('Once they have a real reason to do so, they'll abandon him'). Third, the electoral appeal may have been more a collective one – a desire to keep the Conservative Party in power rather than to retain individual seats – in which case it would not have been detected by this analysis: candidates in the safest of seats should want a party leader that can win elections.

Age and Experience

Table 6 shows the mean age and parliamentary experience (both in years) of the candidates' supporters.

TABLE 6
MEAN AGE AND EXPERIENCE OF CANDIDATES' SUPPORTERS (IN YEARS)

	Confirmed data only		Probable data included		Doubtful data included	
	Age	Exper -ience	Age	Exper -ience	Age	Exper -ience
Major	51.4	11.9	51.7	12.2	51.8	12.3
Heseltine	53.3	15.8	53.9	16.2	53.9	15.9
Hurd	49.4	12.5	49.7	12.9	50.4	13.4
All MPs	51.5	13.2	52.2	13.6	52.3	13.7

Heseltine clearly drew his support from the older echelons of the party: for all three sets of data the mean age and mean experience of his supporters is greater than that of both Major and Hurd's supporters (and the mean for the parliamentary party as a whole). But the hypothesis concerning Major's ability to tap into the Conservative Parliamentary Party's 'youth vote' is not validated. Major's supporters were, on average, just slightly older than Hurd's but, somewhat paradoxically, less experienced.

Multivariate Analysis

Of course, many of the variables identified and analysed above may be artefacts of each other. The variables may, and indeed do, interrelate. Multivariate techniques – such as regression analysis – allow for this, by controlling for the effect of any such interrelationships. Table 7 shows the beta values for a multiple regression analysis – with forward inclusion of variables of significance <0.05 – and the R^2 values (indicating how much variance collectively is explained by these variables).

The R^2 values differ, but none are especially high. In no case does a combination of these variables explain more than 20 per cent of the variance. Although this does *not* mean that the remaining 80–90 per cent can be explained by candidate-centred explanations (a voter-centred explanation not considered here or a different arrangement of one that includes, say ideology, may explain more of the variance), it seems fair to argue that this analysis indicates that candidate-centred explanations were important in 1990. Attempts to portray it solely as a contest of ideologies, or of socio-economic background, or of insiders vs. outsiders are clearly misleading. That said, voter-centred explanations were important, and although the precise figures differ somewhat depending on which set of data is used (and so all three sets are referred to in the discussion below), broad trends are clear.

TABLE 7
MULTIVARIATE ANALYSIS OF 1990 CONTEST

Variable	Major Data Set			Heseltine Data Set			Hurd Data Set		
	1	2	3	1	2	3	1	2	3
Ideology									
Wet	-0.278	-0.282	-0.254	0.225	0.245	0.253			
Damp	-0.234	-0.236	-0.189				0.222	0.221	0.205
Populist				0.126					
Pure Thatch.		0.103	0.104		-0.104				
Career									
Serving				-0.251	-0.144	-0.191	0.201	0.184	0.139
Experience					0.113				
Education									
Oxbridge	-0.154	-0.161	-0.149				0.151	0.159	0.145
Private	-0.134			0.148		0.106			
R^2	0.18	0.19	0.15	0.16	0.15	0.11	0.14	0.13	0.10

Note: Forward inclusion of variables; only variables with significance <0.05 entered. Data set 1=confirmed data only; 2=confirmed and probable data; and 3=confirmed, probable and doubtful data.

Only three groups of variables are significant: an MP's ideology, career status, and education. Of the three, ideology is the most important. In each case, the candidate's support was significantly determined by ideology. In all but one of the rows, an ideological variable has the highest beta value. In fact, in Major's case, the two highest beta values in all three rows are ideological. The directions of the ideological beta values are as expected. Major did badly among the Critics, Heseltine did well among the Wets, and Hurd did well among the Damps. Using just the confirmed data, Heseltine did well among the Populists, but once the data include the probables as well, this effect disappears and is replaced by a Thatcherism effect (which works for Major but against Heseltine). But note that this is a Pure Thatcherism effect. Controlling for other variables indicates that Major did not especially gain support, nor did Heseltine or Hurd lose support, from the other two Thatcherite groupings (the Neoliberals and the Tory Right). Education was also important, and again these effects are in the direction expected. Major did well among those not educated at Oxbridge and (for one set of data) among those educated at state schools. Hurd, by contrast, did well among those educated at Oxbridge even after controlling for other variables. Finally, in two of the rows there is a private school effect for Heseltine. But, as noted above, although important, in the case of all three candidates the effect of socio-economic factors is secondary to ideology.

An MP's career status was also important. But, here, the multivariate analysis reveals slightly different trends from those detected using the bivariate analysis. The tendency for those in government to eschew Heseltine is confirmed, as is the reverse effect for Hurd. But once other variables are controlled for, any insider effect for Major disappears. Similarly, note how, once other factors are controlled for, any marginality or age effects disappear.

Conclusion

A full explanation of the second round of the 1990 contest for the leadership of the Conservative Party requires an understanding of candidate- and voter-centred factors. While both were important, this article has considered only the latter. In most cases the explanations given in the extant literature have been found correct. But in some cases they have been rejected or amended.

An MP's career status was an important factor in determining his (or her) vote, more important than some studies suggest, though not as important as simple bivariate analysis indicates. Heseltine almost totally failed to tap into the so-called 'payroll vote'. This would not matter if the payroll vote was small or if he had received disproportionate support from other outsiders. But it wasn't, and he didn't. Those on the inside voted for Hurd, but any apparent insider effect for Major is caused by other factors. By contrast, class was probably less important than some of the existing studies suggest. There was a class effect certainly, but it diminishes once controls are introduced. Perhaps more importantly, the crucial thing about Major's support was not that he managed to gain disproportionately more support from his 'own', but that he managed to reach beyond his constituency, to gain the support of a large share of the more 'privileged' wing of the party. Since the vast majority of the Conservative Parliamentary Party were privately educated and went to university, and just under half were Oxbridge educated, no prime ministerial hopeful could win without doing well among the more 'traditional' Tories. Major managed this: he managed to gather support from his natural constituency, as well as those with whom he had less in common. This Hurd singularly failed to do. Some other apparent effects – such as the slight individualistic electoral appeal of Major – disappear once controls are introduced. If the electoral appeal of the candidates was as important as some accounts suggest then it must have been a more collective phenomena.

Even when other factors are controlled for, ideology remains the single most important factor determining an MP's vote. The left supported Hurd or Heseltine, and the Thatcherite praetorian guard (Norton's Pure Thatcherites) backed Major. To that extent, it was first and foremost an ideological contest. But there is both a caveat and a paradox here. The caveat is that, once controls are introduced, Major does no better among the two other Thatcherite groupings than do either of the other candidates. The paradox is that because the majority of the Conservative Parliamentary Party is not composed of ideologues, Major's success cannot therefore be put down to the support he received from ideologues. Major's real strength was not that he was able to reach the Wets and the Damps (because, *pace* Norton, he was not), but that he was able to tap into the support of the numerically much more important centre of the party. However, while an advantage at the time, this has a downside. The defining characteristic of the Party Faithful – as their name suggests – is that they are faithful to the Conservative Party, and not to individuals or ideologies. Their support, therefore, was conditional upon the leader providing 'competent – and successful – leadership, with consequent appeal and reward' (Norton, 1990: 49). This may help explain more than a little of Mr. Major's problems since 1992.

APPENDIX

The data for this article were culled from three sources: published lists of supporters in newspapers or books (for example, Watkins, 1992: 214–15); contacts with members of all three campaign teams; and contacts with over 60 MPs or former MPs. Together, these sources helped estimate the intentions of all 372 Conservative MPs. However, while all the estimates were based on evidence, some were based on more evidence than others. Because of this, in addition to being coded with a variable indicating for whom they cast their vote, each MP was also coded with a variable indicating the certainty of that information. A three-level classification was used: confirmed, probable, and doubtful.

For a vote to be classed as 'confirmed', the MP had to have appeared in one or more of the published lists, and members of the campaign teams had to agree. It required, therefore, *at least* two 'sightings' before an MP's vote would be confirmed. And *all* the evidence had to point in one direction. No sources could conflict. A vote was classed as 'probable' if the MP had not appeared in any of the published lists, but where members of campaign teams were sure about their intentions, or where the individual concerned had indicated their vote. However, again there had to be no conflicting information, either from the MP or from any of the published sources. Finally, an MP's vote was classed as 'doubtful' if a) there was no evidence how they voted, or b) the evidence was inconsistent. In these (very few cases), placing MPs relied on educated guesswork (and/or the balance of the evidence). Importantly, this final category was very small. It was possible to confirm the intentions of 62 per cent of MPs, and in total only 34 MPs, just 9 per cent, were classed as doubtful.

It is of course possible that the published lists may be wrong; that contacts, even well informed contacts, may be mistaken or mislead; and that MPs fib. This is, however, extremely unlikely to be a problem. An earlier draft of this article (Cowley, 1995b), using provisional data, found almost identical results to those discussed above, despite moving some 46 MPs from one category to another between drafts, as a result of extra information obtained. The results are, therefore, extremely robust. Fuller details of coding and the tests applied to the data are available from the author.

ACKNOWLEDGEMENTS

Earlier versions of this article were presented to the EPOP Conference in September 1995, and to the Centre for Legislative Studies, University of Hull, in October 1995. The author would like to thank the participants of both for their helpful comments, and especially Philip Norton, Ed Page, and Mark Stuart who read and commented on the earlier draft. He would also like to thank the 60 MPs with whom he corresponded, the five members of the three candidates' campaign teams who spent a considerable amount of time discussing the subject, and David Melhuish and Rachel Nightingale who helped code the data.

NOTES

1. Apart from many references in the works cited above, see Thatcher's own memoirs (1993) which do not detail any of the many non-ideological factors which are supposed to have led other MPs to support Major. Her support is suspiciously lacking in praise for Major's ability or warmth, instead focusing on a belief – which she soon came to doubt – that he shared her political outlook.
2. The majority of the following two paragraphs summarizing the Norton typology are from Cowley (1995a: 95).
3. These numbers are slightly different to those used by Norton (1993), which suffers from two unfortunate typographical errors. Norton (1990) claims to be up to date to July 1989, but is in fact up to date to January 1990 (thus taking into account the death of the Conservative MP, John Heddle). Between January and November 1990, the Conservative Party also suffered the death of Ian Gow, classed by Norton as a Neoliberal. Both Norton's pieces and this article exclude the Speaker, Bernard Weatherill, from our calculations.
4. In what was supposed to be an unrecorded post-interview discussion with ITN's political correspondent in April 1993, Major asked 'Where do you think most of this poison is coming from? – from the dispossessed and the never possessed. You can think of ex-ministers who are going around causing all sorts of trouble. We don't want another three more of the bastards out there.'
5. I am indebted to Mark Stuart, Philip Norton's researcher, for this information.
6. In particular his stint as a whip has been held up as a time when he began to establish a good reputation among his colleagues. See 'Westminster's Secret Service', BBC2, 21 May 1995.
7. One systematic method of examining Major's career is to look at service on standing committees. The Conservative MP who served on committees with the most divisions between 1979 and 1992 was a certain John Roy Major, who served on sixteen bills which saw a total of 634 divisions. Only two other Conservative MPs served on committees with a total of over 600 divisions, and only seven were within one hundred divisions of Major's total. Major was also well ahead of any of his leadership rivals. Hurd served on just six committees, with a total of 298 divisions, while Heseltine did not serve on a single standing committee between 1979 and 1992. Not only was Major's committee service widespread, but he also served on committees which were larger than the norm, enhancing his contacts with fellow Conservative MPs. During his time on the committees, he served with 146 Conservative MPs. Of these, 123 (a full third of his electorate) were still present in the House at the time of the 1990 leadership election. Such contact with Major did not produce any noticeable changes in MPs' votes (Cowley, 1995b), but it is indicative of his career.
8. One variable not mentioned at all in any of the existing accounts of the 1990 contest is gender. With only 17 female Conservative MPs (forming less than 5 per cent of the parliamentary party) it would be astonishing if there were any noticeable differences according to gender. Just for the record, of the 17, the intentions of 15 were confirmed and two were probable. They split 11 for Major, three for Heseltine, and three for Hurd.
9. A separate analysis, not reproduced here, concentrated on those MPs who were state educated but then went on to university. This confirmed the hypothesis advanced above: Major's support was disproportionately upwardly socially mobile (Cowley, 1995b: 15–16).

BIBLIOGRAPHY

Anderson, Bruce (1992) *John Major*. London: Headline.
Baker, David, Andrew Gamble and Steve Ludlam (1994) 'Mapping Conservative Fault Lines: Problems of Typology', in Patrick Dunleavy and Jeffrey Stanyer (eds) *Contemporary Political Studies* (Vol. 1), pp.278–98. Belfast: PSA.
Burch, Martin and Michael Moran (1985) 'The Changing British Political Elite 1945–1983: MPs and Cabinet Ministers', *Parliamentary Affairs* 28: 1–15.
Clark, Alan (1994) *Diaries*. London: Phoenix.
Cowley, Philip (1995a) 'Parliament and the Poll Tax: a Case Study in Parliamentary Pressure', *The Journal of Legislative Studies* 1: 94–114.
Cowley, Philip (1995b) 'How Did He Do That? A Systematic Analysis of the 1990 Conservative Leadership Election', paper presented at the EPOP annual conference, London, September.
Dunleavy, Patrick (1993) 'The Political Parties', in Patrick Dunleavy, Andrew Gamble, Ian Holliday and Gillian Peele (eds) *Developments in British Politics 4*, pp.123–53. London: Macmillan.
Ellis, Nesta Wyn (1991) *John Major*. London: Futura.
Foley, Michael (1993) *The Rise of the British Presidency*. Manchester: Manchester University Press.
Garry, John (1995) 'The British Conservative Party: Divisions over European Policy', *West European Politics* 18: 170–89.
Hague, Rod and Hugh Berrington (1995) '"A Treaty Too Far?" Opinion, Rebellion and the Maastricht Treaty in the Backbench Conservative Party, 1992–94', paper presented at the PSA annual conference, York, April.
Jenkin, John (ed.) (1990) *John Major: Prime Minister*. London: Bloomsbury.
Junor, Penny (1993) *The Major Enigma*. London: Michael Joseph.
King, Anthony (1993) 'The Implications of One-Party Government' in A. King *et al. Britain at the Polls*, pp.223–48. London: Chatham House.
Norton, Philip (1990) '"The Lady's Not For Turning". But What About the Rest? Margaret Thatcher and the Conservative Party 1979–89', *Parliamentary Affairs* 43: 41–58.
Norton, Philip (1993) 'The Conservative Party from Thatcher to Major', in Anthony King *et al. Britain at the Polls*. pp.29–69. London: Chatham House.
Pearce, Edward (1991) *The Quiet Rise of John Major*. London: Weidenfeld and Nicolson.
Shepherd, Robert (1991) *The Power Brokers*. London: Hutchinson.
Thatcher, Margaret (1993) *The Downing Street Years*. London: Harper Collins.
Watkins, Alan (1992) *A Conservative Coup*. (2nd Edn) London: Duckworth.
Young, Hugo (1993) *One of Us*. (Final Edn) London: Pan Books.

Professionalization, New Technology and Change in a Small Party: The Case of the Scottish National Party

Peter Lynch

Introduction

The academic literature dealing with the professionalization of political parties in Britain has almost exclusively focused on the Conservative and Labour parties (Franklin, 1994; Kavanagh, 1995). While small parties such as the Scottish National Party have been recognized as important for their blackmail or coalition potential (Sartori, 1976) in terms of their electoral impact on the party system and role as agenda-setting pressure parties, they have seldom been examined within the growing literature on political communications, political marketing and the professionalization of parties. Despite neglect by scholars, small parties have had to respond to Franklin's (1994) 'new media democracy' as much as large parties. They have done so not only by altering their own political communications and marketing strategies in order to utilize new techniques and technology, but also by responding to the strategies and initiatives of the main parties which are better-funded, better-staffed and gain greater media coverage. Essentially, small parties 'learn' from the large, through a process of copying and emulation. The Scottish National Party (SNP) is a good example of this phenomenon, as it has responded to changing media and technology through its own attempts to embrace new communications techniques while keeping a steady eye on the activities of its competitors to see what can be copied in order to catch up with the new professionalism of the main parties. In its heyday in the mid-1970s, the SNP was seen to have adopted the razzmatazz of an American campaign (Hanby, 1976: 226), but by the 1980s its campaigning efforts fell behind its competitors due to lack of resources. In the 1990s the party has sought to bridge this gap through the adoption of a new political strategy, the use of new technology to raise funds and the development of a more sophisticated, professionalized approach to political communications.

Change in Small Parties

The professionalization of political parties and the dynamics of change within parties have had a prominent role in recent literature on parties and party systems. Some have argued that the modern pressures on political parties have transformed parties into electoral-professional organizations (Panebianco, 1988); others have emphasized the impact of new technology and the media in generating fundamental changes to parties and campaigning (Franklin, 1994). This literature has almost exclusively tended to focus on large parties with significant bureaucracies and organizations. But the same effects and problems can be seen to impact upon small and third parties which often face a more constant struggle with professionalization, new technology and change, because they lack the resources and stability to successfully manage organizational or party system change. Panebianco's analysis of the transformation of mass-bureaucratic parties into electoral-professional organizations cannot be easily applied to small parties. Certainly, small parties have taken on facets of the electoral-professional party, but they seldom operated as mass parties in advance of such developments, so that arguments about party transformation are inappropriate in their entirety.

New technology, new campaign techniques and increased professionalization have been developments that have swept across all political parties. The difference between large and small parties is in the capacity to respond to such developments. In simple terms, it might be expected that small parties were more capable of addressing the new campaign and communications agenda because they were not burdened by large organizations and bureaucratic inertia. However, the flexibility that may come from having slimmer central bureaucracies is undermined by lack of resources and specialist personnel, which can prevent small parties from taking advantage of technological and communications advances. Resource limits impact upon the ability of small parties to embrace new technology and professionalization in two distinct ways. First, they can limit experimentation with professional techniques and new technology because of the high costs of failure. Small parties cannot easily afford to make mistakes with computerization, opinion polling, the hiring of professionals or PR support. Second, lack of funds limits access to professional support from marketing companies and consultants. Small parties simply cannot afford to hire professionals or buy in professional techniques such as private opinion polling. In essence, small parties are reliant upon volunteers from their existing organization or on the skills of a few existing staff members. Such shortcomings are often evident in the heat of an election campaign and can play a significant role in propelling organizational changes within parties. In the case of the SNP, the experience of electoral campaigning in 1992 was to generate changes within the party's political communications efforts and general political strategy, while longer-term problems associated with fundraising and a falling membership were responsible for the adoption of professional techniques to improve the party's organizational and financial position.

The 1992 General Election and the Paradox of Professionalization

The conduct of the general election campaign of 1992 was a significant force propelling change within the SNP in the 1990s. Though the party achieved a substantial increase in its share of support in 1992 to 21.5 per cent (+7.5 per cent, see Table 1), it made no advance in terms of seats, and party managers were dissatisfied with the conduct and message of the election campaign. On the surface, the SNP fought a professional campaign, but closer inspection revealed a campaign that was confused in message, tone and goals, which party leaders saw resulting in a lower than expected level of support. The campaign problems were the result of a political division that lies at the heart of the internal politics of the SNP. While some parties are divided on fairly orthodox left/right lines, the SNP has been divided on strategy between gradualist and fundamentalist tendencies. Fundamentalism and gradualism have been historic divisions within the SNP and even existed within Scottish nationalism before the advent of the SNP in 1934 (Hanham, 1969). The division is not about goals, as each wing of the party supports independence, but differs on the route to achieving independence. Essentially, gradualists see independence occurring through the halfway house of devolution whereas fundamentalists see devolution as a reform which will prevent independence (Mitchell, 1990). These differing views have influenced SNP attitudes to Labour's devolution legislation in the 1970s, involvement in the pro-devolution Scottish Constitutional Convention in the 1980s and co-operation with nationalist-oriented members of the Labour Party in the 1990s. For the purposes of this article, the key thing to understand is that both fundamentalist and gradualist viewpoints were represented in the campaign teams responsible for the 1992 electoral strategy, which produced mixed messages and campaign goals and created the impression that the SNP was running a dual campaign.

TABLE 1
THE 1992 GENERAL ELECTION IN SCOTLAND

Party	Vote %		Seats No.	
Conservatives	25.7	(+1.7)	11	(+1)
Labour	39.0	(-3.4)	49	(-1)
Liberal Democrats	13.1	(-6.1)	9	
SNP	21.5	(+7.5)	3	

Note: The changes since the last election are in parentheses.

One perceived flaw in the SNP's 1992 campaign strategy was the message rather than the medium. The gradualists sought to implement a restrained campaign of positive messages about change and reassurance to supporters, seeking to maximize SNP support in areas likely to return MPs: their primary concern was to avoid scaring off existing supporters. The fundamentalist campaign, in contrast, was a full-blown campaign for national independence that featured aggressive attacks on Labour and party election broadcasts that looked forward to celebrating 'independence day' and encouraged voters to 'take the plunge' and vote SNP. The problem with this type of message was not necessarily its content, but the context in which the message was delivered, and the fact that the context made the message appear highly unconvincing. The message was advanced at a time when the SNP had five MPs out of 72 and was standing at the low 20s in the opinion polls. At the end of the campaign the SNP was left with only three MPs – which showed how ill-judged it had been to fight the election as 'the independence election'. The tone of the campaign also played into the hands of opponents who were primed to fight a negative campaign on the issue of constitutional change. Essentially, the SNP's message enabled its opponents to operate effective 'fear-arousal' strategies about the dangers of voting SNP (O'Shaugnessy, 1990). The over-optimistic campaign message also created problems for targeting and the management of expectations among the party membership and supporters. The fundamentalist section of the campaign team stated that the party was aiming to win a majority of seats in Scotland (38). This extravagant claim created havoc with the party's targeting strategy and created a rod for the party's own back. The tone of the fundamentalist's campaign also created false expectations among SNP supporters which came crashing to the ground when the ballot boxes were emptied. The effect of the campaign was a considerable loss of credibility for the SNP in the post-election period and much of the party's strategy since then has revolved around restoring the credibility it lost in 1992.

The problems within the SNP campaign of 1992, with mixed forecasts and messages from different party figures associated with the gradualist and fundamentalist wings of the SNP, were exacerbated by professionalization and the use of modern political communications techniques – creating the 'paradox of professionalization'. From 1991–92, the SNP had emulated Labour in its efforts to develop a more professional approach to political communications. The party had enjoyed part-time PR advice provided on a voluntary basis by a group of sympathetic individuals within the PR and media sector – the SNP's equivalent of the shadow communications agency. This informal grouping gradually gave way to full-time professionalization. The necessity for full-time PR support was a consequence of the political developments that took place in the early months of 1992, as the issue of constitutional change rose rapidly to prominence ahead of the general election – particularly the BBC's Great Debate' between the four Scottish party leaders at which the SNP's media-savvy leader performed extremely well. This event along with *The Scotsman* opinion poll of January 30th 1992, which revealed that 50 per cent of respondents favoured independence, had a dramatic effect on the SNP which neither the party's press team nor the part-time 'shadow' PR group could cope with.

Around this time, Edinburgh PR consultancy, SMARTS, offered to provide advice and support for the general election campaign on a no-fee, expenses-only basis. This offer was attractive, particularly because it would enable the SNP to catch up and compete with its opponents. However, there were two distinct problems with the new PR approach which were not apparent until during the general election campaign itself. First, hiring SMARTS on an expenses-only basis remained an expensive operation, particularly because it operated alongside the SNP's own campaign efforts. Second, the professional campaign was not effectively integrated into the SNP's wider election campaign. The SMARTS agency seem to have been given a rather vague advertising remit and did not easily handle the requirements of a political party in the heat of an election campaign as opposed to a business during a marketing campaign. The most striking fault with the involvement of professional advertising consultants was that they were monopolized by only one of the dual campaign teams operating inside the SNP, that run by the fundamentalists. The result was that the party election broadcasts produced by SMARTS tended to exentuate the overblown message put across by that side of the party and created a confusion by amplifying a mixed message rather than distilling the SNP's differing gradualist and fundamentalist voices into one message.[1] The professionalization of the 1992 general election campaign therefore paradoxically damaged the cohesive nature of the SNP campaign and electoral message.

The New Strategic Consensus

SNP strategy since 1992 has been dominated by the party's gradualist wing, despite occasional bouts of dissent by fundamentalists. This situation was brought about by the decision of a number of party office-bearers associated with the fundamentalists to stand down from key positions and by the gradualist wing's success in gaining support in the party to make a number of organizational and strategic changes to avoid a repetition of the problems of the 1992 campaign. What emerged from these changes was a new strategic consensus that mapped out a five year campaign strategy to take the SNP from the 1992 election through local and European elections in 1994 and 1995 to the general election in 1996/7: an example of the extent to which advanced planning has become a central feature of modern election campaigning. The most significant aspects of the new strategic consensus were the party's identification of issues and problems to address in the years 1992–97 and the more conservative assessment of party goals and objectives compared to 1992. The new strategy set out four different objectives in two strategy documents produced in 1992 and 1994 (Scottish National Party, 1992, 1994).

Increasing Electoral Support

Since 1992, SNP election campaigns have been notable for their reassuring, voter-friendly messages – a more cautious campaign style that was the opposite of the 1992 campaign. The regional and European elections of 1994 and the local elections of 1995 were mostly fought on non-constitutional themes such as water privatization and VAT on fuel. They were protest elections in which the SNP sought to galvanize hostility to the government and maximize its support, rather then treat every election as the independence election. Because the 1992 general election had brought a substantial increase in the SNP's support but no increase in parliamentary representation, it was crucial that the SNP made real gains in the regional and European elections in 1994. The SNP approached these elections with a substantial degree of circumspection. Cautious forecasts not extravagant predictions were the order of the day, with the result that the SNP's gains in both elections looked more impressive: especially in the European contest, when the SNP took its target seats with large majorities and gained 33 per cent in Scotland, surpassing its previous highest level of support in October 1974 (Lynch, 1994), though the second-order nature of European elections puts this result into perspective.[2] These instances of cautious forecasting and campaigning provide a key pointer to the SNP's campaign strategy for the next general election.

Establishing Institutional Support for Independence

While Labour and the Tories enjoy support from a range of economic and political interest groups and organizations, the SNP has traditionally been bereft of institutional sources of support. This situation has had financial implications for the party's resource base, but even greater implications for its constitutional option of Scottish independence. All too often, the SNP has been the sole voice speaking up for the independence option, which has a tendency to make the party appear isolated as its opponents wheel out the CBI, the Convention of Scottish Local Authorities, the Scottish Trades Union Congress and a range of other organizations and interests. The Scottish Green Party's support for independence was helpful in the late 1980s, but since then the Greens have faded away to nothing. The SNP's response has been to attempt to build its own coalition of support groups for independence. This strategy has not been particularly successful as most of the support groups for independence merely contain existing party members, which have played a very limited public role. The SNP has started to identify and target sub-groups within the Scottish population, such as business, Catholics and the new Scots, but the issue of institutional support remains a problem.

Promoting Independence and Undermining the Union

This aspect of party strategy involves a combination of positive and negative campaigning. The SNP has always been in a good position to benefit from a positive message and the 'vision thing'. National independence is the type of issue that allows a political party to develop positive images and themes. In the 1970s, the SNP came to political prominence through promoting the economic dimension to independence with the imaginative slogan of 'It's Scotland's Oil'. In the latter 1980s, it was the idea of 'independence in Europe' that enabled the SNP to modernize the independence issue and promote the party's constitutional option in a new context (Lynch, forthcoming). Despite these relaunches of independence, there are major obstacles to the SNP's constitutional position. The three most prominent obstacles are the transition to independence itself and the issues of defence and the Scottish economy, particularly the issue of a Scottish currency in the context of European economic and monetary union.[3] The resolution of these problems has developed into a key aspect of the party's effort to establish the political credibility of independence. These issues have been addressed to improve the viability of the independence option and also to remove the possibility of negative campaigning by opponents (SNP, 1995a, 1995b). The SNP was a victim of negative campaigning in 1992, which the party did not handle particularly well. Since 1992, it has been much more prepared to produce special defence mechanisms against negative campaigning – quick responses for one – and also to 'go negative' on the Union and devolution as much as possible.

Establishing the SNP as a European Social Democratic Party

The SNP's final strategic aim for the period from 1992 to the next general election involved the establishment of a clearer centre-left profile for the party. This goal was partly developed in the 1990–92 period under the leadership of Alex Salmond, but has grown in importance over the last year. The fact that the ideological and social profiles of the SNP and Labour supporters are more or less identical is one reason for the SNP to stress its social democratic credentials (Brand, Mitchell and Surridge, 1994). The fact that the SNP wants to become the replacement party for Labour is also influential. Recently, the most important development has been the new populism and rightward movement of the Labour Party under Tony Blair. This development has some potential to open up Labour to attack from the left, and even the centre-left, though the overall popularity of New Labour may act to stem voter defections in Scotland.

The SNP's strategy from 1992 until the next general election is relatively broad, but the fact that the implementation of the strategy has been left in the hands of office-bearers and staff members associated with the gradualist side of the party has meant that the details of policy and campaigning have been easy to deal with. The party's general election campaign team has already been established, with the intention of sketching out campaign themes and preliminary preparations for the pre-campaign and the campaign itself. The campaign team is particularly concerned at setting the agenda on a range of issues associated with the economics of independence, the transition to independence and the provision of targeted messages of reassurance to sections of the Scottish electorate. Alongside these strategic goals lies the issue of professionalization, without which the SNP would face substantial difficulties. The financial, organizational and managerial dimension to election campaigning were clearly problematic in 1992, and the party leadership was determined to overcome these obstacles in the years leading up to the next election. New technology, enhanced fundraising capacities and a more developed political communications strategy were all to play a part in the preparations for the next election.

New Technology and Fundraising

The most striking area in which the SNP has employed a strategy of professionalization has been in the use of new technology to assist fundraising, a venture which pre-dated the 1992 general election, but which was expanded because the party found itself outspent by its rivals during the 1992 campaign. The application of new technology to fundraising and communications activities has been one of the key features of change within British parties over the last decade, though the utilization of new technology has been a slow process within the SNP. The party lacks the funds to invest in new technology (and also the new technology to raise funds) and also lacked a computer-literate activist base to drive the computerization of the party organization. While Labour was blessed with Computing for Labour since the early 1980s, the SNP's own computer support group progressed by fits and starts in the late 1980s before becoming well-established in the 1990s. The area in which the SNP has had most success with new technology is in fundraising and specifically in the operation of a direct mail campaign to increase the party's financial resources.

The SNP has traditionally relied upon its own membership for finance. In the late 1960s, the party was financed by a dramatic growth in membership and the success of a party 'pools' scheme which raised large funds (Brand,

1978: 282). In the 1970s and 1980s, the party relied upon a 'volunteer' approach to fundraising. Its fundraising committee tended to be comprised of party activists with little experience of modern fundraising and a tendency towards amateurism which relied upon traditional methods such as raffles and collections and failed to realize substantial funds. The fact that the party membership shrunk throughout the 1980s meant that the party's income dropped by a dramatic amount, causing a contraction of the party's headquarters and occasional paralysis to the party organization. The SNP managed to survive these lean years through the gift of a legacy left by one of the party's supporters. However, by the end of the 1980s this well was running dry.

The answer to the party's financial crisis involved a prolonged attempt at professional fundraising using new technology. The most significant thing about this development was that it took place in-house, though this may have been unavoidable given the poor state of party finances and the prohibitive costs of using professional marketing consultants. The SNP appointed its own professional fund-raiser and began to develop an American-style direct mail campaign in conjunction with a fundraising consultant who had experience of US campaign communications and was a former SNP staff member. The new personnel, along with key party office-bearers, then fashioned a rolling programme of direct mail to the party membership. Though the SNP lacks a centralized membership list it had computerized its membership on the basis of returns from local parties. This information was used for sporadic financial appeals in the 1980s, but really only came into its own with the development of a direct mail campaign, known as the Challenge of the Nineties, which identified existing party members as the most likely source of new funds.

Soaking the membership for funds via direct mail appeals was seen to be subject to a law of diminishing returns, so the direct mail approach was combined with the mailing of a newsletter to all registered party members, which would usually contain details of how to participate in the new fundraising scheme alongside a member's magazine that featured party news and information. This latter scheme was intended to provide a means for the party to communicate with its membership, organize events and orchestrate political activities. Achieving a balance between these two features of the direct mail campaign has not been easy. Constantly bombarding the members with fundraising mailshots was not seen as an effective strategy, and so the role of the party newsletter has increased markedly as a means of internal political communication that is distinct from fundraising. Despite this, it has contributed greatly to the effective marketing of the SNP amongst its own members, helping to make members feel closer to the party and more likely to donate funds on a regular basis. There is also some expectation that it will prevent membership attrition and compensate for the inactivity of some local parties, thus partly curing Noelle-Neumann's (1974) spiral of silence.

The success of the party's fundraising campaign is evident by the amount of new money that has been raised for the organization. The Challenge of the Nineties began in 1990 and had raised over £200,000 by the autumn of 1994. For a party with an estimated 15,000 members this was a fairly positive achievement – because it was additional funds – even though it is dwarfed by the campaign funds available to the Conservative and Labour parties. It would be something of an unfair comparison to try to compare the SNP with the British party organizations, but the party stands up well in relation to the Scottish branches of the British parties. The Conservatives in Scotland are financially dependent on the British organization, a situation that has worsened in recent years, while the Scottish Labour Party has most of its staff and campaigning costs covered by Walworth Road. Indeed, Scottish Labour's fundraising strategy compares very badly with that of the SNP. At the Scottish Labour Party conference in 1995 the party announced plans to develop a 'pools' scheme to raise funds in addition to organizing a sponsored walk and football competition (Scottish Labour Party, 1995) – examples of the amateur techniques that the SNP has left behind.

While the SNP has been reasonably successful in generating new funds from within its own membership it has had less success in developing external sources of finance. The party has compiled databases of supporters in Scotland, such as the business community, and targeted specific mailshots to canvass for funds, but it has been the development of a direct mail operation in North America which was seen to have greatest potential. The SNP sought to tap the expatriate community on several occasions in the 1980s, but each time the campaign was under-resourced or insufficiently professional to reap rewards. Latterly, the SNP has sought to replicate the success of the Challenge of the Nineties with a direct mail campaign in North America. This attempt was based on the dubious assumption that expatriate Scots would support the SNP and independence with similar enthusiasm to Irish-American supporters of Sinn Féin. However, this has rapidly been proven a false assumption with the party involved in a rather strained marketing campaign in the US which is not generating funds: there has been a considerable drain on resources – a clear case of the professionalization of fundraising leading to organizational over-confidence.[4]

New Technology and Campaign Communications

Similar to other parties, the SNP has made extensive use of new technology in the operation of its central organization, but there seems to have been a much slower diffusion of new technology to the local organization. The party established a computer steering group in the mid to late 1980s, but it has lacked the funds and local infrastructure to generate computerization at the grassroots, though the general absence of permanent local party offices has made this development unlikely anyway.[5] In areas in which the party has strong local organizations with their own premises, computerization of a range of party activities has been achieved: with an emphasis on employing computers for campaigning such as building databases of supporters and issuing targeted mailshots, not merely conducting administrative tasks. However, compared to Labour or the Liberal Democrats, computerization is an undeveloped area within the SNP. Computing for Labour was formed in 1983, and produced software for local party organizations, along with providing computer training, network facilities and common purchasing information (Smith and Webster, 1995: 1232). The Liberal Democrats also have a pedigree in producing and circulating software, clip art packages and information on computer applications. The SNP is a long way behind these developments and it is only very recently that it has begun to examine the production of software and marketing of discs and clip art.

About ten of the SNP's local parties have become computerized, though three of these were MP's offices.[6] Other constituency organizations have some computer capacity but it is not advanced. This situation demonstrates the party's lack of funds but also the grassroots' desire to stick to traditional methods of campaigning. The party's activist culture seems to resist modern techniques or is unsure how to implement new methods. The party's headquarters has invested a good deal of effort trying to popularize computerization, with training and briefings and some software development, but it has mostly failed to get results. Most of the main computer developments amongst local parties have tended to have their roots in efforts by local activists. The problem with this approach, in the words of one of the party's former advisors on computerization, was that local parties would move in 'seventy different directions' in buying and using computer equipment, making for a fragmented computer network that was not actually a network at all.[7]

Telephone canvassing has become widespread in Scottish elections, though it remains a largely hidden phenomenon. The Scottish Conservatives have been most active in the area of telephone canvassing as a result of the adoption of US-style techniques across the Tory party at large, but also as a campaign antidote to the aging and inactive membership of local Conservative organizations (Seyd et al., 1994). The other parties have been much slower to adopt telephone canvassing techniques through suspicion of public reaction to such techniques. Labour is widely believed to have run a covert telephone canvassing scheme at the 1992 general election, which focused on target seats, and mounted a strong challenge at the Perth and Kinross by-election in May 1995 using similar techniques – though this was very much a substitute for an absence of local activists in the constituency. The SNP, meantime, has not gone into telephone canvassing in a very large way. The party operated a limited telephone canvassing campaign in Perth and Kinross which was seen to be highly successful and the extent to which other parties, particularly the Conservatives, have employed telephone techniques, is propelling the SNP towards expanding its phone canvassing efforts at the next general election.

Where the SNP has made no progress at all is in the area of opinion polling. While the Conservative and Labour parties have been able to commission private opinion polls at and between elections, lack of funds has prevented the SNP from using polling in almost all circumstances. The party's new strategic consensus is constructed on secondhand opinion polls from newspapers, the Scottish election surveys and perceptions of the party's image and appeal in Scotland. However, with the exception of one extensive poll in the late 1980s, the SNP has been unable to utilize opinion polls as a marketing device. Resource constraints have prevented even limited professionalization and polling within the party. For example, neither party political broadcasts nor major campaign themes are pre-tested. This situation places the SNP well behind its competitors not merely in Britain, but in Scotland. The Scottish Labour Party has honed its image and political appeal through the use of pre-testing and focus groups, but the SNP has not employed similar techniques. Of course, extensive use of opinion polls can be counter-productive, with considerable funds spent on polling which is not effectively utilized (Shaw, 1994: 63). However, the SNP's inability to commission polls to guide its political strategy is a major weakness.

The Internet is one area in which the SNP has made some progress, largely because it can be propelled by the central organization and is relatively cheap to finance. The party was slower in setting up its home page than were Labour or the Liberal Democrats, but is now working on extending its existing WWW capacity. The SNP's pages were created through the efforts of the new chief executive and members of the party's computer support group, comprised of party members involved in the computer industry or in the computerization of their local organization – not outside professionals but party volunteers. The computer support group has been involved in designing and extending the SNP's home page, with the intention of widening the use of the Internet both as a publishing medium and a means of allowing members, supporters and the curious to access information about the party and its activities. In the short term, the Internet is being used in a limited way as a publishing medium, but over the longer term it is being developed as an internal communications system through the networking of party offices and the intention to use it as an interactive device for party members and supporters.

Political Communications

The SNP has traditionally operated an effective political communications strategy. The party's press team has usually been reasonably skilled at producing and placing stories and getting journalists 'interested' in stories through providing exclusives and presenting stories as a packaged item. These skills have been augmented by the reinforcing of the party's publicity team with new staff and an intention to boost the number of publicity staff for the 1996–7 general election. The level of funds generated by the party's direct mail campaign enabled the party to appoint an overall chief executive, with a range of responsibilities for the party organization in addition to the media relations functions, while appointing further members to the press team. The appointment of a chief executive is another aspect of professionalization as the holder of the position is a former film and TV producer who had run a media consultancy. However, the chief executive is anything but an outsider, being a former party office-bearer and parliamentary candidate. The appointment of a chief executive has not merely added to the party's communications team, but has also created a hierarchy of media managers,[8] with a senior staff member responsible for overall media strategy who can take over operational control of key events such as by-elections while also being available for media work on a daily basis. The party's new chief executive has also been appointed with the management of the next general election in mind, as the key campaign manager responsible for implementing the campaign strategy and avoiding the fragmented message and campaign themes of 1992.[9]

All the techniques of spin-doctoring, the placement of stories, agenda-setting, using media gimmicks, etc., that are found in the Conservative and Labour parties are to be found within the SNP. The party attempts to build some stories and suppress others, while forming close relationships with the community of political journalists in Scotland to their mutual benefit. The symbiotic relationship between politicians and journalists described by Franklin (1994: 15) is certainly present in Scotland, though the Scottish political and media communities are more interrelated than in other parts of the UK as Scotland is a small country with a small and highly familiar political and media élite. The SNP is in a unique position in Scotland as it has to be pro-active in its political communications strategy. The other parties can often rely upon their British leaders and organizations to gain favourable coverage in Scottish and British newspapers, but the SNP is very much on its own in having to maintain a profile within the Scottish media while dealing with the disadvantage of the British parties' ability to dominate network coverage on BBC and ITV.

Most of Britain's opposition parties complain about unfavourable press coverage and blame the Tory-dominated press. However, the SNP has been a rather odd beneficiary of changing newspaper partisanship in recent years. Shortly before the 1992 general election, *The Sun* decided to endorse the SNP and its preference for independence (Smith, 1994). *The Sun*'s decision was circulation-oriented, supporting the SNP was the only way to gain a working class readership in Scotland to challenge the hegemonic *Daily Record* which supports Labour. But *The Sun* itself is not a purely Scottish newspaper, rather it is a Scottish edition of a London newspaper. This means that it will contain Scottish and pro-SNP stories in one section while also containing British and more conservative stories in another section, producing contradictory political messages due to editionalizing.[10] The effect of *The Sun*'s conversion to Scottish nationalism has not merely been to give the SNP a sympathetic popular newspaper, it has also had a knock-on effect on other papers. Since *The Sun* became pro-SNP, there has been a perception that the *Daily Record* and *Sunday Mail* have become more pro-Labour.[11] However, neither *The Sun* nor the pro-Labour papers provide regular political features. Outside of elections or by-elections, these papers give negligible coverage to politics, therefore their impact and importance is difficult to judge.

The growth of political communications staff in the SNP, with the appointment of more experienced staff, has enabled the party to develop a more pro-active media strategy. The Perth and Kinross by-election of May 1995 was a good example of the SNP's pro-active approach as it was expected to win the seat from the Conservatives and had to respond to a substantial amount of negative campaigning by its opponents. There was a widespread feeling that the Conservatives had delayed the by-election to coincide with VE day celebrations and would seek to use the occasion to boost its support. This suspicion was confirmed when the Tories put out a leaflet linking Scottish nationalism with the excesses of nationalism in WW2 – along the lines of all nationalists are Nazis – and sought to develop this theme at press conferences. This piece of negative campaigning was intended to gel with the Union Jack waving aspect of VE day and to give the Conservatives a publicity boost. However, this strategy was anticipated by the SNP which had managed to prepare a number of responses before the election campaign was actually under way. The party's communications team compiled a story about the SNP candidate's father, who had fought in WW2, with a photograph of him in uniform and details of his war record, then placed it in a number of newspapers to coincide with the expected Conservative attack on nationalism at VE day. What could have been a difficult event for the SNP was therefore carefully managed and turned to the party's advantage.

Conclusion

Though developments in new technology and increasing professionalization have led to organizational centralization within British parties (Webb, 1994), it is difficult to see how this process has led to centralization within the SNP.

The SNP is a mixed-type of party, which has both grassroots and élite characteristics which make it appear both as a cadre and mass party. The democratic mechanisms within the SNP linking the party leadership to the grassroots remain strong, despite the party's professionalization and use of new techniques. However, centralization is more evident when it comes to political communications and fundraising. The effects of direct mail in party fundraising certainly has the ability to centralize resources within the national party organization to the detriment of local parties. The central organization can regularly tap local members for funds, thus sidestepping local parties completely and reducing the amount of funds available for local parties. The provision of a members' newsletter as a device for internal party communication may appear as evidence of grassroots activity, but it is controlled by the party organization and leadership. Thus it is a top-down mechanism for political communication within the party.

The use of new technology and development of political communications strategies does raise the question as to whether the SNP has become an electoral-professional party. This question is difficult to answer. Clearly, the SNP has used a number of techniques that are common to parties normally characterized as conforming to the electoral-professional category and has become more concerned with mobilizing electoral support than maintaining its existing organization – there is only one party organizer, but two researchers, three political communications staff and one fundraiser – so that much of the party's work has been directed outwards to voters not inwards towards members and activists (Mair, 1994: 13). This might account for the fact that SNP membership has remained relatively static in recent years, in spite of the fact that electoral support for the party has risen dramatically at elections in 1992 and 1994. The rising electoral-professional dimension of the SNP does bear some comparison with Labour. One of the strongest points about Labour's professionalization in the 1980s was that the party's election campaign's began to be run by outside professionals, such as the shadow communications agency (Webb, 1994). However, the SNP's response to the need to run a more professional campaign has swung towards appointing its own staff and away from using external assistance. While the party has used professionals in both fundraising and political communications, these professionals are not exactly 'outside' the party, but have been sympathizers or former party members. When outside professionals were involved in 1992, with the involvement of SMARTs advertising agency, the results were not deemed a success, contributing to the paradox of professionalization.

ACKNOWLEDGEMENT

The author is grateful for the financial support of the Carnegie Trust for the Universities of Scotland which aided the fieldwork for this article.

NOTES

1. Interview with SNP strategist, 1995.
2. The SNP traditionally gains second-order benefits at European elections (see Lynch, forthcoming).
3. The party established a special committee of academic advisors to assess the procedural aspects of independence and the detailed process of transition to an independent nation-state.
4. *Scotland on Sunday,* 20 August 1995.
5. Labour and Conservative permanent local offices are usually provided by the MP, party social club, trade union organization, etc. The SNP lacks these institutional sources of support, and with only four MPs, it also lacks the funds and organizational ability to create local offices in most areas.
6. Interview with SNP National Organizer, 1995.
7. Report of the SNP's Computer Steering Group to the NEC, 8 January 1988: National Library of Scotland, Acc. 10754.
8. It also gave the party a new media spokesperson equivalent to one of the party's MPs – a definite benefit given the fact that there are only four MPs.
9. There is also the related problem that most of the party office-bearers responsible for designing and running the election campaign are actually parliamentary candidates, often in key seats. This reality removes them almost completely from campaign management when the election is called, leaving a considerable vacuum in the party's campaign which can cause confusion and generate non-decisionmaking in mid-campaign: interview with former National Organizer, 1995.
10. The best two examples of *The Sun*'s support for the SNP were the editions of 23 January 1992, which had the front page and pages 2–7 devoted to Scottish issues and support for independence, and also 8 April 1992, which contained a pro-SNP front page and pages 2–9 dubbed the 'independence special'.
11. Interview with SNP chief executive, 1995.

BIBLIOGRAPHY

Brand, Jack (1978) *The National Movement in Scotland.* London: Routledge.
Brand, Jack, James Mitchell and Paula Surridge (1994) 'Will Scotland Come to the Aid of the Party?', in A. Heath, R. Jowell and J. Curtice (eds), *Labour's Last Chance.* London: Dartmouth.
Franklin, Bob (1994) *Packaging Politics : Political Communications in Britain's Media Democracy.* London: Edward Arnold.
Kavanagh, Dennis (1995) *Election Campaigning.* Oxford: Blackwell.
Hanby, Victor (1976) 'The Renaissance of the Scottish National Party: From Eccentric to Campaigning Crusader', in Louis Maisel (ed.), *Changing Campaign Techniques.* London: Sage.
Hanham, H.J. (1969), *Scottish Nationalism.* London: Faber.
Lynch, Peter (1994) 'The 1994 European Elections in Scotland: Campaigns and Strategies', *Scottish Affairs* 9: 45–58.
Lynch, Peter (forthcoming), *From Versailles to Maastricht: Minority Nationalism and European Union.* Cardiff: University of Wales Press.
Mair, Peter (1994), 'Party Organizations: From Civil Society to the State', in Richard Katz and Peter Mair (eds), *How Parties Organize: Change and Adaptation in Party Organizations in Western Democracies.* London: Sage.

Mitchell, James (1990) 'Factions, Tendencies and Consensus in the Scottish National Party in the 1980s', in Alice Brown and Richard Parry (eds), *Scottish Government Yearbook 1990*. Edinburgh: Unit for the Study of Government in Scotland.

Noelle-Neuman, E. (1974), 'The Spiral of Silence', *Journal of Communication*, 24.

O'Shaugnessy, Nicholas (1990) *The Phenomenon of Political Marketing*. London: Macmillan.

Panebianco, Angelo (1988) *Political Parties: Organization and Power*. Cambridge: Cambridge University Press.

Sartori, Giovanni (1976) *Parties and Party Systems*. Cambridge: Cambridge University Press.

Scottish Labour Party (1995), *Annual Report 1994–5* Glasgow: Scottish Labour Party.

Scottish National Party (1992) *Scottish National Party 4-Year Plan: The Independence Strategy, Stage 1*. Edinburgh: SNP.

Scottish National Party (1994) *Scottish National Party 4-Year Plan: The Independence Strategy, Stage 2*. Edinburgh: SNP.

Scottish National Party (1995a) *Paying Our Fare Share and More*. Edinburgh: SNP.

Scottish National Party (1995b) *Counting the Benefits of Independence*. Edinburgh: SNP.

Seyd, Pat, Paul Whiteley and Jeremy Richardson (1994), *True Blues: The Politics of Conservative Party Members*. Oxford: Clarendon.

Shaw, Eric (1994) *The Labour Party Since 1979*. London: Routledge.

Smith, Colin and William Webster (1995) 'Information, Communication and New Technology in Political Parties', in J. Lovenduski and J. Stanyer (eds), *Contemporary Political Studies 1995*. York: Political Studies Association.

Smith, Maurice (1994) *Paper Lions: The Scottish Press and National Identity*. Edinburgh: Polygon.

Webb, Paul (1994) 'Party Organizational Change in Britain: The Iron Law of Centralization?', in Richard Katz and Peter Mair (eds), *How Parties Organize: Change and Adaptation in Party Organizations in Western Democracies*. London: Sage.

Reference Section

In this edition of the *Yearbook*, the reference section is rather slimmer than normal. Partly this reflects pressure on space, but it also reflects genuine doubts that we have about the value of some of the material which has been included in previous years. In some areas, for example, change is so rapid – as in the editorships of national newspapers – that the information we have carefully gathered is out of date before the book is in the hands of the readers.

We have no doubts, however, about the usefulness of the chronology of the year (prepared, as in all previous editions, by David Broughton) and it is clearly important that we should maintain the series in respect of parliamentary by-election results, opinion poll data on voting intentions, the party leaders and economic expectations, and summaries of the results of local elections. As before, we also provide information about the party organizations and for the first time include estimates of party membership. Two other new features of the reference section are worth pointing out. First, we provide details of the circulations of national newspapers and we intend to continue to update the figures in future editions. Second, we include details of World Wide Web sites that may be of interest to readers. No one can accuse us of failing to keep up with the latest technological developments!

We would like to express our thanks to those who have helped in the gathering and checking of the material contained in this section, including David Broughton, David Cowling, Colin Rallings and Michael Thrasher.

David Denver
Justin Fisher

1. Chronology of Events 1995

JANUARY

3. Three life prisoners escaped from Parkhurst prison on the Isle of Wight. They were re-captured five days later still on the island. The governor of the prison, John Marriott, was 'moved to non-operational duties' as a consequence on 10 January.

4. The first applications were submitted for funds to be distributed from National Lottery receipts.

7. Enid Lakeman, director of the Electoral Reform Society 1960–79, died aged 91.

10. Thirty-two of the sixty-two Labour Euro-MPs placed an advert in the *Guardian* which criticized Tony Blair's plan to rewrite clause four of the party's constitution. Blair accused the MEPs of 'infantile incompetence'.

12. RUC Chief Constable Sir Hugh Annesley announced that troops were to be withdrawn from the streets of Belfast during daylight hours for the first time for 25 years.
    The Labour Party published its proposals for devolution to Scotland and Wales.

17. The Nolan Committee held its first public hearings into standards of conduct in public life.
    Lord Kagan, Labour life peer and creator of the Gannex raincoat, died aged 79.

19. Lord Nolan proposed the introduction of an independent element into MPs' self-regulation of their financial interests.

20. Neil Kinnock, who had been appointed to the European Commission, resigned his seat in the House of Commons, causing a by-election in his Islwyn constituency.

24. Alan Rusbridger was appointed editor of the *Guardian* in succession to Peter Preston.

26. Tony Blair began a series of regional consultation meetings over his proposal to amend or replace clause four of the Labour Party's constitution.

FEBRUARY

1. Animal rights campaigner, Jill Phipps, was killed under the wheels of a lorry carrying veal calves for export.

7. Allan Stewart, junior Scottish Office Industry minister, became the eighth Conservative minister to resign since the 1992 general election amidst accusations that he wielded an axe at motorway protesters. He was succeeded by George Kynoch.
    Andrew Jaspan was appointed editor of the *Observer* in succession to Jonathan Fenby.

9. The Chancellor of the Exchequer, Kenneth Clarke, insisted that a single European currency would not mean the end of British sovereignty.

12. Charles Wardle, the Under-Secretary of State for Industry and Energy, resigned over European Union immigration policy, claiming that it would leave Britain's 'back door' open. He was succeeded by Richard Page.

16. The Islwyn by-election took place. Labour easily retained the seat.

19. Sir Nicholas Fairbairn, Conservative MP for Perth and Kinross since 1974 and Solicitor-General for Scotland 1979–82, died aged 61.
    The *Sunday Times* alleged that Michael Foot, the former Labour Party leader, had been a Soviet agent. In July, the *Sunday Times* apologized in the High Court to Mr. Foot, withdrew its allegations and also paid Mr. Foot substantial damages.

22. The Cabinet approved the joint framework document on the future of Northern Ireland.

23. Trader Nick Leeson disappeared in Singapore hours after Baring's Bank collapsed with debts of £860 million.

MARCH

1.   Norman Lamont, the former Chancellor of the Exchequer, voted with
      Labour after an acrimonious debate over economic and monetary
      union. The government had a majority of five at the end of the debate.

2.   Fugitive bank trader Nick Leeson was arrested at Frankfurt airport,
      ending a seven day search in the wake of the collapse of Baring's Bank.

6.   Baring's Bank was bought by the Dutch banking and insurance group,
      ING.
      Robert Hughes, the minister in charge of the Citizen's Charters,
      resigned from the government over an affair that had ended six months
      before. He was succeeded by John Horam.

13.   Labour leader Tony Blair received the backing of the party's National
      Executive Committee on the wording of the replacement for clause four
      of the party's constitution.

20.   Sir James Kilfedder, Ulster Popular Unionist Party MP for North Down
      since 1970, died aged 66.

21.   The Deputy Governor of the Bank of England, Rupert Pennant-Rea,
      resigned after newspaper revelations of his affair with a freelance
      financial journalist, Mary-Ellen Synon.

APRIL

3.   A judge banned the showing of a BBC *Panorama* interview with Prime
      Minister John Major in Scotland because of its possible influence on
      forthcoming Scottish local elections. In the event, the Conservatives
      did not win one of the 29 new councils they had created.
      Ann Clwyd and Jim Cousins, two Labour foreign affairs frontbench
      spokespersons, were sacked by Tony Blair after visiting Kurds in
      Turkey without permission and consequently missing votes in the
      House of Commons.

5.   The House of Lords ruled that the Home Secretary, Michael Howard,
      had acted outside his powers in introducing a new criminal injuries
      compensation scheme without parliamentary approval.

6.   Labour secured control of 20 of the 29 new Scottish local authorities; the Scottish National Party won control of three, Independents also won control of three, while in three others, there is no overall control. The Conservatives did not win control of any councils and won only 81 of the 1,159 seats at stake.

9.   Richard Spring, Parliamentary Private Secretary to the Secretary of State for Northern Ireland, Sir Patrick Mayhew, resigned after he was named in a story in the *News of the World*.

10.   The Chief Secretary to the Treasury, Jonathan Aitken, issued a writ against the *Guardian* over allegations made about his business affairs. He also launched a crusade against allegations of sleaze in the press, promising to fight the 'cancer of bent and twisted journalism' with the aid of the 'simple sword of truth and the trusty shield of fair play'.

20.   David Tredinnick and Graham Riddick, the two Conservative MPs at the centre of the 'cash for questions' allegations, were suspended without pay from the House of Commons for 20 and 10 working days respectively as recommended by the Privileges Committee of the House.

24.   The whip was restored to eight Conservative MPs from whom it had been withdrawn in November 1994 after their voting actions on the European Communities (Finance) Bill.
Howard Davies was appointed Deputy Governor of the Bank of England with effect from September.

25.   It was announced that the Central Statistical Office (CSO) and the Office of Population, Censuses and Surveys (OPCS) were to be merged by April 1996.

26.   The use of just over £13 million of National Lottery funds to buy Sir Winston Churchill's papers sparked a heated political row.

27.   Peter Wright, the author of *Spycatcher* and an MI5 officer 1955–76, died aged 78.
Lord Mackay, the Lord Chancellor, published a White Paper containing changes in divorce law, effectively abolishing 'quickie divorces' and requiring a period of reflection and mediation.

29.   At a special party conference, Labour party delegates voted in favour of a new clause four for the party's constitution by a majority of 65.23 per cent to 34.77 per cent.

MAY

4.   The Conservatives suffered disastrous local election results, losing about 1,800 seats and control of 59 councils. Labour gained control of 39 councils. The Conservatives were left in overall control of only eight district authorities in England, plus four London boroughs and one non-metropolitan county.

10.   The first direct talks between Sinn Féin and British government ministers for 23 years took place in Belfast.

11.   The Nolan Committee on Standards in Public Life published its first report which included a ban on MPs working for consultancies representing multiple clients and for disclosure by MPs of their outside earnings. On 18 May, the Prime Minister announced that the recommendations would be referred to a parliamentary committee.

12.   Lord Goodman, adviser to both Harold Wilson and Edward Heath, died aged 81.

16.   It was revealed that Sir Jerry Wiggin, a senior Conservative backbencher, had secretly used the name of another MP (Sebastian Coe) to table an amendment to gas legislation in which he had a financial interest. On 22 May, Sir Jerry apologized to the House of Commons for his actions and the case was not referred to the House of Commons' Privileges Committee.

17.   Geoffrey Dickens, Conservative MP for Littleborough and Saddleworth since 1983, died aged 63.

24.   Lord Wilson of Rievaulx, Labour MP 1945–83; Leader of the Labour Party 1963–76; Leader of the Opposition 1963–64 and 1970–74; Prime Minister 1964–70 and 1974–76, died aged 79.
       Gerry Adams, Sinn Fein President and Northern Ireland Secretary, Sir Patrick Mayhew held a meeting in Washington D.C. where both were attending a conference on trade and investment in Northern Ireland.

25.   The Perth and Kinross by-election was won by the Scottish National Party, gaining the seat from the Conservatives with a swing of 11.5 per cent.

JUNE

5.   According to a leaked report of the Scott inquiry, William Waldegrave had written 'untrue' letters to MPs and had indulged in 'sophistry' in defence of the government's policy towards arms sales to Iraq.

6.   The House of Commons approved the establishment of a select committee on standards in public life to advise how the recommendations of the Nolan Committee might be implemented.

12.   The second volume of Mrs. Thatcher's memoirs, *The Path to Power*, was published.

13.   The Prime Minister was reported to have had a tense meeting with 'Eurosceptic' backbench MPs belonging to the Conservative Fresh Start group.

14.   The Old Bailey cleared two police officers of manslaughter over the death of illegal immigrant Joy Gardiner in August 1993.
        The House of Commons approved an order establishing the new parliamentary boundaries in England to take effect at the next general election.

15.   The North Down by-election was won by Robert McCartney of the United Kingdom Unionist party, with a majority of nearly 3,000 over the Official Unionist Party candidate.

20.   The Labour Party suspended all 17 Labour councillors on Monklands district council after allegations of corruption.
        Shell UK announced that it would abandon plans to dump the Brent Spar oil installation in the North Sea after protests by the environmental pressure group, Greenpeace.

22.   The Prime Minister resigned as leader of the Conservative Party in order to force a leadership election; he challenged his critics within the Conservative Party to 'either put up or shut up'.

23.   Douglas Hurd announced that he would resign as Foreign Secretary after the Conservative Party leadership election.
Bill Morris was re-elected general secretary of the Transport and General Workers Union, with 57.6 per cent of the votes, defeating Jack Dromey.

26.   Welsh Secretary, John Redwood, resigned his Cabinet post and announced that he would stand against John Major for the leadership of the Conservative Party.

29.   Nominations for the post of leader of the Conservative Party closed with two candidates: John Major and John Redwood.

JULY

4.   John Major was re-elected leader of the Conservative Party, beating John Redwood by 218 votes to 89. There were 20 abstentions or spoiled ballot papers and two MPs failed to vote.

5.   In a re-shuffle of the Cabinet, Michael Heseltine was appointed First Secretary of State and Deputy Prime Minister; Malcolm Rifkind was appointed Foreign Secretary to replace Douglas Hurd and the Department of Employment was disbanded, with most of its former responsibilities being given over to the Department of Education, which was re-named the Department for Education and Employment. Brian Mawhinney was appointed Chairman of the Conservative Party organization.

6.   Metropolitan Police Commissioner, Sir Paul Condon, provoked anger from the black community by suggesting that most muggings in London are committed by young, black males.

13.   The first of a series of 24-hour rail strikes was called by ASLEF, the train drivers union, after the failure of pay talks.

18.   Roger Freeman, the Chancellor of the Duchy of Lancaster, announced that the government would accept most of the recommendations of the Nolan Committee relating to ministers and former ministers.

20.   Sir Richard Greenbury, the architect of a new plan to tax share options, admitted that the plan would hit ordinary employees as well as 'fat cats' and he advised Chancellor Kenneth Clarke not to enact the plan.

23. George Walden, Conservative MP for Buckingham, announced his intention to resign his seat at the next election on the grounds that 'our politics seem to be increasingly about the management of illusions'.

26. The National Executive Committee of the Labour Party approved a rule change which reduced from 70 per cent to 50 per cent the share of the trade unions in terms of voting power at the party's annual conference.

27. The Littleborough and Saddleworth by-election took place. The Liberal Democrats won the seat from the Conservatives with a swing of over 11 per cent. Labour came second.

AUGUST

6. Lord Lever of Manchester, Labour MP 1945–79 and Chancellor of the Duchy of Lancaster 1974–79, died aged 81.

8. The Labour Party suspended its district party organization in Walsall amidst allegations of intimidation and misconduct.

10. Criticism of Tony Blair's modernization of the Labour Party came from a Labour backbencher, Richard Burden, MP for Birmingham Northfield in an article published in the *New Statesman and Society*. This was followed a week later by other criticism by Ronnie Campbell, MP for Blyth Valley who accused the Shadow Cabinet of being 'power mad'.

15. Prime Minister John Major received what appeared to be an apology from the Japanese government over the conduct of Japan during the Second World War although this interpretation was later denied by Japan.

16. John Redwood announced the establishment of a new 'think tank', Conservative 2000 Foundation.

17. The *Evening Standard* published an article critical of the Labour Party leadership written by the teenage son of Michael Howard, the Home Secretary, but confused it with another article written by Bryan Gould, the former Labour MP and Shadow cabinet member, now Vice-Chancellor of Waikato University in New Zealand.

25.   The Government announced plans for the early release of one hundred prisoners as part of the peace process in Ireland.

28.   James Molyneaux announced his resignation as the Leader of the Official Ulster Unionist Party.

SEPTEMBER

5.   Greenpeace apologized to Shell for errors made in assessing the risk of pollution caused by the Brent Spar oil installation.
      A planned summit meeting between John Major and John Bruton, the Irish Prime Minister, was cancelled after they failed to agree over the timing of the disarmament process in Northern Ireland.

8.   David Trimble was elected leader of the Official Unionist Party by the party's governing council, defeating John Taylor on the third ballot.

11.   The 127th Trades Union Congress opened in Brighton.

14.   Kevin McNamara, the Labour Party's chief spokesperson on the civil service, resigned over his party's policy on Northern Ireland and towards the trade unions.

18.   The Liberal Democrats held their annual conference in Glasgow.
      Michael Howard, the Home Secretary, announced plans for the first 'boot camp' prison for young male offenders.

19.   The Inland Revenue Staff Federation (IRSF) and the National Union of Civil and Public Servants (NUCPS) announced their intention to merge to form the Public Services, Tax and Commerce Union (PTC) from the beginning of 1996.

20.   The Scottish National Party's annual conference opened in Perth.

21.   Plaid Cymru's annual conference opened in Aberdare.

27.   The European Court of Human Rights ruled by a narrow majority that British soldiers had acted unlawfully in killing three IRA members in Gibraltar in 1988.
      The Labour Party's National Executive Committee confirmed the decision to reject Liz Davies as the prospective parliamentary candidate for Leeds North East.

OCTOBER

2.   The Labour Party annual conference opened in Blackpool.

7.   Alan Howarth, Conservative MP for Stratford on Avon since 1983 and
       a junior Minister between 1987–92, announced that he would join the
       Labour Party.

8.   John Cairncross, a former MI6 official, identified in 1964 as the alleged
       'fifth man' in the Cambridge Soviet spy ring, died aged 82.

9.   Lord Home of the Hirsel, Foreign Secretary 1960–63; Prime Minister
       1963–64; Leader of the Opposition 1964–65; and Foreign Secretary
       1970–74, died aged 92.

10.   On the first day of the Conservative Party's annual conference in
       Blackpool, Michael Portillo, the Defence Secretary, launched a fierce
       attack on various aspects of the European Union and affirmed the
       independence of Britain's defence policy.

12.   The Green Party's annual conference opened in Southport.
       At the Conservative Party conference, Michael Howard, the Home
       Secretary, announced plans to increase penalties for serious crimes and
       to abolish the system of early release for many prisoners.

16.   Derek Lewis, the director general of the Prison Service, was sacked by
       the Home Secretary, in the wake of the Learmont report on the state of
       British prisons. Lewis protested that he was being made a scapegoat
       and he issued a writ against the Home Secretary two days later.

18.   Elections to Labour's Shadow Cabinet saw the replacement of Jack
       Cunningham by Clare Short and the return of Tom Clarke. The
       allocation of responsibilities was decided the following week.

18/19. Max Hastings resigned as the editor of the *Daily Telegraph* to edit the
       Evening Standard. Charles Moore moved from the *Sunday Telegraph* to
       the *Daily Telegraph* to replace him, while Dominic Lawson moved
       from the *Spectator* to the *Sunday Telegraph* and Frank Johnson was
       appointed editor of the *Spectator*.

24.   The newly established Referendum Party set out its aims in press
       adverts, proposing the election of MPs who were committed to the

holding of a referendum on the Maastricht Treaty and any successor treaty of the European Union.

27.   A Canadian disc jockey managed to talk to the Queen after pretending to be the Canadian Prime Minister. He asked for advice on the forthcoming referendum in Quebec.

28.   Clare Short, Labour MP for Birmingham Ladywood, suggested in a television interview that cannabis could be legalized.

31.   Derek Enright, Labour MP for Hemsworth since 1991, died aged 60.

NOVEMBER

3.   A ban on homosexuals in the armed forces was upheld by the Appeal Court.

6.   MPs voted to reveal their outside earnings in line with the recommendations of the Nolan Committee by 322 votes to 271, a majority of 51.

13.   Tony Blair told the CBI conference in Birmingham that European legislation on social affairs would not automatically be adopted by an incoming Labour government.
Ian Hargreaves resigned as editor of the *Independent*.

15.   The new session of Parliament opened with the Queen's Speech setting out the government's programme for the next year, including an Asylum and Immigration Bill, a Family Law Bill involving divorce reform, a Broadcasting Bill and a Nursery Education Bill.

16.   News International announced that it would close the *Today* newspaper the next day.

20.   The Princess of Wales gave an interview to the BBC's *Panorama* programme in which she admitted adultery, self-mutilation and periods of bulimia.

23.   Sir Marcus Fox was re-elected chair of the Conservative Party's 1922 backbench committee.

28. The Chancellor of the Exchequer, Kenneth Clarke, made the annual budget statement to the House of Commons. He announced a reduction in the basic rate of income tax from 25p to 24p, increased the main income tax personal allowances by more than inflation, reduced some duties on alcoholic drinks and sharply raised the inheritance tax threshold.

    The UK and Irish Prime Ministers, John Major and John Bruton, signed an agreement on a 'twin-track' process of political talks for Northern Ireland and the decommissioning of paramilitary weapons.

29. The Labour Party NEC suspended the leader and deputy leader of Walsall Council (Dave Church and John Rothery), claiming that the two were leading 'a party within a party'.

30. President Bill Clinton visited Belfast in the wake of the latest moves on talks on the future of Northern Ireland. He flew to Dublin for further talks the next day.

    William Hague, the Welsh Secretary, announced an increased role for the Welsh Grand Committee.

    General Sir David Ramsbotham was appointed to succeed Judge Stephen Tumim as Chief Inspector of Prisons in England and Wales.

DECEMBER

7. The IRA declared that it would never surrender its weapons as a precondition for the commencement of all-party negotiations on the future of Northern Ireland.

12. David Lightbown, Conservative MP for Staffordshire South East, died aged 63.

    The Health Secretary, Stephen Dorrell, announced an increase in the recommended 'safe' levels of drinking based on daily rather than weekly consumption.

13. Chancellor of the Exchequer, Kenneth Clarke, cut interest rates by one quarter of one per cent to 6.5 per cent.

    Rioting erupted in Brixton after a black man died in police custody.

14. The former political editor of the *Daily Express*, Charles Lewington, was appointed as the director of communications of the Conservative Party.

18.   Sir David Ramsbotham, the new Chief Inspector of Prisons, withdrew his team of inspectors from Holloway Prison for women in London until conditions in the prison improved.

19.   The Government lost a division on European Union fishing quotas by two votes in the House of Commons after an acrimonious debate highlighting the divisions between pro-European Conservative MPs and Eurosceptics.
       David Ashby, Conservative MP for Leicestershire North-West, lost his libel case against the *Sunday Times*, which had branded him 'a liar, a hypocrite and a homosexual'.

20.   An independent inquiry set up by the Scottish Secretary cleared Monklands District Council of corruption including nepotism and both political and religious bias.

26.   It was confirmed that the government had paid the legal costs of the families of the three alleged IRA members shot dead by the SAS in Gibraltar in March 1988.

28.   Brian Mawhinney, the Conservative Party Chairman, published his New Year message to party activists in which he exhorted them to 'think votes' and to realize that 'victory must be our only concern'.

29.   Emma Nicholson, Conservative MP for Devon West and Torridge, announced that she was joining the Liberal Democrats, accusing the Conservative government of 'indecision and weak leadership on Europe' and of being 'a government which does not care'.

2. Parliamentary By-Elections 1995

(Note: By-elections are numbered consecutively from the general election of 1992.)

11. ISLWYN 16 February 1995 (Resignation of Mr N. Kinnock)

Result

Candidate	Description	Votes
D. Touhig	Labour	16,030
J Davies	Plaid Cymru	2,933
J Bushell	Liberal Democrat	2,448
R Buckland	Conservative	913
Lord Sutch	Official Welsh Monster Raving Loony	506
H Hughes	UK Independence Party	289
T Rees	Natural Law Party	47

Labour hold: Majority 13,097

Turnout and Major Party Vote Shares (per cent)

	By-election	General Election	Change
Turnout	45.7	81.5	-35.8
Con	3.9	14.8	-10.9
Lab	69.2	74.3	-5.1
Lib Dem	10.6	5.7	+4.9
PC	12.7	3.9	+8.8

12. PERTH AND KINROSS 25 May 1995 (Death of Sir N. Fairbairn)

Result

Candidate	Description	Votes
R Cunningham	SNP	16,931
D Alexander	Labour	9,620
J Godfrey	Conservative	8,990
V Linklater	Lib Dem	4,952
Lord Sutch	Official Monster Raving Loony	586
V. Linacre	UK Independence Party	504
R Harper	Green	223
M Halford	Scottish Conservatory	88
G Black	Natural Law	54

SNP gain: Majority 7,311

Turnout and Major Party Vote Shares (per cent)

	By-election	General Election	Change
Turnout	62.0	76.9	-14.9
Con	21.4	40.2	-18.8
Lab	22.9	13.2	+9.7
Lib Dem	11.8	11.4	+0.4
SNP	40.4	36.0	+4.4

13. NORTH DOWN 15 June 1995 (Death of Sir J. Kilfedder)

Result

Candidate	Description	Votes
R McCartney	UK Unionist	10,124
A McFarland	Ulster Unionist Party	7,232
O Napier	Alliance	6,970
A Chambers	Independent Unionist	2.170
S Sexton	Conservative	583
M Brooks	Free Para Clegg	108
C Carter	Ulster's Independent Voice	101

UK Unionist gain: Majority 2,892

Turnout and Major Party Vote Shares (per cent)

	By-election	General Election	Change
Turnout	38.8	65.5	-26.7
UK Unionist	37.1	-	
UUUP	26.5	-	
Alliance	25.5	14.7	+10.8
Ind Unionist	8.0	-	
Con	2.1	32.0	-29.9

14. LITTLEBOROUGH AND SADDLEWORTH 27 July 1995 (Death of Mr G. Dickens)

Result

Candidate	Description	Votes
C Davies	Liberal Democrat	16,231
P Woolas	Labour	14,238
J Hudson	Conservative	9,934
Lord D Sutch	Official Monster Raving Loony	782
J Whittaker	UK Independence	549
A Pitts	Socialist	466
P Douglas	Conservative	193
Mr Blobby	House party	105
L McLaren	Old Labour/Probity of Imposed Candidate	33
C Palmer		
Lord Manton	21st Century	25

Liberal Democrat gain: Majority 1,193

Turnout and Major Party Vote Shares (per cent)

	By-election	General Election	Change
Turnout	64.5	81.6	-17.1
Con	23.3	44.2	-20.9
Lab	33.5	19.9	+13.6
Lib Dem	38.1	35.9	+2.2

TABLE 2.1 *Summary of By-election Results 1992–95*

Constituency	Turnout Change	Change in Share of Vote			
		Con	Lab	Lib Dem	SNP/ PC
Newbury	-11.5	-29.0	-4.1	+27.8	
Christchurch	-6.5	-31.5	-9.3	+39.7	
Rotherham	-27.6	-13.9	-8.4	+17.4	
Barking	-31.5	-23.5	+20.5	-2.5	
Bradford S	-31.6	-20.6	+7.7	+10.2	
Dagenham	-33.5	-26.4	+19.7	-3.1	
Eastleigh	-24.0	-26.6	+6.9	+16.3	
Newham NE	-24.9	-15.9	+16.6	-7.0	
Monklands East	-4.9	-13.8	-11.5	-2.0	+26.9
Dudley West	-34.8	-30.1	+28.1	-2.9	
Islwyn	-35.8	-10.9	-5.1	+4.9	-+8.8
Perth and Kinross	-14.9	-18.8	+9.7	+0.4	+4.4
North Down	-26.7				
Littleborough & Saddleworth	-17.1	-20.9	+13.6	+2.2	

3. Public Opinion Polls 1995

TABLE 3.1 Voting Intentions in Major Polls 1995 (per cent)

Fieldwork		Company	Sample Size	Con	Lab	Lib Dem	Other
Jan							
	4–9	Gallup	1080	19	62	14	6
	12–13	Harris	957	25	60	12	3
	13–14	ICM	1455	25	56	15	4
	20–23	MORI	1845	27	56	14	3
	25–30	Gallup	1142	24	60	13	4
Feb							
	10–11	ICM	1427	24	58	14	4
	17–20	MORI	1917	24	58	14	4
	22–27	Gallup	1156	21	61	15	4
Mar							
	10–11	ICM	1447	22	59	14	5
	17–20	MORI	1999	25	57	13	5
	24	MORI	1006	25	59	12	4
	29–3/4	Gallup	1098	23	58	15	5
Apr							
	7–8	ICM	1358	20	58	17	5
	21–24	MORI	1937	26	56	15	3
May							
	3–8	Gallup	1033	23	56	17	5
	12–13	ICM	1428	23	56	17	4
	19–22	MORI	1869	22	58	16	4
Jun							
	31/5–6/6	Gallup	1107	20	60	15	6
	9–10	ICM	1416	20	59	18	4
	20–24	MORI	756	32	54	11	3
	23–26	MORI	1921	29	56	13	2
	26–27	MORI	1002	31	55	11	3
	28–4/7	Gallup	1073	26	57	13	5
Jul							
	3	MORI	516	33	52	10	4
	7–8	ICM	1347	26	57	14	3
	20–21	NOP	1628	26	55	14	4
	21	MORI	1104	30	52	13	5
	21–24	MORI	1938	26	59	12	3
	25–31	Gallup	1122	23	58	15	6
	28–31	ICM	1418	24	58	14	4
Aug							
	4–5	ICM	1418	26	56	14	4
	17–18	NOP	1598	24	57	15	4
	25–28	MORI	1782	25	56	15	2
Sep							
	31/8–4/9	Gallup	1082	27	55	14	5
	8–9	ICM	1373	26	55	16	4
	8–11	ICM	1002	30	50	15	5
	14–15	NOP	1538	26	53	16	4
	22–25	MORI	1918	28	51	16	5
	27–2/10	Gallup	1124	26	56	14	5
Oct							
	6–7	ICM	1461	23	57	15	6
	19–20	NOP	1503	23	59	15	3
	20–23	MORI	1929	27	56	13	3
	25–30	Gallup	1062	22	61	15	3
Nov							
	3–5	ICM	1231	26	51	19	4
	16–17	NOP	1540	27	56	13	3
	17–20	MORI	1877	26	56	14	3
Dec							
	29/11–4/12	Gallup	1074	23	62	12	3
	30/11–1/12	NOP	1034	24	58	13	5
	1–4	MORI	1894	28	55	13	3
	8–9	ICM	n.a.	29	53	15	3

Notes: The figures shown are unadjusted voting intention percentages after the exclusion of respondents who did not indicate a party preference. Gallup results are normally reported to the nearest 0.5 but all such cases here have been rounded up.

TABLE 3.2 *Voting Intentions (adjusted) in Major Polls 1995 (per cent)*

Fieldwork	Company	Sample Size	Con	Lab	Lib Dem	Other
Jan						
13–14	ICM	1455	30	48	18	4
Feb						
10–11	ICM	1427	31	49	17	4
Mar						
10–11	ICM	1447	27	52	17	4
Apr						
7–8	ICM	1358	26	51	18	5
May						
12–13	ICM	1428	29	48	19	4
Jun						
9–10	ICM	1416	24	53	19	4
Jul						
7–8	ICM	1347	32	47	17	3
20–21	NOP	1628	27	54	14	5
Aug						
4–5	ICM	1418	31	48	17	5
17–18	NOP	1598	25	54	17	4
Sep						
8–9	ICM	1373	31	48	17	4
14–15	NOP	1538	27	53	17	3
Oct						
6–7	ICM	1461	29	49	17	5
19–20	NOP	1503	26	56	15	3
Nov						
3–5	ICM	1231	30	47	19	4
16–17	NOP	1540	27	55	14	3
Dec						
30–1/12	NOP	1034	25	57	15	3
8–9	ICM	n.a	31	48	16	4

Note: Following criticism of the polls after the 1992 general election, NOP and ICM began to adjust their voting intention figures, publishing the resulting scores as their 'headline' figures. In both cases the adjustment partly involves taking account of past voting.

TABLE 3.3 *Voting Intentions in Scotland 1995 (per cent)*

	Con	Lab	Lib Dem	SNP
Jan	12	56	10	23
Feb	11	52	10	25
Mar	11	53	9	25
Apr	13	52	12	22
May	11	53	9	27
Jun	11	57	8	23
Jul	12	54	11	22
Aug	12	52	8	26
Sep	13	46	11	30
Oct	13	52	10	23
Nov	13	57	8	21

Note: System Three do not poll in December but have separate polls in early and late January. The January figure shown is the average of the two January polls. Rows do not total 100 because 'others' are not shown.

Source: System Three Scotland polls, published monthly in *The Herald* (Glasgow).

TABLE 3.4 *Monthly Averages for Voting Intentions 1995 (per cent)*

	Con	Lab	Lib Dem		Con	Lab	Lib Dem
Jan	24	59	14	Jul	27	56	13
Feb	23	59	14	Aug	25	56	15
Mar	24	58	14	Sep	27	53	15
Apr	23	57	16	Oct	24	58	15
May	23	57	17	Nov	26	54	15
Jun	26	57	14	Dec	27	57	13

Note: These are the simple means of unadjusted voting intentions.

TABLE 3.5 *Ratings of Party Leaders 1995*

| | Major | | | Blair | | | Ashdown | | |
	Pos	Neg	Net	Pos	Neg	Net	Pos	Neg	Net
Jan	18	75	-57	56	18	+38	52	27	+25
Feb	19	74	-55	58	19	+39	52	26	+26
Mar	21	72	-51	59	19	+40	51	27	+24
Apr	21	72	-51	61	18	+43	52	26	+26
May	21	72	-51	65	16	+49	55	23	+32
Jun	22	71	-49	66	15	+51	53	25	+28
Jul	26	65	-39	62	18	+44	51	26	+25
Aug	26	66	-40	59	21	+38	54	24	+30
Sep	26	66	-40	56	24	+32	54	23	+31
Oct	25	67	-42	63	19	+44	54	24	+30
Nov	25	67	-42	62	20	+42	53	24	+29
Dec	27	65	-38	64	19	+45	53	25	+28

Notes: The figures are based on responses to the questions 'Are you satisfied or dissatisfied with
Mr Major as Prime Minister?'; 'Do you think that Mr Blair is or is not proving a good
leader of the Opposition?'; 'Do you think that Mr Ashdown is or is not proving a good
leader of the Liberal Democratic Party?'.
The data are derived from the 'Gallup 9,000', which is an aggregation of all Gallup's
polls in the month concerned.
The difference between 100 and the sum of positive and negative responses is the
percentage of respondents who replied 'Don't know'.
Source: Gallup Political and Economic Index

TABLE 3.6 *Best Person for Prime Minister 1995 (per cent)*

	Major	Blair	Ashdown	Don't Know
Jan	15	44	13	29
Feb	15	43	13	29
Mar	16	43	12	30
Apr	15	42	14	29
May	15	44	13	29
Jun	16	46	12	27
Jul	21	42	11	27
Aug	19	39	13	29
Sep	19	39	14	28
Oct	19	43	13	26
Nov	18	42	13	28
Dec	19	42	12	27

Source: Gallup Political and Economic Index. The data are derived from the 'Gallup 9,000'.

TABLE 3.7 *Approval/Disapproval of Government Record 1995 (per cent)*

	Approve	Disapprove	Don't Know	Approve – Disapprove
Jan	11	80	10	-69
Feb	11	80	10	-69
Mar	11	79	10	-68
Apr	12	79	10	-67
May	10	79	10	-69
Jun	12	78	10	-66
Jul	14	74	12	-60
Aug	14	74	12	-60
Sep	13	76	11	-63
Oct	15	74	11	-59
Nov	14	74	12	-60
Dec	15	75	11	-60

Notes: These are answers to the question 'Do you approve or disapprove of the government's
       record to date?'. The data are derived from the 'Gallup 9,000'.
Source: Gallup Political and Economic Index

TABLE 3.8 *National and Personal Economic Evaluations 1992–95*

	National Retrospective	National Prospective	Personal Retrospective	Personal Prospective
1992				
Apr	-45	+25	-16	+15
May	-35	+26	-11	+9
Jun	-31	+9	-9	+8
Jul	-56	-12	-17	0
Aug	-74	-30	-23	-7
Sep	-83	-30	-33	-18
Oct	-88	-44	-25	-21
Nov	-85	-39	-30	-18
Dec	-78	-25	-22	-9
1993				
Jan	-65	-8	-16	-2
Feb	-67	-23	-29	-16
Mar	-68	-20	-29	-9
Apr	-63	-14	-32	-17
May	-49	+3	-23	-6
Jun	-49	-7	-23	-9
Jul	-41	-7	-21	-10
Aug	-37	0	-19	-7
Sep	-39	-8	-25	-22
Oct	-36	-10	-26	-22
Nov	-46	-13	-29	-23
Dec	-40	-18	-31	-29
1994				
Jan	-28	-5	-23	-16
Feb	-34	-13	-24	-26
Mar	-45	-26	-35	-33
Apr	-52	-28	-38	-31
May	-40	-17	-36	-23
Jun	-38	-16	-35	-17
Jul	-38	-13	-29	-21
Aug	-27	5	-27	-12
Sep	-30	-10	-22	-13
Oct	-34	-13	-28	-20
Nov	-31	-10	-23	-7
Dec	-36	-22	-27	-29
1995				
Jan	-28	-12	-23	-9
Feb	-34	-16	-28	-14
Mar	-47	-26	-25	-17
Apr	-26	-5	-21	-8
May	-34	-17	-30	-13
Jun	-36	-16	-23	-10
Jul	-37	-14	-20	-6
Aug	-35	-15	-20	-6
Sep	-32	-10	-14	-4
Oct	-35	-15	-16	-5
Nov	-39	-15	-24	-6
Dec	-34	-12	-20	-9

Notes: In previous editions of the Yearbook we have used Gallup's 'consumer confidence' series of questions to construct this table. Since publication of this series of data is becoming more intermittent we have switched to the '1974 series' of economic indicators and show the figures from the last general election. The figures are based on answers to the following questions: 'Do you consider that the general economic situation in this country in the last 12 months has improved a lot, improved slightly, remained the same, deteriorated slightly or deteriorated a lot?'; 'Do you think that the general economic situation in the next 12 months is likely to improve a lot, improve slightly, remain the same, deteriorate slightly or deteriorate a lot?'; 'In the last 12 months has the financial situation of your household improved a lot, improved slightly, remained the same, become a little worse or become a lot worse?'; Do you consider the financial situation of your household in the next 12 months will improve a lot, improve slightly, remain the same, deteriorate slightly or deteriorate a lot?'.
In each case entries are the percentage of respondents saying things have deteriorated/will deteriorate subtracted from the percentage saying things have improved/will improve.
Source: Gallup Political and Economic Index.

TABLE 3.9 *Best Party to Handle Economic Difficulties 1992–95*

	Conservative	Labour	No Difference	Don't Know
1992				
Apr	49	31	12	8
May	46	34	11	8
Jun	–	–	–	–
Jul	–	–	–	–
Aug	–	–	–	–
Sep (early)	41	36	13	10
Sep (late)	35	36	17	12
Oct	29	47	14	10
Nov	27	48	14	11
Dec	28	39	20	13
1993				
Jan	32	40	19	10
Feb	30	40	20	10
Mar	27	41	22	20
Apr	28	41	21	10
May	27	41	22	10
Jun	23	41	26	10
Jul	26	40	24	11
Aug	26	38	26	11
Sep	25	42	23	11
Oct	27	41	23	10
Nov	25	41	24	11
Dec	27	41	22	11
1994				
Jan	25	43	21	11
Feb	25	43	21	11
Mar	24	43	22	12
Apr	24	43	22	12
May	23	43	19	15
Jun	22	47	21	10
Jul	22	47	21	11
Aug	21	49	18	12
Sep	22	48	19	11
Oct	21	48	18	12
Nov	21	48	19	12
Dec	19	51	17	13
1995				
Jan	21	50	18	12
Feb	20	49	19	12
Mar	20	47	20	13
Apr	21	48	19	12
May	20	50	18	12
Jun	20	50	17	12
Jul	24	47	17	13
Aug	24	45	18	13
Sep	25	45	18	12
Oct	24	49	17	11
Nov	24	47	18	11
Dec	24	47	18	12

Note: These are answers to the question 'With Britain in economic difficulties, which party do you think could handle the problem best – the Conservatives under Mr. Major or Labour under ......?' (Mr. Kinnock in April 1992, Mr. Smith from May 1992 to May 1994 and Mr. Blair from July 1994). The question was not asked from June to August 1992. From December 1992 the figures are based on the 'Gallup 9,000'.

Source: Gallup Political and Economic Index.

4. Local Elections 1995

Although the annual rounds of local elections attract increasing attention in the media and are important in various ways for the political parties, current changes in the structure make it increasingly difficult to keep track of the various election cycles for the various authorities.

In 1995 there were elections for 29 new unitary authorities in Scotland and 22 in Wales. These new authorities were to 'shadow' the old two-tier authorities for a year and assume power in April 1996. Councillors elected in 1995 will remain in office until 1999.

In England, on the other hand, while London and the metropolitan areas continue as before, change in the areas covered by shire counties has been piecemeal and is continuing. In 1995 there was the regular cycle of elections in metropolitan boroughs and in shire districts with 'annual' elections. On this occasion too, districts with 'all in' elections every four years went to the polls. In addition, however, there were first elections for 14 newly-created unitary authorities with all seats being at stake. These new unitary authorities were Bath and North East Somerset; Bristol; East Riding of Yorkshire; Hartlepool; Isle of Wight; Kingston-upon-Hull; Middlesbrough; North East Lincolnshire; North Lincolnshire; North West Somerset; Redcar and Cleveland; South Gloucestershire; Stockton-on-Tees; York.

It is difficult to know what kind of summary of local election results would be most useful to users of the reference section. On this occasion we provide a summary of the results in the different types of authority with Scotland and Wales being treated separately. We have made no attempt to estimate gains and losses of seats in the new authorities.

Full details of the 1995 local election results, including individual ward results and commentary, can be found in C. Rallings and M. Thrasher, *Local Elections Handbook 1995* (Local Government Chronicle Elections Centre, University of Plymouth) and H. Bochel and D. Denver, The *Scottish Council Elections 1995* (Election Studies, 106 Tay St., Newport-on-Tay, Fife, DD6 8AS).

TABLE 4.1 *Summary of 1995 Local Election Results*

	Candidates	Seats Won	Gains/ Losses	% Share of Vote
Metropolitan Districts (36)				
Turnout 32.8%				
Con	736	49	-137	19.9
Lab	841	682	+156	57.1
Lib Dem	649	101	-5	19.1
Other	349	10	-7	3.8
'Annual' Shire Districts (107)				
Turnout 39.2%				
Con	1608	257	-381	25.5
Lab	1525	831	+233	44.5
Lib Dem	1287	444	+100	25.1
Other	500	119	-14	4.9
'All in' Shire Districts (167)				
Turnout 43.6%				
Con	4863	1611	-1375	26.7
Lab	5512	2911	+1136	34.3
Lib Dem	4350	1877	+390	24.9
Other	2800	1175	-220	14.1
English Unitary Authorities (14)				
Turnout 41.0				
Con	616	95	–	23.6
Lab	725	473	–	42.6
Lib Dem	626	190	–	25.1
Other	203	30	–	8.7
All English Authorities (324)				
Turnout 37.7%				
Con	7823	2012	–	24.5
Lab	8603	4897	–	42.8
Lib Dem	6912	2612	–	23.6
Other	3852	1334	–	9.1
Scottish Unitary Authorities (29)				
Turnout 44.9%				
Con	586	82	–	11.3
Lab	935	614	–	43.8
Lib Dem	527	121	–	9.2
SNP	994	181	–	26.2
Other	469	161	–	9.1
Welsh Unitary Authorities (22)				
Turnout 49.4%				
Con	268	42	–	8.1
Lab	956	726	–	43.6
Lib Dem	361	79	–	10.2
Plaid Cymru	366	113	–	12.5
Other	769	312	–	25.4

Note: Gains and losses are as compared with seats won in the same authorities in 1991 and cannot, of course, be calculated for new authorities.

Sources: C. Rallings and M. Thrasher; H. Bochel and D. Denver.

TABLE 4.2 *Monthly Party Vote Shares in Local Government By-elections 1995 (per cent)*

	Con	Lab	Lib Dem	Oths	N of Wards
Jan	18.8	55.7	16.8	8.6	6
Feb	16.6	48.8	33.9	0.7	5
Mar	20.0	44.8	32.7	2.5	15
Apr	18.8	54.9	24.7	1.6	9
May	35.1	41.4	22.6	1.0	15
Jun	22.3	33.0	33.2	11.5	12
Jul	24.1	40.6	31.9	3.4	20
Aug	24.2	40.3	23.6	11.9	9
Sep	24.7	40.2	31.5	3.7	19
Oct	24.9	45.2	27.0	2.9	23
Nov	31.2	35.0	30.5	3.2	21
Dec	33.5	33.1	24.9	8.5	10

Note: These figures relate to the results of local government by-elections in wards and electoral divisions contested by all three major parties.

Source: David Cowling, ITN.

TABLE 4.3 *Seats Won and Lost in Local Government By-elections 1995*

	Con	Lab	Lib Dem	Others
Held	32	88	42	12
Lost	28	7	16	8
Gained	9	26	19	5
Net	-19	+19	+3	-3

Source: David Cowling, ITN.

TABLE 4.4 *Quarterly Party Vote Shares in Local Government By-elections 1995 (per cent)*

	Con	Lab	Lib Dem	Others	Number of wards
Q1	19.2	47.9	29.3	3.6	26
Q2	28.1	42.2	25.7	3.8	36
Q3	24.3	40.4	30.5	5.3	48
Q4	29.1	38.7	28.1	4.0	54

Note: These figures relate to the results of local government by-elections in wards and electoral divisions contested by all three major parties.
Source: David Cowling, ITN.

TABLE 4.5 *Projected National Share of Votes in Local Elections 1993–96 (per cent)*

	1993	1994	1995	1996
Con	31	27	25	27
Lab	41	42	46	43
Lib Dem	24	27	24	26

Source: The Guardian 2–4/5/96

5. Political Parties

PARTY MEMBERSHIP

The table below shows individual membership levels of UK parties, as declared by the political parties themselves. Some of these figures carry a strong 'health warning', however, since (with the exception of the Labour Party) they are estimates . There is a variety of reasons accounting for this, not least the fact that the parties themselves are unable (or unwilling) to give precise figures where membership records are not held centrally. These figures should, therefore, be treated as indicative levels of membership and readers should take account of the footnotes to the table.

Party	Declared Individual Membership
Conservative Party [1]	750,000
Labour Party	367,992
Liberal Democrats	103,000
Scottish National Party [2]	†
Plaid Cymru	10,000
Green Party	4,000
Liberal Party [3]	n.a.
Ulster Unionist Party	10,000–12,000
Democratic Unionist Party	5,000
SDLP	†
Alliance Party	4,000
Sinn Féin	n.a.

Notes:
†   Party policy not to reveal membership figures.
1.   There is a certain discrepancy in membership figures for the Conservative Party. The figure released from Conservative Central Office is an estimated 750,000 members. However, in *True Blues: The Politics of Conservative Party Membership*, Whiteley, Seyd and Richardson calculate that the Conservative Party is losing on average 64,000 members per year. On that basis, given that their estimate of 750,000 was calculated in 1992, this would suggest an estimated membership figure of 494,000 in 1996.
2.   Estimated membership of the Scottish National Party is 20,000
3.   National membership figure for the Liberal Party is not available as records are kept at a local level.

Data collected April 1996

THE CONSERVATIVE PARTY

Main Addresses
Conservative and Unionist Central Office
32 Smith Square
Westminster
London SW1P 3HH
Tel: 0171-222-9000
Fax: 0171-222-1135

Scottish Conservative and Unionist Central Office
Suite 1/1
14 Links Place
Edinburgh EH6 7EZ
Tel: 0131-555-2900
Fax: 0131-555-2869

Other Addresses
Conservative Research Department
32 Smith Square
Westminster
London SW1P 3HH
Tel: 0171-222-9000
Fax: 0171-233-2065
Director: Daniel Finkelstein
Deputy Directors: Alistair Cooke, Julian Lewis

Conservative Political Centre
32 Smith Square
Westminster
London SW1P 3HH
Tel: 0171-222-9000
Fax: 0171-233-2065
Director: Alistair Cooke

National Union of Conservative and Unionist Associations
32 Smith Square
Westminster
London SW1P 3HH
Tel: 0171-222-9000
Fax: 0171-222-1135

One Nation Forum
32 Smith Square
Westminster
London SW1P 3HH
Tel: 0171-222-9000
Fax: 0171-222-1135
Chairman: Sir Geoffrey Pattie
Secretary: Tom Peet

Board of Management

Brian Mawhinney	Sir Marcus Fox
Sir Peter Bowness	David Kelly
Dame Hazel Byford	Dame Angela Rumbold
Sir Malcolm Chaplin	Lord Sheppard of Didgemere
Sir Basil Feldman	Tom Spencer
	Tony Garrett (Secretary to the Board)

Officers

Party Chairman	Brian Mawhinney
Deputy Chairman	Michael Trend
Vice Chairmen	Dame Angela Rumbold (Candidates)
	Sir Graham Bright (Campaigns, One Nation Forum)
	Charles Hendry (Communications)
	Eric Pickles (Local Government)
	Baroness Seccombe (Women)
Chairman of the Party in Scotland	Sir Michael Hirst

Staff

Directors

Research	Daniel Finkelstein
Communications	Charles Lewington
Fundraising/Treasurer's	Jeffrey Speed
Campaigning	Tony Garrett
Finance	Martin Saunders

Deputy Directors

Research Department	Alistair Cooke, Julian Lewis

Departmental Heads

Local Government	David Trowbridge
Speakers	Penny Brook
Conservatives Abroad	David Smith
Chief Press Officer	Alex Aiken
Training	Geoffrey Harper
Elections Unit	John Earl
Legal Officer	Paul Gribble

Regional Directors

		Telephone
London and Eastern	Tim Cowell	0171-2229000
Yorkshire & North East	Peter Smith	01532-450731
North West	Ron Bell	0161-7971231
Midlands	Rachael Dyche	01455-239556
Southern	David Simpson	01932-866477
Western	Bill Henderson	01392-58231
Wales	Martin Perry	01222-616031
Scotland	Roger Pratt	0131-5552900

Board of Treasurers

Lord Hambro (Chairman)
Lord Harris of Peckham
 (Deputy Chairman)
Sir Malcolm Chaplin
William Hughes

David Davies
Sir Nigel Mobbs
Sir Geoffrey Lee
Alan Lewis
Leonard Steinberg

National Union Advisory Committees
Conservative Women's National Committee
Chairman: Dame Joyce Anelay
Secretary: Mary Shaw

Young Conservatives' National Advisory Committee
Chairman: Jason Hollands
Secretary: Hugh O'Brien

Conservative Trade Unionists' National Committee
Chairman: Derek Beard
Secretary: High O'Brien

National Local Government Advisory Committee
Chairman: David Heslop
Secretary: David Trowbridge

Conservative Political Centre National Advisory Committee
Chairman: Ross Coates
Secretary: Alistair Cooke

Association of Conservative Clubs
Chairman: Sir Marcus Fox
Secretary: Ken Hargreaves

Conservative Party Leadership Election (June 1995)
(Electorate Comprised Conservative MPs)

	Votes
John Major	218
John Redwood	89
Abstentions, spoiled ballots	22

THE LABOUR PARTY

Address
The Labour Party
John Smith House
150 Walworth Road
London SE17 1JT
Tel: 0171-701-1234
Fax: 0171-277-3300

Information
Tel: 0171-277-3346
Fax: 0171-277-3555

Regional Secretaries		*Telephone*
Northern & Yorkshire	Andrew Sharp	01924-291221
North West	Vacant	01925-574913
Central	Roy Maddox	0115-9462195
West Midlands	Fiona Gordon	0121-553-6601
South East	George Catchpole	01473-255668
Greater London	Terry Ashton	0171-490-4904
South West	Graham Manuel	0117-9298018
Wales	Anita Gale	01222-398567
Scotland	Jack McConnell	0141-332-8946

Officers and Staff

Leader	Tony Blair
Deputy Leader	John Prescott
General Secretary	Tom Sawyer
European Coordinator	Larry Whitty
Chief Party Spokesperson	David Hill
Election Campaigning	Peter Mandelson
Organization and Development	Peter Coleman
Policy	Matthew Taylor
Finance	Paul Blagborough
Parliamentary Labour Party Secretary	Alan Haworth
Labour Party News	Virginia Gibbons
Computers	Roger Hough
Women's Officer	Deborah Lincoln
Youth Officer	Tom Watson
Senior Development Officer	Nick Smith

National Executive Committee 1995–96

Chair	Diana Jeuda
Vice-Chair	Tom Burlison
Treasurer	Tom Burlison (GMB)
Ex Officio Members	Tony Blair, John Prescott

Division 1 – Trade Unions

Dan Duffy	(TGWU)	Margaret Wall	(MSF)
Diana Holland	(TGWU)	Alan Johnson	(USDAW)
Vernon Hince	(RMT)	Bill Connor	(USDAW)
John Mitchell	(GPMU)	Nigel Harris	(AEU)
Mary Turner	(GMB)	Richard Rosser	(TSSA)
Maggie Jones	(Unison)	Christine Wilde	(Unison)

Division 2 – Socialist, Co-operative and Other Organizations
John Evans   (National Union of Labour and Social Clubs)

Division 3 – Constituency Labour Parties

Diane Abbott	Robin Cook
David Blunkett	Harriet Harman
Gordon Brown	Mo Mowlem
	Dennis Skinner

Division 4 – Women Members

Margaret Beckett	Diana Jeuda
Brenda Etchells	Joan Lestor
Clare Short	

Youth Representative
Catherine Taylor

Result of Elections to National Executive Committee 1995–96
Names asterisked were elected. Figures for 1994 are shown in brackets if applicable.

Trade Unions (Twelve places of which four must be women.)

* Bill Connor	3,594,000	(3,896,000)
* Dan Duffy	3,700,000	(4,002,000)
* Nigel Harris	3,571,000	(3,827,000)
* Vernon Hince	3,685,000	(3,985,000)
* Diana Holland	3,685,000	(3,922,000)
* Alan Johnson	3,607,000	
* Maggie Jones	3,639,000	(2,319,000)
* John Mitchell	3,683,000	
* Richard Rosser	2,955,000	(3,209,000)
* Mary Turner	3,659,000	
* Margaret Wall	3,611,000	(3,889,000)
* Christine Wilde	1,488,000	
Mike Leahy	1,447,000	
Arthur Scargill	888,000	(1,068,000)

Socialist, Co-operative and Other Organizations (One place.)

* John Evans	43,000	(25,000)
Graham Lane	7,000	
Derek Munn	1,000	
Glenys Thornton	18,000	

Constituency Labour Parties (Seven places of which three must be women.)

* Robin Cook	85,670	(83,923)	Alice Mahon	29,212	(26,668)
* Gordon Brown	79,371	(76,753)	Jeremy Corbyn	22,457	(16,418)
* David Blunkett	75,984	(80,150)	Joyce Quinn	21,903	
* Harriet Harman	69,092	(67,355)	Angela Eagle	21,857	
* Dennis Skinner	64,288	(59,237)	Alan Simpson	12,409	(8,724)
* Mo Mowlem	53,578	(35,045)	Suzanne L'Estrange	7,787	
* Diane Abbott	45,653	(36,539)	Lee Vasey	7,533	
Jack Straw	58,486	(50,850)	Kevin Hutchens	5,066	
Ken Livingstone	53,423	(47,960)	Paul Harrison	5,040	
Peter Hain	32,394	(29,573)	George Stevenson	4,326	(5,313)
Dawn Primarolo	31,766	(33,377)	Charlie Smith	4,261	
Tam Dalyell	30,705	(28,433)	Lynda Struthers	4,225	

Women Members (Five places. Result announced in percentage terms.)

* Margaret Beckett	18.73%	(18.77%)
* Joan Lestor	18.28%	(17.79%)
* Diana Jeuda	17.84%	(16.88%)
* Clare Short	17.15%	(16.72%)
* Brenda Etchells	14.68%	(14.05%)
Hilary Armstrong	9.75%	(10.03%)
Christine Shawcroft	3.57%	

THE LIBERAL DEMOCRATS

Addresses
The Liberal Democrats
Party Headquarters
4 Cowley Street
London SW1P 3NB
Tel: 0171-222-7999
Fax: 0171-799-2170

Scottish Liberal Democrats
4 Clifton Terrace
Edinburgh EH12 5DR
Tel: 0131-337-2314
Fax: 0131-337-3556

Welsh Liberal Democrats
57 St Mary Street
Cardiff CF1 1FE
Tel: 01222-382210
Fax: 01222-222864

Associated Organizations
Association of Liberal Democrat Councillors
President: Baroness Hamwee
Chair: Bill Le Bretton
Tel: 01422-843785
Fax: 01422-843036

Association of Liberal Democrat Trade Unionists
President: Tudor Gates
Chair: Andrew Hudson
Tel: 01375-850881

Youth and Student Liberal Democrats
Chair: Tim Prater
Tel: 0171-222-7999 ext. 587

Women Liberal Democrats
President: Hilary Campbell
Chair: Jo Hayes
Tel: 0171-222-7999 ext. 408

Ethnic Minority Liberal Democrats
Chair: To be elected
Tel: 0181-2658727

Liberal International (British Group)
President: Sir David Steel

Federation of European Liberal Democrat and Reform Parties
97 Rue Belliard
1047 Brussels
Belgium
Tel: (00)-322-284-2207
Fax: (00)-322-231-1907
President: Willy de Clerq
Secretary-General: Christian Ehlers

Regional Contacts

		Telephone
Chilterns	Dave Hodgson	01908-503001
Devon and Cornwall	Noel Thomson	01803-842246
East Midlands	Richard Lustig	0116-2543833
Eastern	Nina Stimson	01223-460795
Hampshire and		
Isle of Wight	Gerald Vernon-Jackson	01703-848484
London	Paul Farthing	0171-2220134
Northern	Philip Appleby	01388-601341
North West	Flo Clucas	0161-2365799
South East	Dave Manning	01273-202300
West Midlands	Jim Gosling	01384-872296
Western	Gill Pardy	01202-516329
Yorkshire and Humberside	Andrew Meadowcroft	01709-816601

Party Officers

Party Leader	Paddy Ashdown
President	Robert Maclennan
Vice-Presidents	Andrew Duff (England)
	Marilyne MacLaren (Scotland)
	Rev. Roger Roberts (Wales)
Chair of Finance	Tim Clement-Jones
Treasurer	Tim Razzall

Scottish Party

Leader	Jim Wallace
President	Roy Thomson
Convenor	Marilyne Maclaren
Chief Executive	Andy Myles

Welsh Party

Leader	Alex Carlile
President	Martin Thomas
Administrator	Judi Lewis

Federal Party Staff

General Secretary	Graham Elson
Press Officer	Elizabeth Johnson
Campaigns and Elections Director	Chris Rennard
Campaign Officers	Paul Rainger, Candy Piercy, Mel ab Owain, Derek Barrie, Willie Rennie, David Loxton, Paul Schofield
Candidates Officers	Sandra Dunk, Garry White
Policy Director	Neil Stockley
Policy Officers	David Cloves, Iain King, Wyn Evans, Candida Goulden
International Officer	Kishwer Khan
Finance Controller	Ken Loughlin
Head of Membership Services	Keith House
Membership Finance Co-Ordinator	Helen Sharman
Conference Organizer	Penny McCormack
Agents' Officer	Paul Bensilum
Director of Strategy and Planning	Alan Leaman
General Election Planning Manager	Alison Holmes
Liberal Democrat News Editor	David Boyle

Periodicals

Liberal Democrat News	Weekly party newspaper
Liberator	Eight times a year, independent forum for debate
The Reformer	Quarterly, independent journal of policy and strategy

OTHER PARTIES

Scottish National Party (SNP)
6 North Charlotte Street
Edinburgh EH2 4JH
Tel: 0131-226-3661
Fax: 0131-226-7373
President: Winifred Ewing
National Convenor: Alex Salmond
Parliamentary Leader: Margaret Ewing
National Secretary: Alasdair Morgan
Director of Organization: Alison Hunter
Communications and Research: Keith Pringle

Plaid Cymru (PC)
51 Cathedral Road
Cardiff CF1 9HD
Tel: 01222-231944
Fax: 01222-222506
President: Dafydd Wigley
General Secretary:Karl Davies

Green Party
1a Waterlow Road
Archway
London N19 5NJ
Tel: 0171-2724474
Fax: 0171-2726653
Chair: Jenny Jones
Press Officer: Penny Kemp

The Liberal Party
Gayfere House
22 Gayfere Street
London SW1P 3HP
Tel: 0171-233-2124
Fax: 01704-539315
President: Michael Meadowcroft
Secretary General: Nigel Ashton
Chair of National Exec.: Rob Wheway

Democratic Left (Political organization, *not* party, since June 1995)
6 Cynthia Street
London N1 9JF
Tel: 0171-278-4443
Fax: 0171-278-4425
Federal Secretary: Nina Temple

Northern Ireland

Ulster Unionist Party
3 Glengall Street
Belfast BT12 5AE
Tel: 01232-324601
Fax: 01232-246738
Leader: David Trimble
Party Chairman: Jim Nicholson
Party Secretary: Jim Wilson

Democratic Unionist Party
91 Dundela Avenue
Belfast BT4 3BU
Tel: 01232-471155
Fax: 01232-471797
Leader: Ian Paisley
Deputy Leader: Peter Robinson
Party Chairman: James McClure
Secretary: Nigel Dodds
Press Officer: Samuel Wilson

Social Democratic and Labour Party (SDLP)
Cranmore House
611c Lisburn Road
Belfast BT9 7GT
Tel: 01232-668100
Fax: 01232-669009
Leader: John Hume
Deputy Leader: Seamus Mallon
Party Chairman: Jonathan Stevenson
Party Administrator: Gerry Cosgrove

Alliance Party
88 University Street
Belfast BT7 1HE
Tel: 01232-324274
Fax: 01232-333147
Leader: John Alderdice
Party Chairman: Stephen McBride
General Secretary: David Ford
President: Jim Hendron

Sinn Féin
Belfast Office
51–55 Falls Road
Belfast BT13
Tel: 01232-230261
Fax: 01232-231723

Dublin Office
44 Cearnog Pharnell (Parnell Square)
Dublin 1
Republic of Ireland
Tel: (00) 3531-8726932
Fax: (00) 3531-8733441
President: Gerry Adams
Vice-President: Pat Doherty
General Secretary: Lucilita Bhreatnach
National Chairman: Tom Hartley
N. Ireland Chairman: Gerry O'Hare
Director of Publicity: Rita O'Hare

6. National Newspapers

TABLE 6.1 *Circulation of National Newspapers*

	Ave. Net Circulation	
Newspaper	Oct 95– Mar 96	Oct 94– Mar 95
Sun	4,072,971	4,064,905
Daily Mirror/Daily Record	3,240,354	3,218,044
Daily Mail	1,981,707	1,765,320
Daily Express	1,262,920	1,288,012
Daily Telegraph	1,044,281	1,064,524
Times	672,292	618,907
Daily Star	667,207	669,214
Guardian	401,988	403,338
Financial Times	304,854	292,953
Independent	288,364	287,510
Today	*Closed Nov 95*	581,838
London Evening Standard	463,146	466,300
News of the World	4,646,791	4,793,828
Sunday Mirror	2,454,204	2,527,512
Mail on Sunday	2,083,384	1,955,232
The People	2,066,608	2,079,626
Sunday Express	1,309,301	1,430,570
Sunday Times	1,285,919	1,280,374
Sunday Telegraph	663,196	673,203
Observer	465,538	486,806
Independent on Sunday	316,794	314,677
Sunday Sport	275,049	327,576

Source: Audit Bureau of Circulations

7. World Wide Web Sites

The Internet and World Wide Web have become an important tool for political scientists. Beyond the common usage of electronic mail, the Internet is increasingly an important research and teaching resource. In this section we list a selection of World Wide Web sites which may be of interest to readers. Of course, listing such sites in 'hard-copy' might run counter to the ethos of the Web, but this guide is intended to simply highlight the availability of information.

For those who use the Web regularly, the best route for political scientists is the Political Studies Association Home Page which provides a gateway to numerous sites. This can be found at

http://www.lgu.ac.uk/psa/psa.html

We hope that readers will also visit the EPOP Home Page at

http://www.lgu.ac.uk/psa/epop.html

We are grateful to Richard Topf at London Guildhall University for his help in compiling this section.

UK Government

http://www.open.gov.uk	HM Government : Main UK Open Government home page
http://www.coi.gov.uk/coi/	Central Office of Information
http://www.dti.gov.uk/	Department of Trade and Industry
http://www.fco.gov.uk	Foreign and Commonwealth Office
http://www.hmso.gov.uk/	HM Stationery Office
http://www.hm-treasury.gov.uk	HM Treasury
http://www.mod.uk	Ministry of Defence
http://www.nics.gov.uk	Northern Ireland Office
http://www.soton.ac.uk/~nukop/index.html	New Official Publications

UK Political Parties

http://www.conservative-party.org.uk/	Conservative Party
http://www.pncl.co.uk/~pwhite/ CHARTER1.HTML	Conservative Party Charter Movement
http://www.poptel.org.uk/labour-party/	Labour Party
http://www.labour.org.uk	Labour Party Conference
http://www.libdems.org.uk/	Liberal Democratic Party
http://www.scotlibdems.org.uk/	Scottish Liberal Democrat Party
http://www.compulink.co.uk/libdems/ reformer.htm	*The Reformer:* Liberal-Democrat Party journal
http://www.wales.com/political-party/plaid- cymru/englishindex.html	Plaid Cymru
http://www.tardis.ed.ac.uk/~alba/snp/	Scottish National Party
http://www.rmii.com/mckinley/sinnfein.html	Sinn Fein

Interest Groups

http://www.tuc.org.uk/	TUC
http://www.gn.apc.org/charter88/index.html	Charter 88
http://www.foe.co.uk/	Friends of the Earth
http://www.greenpeace.org	Greenpeace

Mass Media

http://www.bbc.co.uk/westonline/	BBC Westminster On-Line: Preview of politician of the day
http://www.cnn.com/POLITICS/index.html	CNN Political News Index
http://www.gallup.com	Gallup Polls
http://go2.guardian.co.uk/	*The Guardian*

http://www.cleanroom.co.uk/nss/
NSSHome.html   *New Statesman and Society*

http://www.the-times.co.uk/   The Times Newpaper Group

Academic Sites

http://www.aber.ac.uk/~inpwww/forum/
forum.html   Research on Human Rights

http://sosig.ac.uk/ccss/   Centre for Computing in the Social
                                        Sciences

http://cspo.queensu.ca:8080/cspo.html   Centre for the Study of Public Opinion

http://www.essex.ac.uk/ECPR   ECPR at University of Essex

http://www.unige.ch/ses/sococ/ecpr/   Computers in Political Science Group

http://www.esrc.ac.uk   ESRC

http://dawww.essex.ac.uk/   ESRC Data Archive

http://www.gcdis.usgcrp.gov/   GCDIS: Global Change and Data
                                        Information System

http://www.social-science-gesis.de/   GESIS: German Social Science
                                        Infrastructure Services

http://icpsr.umich.edu/   ICPSR(International Consortium for
ICPSR_homepage.html   Political and Social Research)

http://csf.colorado.edu/   International Political Economy
                                        Network

http://www.ucd.ie/~coakleyj/index.html International Political Science
                                        Association

http://ssdc.ucsd.edu/   Lijphart Election Data Archive

http://www.orst.edu/Dept/pol_sci/pnwpsa/ Pacific Northwest Political Science
                                        Association

http://www.unige.ch/ses/spo/rssp   Swiss Political Science Review

http://www.lsu.edu/~poli/research.html Political Science Resources on the
                                        Internet

http://www.lib.umich.edu/libhome/ Documents.center/polisci.html#pss	Political Sciences Resources on the Web
http://www.niss.ac.uk/subject/32menu.html	NISS Politics Index
http://www.uib.no/nsd/	Norwegian Social Science Data Archive
http://opr.princeton.edu/	Office of Population Research
http://www.esrc.bris.ac.uk	Social Information Gateway
http://lorne.stir.ac.uk:80/ departments/cti_centre	SocInfo
http://ssdc.ucsd.edu/	Social Science Data Collection at UCSD
http://www.shef.ac.uk/uni/academic/ N-Q/pol/EUROTORY.HTML	Conservative Parliamentarians and European Integration Survey, 1994.
http://www.ping.be/~ping0656/	Index of European Political Parties
http://huizen.dds.nl/~benne/pol-parties.html	Political Parties Around the World
http://www.keele.ac.uk/depts/po/psr.htm	Political Science Resources
http://ourworld.compuserve.com/ homepages/timb/	UK Elect: UK Election Resources (including UK-Elect Software)

Political Science Journals

http://www.psci.unt.edu/es/	*Electoral Studies*
http://www.polisci.nwu.edu:8000/	*Party Politics*
http://www.nd.edu/~plofmarx/	*Rethinking Marxism*

European Union

http://www.ispo.cec.be/	Europa : European Commission with linkages to policy documents, speeches, etc.
http://www.cec.lu/europarl/europarl.htm	EUROPARL – European Parliament Server

http://www.cec.lu/en/comm/opoce/wel.html	EUR-OP – Office of Official Publications of the European Communities
http://www.cec.lu/en/comm/eurostat/ eurostat.html	EUROSTAT :Statistical Office of the European Communities

International Sites

http://WWW.StatCan.CA/start.html	Canadian Statistical Office: On-line Statistical Data
http://www.elections.ca/	Elections Canada
http://metro.turnpike.net/S/SPC/	Canada: Socialist Party
http://www.itr.qc.ca/PQ/	Canada: Bienvenue au Parti Quebecois
http://www.liberal.ca/	Canada: Liberal Party
http://fed.ndp/ca/fndp/	Canada: New Democrats
http://www.pcparty.ca/	Canada: Progressive Conservative Party
http://www.whitehouse.gov	USA:White House
http://lcweb.loc.gov/global/executive/ white_house.html	White House: Index of Documentation
http://www.house.gov	USA:House of Representatives
http://www.fedworld.gov	US Government
http://www.access.gpo.gov/su_docs/aces/ aaces001.html	US Government Database of Official Documents
http://www.usia.gov/	United States Information Agency
http://www.census.gov/ftp/pub/ population/www/	US Population Division – US and International demographic data
http://www.democraticparty.com/	US: Democratic Party
http://www.webcom.com/~digitals/	US Democratic Party Activists
http://www.republicanparty.com/	US: Republican Party

http://www.house.gov/CONTRACT.html	US: Republican Contract with America
http://republicans.vt.com/republicans.html	US Republican Web
http://www.nla.gov.au/pmc/pmchome.html	Australia: Prime Minister's Office
http://gov.info.au/	Australia: Government Information Services : Federal, State, and Local
http://senate.aph.gov.au/	Australia: Senate
http://www.uq.edu.au/~e2gjenki/democrats.html	Australian Democrats
http://www.vicnet.net.au/~victorp/vplib1.htm	Australian Liberalism
http://www.govt.nz/	New Zealand: Government
http://www.oenp.or.at/oenp/	Austria: Natural Law Party
http://www.spoe.or.at/	Austria: Social Democratic Party
http://www.oevp.co.at/oevp/	Austria: Volkspartei
http://www.innet.be/cvp/menu.html	Belgium: Christelijke Volkspartij
http://www.interpac.be/ecolo/	Belgium: Ecology
http://www.cvp.be/	Flemish Christian Party
http://www.vld.be/vld/	Belgium: Vlammse Liberalen en Democraten (Flemish Liberals and Democrats)
http://www.agalev.be/agalev/	Belgium: Agalev (Flemish Green Party)
http://www.tiac.net/users/jimanne/index.html	Ireland: The Democratic Left
http://ireland.iol.ie/resource/green/index.htm	Ireland : Green Party
http://www.kaapeli.fi/~vihreat/engl.html	Finland: Greens
http://www.cdu.de/	Germany: Christian Democratic Union
http://www.liberale.de/	Germany: The FDP

NOTES TO CONTRIBUTORS

The manuscript (referred to throughout as an 'article') should be submitted in duplicate, typewritten on one side only, unjustified on the right margin and double-spaced throughout (including notes, but not including tables/figures). Pages should be numbered consecutively, including those containing illustrations, diagrams or tables. A disk should accompany the manuscript. It should be labeled with the name of the article, the author's name and the software system used (ideally IBM compatible).

All tables, figures, maps, etc. must conform to the type area 108mm x 175mm. A clear hard copy of figures and maps must be provided. Sources should be given in each case. The article should be accompanied by a brief abstract (c. 150 words), and notes on the contributors, each in separate files.

STYLE
Font: Times New Roman 12pt. Headings: (1) Bold; (2) Italics (not underlined); (3) Italics, no new paragraph.

Quotation marks: single in text throughout; double within single; single within indented quotations.

Dates and Numbers: 12 July 1994. Abbreviate years: 1983–84; 1908–9; 1920–21; the 1930s (*not* 'the thirties').
Spelling: use the -z- alternative (recognize) except where -yse (analyse); -our rather than -or (favour) except in proper names, e.g. Labor Party, if that is its formal title.

Capitalization: Use capitals sparingly, for titles (the Secretary-General; President Mitterrand) and for unique or central institutions (the European Commission, the International Atomic Energy Authority) but not for general or local organizations and offices (a government minister, the mayor, Brigham parish council). Capitalize Party in a title (the British Green Party), otherwise lower case. Lower case for the state and for the left and the right (but the New Left, the New Right). Capitalize -isms from names (Marxism), elsewhere lower case (ecologism). In general, lower case for conferences and congresses (the party's tenth congress was held in 1995).

Notes and References: Essential notes should be indicated by superscript numbers in the text and collected on a single page at the end of the text. References cited in the text should read thus: Denver (1990: 63–4), Denver and Hands (1985, 1990). Use '*et al.*' when citing a work by more than two authors, e.g. Brown *et al.* (1991). The letters a, b, c, etc., should be used to distinguish citations of different works by the same author in the same year, e.g. Brown (1975a, b).

All references cited in the text should be listed alphabetically and presented in full after the notes, using the following style:

Articles in journals: Anker, Hans (1990) 'Drawing Aggregate Inferences from Individual Level Data: The Utility of the Notion of a Normal Vote', *European Journal of Political Research* 18: 373–87.
Books: McLean, Iain (1982) *Dealing in Votes.* Oxford: Martin Robertson.
Articles in books: Webb, Paul D. (1994) 'Party Organizational Change in Britain: The Iron Law of Centralization?', in Richard S. Katz and Peter Mair (eds) *How Parties Organize: Change and Adaptation in Party Organizations in Western Democracies*, pp.109–34. London: Sage.

Tables: set page width to 108mm (for wider tables, use landscape with maximum width 175mm). Place table in the **text approximate position**, placing a page break at the top and tail: there is no need to include such guidance as '[INSERT TABLE 2 ABOUT HERE]'. **Do not use the 'Table function'** in the word processing package as this causes difficulties at production stage. Instead, use the tab function, as follows: set tabs for columns; align by decimal point; centre the headings. The font size of the Table is not so important; what matters is that the Table should fit **within type area 108mm x 175mm**.

Maps: tints: keep number of gradations to a minimum (if possible no more than 3). Provide a bromide and disk version.

Figures: try to avoid tints. If they are necessary, send a hard copy with tint, and a disk version without tint.